Women's problems in general practice

Oxford General Practice Series 4

edited by

ANN McPHERSON
General Practitioner, Oxford

and

ANNE ANDERSON
University Lecturer, Nuffield Department of Obstetrics and Gynaecology, John Radcliffe Hospital, Oxford

OXFORD   NEW YORK   TORONTO   MELBOURNE
OXFORD UNIVERSITY PRESS
1983

Oxford University Press, Walton Street, Oxford OX2 6DP

London   Glasgow   New York   Toronto
Delhi   Bombay   Calcutta   Madras   Karachi
Kuala Lumpur   Singapore   Hong Kong   Tokyo
Nairobi   Dar es Salaam   Cape Town
Melbourne   Auckland
and associate companies in
Beirut   Berlin   Ibadan   Mexico City   Nicosia

Oxford is a trademark of Oxford University Press

© Ann McPherson and Anne Anderson, 1983.

All rights reserved. No part of this publication may be reproduced, stored in a retrieval system, or transmitted, in any form or by any means, electronic, mechanical, photocopying, recording, or otherwise, without the prior permission of Oxford University Press

This book is sold subject to the condition that is shall not, by way of trade or otherwise, be lent, re-sold, hired out or otherwise circulated without the publisher's prior consent in any form of binding or cover other than that in which it is published and without a similar condition including this condition being imposed on the subsequent purchaser

British Library Cataloguing in Publication Data
Women's problems in general practice.—(Oxford medical
publications)—(Oxford general practice series; 4)
1. Gynecology   2. Obstetrics
I. McPherson, Ann   II. Anderson, Anne B.M.
618   RG101
ISBN 0-19-261345-6

Printed in Great Britain by
Thomson Litho Ltd, East Kilbride, Scotland

Contents

Contributors

Sheila Adam, MB, Ch.B., DCH, MRCP, MFCM
Specialist in Community Medicine, Brent Health Authority; Honorary Senior Lecturer in Community Medicine, Middlesex Hospital Medical School. Evaluated a breast self-examination programme within a general practice in 1978 while a Community Physician in the Department of Community Medicine and General Practice in Oxford.

Anne Anderson, MD., Ph.D., FRCOG
University Lecturer, Nuffield Department of Obstetrics and Gynaecology, John Radcliffe Hospital, Oxford; Honorary Consultant in Clinical Reproductive Physiology. Clinical and research interests in medical aspects of gynaecology, especially endocrinology. Runs a clinic for women at the menopause and is involved in studies in primary dysmenorrhoea, premenstrual syndrome and the control of menstrual blood loss.

David Barlow, MA, BM, MRCP
Consultant Physician, Department of Genitourinary Medicine, St. Thomas' Hospital, London. Has worked in venereology and genitourinary medicine since 1971 and lectures widely to general practitioners on these subjects.

Judith Bury, MA, MB, B.Chir., DCH, DRCOG
Family Planning Doctor, Lothian Health Board Family Planning Services and Edinburgh Brook Advisory Centre. Has a particular interest in pregnancy counselling, sex therapy, and problems of adolescence. Worked in general practice for four years and now teaches on family planning courses for general practitioners.

Mark Charnock, FRCS, MRCOG
Consultant Obstetrician and Gynaecologist, John Radcliffe Hospital, Oxford. Special interest in fertility problems developed while working in St. Mary's and St. Bartholomew's Hospitals, London. Actively engaged in Fertility Clinic in Oxford.

Shirley Elliott, MB, BS, DRCOG, MRCGP
General Practitioner in Oxford. Royal College of General Practice Tutor in Oxford. Has worked in General Practice for four years.

Hilary Graham, MA, Ph.D
Lecturer in Social Policy, University of Bradford. Researches into the family influences on health and health care which has brought her into close contact with the primary health care team.

Judy Greenwood, MB, BS, MRC.Psych.
Fellow in Community Psychiatry, Royal Edinburgh Hospital, Edinburgh. Worked in general practice for ten years before training in psychiatry. Now interested in

community psychiatry in a deprived area of Edinburgh and is also an experienced psychosexual counsellor.

Keith Hawton, MA, DM, MRC.Psych.
Clinical Tutor, University Department of Psychiatry, Oxford.Has had ten years' clinical research and teaching experience in the management of patients with sexual problems and runs teaching seminars for general practitioners interested in these problems. Has also worked on the role of the general practitioner in the management of self-poisoning patients.

Barbara Law, MB, BS, MRCS, LRCP, DCH
Formerly University College Hospital and Whittington Hospital, London. Worked in Family Planning for 30 years and was Chairman of the Joint Committee on Contraception and of the Association of National Family Planning Doctors.

Ann McPherson, MB, BS, DCH, MRCGP
General Practitioner in Oxford. Has worked in general practice for eight years with a special interest in women's health problems, the work of women general practitioners, and health education in primary health care particularly for women and children.

Richard Mayon-White, MB, BS, MRCP, MFCM
Consultant Epidemiologist, Oxford Regional Public Health Laboratory. Currently involved in surveillance of infection in general practice and is running a controlled trial of antimicrobial treatment for cystitis. In the past has studied the application of laboratory tests to the diagnosis of urinary tract infection in general practice and screening for asymptomatic bacteriuria.

Elizabeth Mitchell, MA, Dip. Psych.
Senior Psychologist, St. George's Hospital and Atkinson Morley's Hospital, London. Clinical interests in eating disorders including anorexia nervosa and massive obesity combined with a research interest in the relationship between eating behaviour and emotional arousal. Actively engaged in clinical work in general practice.

Catherine Oppenheimer, MA, MRCP, MRC. Psych.
Senior Registrar in Psychiatry, Warneford Hospital, Oxford. Works with couples referred to the psychosexual problems clinic and has taught psychosexual counselling to general practitioners and family planning doctors. Interested in the ethical issues of counselling.

Katharine Peet, BM, B.Ch., MRCP
Associate Specialist, Department of Neurology, Radcliffe Infirmary, Oxford. Has run the Migraine Clinic in Oxford for the past ten years.

Maureen Roberts, B.Sc., MB, B.Ch., MD
Director and Honorary Consultant, Edinburgh Breast Screening Clinic; Senior Lecturer, Department of Clinical Surgery, University of Edinburgh. Has worked in the field of breast cancer since 1966, first in hospital patient care and therapeutic trials. Currently runs a large breast screening project, involving all the general practitioners in Edinburgh.

Diana Sanders, BA, Ph.D.
Post Doctoral Fellow, Department of Psychology, University of Canterbury, New Zealand. Worked on the Premenstrual syndrome for her Ph.D thesis while in the Medical Research Council Reproductive Biology Unit in Edinburgh. Particularly interested in the relationship between fluctuations in hormones, mood, and sexual responses during the menstrual cycle.

Wendy Savage, BA, MB, B.Ch., MRCOG
Senior Lecturer in Obstetrics and Gynaecology, The London Hospital Medical College. Has been interested in cervical cytology for many years and has also been involved with general practitioner in-service training programmes in obstetrics and with Islington Domiciliary Service.

Acknowledgements

We are indebted to the following people who have helped us enormously by their suggestions and support:

Juliet Cheetham, Gerald Draper, Aidan Macfarlane, Ian Mackenzie, Klim McPherson, Rachel Miller, Alec Turnbull, Charles Warlow, and Charles Webster. We would also like to thank Ginnie Hetherington and Sheila Woodley for their patience in typing this manuscript.

ADDENDUM

Anne Anderson died on 11 February 1983 from breast cancer. It was a mark of her commitment to the understanding of women's health problems that she worked with enthusiasm during her last illness to complete this book and it is sad that she did not live to see it published. The book is dedicated to her memory.

February 1983   Ann McPherson

1 Why women's health?

Ann McPherson

Although there is a large number of recently published books for women about their health problems, there are few such books written specifically for doctors. Obviously many health problems that women suffer are common to both sexes, but there are many that are unique to women. The changing attitudes of society towards women have forced the medical profession to pay more attention to these problems. This book is an attempt to provide general practitioners with an up-to-date critical review of the management and treatment of the sort of problems that women are likely to consult them about—problems which are increasingly being dealt with at a primary care level.

What we have done in this book is to include all the major areas of women's health without trying to be rigidly comprehensive. We have deliberately excluded pregnancy, childbirth, and puerperal problems as these are dealt with in another book in this series. We have also avoided being rigid in our choice of authors, and rather than choosing from a single group, i.e. all general practitioners, or all women, or all consultant specialists, we have instead sought those most appropriate both for their expertise in their subject and their positive attitudes towards primary care.

HISTORY

The development of contemporary medical attitudes to women's health can be best understood within a historical and social context, and we shall give a brief summary here.

There have always been differences between the health problems of men and those of women, and even in primitive hunter–gatherer societies it is not difficult to imagine that the major causes of death would have been different for the different sexes. In more recent history much of the emphasis on women's health has concentrated on childbearing, but, with the advent of more effective contraception and the conquest of infection, the broader and more subtle aspects of women's, as against men's, health became apparent.

The last 150 years

The general health of both women and men has improved dramatically since the 1800s as can be seen from the fall in the death rate. Although death may seem a strange measure of health—and it does not necessarily have a direct relationship with morbidity—it does give some indication of the health of a population and is often the only measure available. Thus, between 1840 and 1978 the death rate of women aged 25 to 34 in England and Wales fell from 10.6 per 1000 to 0.59 per 1000, and the life expectancy of women (at birth) increased from 42 years to 76 years—the equivalent for men was 40 years in 1840 and 70 years in 1978.

The main cause of death in the 1800s, and even in the early part of this century, in both sexes, was infectious diseases. The heroines of novels and opera wasted away with consumption or tragically died in childbirth. Even as late as between 1921 and 1930, records show that tuberculosis accounted for 26 per cent of deaths in women under the age of 45 and that maternal mortality (mainly puerperal fever) over the same period and in the same age group accounted for 17 per cent of deaths. Many factors, both specific to women and general to both sexes, played a part in the eradication of these causes of death, particularly improvements in the general standards of living including better nutrition, improved housing, public health measures, more effective contraception, safer childbirth, the introduction of antibiotics, the treatment of anaemia, and various other medical advances.

Part of the difficulty in assessing the relative importance of the various factors involved is the lack of accurate data about primary health care (hospital records were scarcely better) for the first part of this century. The organization of health care at this time partly explains this. Primary health care was not equally available to all social classes or to either sex. From 1911 the Health Insurance Act entitled specific groups of working men and working women, depending on income, to the services of a panel doctor and free medicine. This, however, did not cover hospital treatment or give help to a dependant—other than a maternity grant to the working man's wife. For example, according to the 1911 census only 10 per cent of married women were working outside the home, so that health care facilities were not available to 90 per cent of married women unless they were paid for. It would be untrue to say that there were no free health care facilities for the women working at home, as provision was made for advice to be given in the local authority or voluntary infant welfare clinics and municipal antenatal clinics which were being developed at this time. These were available to those who were pregnant or who had just had a baby. Women used these clinics, many not till later on in pregnancy, for antenatal advice, but very few were seen for post-natal checkups. General practitioners at that time demanded that these State clinics and infant welfare societies should be responsibile only for preventive care, possibly so as not to threaten their own private practice.

The claims made to National Insurance Schemes begun in 1911 give some documented idea, although in no way an overall view of morbidity among women in the early part of the century. Claims showed that women covered by these schemes, especially young married women, had a higher than expected level of morbidity. The high level of morbidity in these women was due in the main to illnesses which fell within the classically accepted sense of disease. However, the claims to the National Health Insurance Scheme are likely to have underestimated the amount of ill health within the community. It is clear that the organization and method of financing health care affects what is brought to the doctor and who brings it. The evidence suggests that whenever health facilities are made more freely available, more underlying morbidity becomes apparent. For example, a study looking at illness, incapacity, and medical attention among adults in 1947 to 1949 (Logan 1950) reflected the official figures of the changing morbidity patterns immediately before and after the introduction of the National Health Service. The main difference between the years 1947/48 and 1948/49 was that medical consultation rates increased over the whole country. The increase was 6 per cent for men under the age of 65 and 9 per cent for those over that age. For women the increases were much greater, 18 per cent for the younger age group and 22 per cent for the older women. Therefore there can be little doubt that before the start of the National Health Service many women failed to seek medical advice for economic reasons, and once the financial disincentive was removed they consulted their doctors more for the same relative amount of sickness.

Evidence of what these illnesses actually were was provided by the Women's Health Enquiry Committee which in 1939 received over a thousand replies from working-class married women to a questionnaire sent out via health visitors. This attempted to see what women themselves perceived as their health problems. It was found that the ailments most mentioned were anaemia, headaches, constipation, rheumatism, gynaecological trouble, dental problems, varicose veins, and ulcerated legs. Treatment patterns for these conditions varied between no treatment at all, self help, and consultation with a doctor. When looking at the results of this questionnaire, the Committee felt that only a third of women were in good health and that another third were actually in poor health. Although many women who replied had consulted a doctor, only a very small number (5 per cent) felt that they had received any health teaching. In a climate of extreme ignorance about health generally, advice on health and how to keep healthy tended to come from the antenatal clinics, welfare clinics, district nurses, and health visitors. It is difficult to assess how many of the ailments cited above would be classified today. How many would actually reach the primary health care team and how many of them would now be loosely included in the area of psychological or depressive problems that are seen so much in general practice? However, the relationship between economic status and the way the health services are used is still by no means simple. The NHS theoretically provides free health care for all, and although women are no longer discriminated against in the same direct economic way as before 1948, the continuing differences in the use of the health service facilities by different social classes give some indication of the complexities involved.

THE INFLUENCES OF FASHION AND FINANCES ON HEALTH

The classification of ailments raises the question of how society and the individual within society define disease. Changing patterns of what has classically been considered pathological disease and the increasing medicalization of areas such as childbirth, sex, relationship problems, etc. may be in part responsible for the relatively high rate at which women now attend the surgeries of general practitioners (see below). These changes have led to the increasing awareness of 'health fashions' which are based to a variable degree on new scientific evidence. Changes in fashion are particularly abundant in the area of women's health, as highlighted by the changing attitudes towards the menopause and premenstrual tension.

Although there is naturally little direct reference to such *risqué* areas in Victorian literature, it is possible that such characters as for instance Mrs Nickleby were in fact menopausal. However, the lack of references to the menopause in literature may not only have been due to prudery but also to the fact that far fewer women succeeded in surviving long enough to experience it! Recently a more rational basis for the symptomatology of the menopause has been developed and this has been widely written about and popularized. Doctors were slow to accept menopausal symptoms as a problem to which they could offer any contribution until patients and the media forced them to take notice. In this atmosphere of increased awareness the drug companies devoted themselves to producing and marketing suitable hormone therapy. Thus the interdependency of medical, pharmaceutical, and lay interests has increased the sensitivity of people to menopausal symptoms and encouraged the view that symptoms of the menopause are pathological. Nevertheless permanent cessation of menstruation is something that happens to all women and cannot therefore in itself be classified as disease, though it is likely that some women will have symptoms which need treatment. The symptoms themselves are not the only determining factor of therapy. As always in medicine they have to be balanced against the side effects of the therapy used. Therefore, with the recent realization that hormonal therapy is not without its dangers, the balance of attitude towards the treatment of menopausal symptoms has again changed.

SELF HELP

In a perverse kind of way the knowledge of the side effects of drugs used, for example in the treatment of the menopause, has led to the use of untried natural remedies for many disorders. There is a general misconception that the word 'natural', as in natural remedies, automatically means safe. However, this is clearly not so, for example it is possible to take an overdose of vitamin A, and some so-called natural diets are in fact deficient. Ginseng, vitamins, diets, herbs, homeopathy, and so on, though fashionable as natural remedies at the moment, have never been assessed either for their efficacy or for their side effects. Nevertheless, it is likely that there are far more benefits than disadvantages in the movement towards self help, and it is hoped that general practitioners will inform and assist their patients towards this end whenever suitable and possible. On the other hand, one has to beware of the dangers in the idea that self help and health education are a panacea for an under-financed and ailing National Health Service.

Self help for women has always been an alternative to professional care but has recently become something of a growth industry. It is by no means new, and in the past it may have come from a similar impetus to the contemporary movement. There is a manuscript dating from 1500 published in 1981 under the title *Medieval woman's guide to health*. This was produced, as the editor comments, 'because women were dissatisfied with their treatment at the hands of male physicians and were endeavouring to instruct one another as to how to help women with their gynaecological problems'. The publication of *Our bodies, ourselves* as a modern counterpart by a group of non-medical women in Boston in 1971 produced a focus for women on the possibilities and increased self respect that self help in health might offer them. The book challenged the idea that help was only the medical profession's prerogative—the authors all having experienced 'frustration and anger towards specific doctors and the medical maze in general', and the basic aim was 'learning to understand, accept and be responsible for our physical selves'. In the United States the book rapidly became a bestseller but when the first English edition was published in the late 1970s it was unheralded. The difference in the reactions to the text and its philosophy in the two countries may in part have been because in the early 1970s American medicine, including family planning and child health, was almost entirely male dominated (only 7 per cent of doctors were female), whereas in England there were more women doctors, (though they were still in the minority) and certainly in the areas of family planning and child health it was very likely that women patients would come into contact with female doctors.

This apparent predominance of interest by women in self help in health is perhaps because in their role as carers and nurturers women have to be more sensitive to the emotional side of their wellbeing—something that they obviously felt was sadly lacking in many of the medical services provided. The health areas in which women are able to support each other are many—as represented by such organizations as the Mastectomy Association, The National Childbirth Trust, The Postnatal Support Group, the UTI (Urinary tract infection) Club, etc. For a complex variety of reasons women predominate, both as users and as providers, whichever way health in the community is considered.

CONSULTATION RATES

Nowadays the general practitioner sees more women than men as patients, and dispenses them with more medicine. Why is this? Who are these women? What illnesses do they have, and what medicines do they take?

There are, of course, more women than men in the community as a whole—the slightly larger number of males than females in the community up to the age of 45 being more than offset by the longevity of women. In 1977 the proportion of the population who were over 65 was approximately 15 per cent; of this 15 per cent, 61 per cent were women and 39 per cent men. Thus in the average practice of 2500, 375 would be over 65 and of these 229 would be women. The predominance of women in the over 75s is just over 2 : 1.

Consultation rates, which are the average of face-to-face contacts between doctors and their patients during one year, and figures from the General Household Survey, National Morbidity Survey of General Practitioners (1975), and a survey by Cartwright and Anderson (1980) indicate that females consult their doctors more often than males. For instance, the 1975/6 figures from the General Household Survey show a female to male ratio of 3.8 : 3.0 for the average number of consultations per person per year. This ratio has remained fairly constant over the last ten years, even though in most studies the overall consultation rate for both sexes has fallen. Looking more closely at these figures, by age as well as sex, the difference in the rate of consultation in the 15–44 year age group is consistently 2 : 1, even across the social classes gradient.

The reasons for which women and men consult their doctors also show differences (Crombie, Pinsent, Lambert, and Birch 1975). For instance, women consult more for endocrine/nutritional/metabolic diseases, diseases of the blood and reproductive organs, mental disorders, diseases of the circulatory system, genito-urinary disorders, muscular and connective tissue disorders. A further category of complaints entitled 'symptoms and ill-defined conditions' is twice as common in women. The only category for which consultation rates are commoner in males is accidents, poisoning, and violence. Consultation rates are roughly the same in both sexes for infectious and parasitic diseases, neoplasms, diseases of the nervous system (excluding mental disorders), diseases of the respiratory system, and disorders of the digestive system and of the skins, though in nearly all these female/male ratio slightly favours the females.

Although it may appear that women do consult their doctors more often than men, from the crude figures—and crude they are—it does also seem that women actually suffer from more disease and do not simply consult more often for each episode of illness—but at the same time they somehow manage to live longer.

A closer look at these figures reveals further difficulties in interpretation because of the question of who deals with what problems where. For instance, the figures for consultation rates with general practitioners show that there are 122 consultations per 1000 women for genito-urinary problems compared with 24 per 1000 for men. The reasons for these consultations in women cover a wide range of problems such as menstrual irregularities, abortion, menopausal problems, vaginal discharge, etc. The equivalent problems in men, such as urethral discharge, are most likely to be dealt with in hospital venereal disease or genito-urinary clinics where female/male ratio of attenders is 1 : 3, but obviously one is not comparing like with like.

Likewise, although, as already mentioned, many men will consult their general practitioners for injuries, they are also more likely to go directly for treatment to hospital. On the other hand, parents (usually women) have other sources of medical advice, such as child health clinics, which will not be documented as their own consultation. Those who run child health clinics well recognize that the problems they most frequently encounter, such as feeding problems, sleep problems, etc., have as much to do with the stresses and strains on women and parents in our present society as any actual illness in the child.

Consultation rates are, therefore, hardly an accurate reflection of illness. The general practitioner is consulted for only one in 18 illness episodes, while in a recent study it was found that there was an average of 11 lay consultations for every medical consultation. This rate is a reflection of what patients and doctors consider as appropriate to be dealt with by the general practitioner, and goes some way towards demonstrating the actual workload he or she has to deal with.

MEDICATIONS

If women appear to like their doctors' company then it is also clear that they consume a diet rich in pills, both prescribed and non-prescribed. The General Household Survey, for instance, showed that in a fortnight previous to the survey, half the women and a third of the men reported that they had taken prescribed medicine, and another study showed that twice as many women as men had treated themselves (17 per cent versus 8 per cent). This pattern did not apply to girls under the age of 15, where the reverse was true, so that one cannot conclude that early experience plays a significant role, although girls may see their mothers taking tablets as being a part of female adult life.

The prescribing practices of general practitioners can provide valuable information. For instance, Skegg, Doll, and Perry (1977) looked at the prescriptions given by general practitioners to a patient population of 40 000. In the year studied (1974) 66 per cent of women and 54 per cent of men had had at least one drug dispensed, and the proportion of prescribed medicine increased with age and was higher among women at all ages.

Psychotrophic drugs were prescribed more often than any other group and accounted for 20 per cent of all prescriptions: 21 per cent of all women (and 33 per cent of women aged 45–49) compared with 10 per cent of all men received a psychotrophic drug. If the psychotrophic drugs are looked at in more detail the frequency of antidepressive medication is particularly high among middle-aged women, with 11 per cent of all women in the 45–49 age group receiving at least one of these drugs compared to 4 per cent of men. It does seem that women are prescribed more medicine by their general practitioners but it is difficult to compare consultation rates and prescriptions as few studies relate symptoms to prescriptions for specific drugs. Dunnell and Cartwright (1972) have tried to do this and confirmed in their study that women did not take more medicine just because they had more symptoms—they were actually more likely to take medicines for the same symptoms. But the evidence is conflicting as the figures from the General Household Survey show that although women were much more likely to have taken a prescribed medicine, they were just about as likely as men to have taken one that had not been prescribed.

Whether consultation rates and prescribing rates are linked or not, it does seem that women take more pills and it is difficult to find the reason, though obviously both patients and doctors are involved. Regular contact with services such as family planning, antenatal care, and child health clinics might encourage women to think of drug taking as acceptable. Further, women as shopper–consumers—at whom most advertisements are directed—have in shops and elsewhere more easy access to medicines, and women's magazines with their widespread circulation give further credence to the idea of taking medicines to cure certain ills. These ideas must remain speculative and do not give the full explanation. If they did, one would expect to see a more significant difference between the sexes in the self-medication rates compared with the prescribed rates and, as mentioned already, the studies done in this area are conflicting. It may be that historically women have tended to take medicines and pills whereas men have taken alcohol. Laudanum and various other tonics containing psychotrophic components might have been the mother's little helper of the Victorian times, replaced now by diazepam and other such drugs;

throughout this time beer drinking and the group psychotherapy camaraderie in the pubs and other leisure pursuits has probably been the equivalent medication available to men!

The medical component may be that doctors react to the same symptoms in the female or male patient in different ways, giving more prescriptions to females than to males, perhaps because they have a preconceived idea that the male patient should be able to cope without help and that the female 'being the weaker sex' needs the support of drugs. A quick glance through the drug advertising in medical journals certainly reinforces the picture of the downtrodden woman patient as a headachey, premenstrual, depressed person with chronic backache and the lines of all the worldly cares written across her face, in obvious need of immediate help from her general practitioner, probably in the form of a prescription.

ENVIRONMENT, SOCIAL CLASS, AND DISEASE

Women may be represented in advertisements in this way for good reason and sociological studies have helped to give general practitioners insight into some of the environmental influence on the health of women. Brown and Harris (1978), for instance, looked at depression in a random sample of women in South London (there was no similar study for men), and their findings confirmed what had been for many general practitioners a clinical impression. They found that the incidence of depression was significantly greater in the lower social classes and they also identified certain vulnerability factors that preceded the depression. These included the loss of mother in childhood, three or more children aged less than 14 living at home, lack of a confiding or intimate relationship with a husband or boyfriend, and lack of full- or part-time work. The effect of employment was especially interesting, as even when all the other factors were present, many more women developed depression if they did not have paid employment—a finding in line with more recent research on unemployment and having important implications for medical practice with the rising levels of unemployment. Other important findings were that less than half the women with clinical symptoms of depression had seen their general practitioners, and very few of those who had were referred to a psychiatrist.

There has been a reluctance to accept the preventive implications of the interaction between other effects of the environment on health in general and women's health in particular, because in many cases there are serious economic implications. The differing standard mortality ratios in men by occupation and social class are well documented (for example, the Black Report, 1980), but the implications of the differences for women have received less attention. For instance, why is cervical cancer in coalminers' wives so much higher than expected, even allowing for social class, and why is suicide so much higher than expected in doctors' wives? But not only do women appear to suffer from the effects of their husband's occupation, but also more directly from their own specific occupations and their social class. Some evidence for this is the apparent increase of spontaneous abortion rates in female anaesthetists, and the fact that women working in the textile industry appear to have a high incidence of vascular disease. In the United States such findings have led to claims that certain occupations are closed to women, unless they agree to be sterilized, because of risks to a potential fetus. Many factors concerned with the health of women will be, to some extent, dependent on their husband's occupation, though the traditional classification of married women and widows' social class in this way is becoming less relevant and more inaccurate as more women work. Almost all ill health and mortality is increased in social classes IV and V, a fact present from birth with the doubling of perinatal mortality in babies born to women of lower social class and the tripling of infant mortality rates in the same social class. Of course, classifications of social class are traditionally likened to a temperature taken with a thermometer—they tell you something is wrong without being able to define what it is—but the effects of social class on health permeate almost every aspect of health care.

General environmental influences, such as the effects of exercise, weight, etc., on coronary artery disease and the effects of smoking on the incidence of lung cancer, have also been examined more thoroughly in men than in women. Nevertheless, coronary artery disease is a significant cause of death in women (albeit less so than in men) and the consumption of tobacco in women is increasing while the proportion of men smoking is decreasing. In 1950 women in Britain smoked half as many cigarettes as their male contemporaries while in 1980 they smoked nearly as many. Not surprisingly, therefore, the rates of lung cancer in women are soaring. Attempts have been made to aim some of the anti-smoking health education programme at women, although usually only during pregnancy—with notable lack of success. Little attention has been paid to why there are differences in the changing smoking patterns in men and women, but recent information on smoking habits emphasizes the need for the general practitioner to use different tactics when counselling women than when counselling men, and different methods with different types of women.

WOMEN DOCTORS, WOMEN PATIENTS

Women are not only the main users of the Health Service but are, as nurses, midwives, health visitors, hospital ancillary staff, radiographers, physiotherapists, also to a large extent the providers. On the other hand, the majority of doctors are men, but even here increasing numbers of women are training.

There is little information on which sex of doctor a patient prefers to see, but the information that there is a preference appears in Cartwright and Anderson's book *General practice revisited* (1980), and in their earlier survey of general practice. When asked which sex they would prefer their doctor to be, most patients in the study expressed no preference, but where a preference was expressed 20 per cent of women wanted a woman doctor and 25 per cent of men wanted a male doctor—3 per cent of women expressed the preference for a male doctor. Whereas males could easily have their wishes met with regards the sex of their doctor, only 14 per cent of general practitioners are female and the female patient's preference cannot always be fulfilled. Further, in some areas, especially in the country, there are no women general practitioners at all, so that it is actually impossible for some women to see a female doctor. With the increasing numbers of women going into medicine this is likely to change in the future. The family planning clinics and child health clinics, on the other hand, may provide easier access for women to obtain advice from women doctors. Many of these consultations will not only be concerned with contraception and/or child health in the stricter sense of the word, but also deal with other health and family problems.

Women doctors do tend to see more female patients than male, though Cartwright and Anderson (1981) found that, whereas in 1964 75 per cent of women doctors' patients were women, this had decreased to 60 per cent by 1977. There is so much written about women, be they doctors, patients, lawyers, or whatever, perhaps the most surprising finding in Ann Cartwright's study is that there was very little overall difference between the male and female general practitioners in their attitudes and behaviour towards women patients, although this may have something to do with the type of training doctors go through.

We have presented in this introduction some ideas influencing women's health in general, but also more specifically in relation to general practice. It was obvious to us, when reviewing the facts available, that they are open to many interpretations; nevertheless, we hope that the issues raised provide a background for the chapters of this book which deal in large part with the more specific problems for which women consult their general practitioners. Just as it has been traditionally necessary for a surgeon to be aware of the female/male differences in the anatomy, with the increasing specialist training, especially now for general practice, it has become essential that the more subtle female/male differences in behaviour and psychological attitudes towards disease should also be taught and learnt.

REFERENCES AND FURTHER READING

Black, D. (1980). *Inequalities in health*. Report of a Research Working Group. Department of Health and Social Security, London.

Brown, G. and Harris, T. (1978). *Social origins of depression*. Tavistock Publications, London.

Cartwright, A. and Anderson, R. (1981). *General practice revisited*. Tavistock Publications, London.

Crombie, D. L., Pinsent, R. J. F. H., Lambert, P. M., and Birch, D. (1975). Comparison of the first and second national morbidity surveys. *Jnl. R. Coll. Gen. Pract.* **25**, 874–8.

Dunnell, K. and Cartwright, A. (1972). *Medicine takers, prescribers and hoarders*. Routledge and Kegan Paul, London.

Fry, John (1979). *Common diseases* (2nd edn). MTP, Lancaster.

HMSO (1980, 1981, 1982). *Social trends*. HMSO, London.

Leeson, J. and Gray, J. (1978). *Women and medicine*. Social Science Paperbacks. Tavistock Publications, London.

Logan, W. P. D. (1950). Illness, incapacity and medical attention among adults, 1947–49. *Lancet* **i**, 773–6.

Morrell, D. C. and Wale, C. J. (1976). Symptoms perceived and recorded by patients. *Jnl. R. Coll. Gen. Pract.* **26**, 398–403.

Rowland, Beryl (ed.) (1981). *Medieval woman's guide to health*. Croome Helm, London.

RCGP (Royal College of General Practitioners) (1979). *Trends in general practice*. Royal College of General Practitioners, London.

Skegg, D. C. G, Doll, R., and Perry, J. (1977). Use of medicines in general practice. *Br. med. J.* **1**, 1561–3.

2 Menstrual problems

Anne Anderson and Ann McPherson

MENSTRUAL MYTHS

The disorders of menstruation, 'the curse', 'the devil's gateway', or whatever one likes to call them, form a significant part of the general practitioner's work. The information from the general practitioner Second Morbidity Study showed that out of 45 of the commonest specific conditions most
often seen in practice, menstrual problems are included in the top ten.
The annual consulting rate for these disorders in a practice of 2500 would
be approximately 50 (compared to depression 80, hypertension 50, vaginal discharge 30, menopausal disorders 15). Fry found the consulting rate
to be even higher at 68 with a breakdown as follows: 14 who consult will
have regular menses, 19 will consult for amenorrhoea or scanty menses,
14 for heavy and/or frequent menses, 10 for dysmenorrhoea, and 11 for
other menstrual disorders.

Like so many other areas of life, menstruation has its own confused
mythology from which traces of documented normative data can be ex-
tracted. It is likely that both doctors' and patients' perceptions of menstruation will even today be strongly influenced (however unwittingly) by
such myths. These are the subject of extensive documentation and include socially and culturally dependent beliefs, for instance that menstruating women: will turn the milk sour; are unclean; make hives of bees
die; make brass and iron rust; stop the bread rising, and so on. In our
own society mothers often tell their children that they should not wash
their hair or have a bath at the time of menstruation. But one should not
be misled into thinking that mythology is prevalent only in the non-
medical area. Where menstruation and its disorders are concerned, medicine, both in its investigations and in its treatment, has contributed to its
own mythology. Perhaps most notable is the use of dilatation and curettage as a panacea for varying types of menstrual disturbances—a subject
we examine in more detail later in the chapter.

It is however the purpose of this chapter to try and outline the information which is available in the way of recorded normative data and to provide guidelines as to what might be considered abnormal. Using this as a
base we will try to suggest which symptomatology, as usually presented to
the general practitioner, might indicate the need for further appropriate

investigation and treatment either at a primary care level or by the specialist.

At any time women might complain that their periods are:

too short
too long
too frequent
too infrequent
too light
too heavy
too painful
too irregular
too early (menarche)
too late (menarche)
too early (menopause)
too late (menopause)
too awful!

This is excluding the not infrequently voiced complaint that it seems unfair that they should have to have them at all. Looking in more detail at one of these complaints a national opinion poll survey, when interviewing over 500 women aged 15–44, found that 60 per cent suffered from dysmenorrhoea ranging from mild to severe—even of those with severe dysmenorrhoea 45 per cent had not been to the doctor—most used home remedies. The substance to cover these bare statistics is revealed in some of the comments of the women interviewed:

'You just accept it really, because everybody else seems to put up with it so why don't I?'

'I use a hot water bottle for comfort really—it doesn't really work—it warms.'

'I just try everything on the market.'

'It is quite painful but I take aspirin or something and then it's all right—it tends to go off.'

'I think doctors have got more things to do really than to listen to someone moaning on about period pain.'

So faced with patients' ideas and problems about menstruation, one needs standards to be able to judge whether their history, symptoms, and fears indicate any underlying pathology which needs further appropriate investigation, or would more appropriately be dealt with by simple reassurance and explanation of variations of normal, or should be investigated or counselled in the psychosocial area.

Unfortunately modern obstetrics and gynaecology is dogged by the word 'abnormal'—from abnormal labour to abnormal uterine bleeding and menstruation. The number of women labelled as abnormal is so great that it must bring into question just how much of the symptomatology is abnormal or just a variation of normal. There are many other areas of medicine, for example hypertension, where there are similar problems with terminology. The boundaries between what is accepted as pathology and what is accepted as normal is in a continual state of flux, not only over time, but between one culture and another. These boundaries seem to be particularly ill defined in the area of menstruation.

One might, of course, argue that the endless succession of menstrual cycles to which a woman today is subjected *is* abnormal. In primitive communities menstruation was probably a very infrequent event since a late menarche, lactational amenorrhoea, and poor nutrition, as well as pregnancies left the woman little time for menstrual cycles. Today's woman is faced with a much earlier menarche—around the age of 12 years—probably brought about by improved nutrition in childhood—but now occurring several years before she will be ready in most instances to contemplate a pregnancy. Furthermore, the menopause may not come for 40 years beyond the menarche, and women in this time will on average have only two full-term pregnancies and perhaps breast-feed with lactational amenorrhoea for two years at the most. Thus, modern-day woman in our society will probably experience 400–500 menstrual cycles in her reproductive life. It may not therefore be surprising that women today have so many problems with their menstrual cycles, given that they occupy so large a part of their lives. The excesses of childbearing in the past have been exchanged for the excesses of menstruation in the present. One of these problems, premenstrual tension, is dealt with in Chapter 3. In this chapter we shall discuss the problems of menstruation itself, whether excessive, painful, or absent. But before the abnormalities of menstruation are discussed, we shall briefly review the control of the 'normal' menstrual cycle.

THE NORMAL MENSTRUAL CYCLE

Hormone changes

The sequence of hormone events occurring in the menstrual cycle during which ovulation takes place is shown in Fig. 2.1. At menstruation, plasma levels of the anterior pituitary hormone, follicle stimulating hormone (FSH), are already rising, stimulating the growth of several Graafian follicles within the ovary. In general, only one follicle is 'chosen' to house the developing ovum, this follicle therefore grows much more rapidly than the others. The developing follicle produces increasing amounts of oestrogens, notably oestradiol. As levels of oestradiol begin to rise early in the follicular phase of the cycle, production of FSH is suppressed—'negative feedback'—but oestradiol levels continue to increase over the next few days until a critical level is reached. This triggers the anterior pituitary to release about 24 hours later a surge of luteinizing hormone,

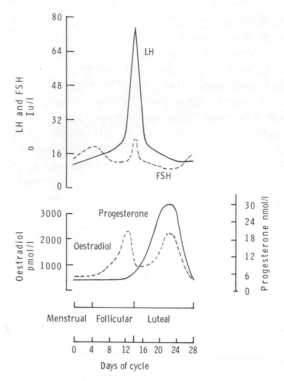

Fig. 2.1. Hormone changes during the menstrual cycle showing fluctuating levels of the pituitary hormones, luteinizing hormone (LH), and follicle stimulating hormone (FSH), and of the ovarian hormones, oestradiol and progesterone.

LH (up to 50 IU/l), and to a lesser extent of FSH (up to 15 IU/l),—'positive feedback'—these high levels of LH and FSH appearing in the circulation on one day only. Ovulation follows this gonadotrophin surge within about 30 to 36 hours and the ruptured ovarian follicle develops into the corpus luteum which secretes both oestradiol and progesterone in the second half or luteal phase of the cycle. Levels of both oestradiol and progesterone therefore rise together after ovulation, reaching peak levels between days 18 and 22 of a 28-day cycle. In the last few days of the cycle, if pregnancy has not occurred, the corpus luteum degenerates and oestradiol and progesterone levels fall before menstruation again occurs. A new cycle begins. The raised levels of progesterone in the second half of an ovulatory cycle are associated with a rise in basal body temperature of about 1 °C, a simple and non-invasive method of monitoring ovulation. Plasma levels of progesterone can also be measured to assess ovulation, levels about 30 nmol/l on days 18 to 22 indicating ovulation. Under the influence of these ovarian hormone changes, the endometrium is converted from a proliferative type under the influence of oestrogen alone in the early part of the cycle to a secretory type with the addition of progesterone after ovulation. Progesterone measurements have largely replaced endometrial biopsy and histology as a more sophisticated means of assessing ovulation. Women do not, of course, have to ovulate to menstruate and in the absence of ovulation menstruation may still occur, although often at irregular intervals. If the ovarian follicle produces enough oestrogen to stimulate endometrial proliferation then endometrial growth can be maintained even if ovulation fails to occur; when levels of oestrogen fall, endometrial shedding and menstruation will take place.

Prolactin, another anterior pituitary hormone, is also probably involved in the control of the ovary, since when levels of prolactin are very high ovulation and even menstruation can cease. In the normal menstrual cycle plasma levels of prolactin do not fluctuate in relation to ovulation in the way that other hormones do.

The anterior pituitary and the ovary must therefore work in close harmony to control ovulation and thus the length of the cycle, the amount of pituitary hormone released at any particular time in the cycle being carefully controlled by signals from the ovary. When these signals fail or are mistimed, ovulation may not occur and there can be alterations in the length of the cycle and in menstrual blood loss.

Physiology of menstruation

A basic understanding of the physiological control mechanisms for normal menstruation is essential if we are eventually to understand what happens when things go wrong, for example, when menstrual blood loss becomes 'too heavy' or 'too light'. The process of menstruation and its initiation are still not understood, although recent work suggests that prostaglandins produced within the uterus may be involved. One feature that distinguishes those species that menstruate from those that do not is the spiralling of the arterioles supplying the endometrium. In the days before menstruation it seems that increasing coiling of the endometrial spiral arterioles occurs as the endometrium itself undergoes regression. Vascular stasis and intense vasoconstriction in the spiral arterioles precedes actual bleeding which is associated with relaxation of the arterioles. It is thought that locally produced prostaglandins, whether from the vessel wall or the surrounding endometrium or myometrium, may be responsible for these important effects on the spiral arterioles. It is obviously critical that those arterioles shut themselves off effectively during menstruation. The wonder is that women do not bleed to death each month, given that spurting of arterial blood can be seen to be taking place! The synthesis of prostaglandins in the uterus may be under the control of the ovarian hormones, oestradiol and progesterone; withdrawal of these hormones over the last few days of the cycle leads to the initiation of menstruation. Certainly the amount of prostaglandins in the endometrium may increase markedly close to and at menstruation, apparently no longer inhibited by the high progesterone levels. On the other hand, this cannot be the whole story since uterine bleeding can occur at the end of anovulatory cycles when there has been no progesterone produced by the ovary and levels of prostaglandins in the endometrium are low. A great deal of research is going on in this area at present and it is hoped that the next few years will bring a further understanding of the control of menstruation. Only then will it be possible to work out ways of altering menstrual blood loss which are more effective than present treatments.

Variation in menstrual blood loss

The amount of menstrual blood lost at each menstruation has been measured in several population studies. In large numbers of women not complaining of any menstrual problem the distribution of menstrual loss is skewed (Fig. 2.2), with a long tail towards the higher losses. On average, women lose 33 ml in menstrual blood loss, with 90 per cent having a loss less than 80 ml and only 1 per cent with a loss of 200 ml or more. Despite variation in the numbers of days of menstruation (average 4–5 days), recent studies suggest that over 90 per cent of the total blood loss for that period is lost within the first three days, no matter the total loss or the total number of days of bleeding. Women find it very difficult to assess their menstrual blood loss, although it is probably when a change occurs that

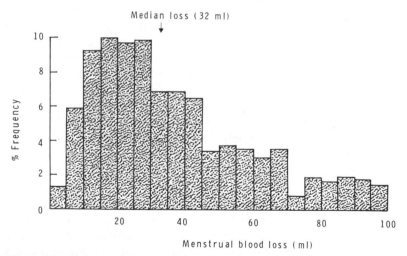

Fig. 2.2. Frequency distribution (%) of menstrual blood loss in several hundred women in Oxford before insertion of an intrauterine device.
Mean menstrual loss is 33 ml; median loss is 32 ml. (From unpublished data of J. Guillebaud with permission.)

they may decide they have a problem. Thus, some women who are losing several hundred ml per period are uncomplaining and do not consider their loss heavy; others with very small loss may complain of menorrhagia. Presumably soon after the menarche women decide that their menstrual loss at that time is 'normal', having no real basis for comparison with friends or siblings, apart from number of tampons or pads used, and will in general only consult a doctor if in the future that loss appears to be changing. There is therefore no way that the woman or her doctor can assess the volume of menstrual blood loss, short of making objective measurements. The woman's own subjective assessment, the number of days of bleeding, or the number of sanitary tampons or pads used are poor indicators of the amount of menstrual blood lost. We will return to this problem later in this chapter when we come to discuss disorders of menstrual blood loss, in particular menorrhagia.

Variation in cycle length

Cyclical vaginal bleeding in women is known to occur at well defined intervals from the menarche to the menopause. Centuries ago it was shown that the length of the menstrual cycle, i.e. from the first day of one period to the first day of the next, approximated to the phases of the moon. Hence the mystical process of periodic vaginal bleeding was designated as occurring every 28 days. For doctors as well as for women the 28-day menstrual cycle has become the symbol of health and normality in relation to reproductive function. Women are programmed for vaginal bleeding at 28-day intervals to such an extent that manipulation of their reproductive system by, for example, steroid contraception or hormone therapy at the menopause, perpetuates this time interval as being the most acceptable and 'normal'. Such is the indoctrination that women clearly begin to worry that something is wrong if their menstrual cycle length deviates from this 28-day 'norm'. Of course, it is convenient to begin to menstruate on exactly the same day of each month and at exactly the same time on that day. Finding oneself unexpectedly bleeding, particularly if the bleeding is heavy, is socially inconvenient to say the least. But the problem is that women may seek, and doctors may prescribe, hormone therapy 'to regulate the periods' if irregular intervals, long or short, have become a worry, even in the absence of pathology. It seems unwise to put women's health at any risk by drug administration if they could accept some irregularity of their periods as part of the normal variation in cycle length. This particularly applies to girls in the first few years after the menarche. Perhaps schoolgirls need to be better informed about the function of their reproductive organs and the limits of normality in terms not only of cycle length but also of menstrual blood loss and discomfort.

The degree of variability in the length of the menstrual cycle from

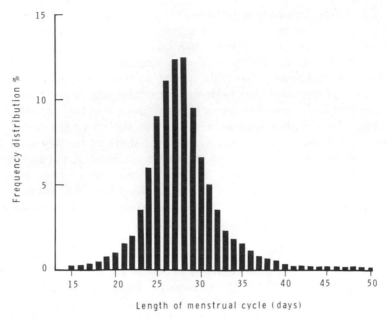

Fig. 2.3. Frequency distribution (%) of length of the menstrual cycle in days from menarche to the menopause. 31 645 menstrual cycle lengths recorded by 656 women aged 11 to 58 years.
(Redrawn from Fig. 33, p. 54 in Vollman 1977.)

menarche to menopause has been well documented in many thousands of women (Vollman 1977). Like most biological functions the length of the cycle has a modal value but a characteristic range of variability and skewness. The famous 28-day cycle happens to be the commonest cycle length recorded (see Fig. 2.3), but only just, and then in only 12.4 per cent of the cycles documented. Cycle length changes with age forming a U-shaped curve from menarche to the menopause. Mean cycle length drops from 35 days at age 12 to a minimum of 27 days at age 43, rising to 52 days at age 55 years. The range of cycle length with age is enormous, from 46 days at age 12 to a minimum of 11 days at age 41, rising steeply to 150 days at age 55 years. These data may not tell doctors too much about the length of the menstrual cycle in the individual woman, but should serve to caution us against over-emphasizing the 'normality' of the 28-day cycle. Clearly in the first few years after the onset of menstruation and in the last few years before the final menstruation there is variation in cycle length such as is not experienced at any other time. This has to be accepted as part of the normal biological function of the menstrual cycle, with its starting phase, an optimal phase, and finally a phase of decay (Vollman 1977).

Against this background of changing cycle length with age, doctors and patients can find it difficult to know if and when an alteration in length of the menstrual cycle indicates serious pathology, particularly in women approaching the menopause. We will return to this later in the chapter since it is an important issue. If one ignores alteration in cycle length as a diagnostic clue, pelvic pathology may be occasionally missed; if one always considers it an abnormal sign then vast numbers of women will be subjected to needless investigation and treatment for what is merely a variation in their physiological function.

THE ABNORMAL MENSTRUAL CYCLE

In this chapter we have tried to get away from the standard gynaecology textbook's listing and classification of menstrual problems. Rather, we have tried to present the problems and ways of dealing with them as seen in general practice. We have therefore deliberately left out the rarities and discussed in detail only the things we think are important for the general practitioner to recognize and treat. This ranges through heavy and painful to absent menstruation and from scanty to prolonged or irregular bleeding.

Heavy menstruation: menorrhagia

Excessive uterine bleeding at menstruation can afflict women at any age during reproductive life. In a survey of the problem on one general practitioner's list (Richards 1979) 7 per cent between the ages of 15 and 50 years had presented with menorrhagia. In about 50 per cent of cases no cause can be found, often called 'dysfunctional uterine bleeding', although this simply means that in the main we are ignorant of the cause; perhaps 'unexplained' is a preferred term. Unexplained menorrhagia is particularly common at the extremes of reproductive life, soon after the menarche before cycles become established in a regular pattern, and close to the menopause. The heavy bleeding at these times is often associated with very irregular cycles, usually anovulatory, but most women with menorrhagia have regular cycles and are ovulating. Menorrhagia can be associated with disease, commonly pelvic pathology such as fibroids, an endocrine disorder such as hypothyroidism, or rarely a hereditary bleeding tendency.

Assessment of menstrual blood loss

It is interesting that the diagnosis of such a common gynaecological problem as menorrhagia rests solely on the patient's subjective assessment of her menstrual loss. Although objective measurement of blood loss can be made, in clinical practice this is never done, and it remains a research tool. Yet major surgery and various forms of drug therapy are commonly advised for a condition which is never quantitated by any means. How many doctors, general practitioners or gynaecologists ever see and examine deliberately during menstruation the woman complaining of menorrhagia, in particular on the day of heaviest flow? Women are often told, certainly in hospital practice, not to come for gynaecological examination during a period, although it is precisely at that time that their symptoms are troublesome. Perhaps if we were to use a speculum to examine the menstrual flow through the cervical os we would learn more about these problems than we do from history-taking, particularly in cases of unexplained menorrhagia. As stated earlier in the chapter, neither the woman's own assessment, the number of days of menstruation, nor the number of sanitary pads or tampons used correlate with measured menstrual blood loss. The passage of large clots is likely to be a better indicator of heavy loss, since clotting occurs in the vagina if flow is very fast and is often noticed when the woman goes to the toilet. Obviously, if a woman wakes in the night and finds the bed sheets soaked in blood, or if in the daytime the menstrual blood suddenly gushes down her legs or soils her clothes excessively, then she is having a very heavy period. But there appears to be a group of women who complain of very heavy periods but in whom objective measurement of menstrual blood loss shows a light loss. Perhaps in them, complaints about menstruation are a manifestation of some other underlying anxiety, or it may be that any increase in menstrual loss is intolerable or causes them concern. Women with true menorrhagia may not necessarily drop their haemoglobin concentration; losses of 800–1000 ml can occur without anaemia. On the other hand, the presence of a hypochromic microcytic anaemia in a woman who menstruates should alert the general practitioner to the possibility that she might have menorrhagia.

Causes and diagnosis

A diagnosis of dysfunctional or unexplained menorrhagia depends on exclusion of local or systemic pathology. Uterine fibroids are the commonest cause and will be discussed later; they usually cause menorrhagia without disturbing cycle length, so periods are regular. Other associated pelvic pathologies are endometriosis (discussed under dysmenorrhoea) and chronic pelvic inflammatory disease often giving pain as well as increasing loss. Endometrial or ovarian carcinoma can present as menorrhagia, although cancer of the ovary often does not reveal itself until a large ovarian mass is present. Endometrial carcinoma rarely presents as increased loss alone with regular cycles, more often being associated with intermenstrual bleeding or blood-stained vaginal discharge in premenopausal women; its commonest presentation is after the menopause with post-menopausal bleeding. Cervical cancer rarely presents as menorrhagia. Polyps, endometrial in particular, can cause menorrhagia, although they more often lead to 'spotting' between or just before periods. Endocrine disorders may lead to increased menstrual loss, notably hypothyroidism, rarely hyperprolactinaemia and adrenal disorders. The intrauterine contraceptive device can increase menstrual loss. Bleeding diatheses, such as in Von Willebrand's disease, deficiencies of factors V, VII, and X, and idiopathic thrombocytopenic purpura are other rare causes of menorrhagia.

History-taking and general physical and pelvic examination should thus allow the general practitioner to reach a diagnosis and decide whether hospital referral is necessary. No one would argue against referring women to hospital when they complain of menorrhagia in the presence of previously undiagnosed pelvic pathology or endocrine or bleeding disorders. The debate centres on whether to investigate the woman who complains of heavy periods in the absence of an obvious cause. Investigation by the specialist will often involve uterine curettage, especially in the woman over 35 years, and thus we must consider the diagnostic and therapeutic role of 'a D and C' in women with menorrhagia. If general practitioners are considering referring the woman with 'unexplained' menorrhagia to hospital for further investigation, then they are, in the main, unless uncertain of their clinical findings, reaching the decision that the patient requires some form of surgery, at least a curettage.

Uterine curettage (D and C)

For long a much favoured operation of gynaecologists, the value of curettage as a therapeutic intervention has recently been called into question. Measurement of menstrual blood loss has shown that there is no long-term benefit for women with menorrhagia, although anecdotally some women say it helped. Its diagnostic role, particularly in younger women (under 35 years), has also been critically examined in recent times. Between 1972 and 1979, in Scotland, for example, D and C was the most frequent in-patient operation recorded; in 1974 24 000 D and Cs were performed under general anaesthetic, accounting for 71 000 bed days in that year (Vessey, Clarke, and MacKenzie 1979). If one excludes any therapeutic benefit of D and C then its main value is as a screening procedure for endometrial cancer, an extremely uncommon condition in women under 35. Knowledge of the histological appearance of the benign endometrium is not helpful in making a decision about treatment of menorrhagia. Furthermore, analysis of over 1000 D and Cs in Oxford in 1973 showed that all endometrial carcinomas diagnosed at curettage had presented clinically with post-menopausal bleeding (MacKenzie 1978). Of course, endometrial carcinoma does occur in premenopausal women but Vessey *et al.* (1979) calculated that in women under 35 years in the whole of Scotland only two endometrial cancers would be expected to present in one year, and 3 to 4 thousand D and Cs would have to be performed at the current rate to discover the two cases. The incidence of endometrial carcinoma does rise quite markedly over 40 and hence curettage is probably needed to exclude malignancy in women with menorrhagia over the age of 40. Between 35 and 40 there is less certainty.

Given that the yield of serious intrauterine pathology diagnosed at curettage is low in younger women, and considering the cost and morbidity associated with the procedure, increasing use has been made of outpatient techniques for sampling the endometrium. Several types of endometrial aspiration curettes are available and although there were initial worries about the reliability of these techniques, several studies have made favourable comparisons between out-patient and in-patient curettage. The out-patient procedure may, of course, be less pleasant for the woman, who often experiences pain when the curette is passed through the cervix, as well as lower abdominal cramps during suction. However, many women seem happy to avoid hospitalization and general anaesthesia if the whole procedure can be got over and done with as part of the initial visit to the gynaecologist. It seems likely that 'office gynaecology' will increase in this country in the next decade.

Who the general practitioner should treat and how

In the light of the evidence presented earlier, women under 35 years complaining of regular but heavy periods are extremely unlikely to have endometrial cancer and referral for specialist opinion and likely curettage in the absence of clinically detectable pathology seems unnecessary. Unless there are other worrying signs such as blood-stained vaginal discharge, intermenstrual or post-coital bleeding, the general practitioner can use medical therapy to try and reduce menstrual blood loss if this is what the woman wants. Some women are prepared to put up with their heavy loss if it is not too debilitating or socially inconvenient, and fear the side effects of drug therapy in the long term. Anaemia should be looked for and corrected. Women over the age of 40 years with menorrhagia (and, some authorities would say, over 35 years) should probably be referred to a gynaecologist. Not all women over 40 will need referral, and the general practitioner may prefer to try medical therapy in women whose loss has gradually been increasing over the years. A sudden change in loss may be more worrying and need earlier referral.

Young girls with heavy periods in the years after the menarche are very unlikely indeed to have any pelvic pathology. Again, probably all that is necessary is for the general practitioner to give reassurance by explaining to the girl (and her mother) that this type of menstrual upset usually settles with time. It is probably part of maturation of the endocrine system, the hypothalamic–pituitary–ovarian links—feedback mechanisms— requiring time to mature and function normally. General practitioners should be cautious about giving girls in the early years after the menarche hormone treatment for heavy periods. We cannot be sure that suppressing the maturing pituitary–ovarian axis is safe in relation to future fertility, and it may be as well to allow it to mature on its own. On the other hand, some young girls with very irregular and heavy periods will have cystic glandular hyperplasia of the endometrium, a problem associated with failure of ovulation and rather high and sustained oestrogen levels. This requires specialist investigation and advice, and a young girl with persistent and intolerable heavy menstrual loss, particularly with irregular cycles, should be referred to a gynaecologist.

Drug therapy

A wide variety of preparations is available to reduce menstrual blood loss in women with unexplained menorrhagia, and these are outlined in Table 2.1.

Table 2.1 *Drug therapy for menorrhagia*

Preparation	Proprietary name	Dose
Hormonal		
Progestagens		
Norethisterone	Primolut-N	5 mg b.d. or t.i.d. days 19 (or earlier) to 26
Medroxyprogesterone	Provera	5 mg b.d., as for Primolut-N
Dydrogesterone	Duphaston	10 mg b.d., days 5 to 26
Combined oestrogen/progestagen pill (high dose) e.g. Gynovlar		
Other		
Danazol	Danol	200 mg daily continuously
Non-hormonal		
Prostaglandin synthetase inhibitors		
e.g. mefenamic acid	Ponstan	500 mg QID during menstruation only
Antifibrinolytics		
Epsilon aminocaproic acid	Epsikapron	1–2 sachets QID during menstruation
Tranexamic acid	Cyklokapron	1–1.5 g 6–8 hourly during menstruation
Drugs reducing capillary fragility		
Ethamsylate	Dicynene	500 mg 4–6 hourly during menstruation

Hormonal.   The most popular therapy has been cyclical progestogens based on the idea that many women with menorrhagia are not ovulating and that replacing the missing progesterone in the second half of the cycle could be helpful. As stated earlier, however, most women with menorrhagia and regular cycles are ovulating so the rationale for progestagen therapy is not clear. It probably suppresses endometrial growth to some extent, but does not appear to have been evaluated properly, i.e. no study has ever been carried out in menorrhagia to assess the effect of progestogens on menstrual blood loss. Various progestogens have been tried and given for differing numbers of days of the cycle, e.g. days 19 to 26, 12 to 26, or even 5 to 26 if shorter courses are ineffective. Side effects of weight gain, breast tenderness, bloating, or breakthrough bleeding can occur. Very large doses of progestogens can be given to arrest torrential vaginal bleeding. Norethisterone up to 30 mg daily will usually stop the bleeding in 24–48 hours; the dose can then be reduced and finally stopped over the next few days. Bleeding of this magnitude needs investigation by the specialist but may require emergency measures by the general practitioner. The combined oral contraceptive pill is undoubtedly very effective in the control of menorrhagia, especially the high oestrogen dose varieties with a large amount of progestagen (e.g. Gynovlar). Of course, menorrhagia is a problem in the over-35s, the very group in whom the high-dose pill is contraindicated, but some authorities feel that it can be prescribed for thin non-smokers who are not hypertensive. Obviously, patients would have to be screened very carefully. The low-dose combined pill is not very effective for menorrhagia. The third type of hormonal therapy which is very effective in the reduction of menstrual blood loss is danazol. The drug probably acts at various levels, hypothalamus, pituitary, ovary and endometrium, leading to endometrial atrophy and amenorrhoea in some women. In a dose of 200 mg daily most patients continue to menstruate regularly, although with dramatically reduced blood loss. Ovulation is usually inhibited at this dose but the drug cannot be relied on as a contraceptive. The drug is expensive and can have side effects of weight, gain, muscle pains, acne, headaches, but can be useful and effective short-term therapy. It does not increase the risk of thrombo-embolic problems.

Non-hormonal.   In recent years drugs that inhibit prostaglandin synthesis have been shown to reduce menstrual blood loss effectively in about 50 per cent of women with menorrhagia. Mefenamic acid in particular has been tested and although the effect is variable from patient to patient, the advantage is that this drug need be taken only during menstruation. This is very attractive to some women who do not want to spend a large percentage of their cycle taking drugs. Mefenamic acid 500 mg four times a day can be prescribed during the heaviest days of the period. It is contraindicated in women with a history of peptic ulceration but seems to have few side effects if taken for only a few days of each cycle. Other non-hormonal remedies include drugs having antifibrinolytic activity such as epsilon aminocaproic acid. These too need be taken during menstruation only and have been shown to reduce blood loss by about 50 per cent. There have been worries, however, about thrombo-embolic risks and these agents should not be given to women with a history of thrombosis or who have risk factors. Ethamsylate is a drug which is said to increase capillary wall strength and can reduce menstrual loss. It is also taken during menstruation but appears to have been studied very little.

Treatment of fibroids

Since these are commonest tumours of the uterus and the commonest pathology associated with heavy menstrual bleeding, they will be discussed here. It has been estimated that one in five of all women will develop fibroids in the uterus but in most cases these will be symptomless and undiagnosed. The tumour probably arises from smooth muscle cells but also contains fibrous tissue—hence its other names: fibromyoma or leiomyoma. It is commonest in nulliparous women and in those of Negro origin. It very rarely becomes malignant. Fibroids usually only give trouble in pre-menopausal women since in most cases they undergo atrophy after the menopause, apparently being influenced by ovarian hormones. Increased menstrual blood loss probably occurs when fibroids project into the uterine cavity, the 'submucous' variety; if this variety become polypoidal, intermenstrual bleeding may also occur.

Fibroids can be single or multiple, and vary enormously in size; they may either cause symmetrical enlargement of the uterus or transform it into an irregular mass. On clinical examination the tumours are rounded, smooth swellings with a characteristic firm consistency and move with the uterus. They usually distort the shape of the uterus and if pedunculated may be mistaken for an ovarian tumour which is the most important differential diagnosis.

Treatment depends in part on size, on the degree of menstrual upset associated with the fibroids, and on how close is the menopause. Near the menopause fibroids may be managed conservatively in the hope that they will atrophy once menstruation ceases; the patient should be examined at intervals, however, to check that rapid growth is not occurring when specialist referral should be made. Oestrogens should be avoided in the treatment of menorrhagia associated with fibroids since these hormones can stimulate growth. Progestogens can be safely prescribed, however, and danazol can also be effective (Table 2.1). In younger women the same medical therapies should be tried and conservative management is safe if the tumours are not too large. If the uterus is enlarged to a size corresponding to a 14 to 16 week pregnancy or there is associated pain, then at any age specialist referral is necessary and surgery will usually be performed, either myomectomy if the woman wants to preserve her fertility, or hysterectomy.

Hysterectomy

The pros and cons of medical as opposed to surgical treatment for unexplained menorrhagia should be discussed with each patient. Women nearing the menopause will often opt for medical therapy, even if there are some side effects, knowing that the treatment should not have to last too long. But younger women, for example those in their 30s, often cannot face the prospect of 15 to 20 years of drug-taking and decide on hysterectomy. It is important that women share in the decision-making with their doctor and are not made to feel that doctors are making decisions for them, particularly since it involves major surgery and loss of an organ that has such obvious sexual implications. If hysterectomy is decided on, the general practitioner is in the ideal position to discuss details of the operation including the vexed question of whether the ovaries are likely to be removed, and possible after effects. This is discussed in more detail in Chapter 6 on ectomies.

Painful menstruation: dysmenorrhoea

Derived from the Greek meaning 'difficult monthly flow', the word 'dysmenorrhoea' has come to mean painful menstruation. Lower abdominal pain, however, is not the only symptom of dysmenorrhoea and other unpleasant features are headaches, faintness, dizziness, nausea, diarrhoea, backache, and leg pain. The symptoms usually appear just before or at the onset of menstrual flow and persist at their worst during the first day or two of menstruation. In some women lower abdominal pain can begin several days before menstruation starts and can persist throughout the total number of days of the period.

Dysmenorrhoea is said to be primary if it occurs in the absence of pelvic disease and this is usually so in adolescent girls. Pain seems to occur in ovulatory cycles only since the early anovulatory cycles after the menarche are painless. It is secondary if it is related to conditions such as endometriosis, fibroids, and pelvic inflammatory disease or if there is an intrauterine contraceptive device. Gynaecological textbooks have laid great emphasis on further subclassifications into spasmodic and congestive but these seem to have no foundation in fact. Congestive dysmenorrhoea is really a description of what we now call the premenstrual syndrome with symptoms of abdominal bloating being ascribed to 'congestion' of the pelvic organs.

The proportion of women in Britain with painful periods is difficult to assess, although recent studies have shed some light on the problem. In one general practitioner's experience (Richards 1979) 14 per cent of women aged 15 to 50 years had presented at the surgery with a primary complaint of dysmenorrhoea. As already mentioned, not all patients with dysmenorrhoea consult their general practitioner.

Aetiology

Various hypotheses have been proposed over the years to explain pain at menstruation. Gynaecological textbooks have frequently expressed the view that primary dysmenorrhoea may be due to a faulty education and outlook on sex and suggest that over-anxious parents, mothers in particular, foster anxiety about pain. Modern textbooks still suggest that exercise and even cold baths may tone up the mental outlook and help the pain. Although psychogenic factors may play a part in some women, the idea that menstrual pain is 'all in the mind' rather than in the uterus cannot be upheld.

Attitudes to dysmenorrhoea, primary in particular, have been changing with increasing evidence that prostaglandins may be involved in the aetiology of the disorder and that drugs that inhibit the synthesis of these hormones are an effective therapy for some women. Secondary dysmenorrhoea is less clearly related to prostaglandins. Since levels of prostaglandins in the uterus are raised in women with primary dysmenorrhoea, painful menstruation may be due to overactivity of the uterine muscle with accompanying abdominal cramps. Escape of prostaglandins from the uterus into the circulation would be responsible for the other symptoms such as gastrointestinal disturbances, faintness, dizziness, and headaches, since these were the side effects noted when intravenous infusion of prostaglandins was used to induce labour in late pregnancy. This is the rationale for treating primary dysmenorrhoea with prostaglandin inhibitors.

Treatment of primary dysmenorrhoea

In most cases, women will seek the help of their general practitioner only if the menstrual pain is severe or there is some other underlying reason, for example a young girl may actually be seeking contraception, knowing that the pill is often prescribed for dysmenorrhoea. In young girls one can assume a diagnosis of primary dysmenorrhoea and it is probably unnecessary to examine them. If dysmenorrhoea is increasing in severity, or appears for the first time after several years of painless menstruation, then a pelvic examination is necessary to try and exclude local pathology. Referral to a gynaecologist may be necessary if pathology is suspected, and laparoscopy may be required to make a diagnosis.

Occasionally no treatment will have been tried at all, and simple analgesics should be suggested. But usually treatment with simple analgesics will have failed if the woman consults her general practitioner. There are two lines of treatment available, prostaglandin synthetase inhibitor drugs or hormonal therapy in the form of an oral progestagen or the combined oestrogen–progestogen pill. The advantage of the prostaglandin inhibitors is that they need be taken only during menstruation at the time of the pain. Several of these drugs have been tested in placebo-controlled trials—indomethacin, mefenamic and flufenamic acid, naproxen, ibuprofen, flurbiprofen, and ketoprofen. Overall results of the trials show a pain-relieving effect in 65 to 90 per cent of patients, significantly better than placebo or ordinary analgesics. Four- to six-hourly medication is probably necessary when the pain is at its worst. There seems no advantage in taking these drugs in the last few days of the cycle before menstruation unless the pain is particularly severe at this stage. It is probably safer to await the onset of menstruation to ensure that pregnancy has not occurred, since it is not known if these drugs are teratogenic in early pregnancy. Although the prostaglandin inhibitors can be effective in primary dysmenorrhoea, they are probably not very useful in the treatment of the secondary variety. The combined pill is undoubtedly effective for the relief of dysmenorrhoea in most women and should, of course, be prescribed if contraception is also required. Many women who do not want contraception, however, much prefer to take treatment for a day or two of the cycle during the time of their symptoms. Oral progestogens, norethisterone 5 mg b.d. or dydrogesterone 10 mg b.d. from days 5 to 26 of the cycle can also be helpful.

Although the general practitioner may feel that pain at menstruation is too minor a complaint to treat with potent drugs, 'a sledgehammer to crack a nut', one must remember that women self-medicate during their periods with common analgesics often taken in large amounts. These analgesics may be no safer than, for example, the prostaglandin inhibitors and in any case we now know that all analgesics owe their efficacy in relief of pain to their inhibitory effects on prostaglandins. To deny women treatment for dysmenorrhoea is not now tenable. Although the pain and symptoms may only last for a few hours of a day, dysmenorrhoea can be devastating, keeping women away from work or school and making it difficult for them to function normally. Doctors have now, we hope, moved away from the old feelings that women tend and even want to be malingerers during menstruation, towards a more sympathetic and positively helpful approach to the problem. The general practitioner is in the ideal position to help, and the acknowledgement by doctors that the problem is real is a help in itself.

A surgical approach to treatment is now largely obsolete. Dilatation of the cervix used to be commonly performed in severe primary dysmenorrhoea but there are worries that forcible dilatation of the nulliparous cervix may disturb its function in a subsequent pregnancy and lead to abortion or premature birth. Presacral neurectomy, aimed at interrupting sympathetic fibres contributing to the pelvic plexus, is occasionally carried out, with claims of a high success rate. It must be regarded as a fairly desperate measure.

Treatment of secondary dysmenorrhoea: endometriosis

Virtually any pelvic pathology can give pain during menstruation and the reader should consult a gynaecology textbook for a detailed account of the diagnosis and treatment of these. Pelvic inflammatory disease is an important problem which can give rise to secondary dysmenorrhoea; it is discussed in this book in Chapter 12. Fibroids have been dealt with earlier in this chapter. Here we will discuss the diagnosis and treatment of endometriosis, an apparently increasing problem in young women, although this may depend on increasing use of laparoscopy in the diagnosis of pelvic pain. Endometriosis can give severe and incapacitating pain before and during menstruation as well as menorrhagia. It can also cause pain during intercourse—a deep dyspareunia—backache and tenesmus. It can be associated with infertility.

The aetiology of endometriosis is obscure but has produced several theories. The most popular has been that menstrual blood containing fragments of endometrium might flow in a retrograde fashion down the Fallopian tubes and out into the peritoneal cavity. The endometrium might then implant on the peritoneal surface of any organ in the pelvis or abdomen, most frequently on the ovary, uterosacral ligaments, or broad ligament, and on the surface of the uterus itself. Another theory is that endometriosis is the result of metaplasia of primitive cells with differentiation into ectopic endometrium. The endometriotic lesions vary in size from very small black spots seen on the peritoneum to large cystic masses in the ovary filled with dark viscous material. These 'chocolate cysts' are probably due to haemorrhage occurring from the endometriotic patches which are influenced in a cyclical way by the ovarian hormones in the same way as the endometrium lining the uterine cavity. Dense pelvic adhesions can eventually occur if haemorrhage is occurring monthly into the peritoneal cavity over several years.

On bimanual pelvic examination the hard fixed nodules of endometriosis may be felt in the uterosacral ligaments, in the pouch of Douglas, the recto-vaginal septum, or on the uterine wall. The uterus can be fixed in retroversion and cystic ovaries may be felt in severe cases. Speculum examination may reveal a bluish nodule in the posterior fornix if the vaginal wall is involved. Moving the cervix usually causes pelvic pain and vaginal examination may be particularly painful. The diagnosis can only be made with certainty by laparoscopy and the GP should consider referral to a gynaecologist if secondary dysmenorrhoea is severe and is associated with infertility, and if attempts at medical therapy have failed.

Treatment may be conservative or radical, medical or surgical, depending on the age of the patient, her desire to preserve her fertility, and the extent of the disease. In many cases pregnancy has a beneficial effect on the disease, so that if the patient is planning to have children she should be encouraged to do so without too much delay since progression of the disease may occur with time and lead to irreversible infertility. If the patient has completed her family and the endometriosis is severe involving many pelvic organs with gross adhesions, radical surgery may be advisable, i.e. hysterectomy and bilateral oophorectomy. Removal of the ovaries is usually advised with extensive disease since it is the cyclical hormone production from the ovaries that fuels the growth of the endometriotic nodules. With less extensive disease, however, and in women who want a pregnancy, endometriotic deposits can be removed surgically with conservation of the ovaries and pelvic adhesions divided.

Medical therapy has become increasingly popular in recent years with the introduction of the drug danazol. This is probably now the drug of choice, although progestagens, for example norethisterone 10–15 mg daily, or dydrogesterone 20 mg daily, given cyclically from days 5 to 25 of each cycle, can give relief of pain, but rarely cure the problem in the long term. The combined contraceptive pill, preferably with a high progestagen content, can be given continuously to stop menstruation. Danazol has the added benefit of causing endometrial atrophy if a large enough dose is given, but may require 600 to 800 mg daily continuously to achieve this effect. At this dose the drug will almost certainly cause amenorrhoea which is the aim of the treatment, the idea being that cessation of menstruation should equate with failure of growth of the endometrium, both inside and outside the uterine cavity. With high doses of danazol, treatment becomes very expensive (about £12 per week at 800 mg daily), and has to be continued for up to 9 months if there is any hope of 'curing' the endometriosis. Side effects are common at these high doses, in particular weight gain, acne, skin rashes, muscle cramps, headaches, which cannot be tolerated by some patients. Unlike the contraceptive pill there seem no thrombotic risks on danazol. Although, in high doses, danazol suppresses both ovulation and menstruation, these both return rapidly on stopping the drug. However, medical treatment may have to be combined with surgical treatment to achieve the best results.

Absent menstruation: amenorrhoea

Absence of periods disturbs women just as much as the other disorders of menstruation. They may feel a loss of femininity or worry about an unwanted pregnancy. There seems no doubt that women in reproductive life prefer to menstruate regularly, not too much and not too little, but not to be without it altogether. In the vast majority of women with amenorrhoea, excluding pregnancy, the cause will be hormonal. There may, of course, be anatomical reasons, for example, absence of the uterus and vagina, but these are rare. There has been a preoccupation in the past and in gynaecological textbooks with distinguishing between primary and secondary amenorrhoea but that should probably be defused. There is so much overlap in causes of primary and secondary amenorrhoea that it is not helpful to consider them as separate entities in relation to diagnosis. Instead, the differential diagnosis of amenorrhoea can be based on the main pathologies that give rise to the problem and these are given in Table 2.2. Congenital disorders usually present as primary amenorrhoea but almost all causes of secondary amenorrhoea can present as primary if they present before the age of 16 years.

Table 2.2 *Main causes of amenorrhoea*

Hypothalamic—pituitary disorders:
  Prolactin hypersecretion ± prolactin-secreting pituitary adenoma
  Tumours
  Weight loss—anorexia nervosa
  Obesity
  Psychogenic
  Post-oral contraception
  Isolated gonadotrophin deficiency (Kallman's syndrome)
Ovarian, uterine, or vaginal disorders
  Polycystic ovarian disease
  Ovarian failure (premature menopause)
  Gonadal dysgenesis (e.g. Turner's syndrome)
  Absence of uterus (e.g. testicular feminization) or vagina
  Haematocolpos
Other diseases
  Thyroid hormone deficiency or excess
  Adrenal disorders (e.g. Cushing's disease, congenital adrenal hyperplasia)
  Severe general disease (e.g. leukaemia or Hodgkin's disease treated with
  chemotherapy)

Clinical and laboratory assessment

It is important to keep foremost in one's mind the possibility of pregnancy even in a woman with primary amenorrhoea. Pregnancy will be excluded from further mention here but the general practitioner should warn women with primary or secondary amenorrhoea of hormonal aetiology that they are not necessarily infertile and are at risk of pregnancy should a sporadic ovulation occur.

History-taking and examination should elicit the following information and physical characteristics in all cases of amenorrhoea:

  age at menarche;
  development of secondary sex characteristics—pubic and axillary hair, breasts;
  menstrual history before amenorrhoea;
  galactorrhoea;
  recent change in body weight; height and weight;
  medication, particularly oral contraception; chemotherapy;
  recent emotional upsets;
  hirsutism;
  hot flushes and sweats, dry vagina;
  symptoms of other endocrine disorders, e.g. thyroid, pituitary, or adrenal;
  abdominal and pelvic examination; inguinal hernias.

Laboratory tests to determine the cause of amenorrhoea involve measurement in serum in all cases of the anterior pituitary hormones LH, FSH, and prolactin. Testosterone levels should be measured in women with hirsutism or where testicular feminization is suspected (see later). The karyotype should be checked if there are suspicions of a chromosomal disorder. Table 2.3 shows the results in the major causes of amenor-

Table 2.3 *Laboratory findings in major causes of amenorrhoea*

	FSH	LH	Prolactin	Testosterone	Karyotype
Hyperprolactinaemia	Normal	Normal	High	Normal	Normal
Premature menopause	Very high	High	Normal	Normal	Normal
Polycystic ovarian disease		Slightly raised	Normal or slightly raised	Slightly raised	Normal
'Hypothalamic'	Normal	Normal	Normal	Normal	Normal
Turner's syndrome	High	High	Normal	Normal	45XO or mosaics
Testicular feminization	High	High	Normal	High	46XY

rhoea. Suspected endocrine problems such as thyroid or adrenal disorders obviously require specific investigation.

Causes

Delayed menarche.   How long should the general practitioner wait before investigating the girl who has never menstruated? Since most girls will have started menstruating by the age of 16 years, this would be regarded as the upper age for the normal menarche. If secondary sex characteristics have not developed or there appear to be anatomical problems on clinical examination then specialist referral is essential. The rarer possibilities are of testicular feminization syndrome (maturation of breasts without maturation of axillary and pubic hair, absent uterus with normal or short vagina; 46XY with testes) or Turner's syndrome (many variants, but typically short stature, sexual infantilism, webbing of the neck, cubitus valgus, 45XO with streak gonads). Haematocolpos is another rare cause when secondary sexual development will be normal, there may be intermittent lower abdominal pain, a lower abdominal cystic swelling or a bulging swelling in the vagina, palpable per rectum. A tense blue-coloured membrane may be seen at the introitus. Referral is obviously necessary for incision of the obstructing membrane under general anaesthesia.

If secondary sexual development is normal or appears to be progressing satisfactorily, albeit delayed, and there is no anatomical problem, then the cause is likely to be hormonal. Measurement of the pituitary gonadotrophins LH, FSH, and prolactin will help sort out the endocrine problem (Table 2.3).

Hypothalamic amenorrhoea.   Secondary amenorrhoea of a month or two's duration is common and usually corrects itself. Six or more months' amenorrhoea may merit investigation unless it is considered that the woman has reached a natural menopause. Very often the findings are of normal LH, FSH, and prolactin levels, suggesting a 'hypothalamic' cause the exact nature of which is seldom established. This is the picture one sees when weight loss has led to amenorrhoea, or in anorexia nervosa (see Chapter 17 on eating problems), and so it is obviously important for the general practitioner to enquire about recent weight changes and to check weight for height. It is also the typical picture in the student who always menstruated regularly until leaving school and home and coming up to university or college; menstruation often returns once the final examinations are passed. Reassurance that there is nothing seriously wrong may be all that is required from the general practitioner. Post-pill amenorrhoea also can give the biochemical picture of normal LH, FSH, and prolactin, although there is no need to investigate this for 4–6 months after stopping the pill since spontaneous return to menstruation can occur in this time.

For many of these women acceptance of their amenorrhoea even if 'nothing is wrong' is very difficult. A feeling of loss of femininity can be a problem, particularly in young girls who have never menstruated and who often want to know what it is like to be the same as other girls, and to be reassured that their periods can be switched on if need be. The problem is that the switching-on process for hypothalamic amenorrhoea is by choice with a fertility drug like clomiphene so that not only menstruation but also ovulation and potential fertility occur. This has to be explained to the woman and contraceptive methods discussed. Sometimes after a few months of menstruation the woman is happy to stop taking the clomiphene, having satisfied herself that she is capable of having periods. Psychologically this can be very helpful and should not be denied women even if they do not wish to conceive. On the other hand, it may be wise from the point of view of future fertility that women do not stay on prolonged courses of clomiphene just to produce menstruation, but rather should be encouraged to 'save' the fertility drug until the time comes when they want to have a pregnancy.

If women with hypothalamic amenorrhoea do not want to menstruate or conceive then contraception must be discussed, given that they may spontaneously begin to ovulate and menstruate at any time. The pill is not necessarily contraindicated (see Chapter 7 on contraception), but barrier methods are obviously preferable. The progestagen-only pill is probably the pill of choice. On the other hand, the combined pill may cause regular withdrawal bleeds and be psychologically more acceptable. The woman should be reassured that her future fertility will not be further impaired in these circumstances if she takes the pill.

Hyperprolactinaemia.   The discovery of human prolactin about ten years ago, and the realization of its involvement in reproductive function, opened new doors in the management and treatment of some menstrual disorders and infertility. High levels of prolactin are found in about 25 per cent of patients with amenorrhoea; about 30 per cent of these also have galactorrhoea. However, galactorrhoea alone, in the absence of severe menstrual disturbances such as amenorrhoea, is rarely associated with

elevated prolactin levels. The exact mechanism whereby hyperprolactinaemia leads to amenorrhoea is not fully understood but the high levels
of prolactin seem to interfere with hormonal events at the level of the
hypothalamus. Consequently, there are effects on the ovary suppressing
ovulation and finally menstruation stops when oestradiol levels fall.

There are many causes of high prolactin levels. The most important
cause is a prolactin-secreting tumour of the anterior pituitary. Therefore,
women with amenorrhoea and hyperprolactinaemia should have an X-ray
of the pituitary gland, followed by tomography and visual field assessment
if a tumour is suspected. Hospital referral is obviously essential if the
pituitary fossa X-ray shows any suspicion of a pituitary tumour. But there
are other causes of hyperprolactinaemia, often associated with drugs such
as the phenothiazines, reserpine and methyldopa, hormonal therapy in
particular oestrogens, and more recently cimetidine has been implicated.
If the hyperprolactinaemia is drug-related the general practitioner has to
weigh up the pros and cons of stopping the offending drugs as opposed to
reassuring the patient that the amenorrhoea should be left untreated.
Lowering drug-induced high prolactin levels with another drug such as
bromocriptine is to treat the side effects of one drug with another and is
probably unwise. In many cases of hyperprolactinaemia there is no
obvious cause.

Menstruation, ovulation, and fertility can be restored in patients with
hyperprolactinaemia by use of the drug bromocriptine which lowers prolactin levels very effectively. The starting dose should be small, one-
quarter tablet taken in bed at night with a small amount of food to minimize the side effects of nausea, and faintness due to hypotension. The
dose can be gradually increased to one-half tablet, then one tablet
(2.5 mg), up to whatever dose is necessary to bring down the prolactin
level into the normal range. If the patient wishes her fertility restored
then obviously she should be treated with bromocriptine. But women
who do not want a pregnancy are in a more difficult position. If they want
to take bromocriptine to allow them to menstruate (and often this is
psychologically beneficial, making women feel more feminine again), but
also require contraception, then a barrier method or the IUCD should be
recommended. The combined pill should not be prescribed because of the
probability that the oestrogenic component can raise prolactin levels; the
progestagen—only pill is probably safe. How long bromocriptine therapy
should be continued is not known. There is some evidence that in the absence of any predisposing cause, hyperprolactinaemia may resolve after
1–2 years on bromocriptine. Short-term treatment is probably not curative.

Polycystic ovarian disease. First described by two gynaecologists, Stein
and Leventhal, in the early 1930s, this syndrome was originally ascribed
to patients with amenorrhoea, hirsutism, obesity, and bilateral polycystic

ovaries. It is clear, however, that any form of menstrual irregularity can occur—oligomenorrhoea, or menorrhagia with regular or irregular cycles —and the term polycystic ovarian disease or syndrome is now preferred. The aetiology of the disease is unknown. Hormonal estimations give a picture of an elevated LH level, normal or low FSH, mildly elevated prolactin in some patients, and elevated testosterone. Laparoscopy will confirm the diagnosis but is not necessary if there is a typical biochemical picture.

In the patient with amenorrhoea and polycystic ovarian disease normal ovulation and menstruation can usually be induced using clomiphene (25 to 50 mg daily for 5 days of each cycle) (see Chapter 12 on infertility). If the patient does not want her fertility restored, the excess LH and hence androgen production from the ovary can be suppressed using the combined pill. Alternatively, and particularly if hirsutism is severe, the anti-androgen drug cyproterone acetate 50 to 100 mg daily, days 5 to 14 of the cycle, along with ethinyloestradiol 30 to 50 μg daily from days 5 to 25 can be given. Surgery in the form of bilateral ovarian wedge resection used to be a favoured treatment although nobody knew why it helped. The benefit of surgery was short-term, however, and there were worries about subsequent adhesions so that surgery is now resorted to only if medical therapy fails or is contraindicated. Most of all, the patient with polycystic ovarian disease needs help from her general practitioner to come to terms with her disease since the androgenic symptoms of obesity, hirsutism, and often acne may make the patient wonder if she is 'turning into a man'. She needs encouragement to reduce her weight, advice about the control of excess hair, facial in particular, and reassurance about her femininity and potential fertility.

Premature menopause.   This is characterized by high FSH and LH (FSH in particular > 20 U/l on two occasions) with normal prolactin levels. Other symptoms of the menopause may be present such as hot flushes or sweats, a dry painful vagina and atrophic vaginitis, indicating low oestrogen levels. Sadly, premature ovarian failure can occur at any age and youth is no protection against the possibility. If the woman has not started or completed her childbearing, specialist referral is necessary for laparoscopy and ovarian biopsy. The 'resistant ovary syndrome' may be amenable to therapy with gonadotrophins and the possibility of pregnancy although little hope should be given. This is discussed further in Chapter 4. Treatment with cyclical oestrogen/progestagen therapy is indicated in women with premature ovarian failure, both to treat symptoms and possibly protect against premature heart disease and osteoporosis.

Infrequent and scanty menstruation: oligomenorrhoea

A woman with infrequent periods should be investigated in the same way as a woman with amenorrhoea, since the causes in general are the same.

Scanty but regular menstruation probably needs no investigation. It may herald the menopause or rarely have an endocrine cause but in general is not a worrying symptom.

Prolonged menstruation

On average, women menstruate for five to six days of each cycle and anything over this may be considered prolonged. As discussed earlier, the number of days of bleeding does not relate to menstrual blood loss since most of the loss is passed in the first two to three days, whether the overall loss is light or heavy. Prolonged menstruation in itself does not need special investigation but usually, of course, goes along with other complaints such as menorrhagia. Periods can be prolonged, the period proper often being preceded by spotting, in association with an IUCD or the progestogen-only pill; reassurance is all that is required unless the woman wishes to change the method of contraception if the number of days of bleeding is unacceptable. Several days of spotting before a period can be a sign of an endometrial or cervical polyp and even of malignancy, and visualization of the cervix, a cervical smear, and pelvic examination should be carried out by the general practitioner with referral to a gynaecologist if there are suspicious findings.

Irregular menstruation and bleeding

Irregular periods

Women often worry if their previously regular periods become irregular, but, as discussed earlier, this is most likely to be no more than a variation on the physiological. Irregular menstruation, both short and long cycles, is most common at the extremes of reproductive life, soon after the menarche or before the menopause. These cycles are usually anovulatory. In adolescent girls it does not need investigation unless there are obvious signs of endocrine disease (see amenorrhoea), and should not be treated with hormonal therapy 'to regularize the periods'. Rather, the general practitioner should reassure a young girl that this is part of the maturation process and convince her of the likelihood that her periods will gradually become more regular. Suppressing the maturing pituitary–ovarian axis with large amounts of synthetic steroids as in the contraceptive pill may give a girl regular vaginal bleeding but is probably unwise in the immediate post-pubertal years. Of course, if she needs contraception this may outweigh all other considerations. In later life, nearer the menopause, irregularity of periods is so common that not all women could be investigated. If the period becomes heavy as well as irregular, referral to a gynaecologist is wise, particularly if there are any other problems such as intermenstrual or post-coital bleeding.

feels better at or shortly after the onset of menstrual bleeding and feels well and back to normal for the rest of the cycle until the symptoms start again. Women who experience PMT report that the severity can vary from cycle to cycle, often depending to a large extent on what is going on in their lives: and in some months the premenstrual phase may pass almost unnoticed. Often, however, the individual can predict the day on which her symptoms will inevitably start each month. The most important defining feature is its cyclical nature and its disappearance around the start of menstruation. This is an important feature which distinguishes it from discomfort associated with menstruation itself such as dysmenorrhoea. Until the relationship to the menstrual cycle is established, some features may be wrongly diagnosed by the woman or her doctor as more generalized emotional or physical problems. Unfortunately, the variable nature of PMT and its many definitions and manifestations often make it hard to recognize. Establishing the timing and duration of the changes in well-being is the first step in recognizing the problem and finding appropriate treatment.

INCIDENCE

It is hard to evaluate how many women experience PMT since the distinction between PMT and more common but less severe cyclical changes is not always clear. Many women notice mild mood changes, such as feelings of tiredness, sadness, or irritability in the day or two before menstruation, with some breast tenderness and feelings of swelling. Epidemiological studies of large randomly selected groups of women indicate that between 75 and 90 per cent of menstruating women notice these changes at some time. For most they are in no way a problem but more a herald of the onset of menstruation each month, and can be regarded as normal 'physiological' aspects of the menstrual cycle.

Severe and distressing PMT which leads the individual to seek medical advice is less common. However, studies estimate that almost ten per cent of women noticing cyclicity in their well-being find these changes a problem and would like help (van Keep and Utian 1981). Clearly this is no small number of individuals. There is a great range from 'normal' cyclical changes to severe and troublesome ones, in between being women who notice moderate premenstrual symptoms but do not find these a particular problem and would not regard themselves as requiring medical treatment. This range leads to the question of whether PMT is a distinct entity or whether it is a more marked version of these milder premenstrual changes.

It is not easy to draw a clear line of demarcation between normal and problematical changes but research by the author indicates that the distinction may be one of degree. Three groups of women with different experiences of cyclical changes rated their moods, physical health, and sexual feelings for one month and frequent blood samples were used to relate the ratings to fluctuating levels of hormones. Women who reported no symptoms showed only mild changes in their moods in the premenstrual phase, although premenstrual breast tenderness was common. In contrast, women attending a clinic complaining of severe PMT showed a marked deterioration in their well-being which started shortly after ovulation. This included feelings of depression, tiredness, and irritability, combined with breast tenderness and swelling, increasing in severity throughout the luteal phase. Women who reported symptoms but had not found it necessary to seek medical advice showed similar changes but these were less marked and the deterioration in well-being started later on, in the mid-luteal phase. This suggests that distressing PMT which leads the individual to seek medical advice may differ from the normal and less troublesome range of cyclicity, not in the nature of the changes, but more in their *severity* and *timing* during the cycle, being related to the entire luteal phase rather than just the few days before menstruation. Experience with talking to women indicates that what brings a woman to a clinic or doctors' surgery is usually the effects of PMT on her life: women require help when it interferes with their working, personal, social, or home life and the best judge of the 'normality', severity, or significance of cyclical changes is the woman herself.

PMT AND SEXUALITY

The influence of PMT on a woman's sexuality is an aspect which has received little attention. There is no doubt that mood changes interact with sexual feelings, sexual activities, and how the individual feels about herself, and women with severe premenstrual tiredness or breast tenderness may also feel less sexually interested at this time. These women may feel more sexual after menstruation when their general well-being improves. However, some women with PMT feel more sexual in the premenstrual phase. These fluctuations in sexual interest may cause worry to the woman and possible difficulties within a relationship unless the links to the menstrual cycle and cyclical mood changes are understood.

WHO EXPERIENCES PMT?

There are no rules as to the type of woman likely to experience the problem; it is reported by young women soon after the menarche as well as those approaching the menopause, and by both nulliparous and parous women. However, severe symptoms are more common in the 30–40 age range than in the 'teens and twenties, and married women with children are common among those who seek medical advice from the general practitioner. This indicates either that PMT gets worse with age or that cyclical changes become less easy to cope with in certain circumstances. For example, stresses associated with family life and responsibility for children may exacerbate the symptoms.

There are claims that PMT is a manifestation of a 'neurotic' personality, but research indicates that there is little consistent relationship between a woman's personality or degree of neuroticism and the presence or severity of the syndrome. It is obviously important to consider the effects of recurrent emotional or physical distress on the personality. Unfortunately in the past PMT has been dismissed as a feature of certain types of women.

EFFECTS

The most important effect is on the woman. It can cause her to feel unwell and distressed for up to half her cycle. However, individuals may report concern about the effects PMT has on other people, especially small children who may not understand apparently unpredictable mood changes in their mother. A proportion of women find that their ability to carry out some aspects of their daily work is temporarily impaired in the premenstrual phase, although this can usually be coped with by reorganization of work schedules. In fact research has indicated that overall work performance is not impaired in the days before menstruation, any impairment being overcome by increased concentration or effort.

More seriously, it is alleged that certain events are exacerbated in the premenstrual phase or are more likely to occur at this time. Crimes, accidents, attempted or successful suicides, examination failures, absenteeism from work, admission to general or psychiatric hospitals, bringing a child to a medical unit, baby battering, and marital disturbances have all been claimed to occur more often around menstruation (Dalton 1977). Indeed, in France acceptance of PMT as a 'risk' has been embodied in legal statutes so that if a woman is convicted of a crime committed before her period, she may use this in her defence, claiming temporary insanity. Recently in Great Britain, amid much controversy, PMT has been considered as a mitigating condition in a woman accused of murder.

Unfortunately, this evidence has been illogically and incorrectly interpreted as indicating that the premenstrual phase is a time when all women are 'at risk' and may batter a child or commit a crime or attempt suicide. It is more likely that women who are predisposed to these events and who experience PMT may become more sensitive and vulnerable to stresses in the premenstrual phase. For example, women who commit crimes may be more likely to be found out at this time or women with PMT who are in a difficult situation at home may become more sensitive to difficulties which they usually stoically tolerate so that flare-ups are more likely to occur premenstrually.

For various reasons troublesome PMT may be experienced by increasing numbers. Women now have a greater number of menstrual cycles during their lifetime than ever before, menarche occurs earlier, pregnancy less often, and there is a decline in the time spent in lactational amenorrhoea. It is possible that the reproductive system is not adapted for repeated menstrual cycles and PMT is an unfortunate indication of this. Social changes may mean that PMT is more of a problem. Increasing numbers of women are employed outside the home and are expected to be full-time mothers and home-keepers, all without the help once available from more community orientated lifestyles or the extended family. Alternatively, because of the increasing isolation of the family, women who are involved in full-time work at home, looking after children and keeping house, may find this situation contributes to feelings of depression or anxiety. These stresses and responsibilities may be felt more acutely in the premenstrual phase such that mood changes which would normally be tolerable are exacerbated and become distressing.

PMT is now becoming recognized and accepted. The swing towards greater openness and discussion of women's health and problems means that women who have put up with distress and discomfort perhaps for years are now learning that others share their problems and are seeking advice and treatment, often from the general practitioner. Until recently, the general practitioner has been ill-equipped to help. Although research on the problem started back in the 1930s, there has been poor understanding of its aetiology, a situation which has not been helped by either denial of PMT as a real phenomenon or dismissal of it as a purely psychological problem. However, recent research has meant that we are beginning to further our understanding of the complex interactions between physiological and psychological factors in the aetiology. We are still a long way from fully understanding this condition, but women experiencing distressing premenstrual changes can now expect both a sympathetic reception and practical suggestions for help. The rest of this chapter evaluates the causes of PMT, various ways women can help themselves to deal with it, and the medical treatments available.

CAUSES

There are many aetiological hypotheses including the involvement of the ovarian hormones, oestradiol and progesterone; an imbalance of fluids and salts; the action of non-ovarian hormones, aldosterone and prolactin; a deficiency in vitamin B_6, pyridoxine; and hypoglycaemia. None of these theories are sufficiently convincing to explain all the various physical and emotional changes. Since the symptoms vary so widely between individuals it is likely that different aetiological factors apply to different women. PMT most probably results from a combination of several factors, physiological and psychological. The interaction with the woman's lifestyle, particularly stressful situations or events, is also vital to any consideration of its causes. The aetiology has been comprehensively reviewed elsewhere (Smith 1975; Steiner and Carroll 1978; van Keep and Utian 1981). The next section discusses research and theories which are most relevant to treatment.

Hormones

Ovarian hormones

Several facts suggest strongly that hormones in some way contribute to PMT. The defining characteristics of PMT are its cyclical nature and the restriction of the symptoms to the luteal phase. Cyclical mood changes, corresponding to fluctuating levels of oestrogens and progesterone persist in women after hysterectomy where the ovaries are not removed and continue to function. There is some debate as to whether premenstrual symptoms occur in anovulatory cycles although the general consensus is that they are not equivalent to that found in ovulatory cycles (Smith 1975). Women find that their cyclical changes disappear during pregnancy and after the menopause.

Hormonal theories go back a long time: research as long ago as the 1930s claimed to find an imbalance of oestrogens and progesterone. However, only in the last two decades have radioimmunoassay methods become available for accurate and reliable measurements of hormone levels. This has allowed an evaluation of the involvement of hormones and whether women with PMT have any endocrinological abnormality or hormone imbalance in the luteal phase. The most popular theories point to the withdrawal of oestradiol and progesterone before menstruation, excess oestrogens, a progesterone deficiency, or an imbalance in the oestrogen to progesterone ratio. On the basis of these theories treatment with hormones is advocated. The involvement of luteal phase hormones was investigated by the author. Women with severe PMT rated their moods and physical well-being each day throughout one menstrual cycle and daily blood samples were taken for measurement of oestradiol and progesterone. Although the women were most distressed in the last five days before menstruation, the changes started at the beginning of the luteal phase parallel with the development of the corpus luteum. When menstruation started the premenstrual symptoms decreased and the women felt well during the follicular phase and at their best during the midcycle oestradiol peak (Fig. 3.1). This establishes a temporal relationship between the entire luteal phase and PMT and indicates the involvement of more than simply the withdrawal of hormones in the last few days before menstruation.

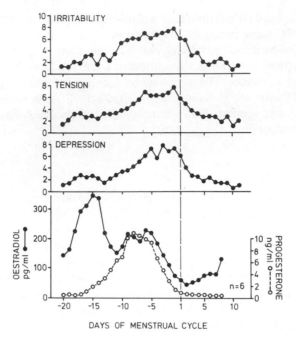

Fig. 3.1. Daily ratings of mood related to the hormonal changes during the menstrual cycle in 19 women with severe PMT. (From Backström 1981.)

It is far from certain precisely what it is about the luteal phase which contributes to these women's marked distress at this time. There is no general agreement about the role of oestrogen and progesterone. Symptoms can occur in the absence of any endocrine abnormality; levels of hormones and the pattern of fluctuation throughout the cycle are generally within the normal range. There are claims that women with PMT have a deficiency of progesterone relative to oestradiol in the luteal phase. However, this has not been confirmed in all studies. In the author's research, levels of oestradiol and progesterone and the oestradiol:progesterone ratio were no different between women with different degrees of cyclical mood changes. There is generally a wide overlap in hormone levels between women with PMT and symptom-free groups, so a progesterone deficiency or hormone imbalance is not a general rule. In the author's research two aspects of the hormonal variations in the luteal phase differed slightly in women with PMT. Compared to the no-problem group, the premenstrual fall in progesterone occurred earlier and there was also a greater drop from mid-luteal to premenstrual levels of oestradiol and progesterone. This indicates that both the length of time that hormone levels are falling and the size of change may contribute to the severity of the emotional and physical distress, although this is as yet speculative.

A further suggestion is that some women may be sensitive to hormones. Although there may be no differences between individuals in circulating levels of hormones, their effects on emotional or physical well-being might vary depending on the woman's constitutional sensitivity, just as tolerance of drugs or alcohol varies between individuals. Some evidence for this comes from research on oral contraceptive agents. In a double-blind study of combined pills containing different oestrogen: progestogen doses, Cullberg (1972) found that women with a history of PMT reacted adversely to the more oestrogenic pills, indicating that these women may be sensitive in some way to oestrogens. In the author's research many of the women with severe PMT had in the past used oral contraceptives and had to stop due to unpleasant side effects, often feeling 'premenstrual' all the time. It is not unlikely that women's reactions to hormones may vary and that there are individual differences in how and whether emotional and physical changes relate to endogenous or exogenous hormones. PMT could represent a woman's sensitivity to her own hormones: there is little research as yet to back this up but it remains an interesting possibility.

Aldosterone

Another popular theory is that a disturbance of water and salt balance is involved with retention of fluids and sodium in the tissues and depletion of potassium. The basis is that a proportion of women notice uncomfortable fluid retention during the premenstrual phase, with swelling of the abdomen, breasts, face, fingers, ankles, or legs, which is relieved in a time of marked diuresis when menstruation starts. Actual weight gain has been recorded, some women gaining as much as 4 kg before menstruation, although this may not always occur and feelings of swelling may be caused by a redistribution of fluid in the body (Andersch, Hahn, Andersson, and Isaksson 1978). No doubt fluid retention and emotional distress are interrelated and women find that the heavy swollen feelings will influence their moods and energy. Dark-skinned large-breasted women may be more prone to fluid retention and associated swelling and heaviness of the breasts than tall thin women with light complexions (Reitz 1979).

An absolute or relative change in levels of aldosterone may contribute to fluid retention, although this theory has little experimental support. Plasma concentrations of aldosterone are higher in the luteal phase than the follicular phase but premenstrual levels are no different between women with or without PMT (Munday, Brush, and Taylor 1981) and it is unlikely that a simple excess of aldosterone occurs cyclically; there are probably complex interactions with other hormones.

Prolactin

Raised levels of prolactin may contribute to PMT, although there are not necessarily significant differences in prolactin levels between women with and without PMT. Some women have levels of prolactin in the high–normal range but hyperprolactinaemia occurs in only a few individuals. Prolactin levels vary during the menstrual cycle. Since this hormone may be involved in salt and fluid retention and acts on breast tissue it is possible that varying levels within the individual could contribute to fluid retention and breast discomfort.

Pyridoxine—vitamin B₆

A lack of pyridoxine has been postulated as a possible factor in depression related to the use of oral contraceptives and supplementation of this vitamin has been successfully used by women who become depressed while taking the pill (Adams, Wynn, Rose, Seed, Foulkard, and Strong 1973). Pyridoxine, in the form of pyridoxal phosphate, is a co-factor in a number of enzyme reactions in the body, particularly those leading to the production of dopamine and serotonin (Fig. 3.2). Thus a reduction in pyridoxine could lead to reduced dopamine and serotonin. Dopamine inhibits prolactin and so its reduction may lead to raised prolactin production with adverse effects on ovarian and breast function and possible fluid retention. Decrease in serotonin has been implicated in emotional disturbances, particularly depression. Pyridoxine may be in short supply in women who suffer from PMT, possibly due to a defect of absorption of the vitamin from the gut or faulty metabolism of pyridoxal phosphate. Its role in this condition is an exciting possibility and merits further attention and research. It gives both a logical explanation of some of the emotional and physical changes and a basis for treatment. A number of women are finding marked relief with large doses of this vitamin.

Hypoglycaemia

Premenstrual feelings of weakness, faintness, or lethargy and cravings for carbohydrates suggest that low blood sugar may be involved, and there is some research indicating that some women have a flattening of the glu-

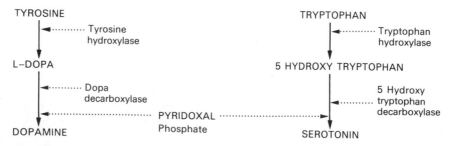

Fig. 3.2. The role of pyridoxine as a co-factor in the metabolism of dopamine and serotonin.

cose tolerance curve in the premenstrual phase. However, sugar cravings may be linked to the emotional changes since physical and emotional distress may influence some women's appetite.

Psychological factors

It is doubtful whether PMT can be explained on a purely physiological basis in terms of a hormone imbalance, pyridoxine deficiency, or fluid retention. These factors no doubt contribute but interact with the woman's constitution, occupation, and events and people in her life to result in the complex physical and emotional distress that is so characteristic of the syndrome. Some advocate that psychological factors are of decisive importance and that it is a 'psychosomatic' disorder characteristic of certain types of women. However, as discussed above, many different women experience PMT and there is no convincing relationship between its existence or severity and personality. Personality factors are more likely to influence the types of emotional changes than to be a simple cause. There are claims that because women are brought up to expect mood changes before menstruation they therefore experience PMT. This theory is not supported by the research demonstrating the persistence of cyclical changes after hysterectomy.

No doubt there are interactions with many aspects of life, especially difficult or stressful times. Many women find their symptoms vary according to what is going on in life: on holiday they may be free from any premenstrual symptoms, whereas a busy, stressful, or challenging time may be accompanied by more premenstrual discomfort. Many women who attend general practitioners for help with premenstrual problems are married and responsible for small children and also may have full- or part time employment outside the home. It is possible that such situations are associated with stress. Research indicates that the development or exacerbation of PMT relates to stressful life events but one can only speculate as to whether this is mediated by physiological factors. The reproductive system is sensitive to stress and environmental changes, as illustrated by examples of amenorrhoea associated with moving, travel, or new environments. Clearly, life events interact with the physiological and psychological factors involved in cyclical changes in well-being, and these interactions require consideration in understanding the aetiology.

MANAGEMENT AND TREATMENT

PMT is a distressing and common problem, and requires both sympathetic attention and appropriate treatment. A major problem is that it is not in itself an illness and often it seems inappropriate for a woman to have 'medical' treatment. Many women find that with information, patience, and encouragement they can work out ways of helping themselves to cope with distressing cyclical changes. Often the first step is recognition and acceptance of the problems and this may lead to a visit to the general practitioner for advice and help. This does not inevitably mean that drug treatment is necessary: a useful start is advice about what the woman can do to help herself. If problems persist then some of the medical treatments can be tried. Before discussing these, the next section covers a 'self-help' approach to PMT.

Self help

The self-help approach to health is growing in popularity and has especially contributed in helping women to work out ways of dealing with specifically female problems. There is now much more information on women's health available through the popular press. Of course, there is nothing new about this. Before the advent of modern medicine there were many cures and treatments for all kinds of ailments, including problems associated with menstruation, which incorporated common sense, support from others, and a variety of herbal remedies: old wives' tales may be founded on centuries of wisdom. Unfortunately much of this has got lost with medical technology and the ready availability of potent and fast-acting drugs. We have too much faith in medicine and too little in our abilities to find solutions and we readily turn to instant treatment rather than taking time to work out the possible causes of problems and how to deal with them. Medicine may not always have the treatments for what are, after all, women's natural functions.

The first step towards help is for the individual to come to terms with PMT and realize that her problems are real and shared by other women. Talking about it is a great help, either with other women, friends and family, or with a doctor. A menstrual diary is useful. This involves daily recording of physical and emotional well-being, as shown in Fig. 3.3. A diary kept over a few months can reveal particular moods and physical changes and their relationship to the cycle. This means that the individual can understand more about her own cycles and can predict how she is going to feel, which is helpful in accepting and dealing with symptoms when they arrive. These records should also be continued throughout times of treatment, in order to assess whether the treatment is effective. Women who can rearrange their daily schedules of work and activities find it helpful to make allowances for times when they feel less energetic or able to cope. Those who are responsible for the domestic side of life can recruit support and help with household tasks from their families. The times after menstruation are often more energetic and creative and can be put to good use in catching up with undone work.

A check on general health is important. Many women spend so much time looking after others' health that they forget themselves in small but vital ways, especially as regards nutrition. Much of our food is relatively

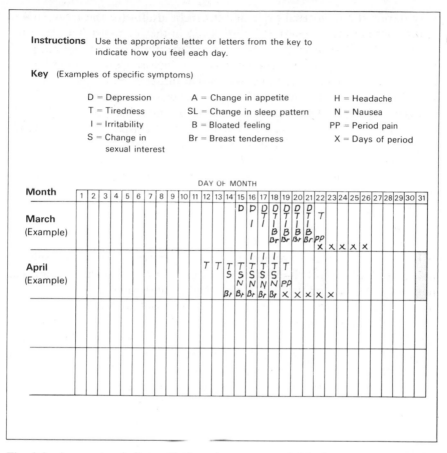

Instructions Use the appropriate letter or letters from the key to indicate how you feel each day.

Key (Examples of specific symptoms)

D = Depression	A = Change in appetite	H = Headache
T = Tiredness	SL = Change in sleep pattern	N = Nausea
I = Irritability	B = Bloated feeling	PP = Period pain
S = Change in sexual interest	Br = Breast tenderness	X = Days of period

Fig. 3.3. A menstrual diary. Similar charts are available from *Drug and Therapeutics Bulletin.*

low in vitamins and minerals as a result of processing. There is little known about the relationship between nutrition and menstrual problems but some women find that careful attention to diet is helpful, making sure of a balanced diet with enough vitamins, minerals, roughage, fresh fruit and vegetables, and avoiding too much processed food. Women's dietary needs are not necessarily the same as men's or children's, but this may be overlooked by women who are responsible for others' nutrition. Exercise can be very helpful for many of the physical and emotional aspects of PMT. Premenstrual tiredness is a common problem and exercise is the last thing desired at this time. However, more physical activity in general can help. Women find that taking or making time for walking, swimming, learning a sport, or yoga can have beneficial effects on general health and make the premenstrual phase more tolerable. Sleep requirements may vary during the menstrual cycle and it can be useful for the individual to realize her pattern. Some need more sleep in the premenstrual phase but do not make allowances for this and consequently premenstrual fatigue is exacerbated. However, some need less sleep before menstruation but are concerned at being unable to get to sleep at this time. It may be helpful to wear loose and comfortable clothing if bloating occurs premenstrually and a well-fitting support bra can help swollen or tender breasts.

A number of remedies can be tried for specific aspects of PMT. However, as with so many of the drug therapies said to be effective in the treatment of this problem, there is lack of scientific evaluation of these remedies. Results are not always instant and often experimentation is necessary to find out what suits the individual. Talking to women about their own pet remedies reveals a wealth of esoteric suggestions including yoga, hot baths, a long walk or run to work off tension, sex, an occasional well-timed alcoholic drink, herbal teas, massage, or a visit to the sauna.

If fluid retention is a problem then cutting down on fluids and salt can make a difference. Much drinking of tea and coffee is habitual rather than necessary and can be usefully replaced by, say, eating some fruit. Many foods, especially those in tins and packets, contain hidden salt. Some foods are naturally diuretic (e.g. prunes, figs, celery, cucumber, and parsley); others are rich in potassium (e.g. bananas, oranges, dried fruits, soya beans, and tomatoes), and it is useful to increase the intake of these in the premenstrual days. A small amount of strong coffee is also diuretic. Constipation is best avoided by increasing roughage in the diet and it is helpful to avoid too much refined carbohydrate. Hypoglycaemia may be involved in premenstrual weakness, faintness, fatigue, and sugar-cravings. Careful attention to diet can help: eating frequent, small, protein-rich snacks is better than missing meals or eating sugary foods. Pyridoxine (vitamin B_6) supplements are increasingly popular to help depression, irritability, fatigue, and breast tenderness. This is available from chemists and health food shops as well as on prescription, but dosages in each tablet are variable and may be very small.

A number of people now try herbal remedies for ill-health, believing them to be gentler and safer than conventional drugs. Women have reported that borage, sage, and fennel are helpful for depression, fatigue, and irritability. For bloatedness and breast tenderness, pennyroyal, rosemary, camomile, or dandelion are reported as useful. Herbs are taken as a tea. Some women who suffer from premenstrual headaches or migraines find help from relaxation techniques such as yoga or breathing exercises. These can lessen the severity of a headache or shorten the time of a migraine attack, especially if they are predicted in advance and a conscious attempt is made to relax before the headache becomes severe. Relaxation in general might help both to reduce the strain during the premenstrual phase and reduce stress.

Women can be advised that many books on PMT and 'self-help' remedies are available from bookshops and libraries: some are listed at the end of this chapter. The Health Education Council and Women's Health Concern provide further information.

Medical treatment

There are many different medical treatments described and their use depends both on the principal symptoms reported by the woman and on the aetiological hypothesis adopted by the doctor (Table 3.2). As for self-help remedies, there has been little scientific evaluation, few controlled trials of these treatments have been carried out, uncontrolled trials or anecdotal reports being the rule. In the absence of controls a fair degree of success is found for many treatments and a proportion of women are helped for some time at least. However, such controlled trials as have been performed have been disappointing since they have indicated that very often the medication is overall no more effective than placebo or self help. Perhaps the most useful contribution to treatment by the general practitioner is to acknowledge to the woman that the condition exists. A key feature is that different things suit different women and so experimentation is required. Even in controlled trials with a strong placebo effect the medication is helpful to some and the problem is to find the appropriate treatment for the individual. Measurement of hormone levels is of no value in deciding which treatment is going to help. Although much has been written about progesterone deficiency in PMT, as stated earlier plasma concentrations of progesterone are in general within the limit of normal or are low–normal and knowledge of the exact level does not allow more rational therapy. Drug therapy appears blunderbuss and the general practitioner can only offer to work through the range of medications available in the hope of finding one that is helpful. Women should also be warned that some of the drugs may make their premenstrual symptoms worse but that this cannot be predicted. They should, of course, stop any therapy that exacerbates the problem. In addition, it would be unwise to prescribe any drug for premenstrual problems if a woman is trying to conceive; the teratogenic effects on the fetus are largely unknown but all drugs are best avoided in these circumstances.

Pyridoxine—vitamin B₆

The possible role of pyridoxine in the aetiology has implications for treatment and there are many reports from doctors and women themselves that this vitamin can dramatically improve some women's premenstrual distress. Kerr (1977) reported that pyridoxine, in doses 40–100 mg daily, relieved depression and irritability in 50–60 per cent of users and headaches in 80 per cent. Other recent trials have been encouraging. In one study 63 per cent of women improved on pyridoxine, depression,

Table 3.2 *The relationship between symptoms, possible causes, and treatment of PMT*

Symptoms	Possible cause	Treatment	Effectiveness
Mood changes including depression, breast tenderness, fluid retention, headaches	Pyridoxine deficiency	Pyridoxine	Improvement of breast tenderness, depression, irritability, and headaches at appropriate dosage No known side effects or contraindications.
Emotional distress Physical symptoms	Hormone imbalance	Natural progesterone	Effective in uncontrolled trials. Strong placebo effect in controlled trials. Inconvenient since cannot be taken orally. Rectal or vaginal administration
		Synthetic progesterone Dydrogesterone	Helpful for fluid retention, depression, and headaches. Little effect on breast tenderness. Occasional side effects.
		Oral contraceptive pills—combined or progestogen-only	Some improvement, *or* PMT limited to 1–2 days, *or* adverse reactions.
Swollen or bloated feelings	Fluid retention	Diuretics	Improve symptoms of fluid retention and weight gain. Little effect on mood disturbances.
Swelling of abdomen, breasts, face, fingers Breast tenderness Headaches Associated emotional distress including tiredness	Increased aldosterone	Aldosterone antagonist spironolactone	Improves symptoms of fluid retention.
Breast tenderness Fluid retention	Increased prolactin	Bromocriptine	Useful for breast tenderness May cause nausea or dizziness
Faintness, tiredness, irritability, depression, appetite changes	Hypoglycaemia	Careful attention to diet	Helpful

irritability, lethargy, breast tenderness, and headaches being especially helped (Day 1979; Taylor and James 1979), although it is less effective for fluid retention. These trials were, however, uncontrolled and other studies comparing its action with placebo are less favourable. But as the vitamin may definitely help some women it is a useful treatment to try before the stronger drugs described below, particularly since it seems safe even in doses much larger than those normally used. To date no significant side effects have been noted apart from a tendency to gastric acidity and headaches at doses above 200 mg daily, a dosage which should not be exceeded except in exceptional circumstances. Some patients have reported sleep disturbance and alteration in the length of the menstrual cycle on 100 mg daily.

The dose of pyridoxine has not been worked out. Most women with moderate to severe symptoms probably require 100 mg daily. If this dose is not effective it may be worth increasing to a maximum of 200 mg daily. Pyridoxine may be prescribed on a twice-daily basis or as a daily sustained-release preparation (Complement, 100 mg). The tablets may be started a few days before the expected onset of symptoms and stopped when menstruation starts or when the symptoms usually disappear. Some women prefer to take them every day if the time of onset is unpredictable. Compared with hormonal therapies, pyridoxine is relatively cheap and free of side effects, and for these reasons general practitioners may consider prescribing it before resorting to other drugs.

Diuretics and aldosterone antagonists

Diuretics are helpful to women whose principal symptoms relate to fluid retention—feelings of swelling or bloatedness or weight gain. Improvement of emotional distress is less predictable and controlled trials of diuretics have not demonstrated any beneficial effects on moods. Long-term use of diuretics can lead to potassium depletion and consequent tiredness and weakness. This can be avoided by prescription of potassium with the diuretic, a potassium-supplemented diuretic, or if the woman increases her intake of potassium-rich foods.

The aldosterone antagonist spironolactone, 25 mg taken twice daily from days 18 to 26, has been found to be effective in relieving fluid retention in 80 per cent of women in small trials of this drug, and potassium depletion is avoided.

Progesterone and progestogens

There is much controversy surrounding the use of progesterone and its synthetic derivatives. On the one hand some doctors and the manufacturing companies claim that natural or synthetic progesterone can have dramatic effects in alleviating severe PMT. On the other, since the syndrome is not necessarily associated with progesterone deficiency, there may be no rational basis for this treatment. However, progesterone does appear to be of benefit to some women and may be appropriate for those not helped by 'self-help' measures, pyridoxine, or diuretics.

Natural progesterone.   The use of natural progesterone is enthusiastically advocated, particularly by Dr Katharina Dalton (Dalton 1977). Since progesterone is not absorbed if taken by mouth, she prescribes 100–400 mg daily by suppository or pessary (Cyclogest) or from 50 mg on alternate days to 100 mg daily by injection. The treatment is started 5 days before symptoms usually appear. For most women progesterone is commenced on day 14 and stopped with the onset of menstruation or after 14 days. The dosage has to be adjusted to suit the individual which can be a lengthy process so results may not be instant. If the symptoms improve, the duration and dosage can be reduced.

In an uncontrolled study of 100 women (Dalton 1977) 75 found suppositories or pessaries helpful and 9 were relieved by injections, indicating a very good response rate. However, two double-blind controlled trials comparing progesterone with placebo are less favourable. Sampson (1979) found that progesterone by suppository (200 mg b.d. from days 16 to 26) was no more effective than placebo and at doses of 400 mg progesterone had adverse effects. Smith (1975) found little difference between progesterone and placebo in relieving PMT. These results mean that it is hard to ascertain whether any improvement reported by women on progesterone is actually due to the effects of the hormone or other, possibly placebo, effects.

In some women progesterone can exaggerate their premenstrual symptoms and they should stop the therapy. Cycle control can be disturbed with shortening or lengthening of the cycle, heavy menstrual loss, or rarely amenorrhoea. This disturbance may sometimes be unacceptable but rarely needs investigating. Natural progesterone is not, of course, contraceptive.

Progestogens.   Unlike natural progesterone, synthetic derivatives are absorbed if taken by mouth and may therefore be more acceptable and convenient. Dydrogesterone (Duphaston) has been promoted in recent times and its efficacy tested in several clinical trials. It is very similar in chemical composition to progesterone. Other progestogens such as norethisterone (Primolut-N 5 mg once or twice daily in the second half of the cycle) or the progestogen-only contraceptive pill may also be tried but do not appear to have been evaluated scientifically.

Dydrogesterone.   Encouraging results with this drug have been reported at a dose of 10 mg twice daily from days 12 to 26 of the cycle. A controlled trial from St. Thomas's Hospital, London (Day 1979), found that 74 per cent of women reported improvement in premenstrual irritability, depression, and fluid retention, although the effect on breast symptoms was negligible. In this trial, however, 43 per cent of women showed an overall improvement on placebo. A more recent trial (Haspels 1981) also showed a high placebo effect with over half the women reporting improvement of their symptoms (73 per cent of 123 women in the study) being in the placebo group. These studies and other clinical evidence demonstrate that although there may be quite a high placebo response, some women do find it a very effective treatment for their premenstrual discomfort. Interestingly, improvement occurs regardless of whether the woman has low or normal progesterone levels, indicating that the rationale for its use may not necessarily be low progesterone. This means it is not possible to use plasma progesterone levels to identify those women who are likely to find dydrogesterone helpful, apart from through trying it. It is most effective for symptoms of fluid retention and depression, symptoms which may not respond so well to pyridoxine. At least three months' trial is necessary to make a reasonable assessment of its efficacy. Side effects such as breakthrough bleeding may be controlled by increasing the dosage. Nausea, weight gain, breast discomfort, and changes in cycle length and the amount of menstrual bleeding have been reported. Dydrogesterone, like natural progesterone, is not contraceptive.

The contraceptive pill

There is debate as to whether the combined pill improves premenstrual problems or makes them worse (Smith 1975). Indeed, Cullberg's study (1972) indicated that women with a history of PMT may react badly to the oestrogen component of the pill. However, some women taking the combined pill find that they experience relief of premenstrual symptoms, and that this relief may continue even after they have stopped taking the pill. A short time on oral contraceptives may therefore be helpful. Similarly, the progestogen-only pill can relieve or make worse premenstrual problems. There is little research to date to evaluate the efficacy of the pill in women with PMT.

Bromocriptine

Controlled studies indicate that the prolactin antagonist, bromocriptine, is particularly effective in relieving breast tenderness, although beneficial effects on fluid retention and mood disturbance have also been reported. The mastalgia does not appear to be necessarily associated with raised levels of prolactin, although bromocriptine will lower plasma concentrations of prolactin. Occasionally women with severe premenstrual symptoms have raised prolactin levels, but this is likely to be associated with menstrual disturbance and bromocriptine would be appropriate therapy (see Chapter 2).

If used for mastalgia in the absence of hyperprolactinaemia a small dose of bromocriptine (2.5 mg daily) is all that is required. Higher doses may be necessary if the patient has raised prolactin levels but this requires specialist advice. The drug should be taken in a low dose to begin with, e.g. a quarter of a tablet taken in bed before going to sleep, preferably with some food, thus avoiding the side effects of nausea and faintness due to its hypotensive effects. After a few days on a small dose, increasing to half a tablet then one tablet (2.5 mg) is usually tolerated.

Antidepressants and tranquillizers

PMT is distinct from general emotional disturbances in that the individual feels distressed only for a proportion of her cycle and is back to normal for the rest of the month. However, antidepressants and tranquillizers, for example diazepam, are sometimes prescribed. These are generally not very helpful and may exacerbate other aspects such as tiredness or lethargy.

CONCLUSIONS

Premenstrual tension includes a wide range of physical and emotional changes varying in the severity, duration, and effects on a woman's life. It is unlikely that there is a simple or single cause but rather any understanding of the aetiology must include both physiological and psychological factors and their interactions with the woman's lifestyle and situation.

The answer is not necessarily simple but there is now greater acceptance and understanding of the problem and more remedies and treatments. Women need to devote time for experimentation in working out the appropriate solution and may require help from their general practitioner to evaluate how they can help themselves and, if necessary, how medical treatments may benefit.

Often the first steps are sympathetic discussion of the problems and some reorganization of aspects of life to help cope with the times of feeling low. For some women a 'self-help' approach is useful, such as changes in diet and exercise, control of fluid and salt intake, and some herbal and vitamin remedies. For others medical treatments are required. Trials of pyridoxine indicate that a substantial number of women find their distressing symptoms are relieved once the appropriate dose is found. For women who do not respond to pyridoxine other drugs such as diuretics, natural or synthetic progesterone, aldosterone antagonists, and bromocriptine may be useful for specific symptoms.

In treating PMT perseverence is often necessary. Solutions may not be instant and a number of different remedies can be tried to find one or a combination to suit the individual. However, once a successful treatment has been found the dramatic improvement in these women's quality of life and their relief after perhaps years of distress is no small reward for either the woman or her doctor.

ACKNOWLEDGEMENTS

I am grateful to Judy Bury and Joan Rogers for their valuable comments on the chapter, and to T. Backström for permission to publish Fig. 3.1.

REFERENCES AND FURTHER READING

Adams, P. W., Wynn, V., Rose, D. P., Seed, M., Foulkard, J., and Strong, R. (1973). Effect of pyridoxine hydrochloride (vitamin B_6) upon depression associated with oral contraception. *Lancet* 1, 897.

Backström, C. T. (1981). In *Progesterone and progestins* (ed. C. W. Bardwin, P. Mauvais-Jarvis, and E. Milgrom). Raven Press, New York.

Andersch, B., Hahn, L., Andersson, M., and Isaksson, B. (1978). Body water and weight in patients with premenstrual tension. *Br. J. Obstet. Gynaecol.* **85**, 546.

Cullberg, J. (1972). Mood changes and menstrual symptoms with different gestagen/estrogen combinations—a double blind comparison with placebo. *Acta psychiat. scand.* (Suppl.), **236**, 1.

Dalton, K. (1977). *The premenstrual syndrome and progesterone therapy.* Heinemann, London.

Haspels, A. A. (1981). A double-blind, placebo-controlled, multi-centre study of the efficacy of dydrogesterone. In *The premenstrual syndrome* (ed. P. A. van Keep and W. H. Utian). MTP Press, Lancaster.

Munday, M. R., Brush, M. G., and Taylor, R. W. (1981). Correlations between progesterone, oestradiol and aldosterone levels in the premenstrual syndrome. *Clin. Endocrinol.* **14**, 1.

Reitz, R. (1979). *The menopause—A positive approach,* Penguin, Harmondsworth.

Sampson, G. A. (1979). Premenstrual syndrome: a double blind controlled trial of progesterone and placebo. *Br. J. Psychiat.* **135**, 209.

Smith, S. L. (1975). Mood and the menstrual cycle. In *Topics in Psychoendocrinology* (ed. E. J. Sachar) pp. 19–58. Grune and Stratton, New York.

Sommer, B. (1973). The effect of men on cognitive and perceptual-motor behaviour—a review. *Psychosomat. Med.* **35**, 515.

Steiner, M. and Carroll, B. J. (1978). The psychobiology of premenstrual dysphoria: a review of theories and treatments. *Psychoneuroendocrinology* **2**, 321.

van Keep, P. A. and Utian, W. H. (ed) (1981). *The premenstrual syndrome,* MTP Press, Lancaster.

The following articles are to be found in *Current Medical Research and Opinion:* (1977) **4**, Supplement 4; (1979) **6**, Supplement 5:

Claire, A. W. (1979). Psychological aspects of women with the premenstrual syndrome. **6**, 11.

Day, J. B. (1979). Clinical trials in the premenstrual syndrome. **6**, 40.

Kerr, G. D. (1977). The management of the premenstrual syndrome. **4**, 29.

Taylor, R. W. (1977). The treatment of premenstrual tension with dydrogesterone. **4**, 35.

—— and James, C. E. (1979). The clinician's view of patients with premenstrual syndrome, **6**, 46.

Further reading for patients

Birke, L. and Gardner, K. (1979). *Why suffer? Periods and their problems*. Virago, London.

Kingston, B. (1980). *Lifting the curse*. Ebury Press, London.

Lever, Judy, Brush, M., and Haynes, B. (1979). *Premenstrual tension: the unrecognised illness*. New English Library, Times Mirror, London.

Rakusen, J. and Phillips, A. (1978). *Our bodies, ourselves*. Penguin, Harmondsworth.

The Health Education Council publishes a leaflet on PMT.

4 Menopause

Anne Anderson and Ann McPherson

INTRODUCTION

The word menopause is derived from the Greek words '*men*' month and '*pausis*' halt. It means simply the end of menstruation and therefore the end of reproductive life. The transitional phase during which reproductive function begins to fail is called the climacteric, defined in the *Concise Oxford Dictionary* as 'occurring at a period of life (45–60) at which vital force begins to decline'. Faced with such a dismal prospect at the 'change of life' it is little wonder that middle-aged women sank into involutional melancholia! For some women the end of reproductive life may be depressing, representing loss of femininity, a symbolic castration and entry into old age. For others it is a welcome release from menstruation and its associated problems, the end of contraception with a new-found sexual freedom.

For most women, the menopause passes almost unnoticed, the occasional hot flush being the only physical symptom experienced. But for about 10 per cent of women the menopause is a miserable time of life, with hot flushes and sweats disturbing their sleep and atrophic changes in the vaginal mucosa making intercourse painful. It seems wrong to deny these women treatment if the therapy is safe and effective. Of course, some doctors have argued that hormone therapy is neither of these things and that the risks outweigh the benefits. In addition, the psychological disturbances occurring at the time of the menopause in some women have served to emphasize that the symptoms may be 'all in the mind' and not deserving serious medical consideration.

Presumably women have always had symptoms at the menopause, although the problems associated with the end of reproductive life have been surrounded by as much mystique and mythology as have the problems surrounding menstruation. In Britain until the early 1970s the medical profession had paid little attention to women at the menopause. In medical schools it was probably rarely considered as a topic in gynaecology which deserved the serious attention of teachers or medical students and women were supposed to bear their symptoms with preconditioned stoicism. Treatment was considered by many doctors unnecessary and in any case dangerous; the menopause was a physiological process and therefore had to be endured as part of the normal change with age in women's bodily functions.

There is no doubt in Britain about 1972 the media, led by a few articulate and highly motivated women journalists, changed doctors' attitudes to the treatment of menopausal problems. Television and radio programmes and articles in women's magazines and newspapers alerted women and probably also doctors to the possibility that hormone therapy— the 'happiness pill'—could help the symptoms of the menopause. In the wake of this media campaign the first hospital menopause clinics were established in Britain, the gospel of 'hormone replacement therapy' was spread, and it seems that gradually treatment of women with problems at the menopause has become an accepted part of medical practice.

The upsurge of interest in menopausal women, their problems and potential treatments, has in recent years led to a great deal of useful research in this area. The possible risks of hormone therapy have been critically assessed and recognized and potentially safer treatment developed. We are now in a position to offer women treatment for their menopausal symptoms which should not jeopardize their health and to discuss with them the pros and cons of such treatment.

As evidence of the increasing attention being paid to the treatment of women at the menopause, the number of prescriptions issued in Britain by general practitioners for hormones for the treatment of menopausal symptoms increased threefold to about 1.2 million between 1971 and 1977 (Vessey and Bungay 1982). By 1979, however, the number had fallen to 940 000, possibly the result of increasing worries about the risk of endometrial cancer with this type of therapy. Vessey and Bungay (1982) also point out that hormone therapy for women at the menopause has considerable implications for health service resources. For example, if all post-menopausal women in Britain were to be treated, the prescription bill might be of the order of £120 million per annum; in addition checks on blood pressure and breast and pelvic examinations including endometrial biopsy would add considerably to the annual cost. We therefore need to consider carefully who will benefit from hormone therapy at the menopause and whether long-term therapy is beneficial and justified in view of the cost involved.

Age at the menopause

In Western society the menopause occurs on average in the early fifties, 50 per cent of women having ceased menstruating by the age of 50 years. There is of course a wide range of age at which the menopause is reached, from adolescence through to the late fifties. Factors that affect the age of the menopause have been examined critically in recent years. The belief that age at the menarche relates to age at menopause is not upheld in a great number of studies. Nor do socio-economic factors influence menopausal age. There is some evidence that women who have had no children reach the menopause at an earlier age than those with children. In addition genetic factors such as race and familial patterns may affect this age. These influences on age at the menopause are relatively minor, however, and are not of much help clinically in prediction.

HORMONE CHANGES AT THE MENOPAUSE

The sequence of hormonal events that leads up to the last menstruation at the menopause is still not understood despite a great deal of research in recent years. It is increasingly clear, however, that the menopause is not a sudden hormonal event but rather that in the years leading up to the final menstrual period gradual changes occur in the function of the ovary and anterior pituitary gland. There is probably a gradual decline in ovarian function with falling levels of oestrogens, oestradiol in particular. In response to this and the removal of the negative feedback effect of oestradiol on the anterior pituitary, levels of the gonadotrophins, luteinizing hormone (LH) and follicle stimulating hormone (FSH) in particular, rise dramatically. There can be increasing irregularity in the length of the menstrual cycle in some women in the years approaching the menopause, often associated with increasing variation in menstrual blood loss and an increase in the incidence of anovular cycles. In these years menopausal symptoms, for example hot flushes and sweats, may begin despite regular menstruation.

Within a year of cessation of menstruation serum FSH levels have risen on average about 13-fold over that found in the premenopausal period; LH levels rise about threefold. Oestradiol levels fall to approximately one-tenth of those found at the lowest level in the menstrual cycle, for example during menstruation. These major hormone changes found at the menopause are shown in Table 4.1. Why the last menstruation occurs is still puzzling; presumably levels of oestrogens fall to such an extent that endometrial growth is no longer induced and the cyclicity of ovarian function ceases. Despite high levels of FSH the remaining ovarian follicles fail to be stimulated. That there are still several thousand primordial follicles in the ovary at the onset of the menopause is well documented, although

Table 4.1 *Hormone levels after the menopause compared with during reproductive life*

	FSH IU/l	LH IU/l	Oestradiol pmol/l
After menopause	30–100	50–100	15–30
During menstruation	2–8	2–8	150–250

why they fail to respond to the rising levels of pituitary gonadotrophins is ill understood. It may be part of a biological aging of both the ovary and its hormonal links with the pituitary. It is important to remember, however, that the post-menopausal ovary is not a dead structure but continues to secrete hormones, oestrogens and androgens, for many years after the menopause. Removal of the ovaries surgically may therefore deprive even the post-menopausal woman of a source of hormones.

Women are therefore not deprived of all sex hormones after the menopause. Apart from the ovary, the adrenal gland contributes through its production of the androgens, androstenedione and testosterone. In turn these androgens can be converted to the oestrogens, oestrone and oestradiol, in 'extraglandular' sites such as fat, skin, and muscle. Oestrone is the main oestrogen produced after the menopause and although biologically not as active an oestrogen as oestradiol, must provide the menopausal woman with reasonable amounts of oestrogenic activity. Therefore the idea that the menopause is associated with 'oestrogen deficiency' is probably not tenable for most women who reach a natural menopause. Women who have a surgical menopause, i.e. both ovaries removed, will experience more rapid hormone changes and will lose a major source of oestrogens and androgens.

Value of hormone measurements in diagnosis of the menopause

FSH levels in the serum or plasma are the most useful hormonal guide to ovarian failure at the menopause since levels of this hormone rise to heights never seen in reproductive life even at their peak just before ovulation. It is no added help to measure LH levels after the menopause since they do not rise to the levels found at mid-cycle in reproductive life and this can be confusing. But measurement of FSH levels in clinical practice is only of value in a few women. It is useful where a premature menopause is suspected, say in women under 40 years with amenorrhoea; or where a woman has had a hysterectomy with conservation of the ovaries and assessment of ovarian function is necessary. It is of no value to measure FSH in women reaching a natural menopause at the normal age unless she has been on the contraceptive pill, has amenorrhoea on stopping it, and wants to know if she has reached the menopause and can cease using contraceptives. Otherwise cessation of menstruation is the only clinical guide required for diagnosis of the natural menopause. As will be described later in this chapter, the decision whether or not to treat menopausal symptoms does not depend on hormone levels but rather on clinical assessment of the severity and nature of symptoms. All women undergo these same hormone changes at the menopause, but not all get symptoms. Measurement of oestrogen levels is similarly of no value in the management of patients at the menopause since levels are no different whether women have severe menopausal symptoms or none at all. The idea that assessment of hormonal status is helpful and even essential for the correct management of symptoms at the menopause cannot be upheld. Nor is there any truth in the notion that measurement of oestrogen levels before oestrogen therapy is necessary to enable the doctor to decide on the correct dose of oestrogen. Treatment of menopausal symptoms with oestrogens can be regarded as blunderbuss therapy not based on the refinements of hormone measurements in the circulation and in the realms of pharmacology rather than physiology.

In summary, FSH levels may be usefully measured to diagnose premature menopause or ovarian failure where hysterectomy has been performed but the ovaries remain; FSH measurements are rarely of value in the diagnosis of a natural menopause. Measurement of LH or of oestrogens are not of added help in the management or diagnosis of the menopause.

SYMPTOMS AND SIGNS OF THE MENOPAUSE: RELATIONSHIP TO HORMONE CHANGES

The evaluation of the clinical features thought to be entirely the result of the menopause is difficult. It seems likely that the only symptoms that can be truly ascribed to the menopause are hot flushes and sweats, and those arising from atrophic changes in the vagina and urethra. Later metabolic effects such as osteoporosis are also recognized as relating to hormone changes at the menopause. The area of controversy is whether the host of psychological symptoms that may occur in middle age are causally related to the hormone changes of the menopause. These issues and others such as effects of the menopause on the cardiovascular system will now be discussed.

Hot flushes and sweats

The hot flush (or 'flash' as the North Americans prefer to call it), often accompanied by palpitations and followed by profuse sweating, are the commonest symptoms compelling menopausal women to seek medical help. Approximately three-quarters of women will have flushes at the menopause, but in only about 10 per cent are the symptoms severe enough to warrant treatment. Although for long in our society more of a music hall joke than a symptom demanding serious medical attention there is no doubt that the symptom is real. Peripheral circulatory changes have been demonstrated in several studies during a hot flush with a rapid increase in peripheral blood flow and pulse rate, followed by a rise in skin temperature; blood pressure does not alter. The flush, the sweating, and the sensation of increased body heat suggest some degree of disturbance of thermo-regulatory control at the menopause although what triggers the hot flush is unknown. It is thought to be a hypothalamic mechanism since the symptoms occur at the same time as the pulsatile release of luteinizing hormone and can occur in people who have had their pituitary gland removed. On the other hand one can argue against hormonal mechanisms being involved since not all women experience hot flushes at the menopause yet all women go through the same hormone changes. In addition, there is no difference in oestrogen levels between post-menopausal women who have severe hot flushes and those who do not. We do not therefore know what determines the individual variation in response but the most intense symptoms do seem to occur when hormone levels fall sharply such as after surgical removal of the ovaries or when hormone therapy is abruptly discontinued. Although the frequency and intensity of hot flushes are generally relieved by hormone treatment, oestrogens in particular, why this should be so is not understood. It is not due simply to a rise in oestrogen levels *per se*.

Because hot flushes and sweats tend to be more severe at night they may also be responsible for secondary disturbances including insomnia, fatigue, irritability, and even depression. Relief of hot flushes by enabling a woman to sleep soundly may thus improve greatly her general well-being.

Genito-urinary problems

Atrophic changes after the menopause can occur in both the vaginal and urethral epithelium since the two share a common embryological origin. Thinning of the epithelium of the genital tract is one of the few signs that do seem to result from oestrogen deficiency although regular sexual intercourse possibly prevents vaginal atrophy in many women. Although women often complain of vaginal dryness at the menopause severe atrophic changes do not usually occur until many years later. The thinning of the vaginal epithelium results in reduced secretions, and alteration in pH can create a more favourable environment for the introduction of infection. Thus the main symptoms of atrophic changes in the vagina are dryness, burning, itching, dyspareunia, discharge often yellow or brownish, and occasionally bleeding. Atrophic changes in the urethra can give rise to dysuria and urinary frequency in the absence of positive urine cultures.

Oestrogen therapy undoubtedly can reverse these atrophic changes with relief of symptoms. Either topical or systemic oestrogens can be used although vaginal oestrogen creams are absorbed into the bloodstream and some authorities feel that topical oestrogens should be avoided in women with contraindications to oestrogen use (see p. 78).

Psychological symptoms

There has been a great deal of controversy about the role of women's hormones on their psyche and on whether the hormonal changes at the menopause are responsible for the various psychological symptoms described at this time. A survey using a general health questionnaire of over 500 women on the lists of six general practitioners indicated a high prevalence of minor psychiatric illness in women aged 40–55 years (Ballinger 1975). There was also evidence in this study of an increase in psychiatric morbidity before the menopause and lasting until one year after menstruation stopped. The increased psychiatric morbidity seemed to be associated in particular with environmental factors relating to problems with children. Another study by postal questionnaire (Bungay, Vessey, and McPherson 1980) showed a clustering around the time of the menopause of minor psychiatric problems such as loss of confidence and difficulty in making decisions. The years around the menopause therefore can be stressful for some women and lead to a multiplicity of complaints such as depression, irritability, tearfulness, loss of concentration, sleep difficulties, and headaches. There is no evidence that these psychological disturbances relate to oestrogen lack although oestrogen therapy is said by some to have a 'mental tonic' effect. In several placebo-controlled trials there was no benefit shown for oestrogens in the control of these psychological problems. For example a study in general practice by Jean Coope (1981) showed oestrogen therapy was no more effective than placebo in treating depression. Thus, there is probably no place for oestrogen therapy in the treatment of these problems; psychotherapy or anti-depressant drugs, or both may be more appropriate. On the other hand, hormone therapy may be helpful if the psychological symptoms are secondary to, for example, hot flushes and sweats causing sleeplessness, or to sexual problems associated with atrophic changes in the vagina.

Osteoporosis

There are many population studies which have clearly demonstrated that while both men and women tend to lose bone mass after the age of 40 years, the rate of mineral loss is about three times greater in women, falling at a mean rate of 1 per cent per annum. Thus by the age of 70 years in women a 30 per cent reduction in skeletal mass will have occurred. There does appear to be a clear-cut association between osteoporosis and the susceptibility to bone fractures in women. Since these changes begin to occur in middle life about the time of the menopause, a causal relationship has been assumed between loss of ovarian function and loss of skeletal mass. The sites most commonly affected by osteoporotic fractures are the vertebral bodies, the distal radius and the neck of the femur. There is certainly a direct relationship between the incidence of Colles' and femoral neck fractures and age beyond 45 years in women; there is no significant increase with age in the fracture rate in men.

Evidence to support the hypothesis that there is a causal relationship between loss of ovarian function and osteoporosis comes from several studies. Placebo-controlled trials have shown a benefit for oestrogen therapy after the menopause in terms of prophylaxis against bone loss. Oestrogen administration cannot, however, reverse already established osteoporosis but can retard its further progress. Other studies show a reduction in the incidence of fractures with long-term oestrogen therapy in post-menopausal women. Although both clinical and epidemiological evidence suggest a beneficial effect of exogenous oestrogens on bone mass after the menopause it is difficult to determine the population at risk of severe osteoporosis. This means that all post-menopausal women would have to be given oestrogen therapy. One is then faced with weighing up the benefits against the risks of long-term oestrogen therapy as well as the cost–benefit of such treatment. The issues are important but unresolved and there is no evidence of British women clamouring for long-term hormone therapy or of British doctors considering seriously the potential benefit in relation to osteoporosis. This is in contrast to attitudes of many patients and doctors in North America; in the United States the Federal Drug Administration has designated oestrogen as effective in preventing early osteoporosis. But it has to be remembered that several factors other than oestrogen loss may influence the acceleration of bone loss after the menopause. These include an insufficient dietary intake of calcium, cigarette smoking, and inactivity. Correction of these may therefore be part of a therapeutic regimen to help prevent osteoporosis. In order to prevent or reduce the incidence of femoral neck fractures therapeutic measures would have to be taken for many years after the menopause since the percentage of women at risk of this particular fracture does not rise to any great extent until the early seventies. If women are to take an oestrogen/progestogen type of preparation, as will be discussed later in this chapter, then they will have to accept monthly withdrawal bleeding into old age. This factor alone will probably be the main deterrent for many women contemplating long-term hormone therapy to reduce the risk of osteoporosis or of major fractures.

Aging

Noticeable signs of aging occur in the skin with generalized thinning and loss of elasticity leading to wrinkling. Breasts may lose their firmness and become 'droopy'. But the belief that this aging process can be prevented by oestrogens has not been substantiated in scientific studies; nor is there any evidence that oestrogens help women feel younger or 'feminine forever'. The use of hormones for these reasons cannot therefore be recommended.

Cardiovascular problems

Women seem to be protected against cardiovascular disease during reproductive life, having much lower rates than men at this time. After the age
of 50 years the death rates from ischaemic heart disease increase more
rapidly in women than in men, and in women increase more rapidly after
50 years than before.

This epidemiological evidence raises the possibility that women's hormones, possibly oestrogens, protect them from heart disease in their pre-
menopausal years and this leads on to the possibility that oestrogen therapy after the menopause may reduce the risk of cardiovascular problems.

There is no conclusive evidence that it is oestrogens that protect pre-
menopausal women against heart disease or that exogenous oestrogens
given to post-menopausal women are either beneficial or harmful to the
cardiovascular system. The discrepancy between men and women in the
risk of coronary artery disease and myocardial infarction may be in part
due to the relative absence in women of risk factors such as hypertension,
smoking, and obesity rather than to the presence of a protective factor
such as oestrogens. Alternatively it has been suggested that women do
not have protection from coronary heart disease after the menopause.
Rather, at around the age of 50, men begin to lose a factor, possibly hormonal, that before this age put them at increased risk compared to
women. Consideration of all the available evidence leads to the conclusion that it is not justified to use oestrogen therapy in post-menopausal
women in the prevention or treatment of cardiovascular disease.

TREATMENT

This chapter will concentrate on the use of hormonal therapy for treatment of the menopause, not because we think it is necessarily the most
important therapeutically but because there has been so much controversy about it in recent times. Women have read and heard of these
controversies through the media and women's magazines and will want to
discuss with their general practitioner the pros and cons of therapy. We
recognize that it may be more important to help the menopausal woman
to come to terms with the problems of her life which may arise in middle
age—a listening ear and sympathy may be more valuable than hormone
pills. Nevertheless, treatment of the physical symptoms of the menopause, hot flushes and sweats and atrophic vaginitis in particular, should
be amenable to hormone therapy.

The treatment of women at the menopause should almost always be
carried through by the general practitioner; only rarely is hospital referral
necessary unless there are contraindications to hormone therapy when
further advice may be welcome. Menopause clinics were set up in several
areas of Britain in the mid-1970s but there is certainly no need now for

the majority of women to be sent there by their general practitioner. These clinics played an important role in the research carried out into the safest forms of therapy and in disseminating knowledge at a time when there was uncertainty and worry about hormone treatment. But the mystique has been taken out of hormone therapy at the menopause and general practitioners are now able to deal with these problems safely and effectively.

Hormonal

A wide assortment of hormone preparations, mainly oestrogens with or without added progestogen, but also testosterone, is now available for the alleviation of menopausal symptoms. There is also a variety of routes of administration, oral, topical, and subcutaneous. Faced with such a bewildering array of hormone treatments the general practitioner may find it difficult to know how to choose the most appropriate therapy, dosage, and route of administration for the individual patient.

Oestrogen alone

Oral preparations (Table 4.2).   Because of the concerns discussed later in this chapter that unopposed oestrogen therapy can cause hyperplasia of the endometrium, which may progress to adenocarcinoma, and because of the studies suggesting an association between oestrogen therapy and endometrial cancer in menopausal women, it would seem unwise to give unopposed oestrogens to women with an intact uterus. Yet this is still the most commonly prescribed form of hormone therapy given at the menopause. General practitioners may feel that women will find unacceptable the almost certain withdrawal bleed if combined oestrogen/progestogen preparations are used. In practice, most women seem to accept a return to 'menstruation' even if their natural menstruation has ceased for some time, provided that the reasons for using preparations causing withdrawal bleeding are fully explained to them. On the other hand, the introduction

Table 4.2 *Oral oestrogens for treatment of menopausal symptoms*

Proprietary name	Active constituents	Dose
Harmogen	Piperazine oestrone sulphate	1.5 mg
Hormonin	Oestriol + oestrone + oestradiol	0.27 mg + 1.4 mg + 0.6 mg
Lynoral	Ethinyl oestradiol	0.01 mg (10 µg)
Ovestin	Oestriol	0.25 mg
Pentovis	Quinestradol	0.25 mg
Premarin	Conjugated equine oestrogens	0.625 mg
		1.25 mg
		2.5 mg
Progynova	Oestradiol valerate	1 mg
		2 mg

of most combined preparations came a few years after the upsurge of interest and use of oestrogens alone in the early to mid-1970s. Both patients and doctors may be unwilling to change to new, often more expensive preparations which may be viewed as 'new-fangled', costly inventions of the pharmaceutical industry and unnecessarily complex for the treatment of a few hot flushes. The consensus of opinion is that unopposed oestrogens should be used only in women who have had a hysterectomy or who cannot tolerate progestogens on account of side effects. If the uterus has been removed then continuous oestrogen therapy can be given; cyclical regimens are unnecessary since the purpose of a break in the treatment schedule is to allow endometrial shedding to occur. There has been recent debate, however, that unopposed oestrogen therapy may be associated with an increased risk of breast cancer (see later) and that addition of progestogens might reduce this risk. There is therefore an argument for using oestrogen plus progestogen therapy even in women who have had a hysterectomy. There is one form of oral oestrogen, quinestradol (Pentovis) which does not stimulate the endometrium but is said to be selectively taken up by the vaginal and urethral mucosa. This preparation can be of value in the treatment of atrophic vaginitis or urethritis and is taken in short courses of two to three weeks daily treatment every few months.

Implant preparations.   Although there is no reason *per se* why implants should not be inserted by the general practitioner in the appropriate patient, they will usually be done in the hospital setting. Relatively few patients need them and therefore each general practitioner's experience is likely to be very limited. 'Pure' oestradiol is available in implant form as a very small hard-packed pellet, 50 and 100 mg, which can be inserted under the skin usually of the lower abdominal wall as an out-patient procedure. It can also be left under the rectus sheath following abdominal hysterectomy when the ovaries have been removed. The oestradiol is slowly absorbed from the implant over the course of about a year. Return of menopausal symptoms can therefore be expected within 9 to 12 months of insertion but the implant can be renewed as often as is necessary to control symptoms. In the main, an oestradiol implant is inserted only in women who have had a hysterectomy, although some gynaecologists use this form of oestrogen administration in women who have an intact uterus and give oral progestogens for 7 to 10 days of each month to induce cyclical bleeding following withdrawal of the progestogen. Removal of an implant may be difficult due to problems of identification of the exact site and probably requires a general anaesthetic.

Vaginal creams.   If atrophic vaginitis is the only problem, then oestrogen vaginal creams, used daily at first, then gradually reducing to perhaps once weekly or less, can be helpful. Two preparations are available, dienoestrol and conjugated oestrogens (Premarin), the latter as a non-liquefying preparation which is said not to leak out of the vagina so readily. But some women find them unpleasant to use, complaining that they are 'messy' or 'smelly'. Oestrogens are absorbed through the vaginal mucosa and raise levels of oestrogens in the peripheral circulation. Some people therefore feel that if there are contraindications to oestrogen therapy, then this applies as much to vaginal use as to other routes of administration. But if used sparingly and infrequently, vaginal oestrogen creams should not lead to consistently raised circulating oestrogen levels, as do other oestrogen preparations.

Oestrogen/progestogen preparations (Table 4.3)

For women who are still menstruating or who are post-menopausal but with an intact uterus, the risk of endometrial hyperplasia and possibly of endometrial carcinoma, may be reduced by prescribing preparations designed to give women at least 7 to 10 days of progestogen in each monthly 'cycle'. All these preparations can be classified as a sequential type of therapy with 10 to 13 days of unopposed oestrogen followed by 7 to 13 days of oestrogen combined with progestogen (Table 4.3). Some are given on a three weeks on treatment, one week off regimen (Cycloprogy-

Table 4.3 *Oral oestrogen plus progestogen preparations for treatment of menopausal symptoms*

Proprietary name		Oestrogen	No. of days	Progestogen	No. of days
Cycloprogynova	1 mg	Oestradiol valerate 1 mg	21	Levonorgestrel 0.25 mg	10
	2 mg	Oestradiol valerate 2 mg	21	Norgestrel 0.5 mg	10
Menophase		Mestranol 20 to 50 µg depending on day of cycle	28	Norethisterone 750 µg to 1.5 mg depending on day of cycle	13
Prempak	0.625 mg	Conjugated equine oestrogens 0.625 mg	21	Norgestrel 0.5 mg	7
	1.25 mg	Conjugated equine oestrogens 1.25 mg	21	Norgestrel 0.5 mg	7
Trisequens		Oestradiol or 1 or 2 mg plus Oestriol 1 or 0.5 mg	28	Norethisterone acetate 1 mg	10

nova; Prempak); others (Menophase, Trisequens) give continuous therapy. Of course, one can prescribe separately an oestrogen preparation for three weeks in four and a progestogen for the last 7 to 10 days of oestrogen therapy. But patients prefer the proprietary preparations, packaged to make it easy to understand the sequence of tablet-taking. Women who have not stopped menstruating can start the first pack early in the cycle, usually on day 5. Post-menopausal women must be warned that they are likely to have several days of vaginal bleeding in the week off therapy if the 21-day preparation is used or in the final week of therapy in the 28-day preparations but the bleeding should not be heavy or painful. If the bleeding is prolonged (say more than 5 days' duration), heavy or painful, gynaecological examination including endometrial curettage is advisable. Breakthrough bleeding or irregular bleeding can never be ignored and again warrants pelvic examination and curettage for endometrial histology to exclude carcinoma. Not all post-menopausal women will have cyclical bleeding particularly on low-dose therapy, indicating lack of endometrial stimulation. Absence of vaginal bleeding is therefore probably perfectly safe and does not require investigation.

Progestogen alone

Oral progestogens are rarely prescribed but can relieve the hot flushes and sweats of the menopause but are of no value in atrophic vaginitis. They could therefore be prescribed where there are contraindications to oestrogens, for example in women with a history of possibly hormone-dependent cancer of the breast or genital tract although whether progestogens are safer than oestrogens in these circumstances is not known. If given on a cyclical basis, vaginal bleeding is unlikely to occur in post-menopausal women. The two progestogens which can be used are norethisterone 5 mg daily or medroxyprogesterone acetate 5 mg daily. The dose of progestogen in the progestogen-only contraceptive pill is too small to control menopausal symptoms.

Testosterone

There is some evidence that androgens may be involved in women's sexual responses. A placebo-controlled trial of testosterone implants in menopausal women complaining of loss of libido was carried out at King's College Hospital in London and showed a significant benefit of the hormone. Young women who have reached a premature menopause through surgical removal of both ovaries and who complain of loss of libido may benefit in particular, since the ovary is a major source of testosterone. Of course, not all women who have diminution of libido at the menopause should be given an implant of testosterone; the complexities of the control of women's sexual response and possible treatments are discussed in Chapter 11 on women's sexual problems. An implant of testosterone

100 mg can be inserted subcutaneously using local anaesthesia as an out-patient procedure. It should be considered especially in women who have had surgical removal of the ovaries who can encounter total and devastating loss of libido to the extent that they find any physical contact with their partner to be repulsive. Replacing oestrogen alone in such women often does not restore their libido, despite oestrogenizing the vaginal walls and making intercourse physically comfortable; additional androgen can be helpful. This may be because the ovary is an important source of testosterone and replacement of this hormone is as necessary as that of oestrogen.

Testosterone implant does not appear to cause masculinization or increased hirsutism, although women can be concerned that they may 'turn into a man' with this type of treatment and they therefore need reassurance.

Non-hormonal therapy

The only drugs of any value in the control of hot flushes and sweats are clonidine (Dixarit) and a mixture of phenobarbitone, ergotamine, and belladonna alkaloids (Bellergal). Clonidine may act peripherally to reduce vascular reactivity and in a dose of 50 to 75 µg once or twice daily, will also have mild hypotensive properties. Bellergal, with its sedative properties as well as effects on peripheral vessels through ergotamine, may help relieve sleeplessness associated with hot sweats. Neither of these preparations is as effective as oestrogens in the relief of menopausal symptoms but may be tried when there are contraindications to hormonal therapy.

POTENTIAL RISKS OF OESTROGEN THERAPY AT THE MENOPAUSE

The major concerns about this type of hormone treatment have been that there may be an increased risk of endometrial or breast cancer, thrombo-embolism, or gall bladder disease.

Endometrial cancer

Over the last five years many reports from the United States have suggested firstly an increase in the incidence of endometrial carcinoma which paralleled in the 1960s and early 1970s increasing sale of oestrogens. Secondly, case control studies show an apparent association between oestrogen usage in post-menopausal women and endometrial carcinoma. These latter reports claim an average fivefold increase in the likelihood of developing endometrial cancer in post-menopausal oestrogen users. Several studies suggest that the risk is increased the bigger the dose of oestrogen and the longer the duration of use. The frequency of endometrial cancer among post-menopausal women who never use oestrogens is of the order of 0.7 per 1000. Prolonged use of oestrogens may raise this risk to around 3 per 1000. The risk of dying of the disease is, however, remote, about 1 woman in 4000 so exposed, since the five-year survival rate exceeds 90 per cent if the disease is localized to the uterus.

Although there has been a good deal of criticism of the retrospective studies from the States, mainly in relation to the selection of control subjects, the agreement in so many studies that there is an increased risk makes it difficult to ignore the conclusions.

Worried by these reports, British gynaecologists in the mid-1970s began to introduce a progestogen into the oestrogen therapy for menopausal women. It was shown in histopathological studies that unopposed oestrogens, as used in the United States, cause hyperplasia of the endometrium in a large percentage of post-menopausal women and this might be a precursor for cancer. If a progestogen was added for 7 to 10 days of each monthly treatment cycle then the incidence of endometrial hyperplasia could be reduced to almost zero. Theoretically, therefore, addition of progestogen should prevent development of the severer forms of endometrial hyperplasia and thus of carcinoma. It will take many years of prospective studies to show whether or not including progestogen in the post-menopausal oestrogen therapy will reduce the apparent risk of endometrial carcinoma associated with unopposed oestrogen use. In the meantime it seems wiser to use the combination therapy but women have to accept a monthly withdrawal bleed in return for this theoretical increase in safety.

Breast cancer

Several case-control studies in the past showed no significant association between oestrogen use and breast cancer, although recent studies have not been so reassuring. One study suggested that the relative risk increased with follow-up duration progressing to 2.0 after 15 years. Three more recent case-control studies each suggest an increased risk of breast cancer in oestrogen users although there are discrepancies between the studies. It is therefore difficult to draw firm conclusions but there is some cause for concern. Perhaps women contemplating hormone therapy at the menopause should be told that we are not certain about the risk of breast cancer on this treatment, that some studies suggest a risk while others do not. Only time and further careful studies will tell.

Thromboembolic disease

Concerns about risks of hypertension and thromboembolic disease in post-menopausal women on oestrogen therapy have arisen because of the risks in older women using oral contraceptives. The dose of oestrogen used to treat menopausal symptoms is however, very much lower than that in the contraceptive pill. For example, oestrogen therapy at the menopause is not contraceptive and does not suppress the hypothalamic–pituitary axis in the way the pill does; it does not lower the very high LH and FSH levels to any great degree. Perhaps therein lies the relative safety of menopausal oestrogen therapy in relation to the cardiovascular system compared to the pill in women over 35 years. On the other hand there is no doubt that steroid hormones, oestrogens, and possibly also progestogens, can influence the components of the blood coagulation and fibrinolytic systems in an adverse direction. Some studies have suggested that natural oestrogens in low dosage as used at the menopause might have some adverse effects on blood-clotting factors and platelet function although these are minimal when compared to larger doses of synthetic oestrogens. Epidemiological evidence is reassuring. Post-menopausal women treated with unopposed oestrogens do not appear to have an increased incidence of stroke, subarachnoid haemorrhage, thrombophlebitis, myocardial infarction, or death from coronary heart disease but one study has suggested an increase in angina. Occasionally hypertension may be produced or exacerbated in women taking hormone therapy after the menopause but this seems reversible if the medication is stopped. The evidence is thus not clear-cut, indicates a small degree of risk and should make us cautious and watchful about giving hormone therapy to menopausal women with any previous history of cardiovascular disease or with established hypertension. In addition concerns about the role of progestogens in arterial disease may indicate that the combined oestrogen/progestogen preparations are not entirely safe in relation to the cardiovascular system. It should be remembered that the epidemiological data so far relate to unopposed oestrogens only.

Gall bladder disease

There is conflicting evidence about the risk of gall bladder disease in menopausal women treated with oestrogens. One study suggested a 2.5-fold increase in surgically diagnosed gall bladder disease; another study failed to confirm this finding. Perhaps caution is indicated in prescribing oestrogens for women with established gall bladder problems.

CONTRAINDICATIONS TO HORMONE THERAPY AT THE MENOPAUSE

Absolute contraindications to oestrogen therapy would be previous hormone-dependent cancers of the breast, endometrium, or ovary. Progestogens may be safer than oestrogens in these situations but this is not known with assurance; non-hormonal therapy should be tried first. Since oestrogens and progestogens are metabolized in the liver, acute liver disease or chronic impaired liver function would also be absolute contrain-dications.

Relative contraindications are pre-existing hypertension, previous thrombo-embolic disease, myocardial infarction, especially in association with obesity and heavy smoking, benign breast disease, diabetes, endo-metriosis or fibroids, gall bladder disease, and familial hyperlipi-daemias. It may be wise for the general practitioner to seek specialist advice for a woman with any of these relative contraindications to hor-mone therapy but whose menopausal symptoms are severe and where non-hormonal therapy has failed. If hormone therapy is prescribed in these circumstances, then close surveillance of the patient is of course necessary.

CHOICE OF HORMONE PREPARATION

The various oestrogen or oestrogen/progestogen preparations probably have little to choose between them although trials comparing the efficacy and side effects of therapies in the same patient have not been done. Two of the oral oestrogen preparations oestradiol valerate (Progynova) and piperazine oestrone sulphate (Harmogen) are probably identical, certain-ly in their effect on circulating levels of oestrogens in post-menopausal women. Following ingestion of either oestrogen, plasma levels of oestra-diol, oestrone and oestrone sulphate are identical, metabolism of oes-trogens occurring in the gastric mucosa or in the enterohepatic circula-tion. The conjugated equine oestrogen preparation (Premarin), manufac-tured from pregnant marcs' urine, contains a mixture of oestrogens. About 50 per cent is oestrone sulphate, the remainder being mainly equine oestrogens. Whether or not these equine oestrogens have any biological action in women is not known and they may owe their efficacy to the high content of oestrone sulphate. The practical application of this is that if patients are not helped or have side effects on one of these so-called 'natural' oestrogens then the others are likely to be equally unhelpful. In women who have had a hysterectomy an oestradiol implant may be more effective and give less side effects than oral oestrogens. This is because absorption of oestradiol from a subcutaneous implant is direct into the bloodstream and the oestradiol is not metabolized to other oestrogens as happens during absorption from the gastro-intestinal tract. As discussed earlier, an oestradiol implant leads to levels of oestrogen much closer to those in the menstrual cycle than do oral oestrogens and this may be re-sponsible for its superior efficacy in many women.

Oestriol is regarded as a weak oestrogen in comparison to oestradiol or oestrone but has been used to treat menopausal symptoms particularly in Europe. Doses of 4 to 6 mg daily of oestriol may be needed to control menopausal symptoms.

In relation to the sequential oestrogen/progestogen preparations each offers something different although in terms of efficacy there may be little to choose among them. The number of days of progestogen varies from 7 to 13 but all preparations probably contain adequate amounts of progestogen to modify the endometrial hyperplasia induced by unopposed oestrogens. Two of the sequential preparations are taken as a three-week therapy, one-week break regimen (Cycloprogynova; Prempak). The other two (Menophase; Trisequens) are taken without a break but with lower amounts of hormone in the fourth week of treatment during which vaginal bleeding will occur. The 28-day preparations are more expensive than the 21-day packs (Prempak is considerably cheaper than all the others) but may be useful for patients who find they cannot tolerate return of their symptoms in the week off therapy. There have been concerns however about the relatively large amount of synthetic oestrogen (up to 50 μg mestranol) given on some days with one of these preparations (Menophase).

Natural versus synthetic oestrogen

Both types of preparation are effective in the relief of symptoms but there are implications that synthetic oestrogens are less safe than natural oestrogens particularly in relation to the risk of vascular thrombosis. The worries about the thrombo-embolic risks of synthetic oestrogens have arisen because of the potential risks of the combined oral contraceptive pill in older women. But the dose of, for example, ethinyl oestradiol required to relieve hot flushes and sweats (10 to 20 μg daily) is below the dose found in most contraceptive pills. Moreover these low doses of ethinyl oestradiol do not appear to alter blood coagulation factors significantly more than some of the 'natural' oestrogens.

Synthetic oestrogens do, however, alter plasma lipid profiles to a greater extent than do the naturally occurring oestrogens. The effect of synthetic oestrogen is to cause elevation of plasma triglycerides and lowered concentrations of high density lipoprotein (HDL) cholesterol. In contrast, some of the natural oestrogens lower plasma levels of triglycerides and increase HDL cholesterol levels and may therefore be considered 'safer' than synthetic compounds. No controlled trials have compared the risks of low-dose synthetic and natural oestrogens in the treatment of menopausal symptoms.

In terms of efficacy and safety, therefore, it is difficult to advocate prescribing natural rather than synthetic oestrogens provided the dose is kept low. In addition the low cost of ethinyl oestradiol compared to the natural preparations (5 p for a 21-day course of 10 μg daily) is attractive and this preparation should certainly be considered among the armamentarium of oestrogen products used at the menopause.

DOSAGE AND DURATION OF THERAPY

There are no clear rules but it is probably wise to adhere to the maxim of giving the lowest effective dose for the shortest possible time. Most women with symptoms severe enough to warrant treatment will require therapy for at least a year but some may need treatment for several years until symptoms disappear. A few women seem to get severe flushes into old age and if there are no contraindications to hormone therapy there is probably no good reason to deny them long-term therapy. The duration of symptoms is so variable that each woman has to find out for herself when her symptoms have disappeared. The only way is for her to stop the therapy, preferably reducing the amount gradually, and assess her symptoms over a few weeks. There is no evidence that taking hormone therapy merely delays the time of cessation of symptoms.

GENERAL MANAGEMENT OF PATIENT BEFORE AND DURING HORMONE THERAPY

Before starting hormone therapy a clinical history should be taken with particular reference to contraindications. The menstrual history is of importance. Abnormal vaginal bleeding such as intermenstrual, post-coital, or post-menopausal must be investigated and hospital referral is essential. Gynaecological examination should be made paying particular attention to the size of the uterus and ovaries and to the appearance of the cervix with smears if appropriate. The blood pressure should be checked and the breasts examined.

During hormone therapy the patient should probably be seen every few months. With women who have a uterus, enquiry about withdrawal bleeding should be made. Regular withdrawal bleeding is almost certainly associated with a normal endometrium but any unscheduled vaginal bleeding must be investigated and the patient referred to a gynaecologist for endometrial biopsy or further investigation. Some gynaecologists feel that if unopposed oestrogens have been taken for a year or more it is probably wise for the woman to be referred for endometrial out-patient sampling even if there has been no irregular bleeding but definite recommendations cannot yet be made. Since hormone therapy may occasionally cause hypertension, the blood pressure should be checked at least once after the first few months on therapy. Other routine checks, for example pelvic examination or cervical smears are not a necessary part of follow-up on hormone therapy unless there are particular indications. Women should be encouraged to examine their own breasts and a regular breast examination should be part of the follow-up. Women with a history of previous benign breast disease especially need breast surveillance on hormone therapy.

The following is a summary of the main points of management in a woman on hormone therapy who has an intact uterus:

1. The lowest effective maintenance dose should be found for each patient.
2. Cyclical treatment, i.e. 3 weeks on therapy, 1 week off, is preferred.
3. A progestogen should be added towards the end of the treatment cycle for 7 to 10 days.
4. Regular withdrawal bleeding is normal. Any atypical bleeding warrants referral to a gynaecologist for investigation.

PREMATURE MENOPAUSE

Although not commonly encountered in general practice, we have included a short description since it can cause many problems in a young woman in whom the diagnosis is easily missed.

The menopause may occur prematurely, i.e. before the age of 40 years, for several different reasons. The ovaries may be removed surgically at an early age or premature ovarian failure may occur. The incidence of premature ovarian failure is difficult to assess; one study suggested that almost 4 per cent of women have reached the menopause before the age of 30 years. The exact cause is not clear but is probably a multifactorial syndrome in which genetic, environmental, for example, viruses or drugs, and immune factors can play a part. The general practitioner must be sensitive to the possibility of a premature menopause in young women who have had a hysterectomy with conservation of the ovaries. Possibly due to disturbance of the ovarian blood supply or related to the reasons for which hysterectomy was performed a small proportion of women have premature ovarian failure following hysterectomy.

The diagnosis is made by finding high FSH levels and normal or low oestrogen levels; prolactin levels will be normal. The majority of patients will have a normal 46 XX karyotype but a small percentage have 45 XO (Turner's syndrome), mosaic XO or 47 XXX. In young women who are concerned about fertility it is necessary to refer to a gynaecologist for ovarian biopsy since only histology will distinguish the 'insensitive ovary syndrome' in which normal ovarian primordial follicles are found from true premature ovarian failure when the ovaries will contain only atretic follicles. The importance of distinguishing between these two syndromes is that in patients with the insensitive ovary syndrome, ovulation and even pregnancy can sometimes be induced with high doses of exogenous gonadotrophins. A firm prognosis that irreversible ovarian failure has occurred and that pregnancy is out of the question should probably not be given without knowing the histopathology of the ovarian tissue.

REFERENCES AND FURTHER READING

The following articles and books are reviews of the current status of knowledge in the menopause:

Beard, R. J. (ed.) (1976). *The menopause* MTP Press, Lancaster.

Greenblatt, R. B. and Studd, J. (1977). The menopause. *Clins Obstet. Gynaecol.* **4.**, Saunders, Eastbourne

Ballinger, C. B. (1975). Psychiatric morbidity and the menopause: Screening of general population sample. *Br. Med. J.* **2**, 344.

Bungay, G. T., Vessey, M. P., and McPherson, C. K. (1980). Study of symptoms in middle life with special reference to the menopause. *Br. Med. J.* **281**, 181.

Coope, J. (1981). Is oestrogen therapy effective in the treatment of menopausal depression? *Jnl. R. Coll. Gen. Pract.* **31**, 134.

Vessey, M. P. and Bungay, G. T. (1982). Benefits and risks of hormone therapy in the menopause. In *Recent advances in community medicine* (ed. A. Smith). Churchill Livingstone, Edinburgh.

Further reading for patients

Cooper, Wendy (1979). *No change.* Arrow Books, London.

Evans, Barbara (1979). *Life change.* Pan Books, London.

Health Education Council. *The change of life.* Health Education Council, London.

Reitz, R. (1981). *The menopause—a positive approach.* Penguin, Harmondsworth.

5 Breast cancer and benign breast disease

Sheila Adam and Maureen Roberts

It has been estimated that in countries such as the USA and the UK which have a high incidence of breast cancer, 1 in 14 women will develop the disease at some stage in their lives (Zdeb 1977). In recent years over 20 000 new cases of breast cancer have been diagnosed annually in England and Wales (OPCS 1980a), and around 12 000 women die each year (OPCS 1980b). About half of these women are under the age of 65 years and breast cancer is the commonest cause of death in women aged 35 to 54 years. The diagnosis of breast cancer almost inevitably leads to considerable physical, mental, and emotional difficulties for the woman and for her family. Apart from the fears of illness and death, the treatment itself may cause many additional problems, but at the same time can offer no guarantee of success.

In this chapter we begin by summarizing the epidemiology of breast cancer, continue by considering strategies to promote its early diagnosis, and then discuss the management of a woman with symptoms of breast disease and the various treatments which are available. We also provide some notes on the best way to examine the breasts. Some discussion of the management of benign breast disease is included, but the emphasis throughout is on breast cancer. Although this is a relatively uncommon cause of breast symptoms, only a small proportion of benign disease requires any treatment other than reassurance, and its main importance lies in the need to exclude malignant disease from the differential diagnosis.

EPIDEMIOLOGY OF BREAST CANCER

The size of the problem

During the past 20 years there has been a small increase in the mortality rates from breast cancer across all age-groups. Similar small increases have been reported in the incidence rates (that is, the numbers of new cases of breast cancer diagnosed each year) reported by the cancer registries, which were established in each Health Region during the 1960s. A survey carried out during 1971–72 estimated that every year 1 in 1000 women in England and Wales consulted their general practitioner at least once with symptoms resulting from breast cancer (RCGP/OPCS/DHSS

1979). A more recent study showed that for every woman presenting for the first time to her general practitioner with breast cancer, another 19 consulted with breast symptoms resulting from non-malignant conditions (Adam 1981). The hospital workload is also considerable, with out-patient attendances, admissions for diagnosis and initial treatment, and lengthy follow-up, often including radiotherapy and cytotoxic therapy. Other forms of treatment may also be required, often to counteract the adverse effects of curative therapies—for example, the provision of prostheses, physiotherapy, psychological and social support, and drugs such as analgesics and anti-emetics. The primary care team may play a major role in the care of these women and their families.

The aetiology of breast cancer

Many studies investigating the aetiology have been reported and only a very brief summary can be provided here. Two reviews of the epidemiology have been published, and these provide much more comprehensive information (MacMahon, Cole, and Brown, 1973; Kelsey 1979).

Reproductive factors

Perhaps the most consistent finding in aetiological studies has been the protection from breast cancer afforded by an early full-term pregnancy. Women who deliver their first child before they are 20 years old have approximately half the risk of breast cancer of nulliparous women, or of women whose first child is born when they are aged 30 to 35 years. The risk is highest in those women whose first full-term pregnancy occurs after the age of 35 years. Parity is associated with age at first birth but some epidemiologists believe that high parity provides some extra protection. Women with an early first birth are more likely to breast-feed, and some studies noted an apparent protective effect of lactation. However, when age at first birth is allowed for, breast-feeding does not seem to reduce the risk of breast cancer. The protection gained from an early first pregnancy only exists as long as the pregnancy continues to term; abortion, either spontaneous or induced, at an early age may even increase the breast cancer risk, although these findings are so far not conclusive. It has been suggested that infertility is associated with an increased risk, perhaps because of altered hormonal levels.

Endogenous hormones

As well as the relationship between pregnancy and breast cancer, other associations with hormonal status exist. Both early menarche and late menopause increase the risk of subsequent breast cancer; artificial meno-pause reduces the risk of breast cancer, and the earlier the menopause, the lower the risk. These findings indicate a positive association between the number of menstrual cycles and the risk of breast cancer. Interest has centred on the possible carcinogenic role of oestrogen. Other hormones have also been investigated, but the precise relationship between endogenous hormones and breast cancer remains unclear.

Exogenous hormones—oral contraceptives (OCs) and hormone replacement therapy (HRT)

On the whole, the results of published studies do not show any increased risk of breast cancer in women who have used OCs or HRT. Oral contraceptives reduce the risk of benign breast disease. However, because OCs have been available for only 20 years, very few women who have used them either for a relatively long period of time or before their first pregnancy have been included in these studies. Similarly with HRT, most of the published work is reassuring, although two studies report an increased risk—one in women 10–15 years after HRT use, and the other in women who received large cumulative doses of oestrogen.

Benign breast disease

Most studies have shown that women who are diagnosed by biopsy as having fibrocystic disease of the breast have two to four times the risk of developing breast cancer. When this is studied in detail, the increase in risk is linked to a small sub-group of women with epithelial hyperplasia. It is uncertain whether epithelial hyperplasia and breast cancer share common aetiological factors, or whether the former does in fact predispose to the latter.

Social class

Breast cancer is about twice as common in women from social class I as in those from social class V (Registrar General's classification). However, most of this difference is due to the protective effect of the earlier age at first birth in working class women.

Family history

Women with a first-degree female relative (mother or sister) with breast cancer have two to three times the chance of developing breast cancer as have all other women. This effect seems to be greater when the index case develops breast cancer before the menopause, or when she has bilateral disease.

Ionizing radiation

Studies of women who received large doses of radiation to their breast for various reasons all show increased incidence and mortality rates of breast cancer. It also seems that there is a linear, non-threshold, dose-response relationship between radiation and breast cancer, so that even low doses of radiation would cause a small increased risk of cancer. The calculated figure is an extra 6 cases of breast cancer per million women per rad of exposure after a latent interval of 10 years.

Nutrition

Population-based data have indicated that nutrition and breast cancer may be linked in two ways. Countries with a high *per caput* consumption of fats and oils have high breast cancer rates. Japanese migrant studies show an increase in breast cancer incidence associated with an increase in fat consumption and thus a high fat diet may predispose to breast cancer. It has also been suggested that breast cancer may be associated with a diet containing excess calories, thus predisposing to obesity, or with a diet which is low in dietary fibre. However, despite these interesting associations at a population level, case-control studies have failed so far to show any consistent relationship between nutrition and breast cancer.

Other factors

Conflicting results about the association of breast cancer and other factors such as reserpine and hair dyes have been obtained, but there is no clear evidence of any causal relationship.

Summary

Epidemiological studies have shown that a variety of factors are associated with breast cancer. However, these associations may not, of course, be causal, and the aetiology of breast cancer remains unclear. Despite this there has been some interest in attempting to define and identify women at high risk of developing breast cancer. Unfortunately, the different risk for women with each described factor (that is, the relative risk) is not great enough to allow useful prediction of the likelihood of the disease. At best, it is theoretically possible to identify the 40 per cent of women who will develop 60 per cent of the breast cancers; selective screening or health education is not therefore realistic. Public health measures aimed specifically at high-risk women will not be feasible unless more precise, and therefore predictive, risk factors (or combinations of risk factors) can be defined. Our inadequate understanding of the aetiology of breast cancer also frustrates any attempt at the primary prevention of the disease. There is no substance that can be added to or removed from the environment, no type of behaviour that can be modified, and no medical intervention which will significantly reduce the incidence of breast cancer. Despite this there are strategies, which can be considered as types of secondary prevention, intended to promote the early diagnosis of breast cancer, and these are considered in the next section.

STRATEGIES TO PROMOTE THE EARLY DIAGNOSIS AND TREATMENT OF BREAST CANCER

These strategies are based on the belief that the outlook for a woman with breast cancer is improved by early diagnosis. Although this belief is intuitively attractive, the benefits of early diagnosis have been questioned. It has been argued that the behaviour of an individual breast cancer can be placed on a spectrum between two points representing 'aggressive' and 'limited-potential' disease. The aggressive form is much more likely to present as advanced cancer, and will also have a worse prognosis. Thus the apparently poorer outcome for women with advanced disease may only be reflection of the different biological characteristics of their tumour.

However, the present weight of evidence does seem to indicate that earlier diagnosis is associated with a better outcome. It has been found consistently that women with stage I disease (small tumours confined to breast tissue) have the best prognosis, those with stage II and III disease (tumours which have spread locally to axillary nodes, skin and chest) will have intermediate prognoses, and those with stage IV disease (with distant metastases) have the worst outcome. Similarly, survival is best in those women without histological involvement of the nodes and worst in those with four or more nodes showing evidence of metastatic disease. These data are discussed in more detail in a recent review article on the management of breast cancer (Henderson and Canellos 1980).

The early diagnosis of breast cancer may be promoted in one of three ways—by screening, by encouraging breast self-examination, and by reducing any delay between the woman's noting an abnormality and receiving definitive treatment.

Screening

Techniques for breast cancer screening were developed during the 1950s employing the three modalities of clinical examination, mammography, and thermography. So far only one randomized study has been reported—the Health Insurance Plan (HIP) study in New York. This study (described by Shapiro *et al.* 1973) of 62 000 women aged 40–64 years found that, after 9 years of follow-up, the numbers of deaths from breast cancer were about one-third lower in women who were offered four annual screening examinations (91 deaths) than in those who received only their normal health care (128 deaths) (Shapiro 1977). However, this benefit from screening was confined to those women aged 50 years and over, and appeared to be due to the very good prognosis for women whose cancers were found on mammography, but were not palpable clinically.

In evaluating any screening programme, certain criteria should be considered, for example the natural history of the disease without treatment, the acceptability, accuracy, safety, and frequency of the screening tests, the costs of both 'over-diagnosis' and 'under-diagnosis', the availability of effective treatment and economic evidence that the screening programme justifies priority over other possible expenditures (McKeown 1968). Unless these criteria are considered, the screening programme may incur greater costs than benefits.

Breast cancer screening raises several such issues. For example, the HIP study showed that the women with the best prognosis were those whose cancer was detected by mammography rather than by clinical examination. However, any irradiation of breast tissue may itself initiate malignant change; mammography would have to be repeated at intervals and thus the risk to each woman would depend on the cumulative dose which she received. Fortunately breast tissue is less sensitive to radiation after the age of 35 years and most screening programmes involve women who are older than this. It should also be noted that with current techniques of mammography, the dosage to the breast should be very small— of the order of 0.5 rads skin dose per examination. Nevertheless a critical watch must be kept on radiation dosage.

Screening by mammography is capable of detecting very early lesions, and it has been suggested that some of these might regress spontaneously rather than develop into the metastasizing form of breast cancer—a similar model to that proposed for cancer-*in-situ* of the cervix. Thus, there may be an element of over-diagnosis which results in the woman receiving unnecessary treatment. The screening test will also detect benign breast lesions, which may have remained asymptomatic and never required any treatment. For example, in Manchester only 1 in 3 (George *et al.* 1976) and in Edinburgh only 1 in 7 (Edinburgh Breast Screening Clinic 1978) women with positive results on screening were found at biopsy to have cancer.

The evidence suggests that those women who do accept invitations to attend for screening are generally very grateful. However, only 2 in 3 women on average will come for the initial examination, and gradually the number attending each year will fall. Thus any screening programme could expect to cover only one-half to two-thirds of the target population. There are also continuing uncertainties about the screening timetable, for example, when screening should begin and end, and how often it should be performed. In addition, there is debate about which modalities should be used at different ages and levels of risk.

A national breast screening programme would require a major investment of NHS resources, both money and staff. Screening is a labour-intensive activity and has traditionally been done by the most expensive health service staff—doctors. Additional clinical facilities are also required to carry out biopsies on the women with positive screening results, and to provide treatment, follow-up, and support for those who are found to have breast cancer. A study sponsored jointly by the DHSS and MRC is currently evaluating breast screening in this country by comparing the results in two centres with screening programmes with those in two centres in which breast self-examination (BSE) is being promoted and four control centres. In Edinburgh the study takes the form of a randomized trial. Until the results are available we do not feel that women other than those participating in these studies should be encouraged to undertake breast screening.

Breast self-examination

BSE has been advocated as a means of promoting the early diagnosis of breast cancer, both as an adjunct to screening and as a technique in its own right. The breasts are first inspected in a mirror and then palpated systematically, including the axillary tails and axillae in a similar way to the clinical examination described on p. 93. The examination is intended to allow each woman to learn what is normal for her, and having done this to be able to detect any slight change. BSE should be repeated at monthly intervals, and, in women who are still menstruating, should be performed soon after the end of each period, when the breasts are least lumpy. (Leaflets can be obtained from the addresses given on p. 104.) Most breast cancers are found by the women themselves, and thus BSE seems a simple, safe, and inexpensive method of improving their efficiency. However, although three studies have shown that women with breast cancer, who say that they practise BSE, are diagnosed at an earlier stage there is as yet no evidence that their eventual outcome is improved. It remains difficult to evaluate BSE; for example, it is impossible to check whether a woman does in fact practise regular monthly BSE, and it may be complicated to judge whether her technique is correct.

Similar problems apply to the assessment of education programmes designed to promote BSE. Most programmes appear to produce a modest increase in the level of BSE practice which is reported. Programmes which include one-to-one teaching by a health professional have been found to be the most effective. For example, instruction by the doctor in a Canadian breast clinic increased the percentage of women who said that they carried out BSE from 10 per cent to 70 per cent. In Finland a community-based programme which included person-to-person education and instruction appeared to result in two-thirds of women practising regular BSE. Women who have received personal instruction from their doctor also seem to develop a better BSE technique. However, the level of reported BSE practice in the general population remains low. Although several studies have shown that the majority of women have heard of it only about 1 in 6 say that they regularly examine their breasts. BSE may cause anxiety on several counts. Women will obviously associate it with breast cancer, and may feel that it would stimulate rather than allay their fears. Many women may be reluctant to touch their breasts, a reluctance which may be circumvented by encouraging them to examine themselves during a bath or shower. BSE is not an easy examination to perform, and women may worry that they are not doing it correctly, or may be alarmed by the rather lumpy nature of normal premenopausal breast tissue.

BSE is therefore a procedure for which there is as yet only fragmentary evidence of benefit, and which only a minority of women practise, although many other women may carry out less formalized breast checks. If it is to be taught, this is most effectively done at the one-to-one level and general practitioners can play a particularly important role, as patients attach great importance to their advice about health. Teaching about BSE should be combined with information about the normal breast and breast abnormalities, and the importance of early diagnosis and the treatment of any symptoms should be stressed.

Reducing the delay in obtaining treatment

The delay between the onset of symptoms of breast cancer and definitive treatment has been described in several series of patients (Bywaters and Knox 1976; Bywaters 1977; Adam *et al.* 1980; MacArthur and Smith 1981, Nichols *et al.* 1981). Some of the delay is attributable to the woman herself; for example, she may decide that the symptoms are unimportant or her domestic responsibilities may make it incovenient to be ill. A few women say that they are too frightened to consult their doctor, but the majority produce a rational explanation for their delay. The characteristics of women who delay have been summarized recently (Ray 1980). Compared with women who present early they are more likely to be older, working class, of lower educational status, to be anxious or depressed, to deny the possibility of cancer and to express fears of mastectomy, malignancy, and hospitalization. However, the underlying reasons for delay are likely to be complex and by no means entirely due to the women. Delay also occurs after the general practitioner consultation. For example, there may have been difficulties in reaching a diagnosis, or administrative delays in arranging hospital admission. Delay at any stage is particularly likely to occur when the presenting symptoms differs from the classical 'painless lump', despite the fact that a significant proportion of cancers may not present in this stereotyped way (MacArthur and Smith 1981; Nichols *et al.* 1981).

Summary

Strategies designed to promote the early diagnosis and treatment of breast cancer involve both women and doctors. Women can be encouraged to attend for screening if this is available, to check their breasts regularly (by means of either BSE or a less formal procedure), and to report any symptoms to their general practitioner as soon as possible. Even though the chances of cancer may be very low, she will have the benefit of either very early diagnosis and treatment, or reassurance that she does not in fact have cancer. If there is any reason to suspect cancer, the general practitioner should refer to hospital immediately, accepting that reducing delay may involve a higher referral rate. If the abnormality is of no significance it is equally important to provide appropriate reassurance so that the woman knows not only that all is well, but also that she was right to consult her doctor.

THE FIRST CONSULTATION WITH A WOMAN WITH BREAST SYMPTOMS

A woman of any age may present to her general practitioner with a problem related to her breasts. Although a lump in the breast is a relatively common symptom, the woman may also complain of pain or discomfort, nipple discharge or retraction, skin changes, or just feeling that her breasts have altered in some way. It is probably true to say that almost *all* women consulting with a breast problem are anxious about it, and some present with a very high level of anxiety. Indeed, they may be so anxious or embarrassed that they find it hard to talk about their breast symptom, and initially give another reason for the consultation.

The general practitioner has the difficult task of deciding:

    (i)   whether an abnormality is present;

    (ii) whether the woman should be referred to hospital.

These decisions are not always straightforward. For example, many women who consult their general practitioner with breast symptoms have only physiological changes due to hormonal fluctuation. On the other hand, even though the general practitioner may not be able to find any definite physical abnormality, further investigation may be warranted by the nature of the woman's complaint.

The following paragraphs offer some guidelines on the management of this first consulation, intended to help the general practitioner in making the correct decision. This process will, of course, be influenced by the wishes and anxieties of the woman herself.

History and symptoms

The age and menstrual status of the patient should be noted, together with an accurate account of the symptoms, including when the woman first noted them. If the symptoms include either a lump or pain or discomfort then any fluctuation during the menstrual cycle must be noted. If she complains of a nipple discharge, ask whether it was bloodstained, milky, or clear, from one or both breasts, and its frequency. This is important, because a discharge is only occasionally reproducible on clinical examination. Check whether the patient is on any drugs.

A carefully taken history will begin to shape one's 'index of suspicion'. A woman aged over 45 years who complains of a lump has more than a 50 per cent chance of having breast cancer. A woman in her 20s who has no lump but pain related to her menstrual cycle almost certainly does *not* have breast cancer. Stereotypes and 'classical symptoms' can be misleading, however, and recent studies suggested that only about two-thirds of women with breast cancer may present with the 'typical painless lump'. The presence of pain or absence of a lump does not rule out cancer. Finally, women still present for the first time with symptoms due to metastatic breast cancer. Remember the possibility in patients with unexplained backache, anaemia, or other generalized symptoms.

Clinical examination

Although the main objective is to determine whether a mass is present, the breasts should always be examined systematically. First, because inspection is such a valuable diagnostic aid, the patient should remove all clothing above the waist and sit facing the doctor. Full inspection may reveal asymmetry between the breasts or in the contour of either breast, nipple retraction, skin changes or a visible mass. These signs are all accentuated if the patient presses her hands on her hips. The arms should be raised above the head to give a full view of the lower surface of the breasts and, if the breasts are large they should be lifted up by hand.

Palpation should always be carried out with the patient lying flat with her hands behind her head, so that the breast tissue is spread out over the ribs. Each breast should be palpated with the flat of the fingers starting at the nipple and working around the breast in a spiral fashion. Some prefer to palpate quadrant by quadrant; it does not really matter as long as the examination is thorough and firm but gentle pressure used. The periphery and the axillary tail must not be forgotten, and it is a good idea to palpate up to the clavicle as breast tissue extends well up the chest wall. The axillary tail and lateral part of the breast is best examined with the patient's arm at her side. Particular attention must be paid to the area pointed out by the patient, and if the lump to which she refers cannot be found, she should be asked to put a finger on it, even if this necessitates her changing position. Even Haagensen recommends enlisting the patient's help and says that the woman is usually right!

Examining in this way enables the doctor to establish the presence or absence of a discrete mass; it also provides an indication of the degree of nodularity or lumpiness (physiological) so important in the premenopausal woman. Any tenderness or discomfort can be noted. If a mass has been found, its size, consistency, and degree of mobility should be noted, *any* fixation increasing the suspicion of malignancy. To complete the examination, the axillae should also be palpated. This can best be done with the patient sitting up with her hands on the doctor's shoulders. This produces relaxed pectoral muscles with improved access to the axilla.

Diagnosis

The general practitioner is now likely to have found that:

    (i) the patient has no lump and no other significant abnormality. It is easier to reach this conclusion if the woman herself has only vague and indefinite symptoms, if she is young, if some explanation can be found (e.g. trauma, hormonal disorder) and if she is simply seeking reassurance. If the symptom is of discomfort only, then it is important to establish that it is related to the menstrual cycle. In these circumstances the woman should be reassured that she was right to seek advice and that there is no need for hospital referral.

or (ii) the patient has a discrete lump in her breast. Even if the lump appears to be benign (and 9 out of 10 lumps *are* benign) the patient should be referred to hospital; the clinical diagnosis can never be certain and she herself may believe that her lump is malignant until proved otherwise. There should be no delay in arranging an appointment as this may lead to additional anxiety although there should also be no implication that this is an emergency—fears may be unnecessarily reinforced. The general practitioner should discuss with her what is likely to happen at the hospital, as this will increase her confidence.

or (iii) it is unclear whether the patient has a significant abnormality. Many women fall into this category, particularly those in their 30s and early 40s who have lumpy breasts, with vague 'thickenings' that may cause alarm. It is of great help to re-examine this kind of patient at a different phase of her menstrual cycle, preferably immediately after the period is over. If there is still marked nodularity or lumpiness or any doubt, it is safest to refer her for further investigation. This is easier for the general practitioner who works in an area with access to a specialist breast clinic. Most of these patients turn out to have fibroadenosis or fibrocystic disease, but it is easy to miss malignancy. The woman herself often requires the further reassurance of a specialist consultation.

or (iv) the patient has unexplained nipple discharge. If she says it was bloodstained, then further investigation is essential, even though the majority of these women do not have cancer. Galactorrhoea should not be ignored as occasionally it is due to a prolactin-secreting pituitary adenoma. If the discharge is clear or greenish in colour, coming from both nipples or multiple ducts, it is (in the absence of other findings) unlikely to be serious. The woman should be encouraged not to express it. Remember to check whether the patient is on drugs as nipple discharge may be caused by some tranquillizers, steroids, the oral contraceptive pill, and occasionally, by digoxin and diuretics.

THERE IS NO DOUBT THAT ANY WOMAN WHO COMPLAINS OF A SYMPTOM OR CHANGE RELATED TO HER BREAST REQUIRES CLINICAL ASSESSMENT AND EITHER REFERRAL, RE-ASSESSMENT, OR REASSURANCE.

TREATMENT OF BREAST DISEASE

Breast disease will usually be treated in hospital, not by the general practitioner. However, as the general practitioner will be involved in the initial discussion with the patient about hospital referral and the treatment options, and may be required to manage the side effects of treatment or the consequences of recurrent disease, a summary of current practice is given.

BENIGN DISEASE

Cysts

These usually occur in the somewhat older woman, commonly arise almost overnight, are often painful, and may be associated with skin discoloration, or slight tethering of the skin. The surgeon might aspirate the cyst, which will relieve pain and anxiety immediately. In three-quarters of such cases operation is avoided, but certain precautions must be taken as cancer within or near to a cyst can occur. The patient must be seen after three weeks to check that the cyst has not refilled and the breast should be examined after aspiration both clinically and by mammography. The cyst fluid may be examined cytologically, but this is rarely helpful.

Dysplasia and 'mastalgia' (breast pain)

This is a common condition, in which the breasts are generally lumpy or nodular. If the woman is aged over 30 years, mammography is a sensible precaution. Providing there is no indication of malignancy and no discrete lump palpable, the patient should be given an explanation of the physiological nature of the problem and reassured that no serious disease is present. It is important to point out the relationship to the menstrual cycle, and to other signs of the 'premenstrual tension syndrome'. Breast pain not only waxes and wanes during the menstrual cycle, but also during reproductive life, often spontaneously subsiding for years. It subsides naturally after the menopause (though not necessarily after hysterectomy). Pain occurring in the older post-menopausal woman should be taken seriously. If the pain or discomfort is severe and a woman's lifestyle is adversely affected (for example, she can no longer swim, or flinches if touched) various treatments may be tried.

Mastalgia is a very difficult symptom to treat but certain treatments have been tried; some suit some women better than others. There seems no way of predicting who will be helped by any particular treatment. A good supporting bra, worn day and night, may improve the situation. An old favourite is to give diuretics in the premenstrual phase and these may give symptomatic relief, even though there is no scientific basis for their use. The anti-oestrogen, tamoxifen, at a dose of 10 mg each day, may give temporary relief in two-thirds of cases, and is relatively free of side effects. This dose does not inhibit ovulation. Danazol may be given at a dose of 200 mg each day and frequently gives prolonged relief from pain. Because it inhibits ovulation, it may interfere with menstrual patterns. It causes weight increase in the majority of patients, and occasional headaches are reported. Other rare side effects are nausea, rashes, acne, and muscle spasm. Progestagens alone may also help, e.g. dydrogesterone 10 mg b.d. in the second half of the cycle. Oral contraceptive preparations may also given relief—either progestogen-only pills or a low-oestrogen combined preparation. Bromocriptine has been shown to relieve cyclical mastalgia, 2.5 or 5 mg daily, even although these patients usually have normal prolactin levels (see Chapter 2 on menstrual problems).

The relationship of breast pain and dysplasia to hormone levels is unknown. So also is the relationship of pain to the psyche, although psychological reasons for pain have been suggested in the past. These are now largely discounted, but psychiatric help may be indicated for the occasional patient.

Fibroadenoma

This is a relatively common cause of benign breast disease in women aged 20–30 years, and usually presents as a small, highly mobile lump (the 'breast mouse'). Most surgeons prefer to excise a fibroadenoma, and this may be done under local or general anaesthesia leaving only a small scar.

Nipple discharge

There is no specific treatment for nipple discharge due to dysplasia, although the woman should be encouraged not to express her breasts. If only one duct is involved, and the discharge is troublesome, then the duct and its associated lobule can be removed surgically (microdochectomy). In galactorrhoea without underlying cause bromocriptine is used, but can have side effects.

Benign disease and the oral contraceptive pill

Evidence suggests that benign disease, especially dysplasia, is less common in women who are taking the oral contraceptive pill. However, some women experience increased breast discomfort, and it is worth trying several varieties of preparation to find that which is most satisfactory.

PRIMARY BREAST CANCER

The patient will usually be referred to a surgeon, who, often in collaboration with the radiotherapist or oncologist, will:
   (i) confirm the diagnosis;
  (ii) determine the extent of the disease;
 (iii) plan and carry out the appropriate treatment.
The diagnosis should always be confirmed by pathological examination either through a closed needle (Trucut) biopsy, or an open biopsy under local or general anaesthetic. Careful clinical staging of local disease is mandatory as this determines whether the tumour is 'operable' or not. Extensive skin involvement, peau d'orange, chest wall fixation, fixed axillary nodes, arm oedema or the presence of supraclavicular nodes renders the local disease inoperable.

Staging for distant metastases is usually carried out by skeletal survey, chest X-ray, haematology, and liver function tests. Sometimes bone scans are employed but these are not always available. It is important to remember that most women understand the reason for these tests, and are very frightened of the possibility of metastatic disease. It is therefore helpful to be open with the patient and to reassure her if there is no evidence of secondaries.

Treatment options

There are essentially four different methods of treatment, the first two treating local and the second two systemic disease:
   (i) surgery to the breast;
  (ii) radiotherapy;
 (iii) hormonal manipulation;
 (iv) cytotoxic therapy.
These may be used individually or in combination, and the treatment plan for each patient depends on the stage of her disease. Until recently, women whose disease was thought to be limited to the breast were treated by local therapy alone. Nowadays, increasing attention is paid to the concept that although there may be no clinical evidence, occult spread of the disease may have occurred by the time of diagnosis, requiring some form of systemic or 'adjuvant' therapy in addition to the local treatment. These systemic treatments are similar to those given for advanced disease, in which the aim is to induce remission rather than produce a cure. We describe the different treatments in general terms, though obviously these will vary from hospital to hospital. The adverse effects of each treatment will also be discussed.

Local treatment

(i) Surgery to the breast. If the disease if confined to the breast and the tumour is considered operable, a simple mastectomy is most common-

ly performed, although some surgeons recommend axillary clearance (modified radical mastectomy). At least one representative axillary node should be examined pathologically, as if tumour has spread to the axilla additional treatment will be required.

If the tumour is less than 3 cm in diameter, and neither too central nor too peripheral within the breast, mastectomy can sometimes be avoided. A quadrantectomy or wide excision of the lump, followed by radiotherapy, may be carried out instead, although it is still essential to biopsy at least one axillary node. If the tumour is very small, impalpable, or non-invasive in type, wide excision (lumpectomy) alone may be sufficient. We favour the woman taking part in this decision-making.

The use of prosthetic silastic implants in women who have undergone mastectomy is increasing. This may be done either immediately or as a delayed procedure, and although the implant may occasionally become hard or be rejected the results are often good. Any woman who feels strongly that she would like an implant should be given the option, although she should understand that, even given the best possible results, her breast will not look the same as before. Incidentally, radiotherapy may be given even when an implant has been inserted.

(*ii*) *Radiotherapy*.   If the axillary nodes are found to be involved by tumour, the patient is usually treated with radiotherapy after mastectomy. The practice varies in different parts of the country, but the chest wall and node areas (axilla, neck, and internal mammary chain) are generally treated. The axilla should not be irradiated if surgical clearance has been performed. Trials are under way to determine the safety of the procedure described above, in which radiotherapy is combined with excision of the tumour, thus conserving the breast. Cosmetic results are often good, but there is still some uncertainty over both the long-term results and the rate of local recurrence. Radiotherapy is the best form of treatment when the tumour is inoperable and may control local disease for many years.

Systemic treatment

At the present time, a number of centres in this country offer systemic therapy as part of the treatment of primary breast cancer.

(*iii*) *Hormonal manipulation*.   It is now known that response to hormonal treatment is related to the presence of the oestrogen receptor molecule in the cytoplasm of the tumour cell. These receptor molecules conjugate with oestrogen, enter the cell nucleus, and initiate cell division. The absence of oestrogen thus inhibits cell division and hence tumour growth. Hormonal manipulation, which reduces oestrogen uptake by the cell, has no effect in the absence of the receptor protein. About three-quarters of malignant breast tumours contain receptors.

Although a wide range of hormonal treatments, both additive and ablative, is available in recurrent or advanced disease, only two are currently being used in the systemic treatment of primary breast cancer. Tamoxifen, an anti-oestrogenic drug, is currently being evaluated in a multi-centre trial. Oophorectomy or irradiation of the ovaries is sometimes performed in pre-menopausal women.

Oestrogens should *never* be given to pre-menopausal women with breast cancer as they may stimulate tumour growth. Likewise, the oral contraceptive pill should *not* be prescribed.

(*iv*) *Cytotoxic therapy.* Several studies (e.g. Bonnadonna *et al.* 1976) have shown the value of cytotoxic therapy following mastectomy for primary breast cancer. Although the follow-up is still relatively short-term, recurrence rates appear to be lower in women who were randomly allocated to receive either one only or a combination of these drugs. Unfortunately the present drug regimes cause significant adverse effects. In this country, the use of cytotoxic therapy after mastectomy is on the increase, but while the long-term effects remain uncertain, it is not used routinely.

Results of treatment. Overall, about 50 per cent of women will be alive and well ten years after mastectomy and long-term follow-up studies, for example, Brinkley and Haybittle (1975) show that 25 per cent of women are still alive and free of recurrence after 25 years. Although prognosis is related to the stage of disease at first diagnosis, it is very variable for the individual patient. A minority of patients experience recurrence within twelve months of first treatment, whereas a small number of others may recur even up to 40 years following mastectomy. Prognosis is worsened by increasing size of tumour, the presence of any of the signs described earlier, involvement of axillary nodes, and obviously the presence of metastatic disease. Whether any improvement in survival will occur with adjuvant therapy is still uncertain, as most studies to date report only recurrence rates. Nevertheless, these early reports are encouraging.

Continuing care

The woman with newly-diagnosed breast cancer has to cope with at least two major problems. The first is the shock of discovering that she has it. Many women will have direct knowledge of breast cancer in a friend or relative and will be worried about the possibility of a recurrence of their disease, of progressive pain and disability leading to death, and the effect of this on others who are close to them. The second is the inevitable consequences of the treatment—for example, the mutilation of mastectomy and the nausea and vomiting of cytotoxic therapy. Some of these problems can be prevented and others alleviated, especially if they are anticipated. The difficulties in coming to terms with the diagnosis should not be underestimated, and may occur even when the woman has an apparently straightforward post-operative course. Such difficulties may represent her major concern, although some symptom of iatrogenic disease may be used as a presenting symptom. Some problems may surprise the doctor—

for example, the elderly, the thin, and the apparently unattractive *do* mind losing a breast, and the woman's sexual partner may also experience considerable fear about her diagnosis and treatment.

The general practitioner and the primary care team are ideally placed to provide the woman and her family with continuing care and support, although in most cases the hospital consultant will also wish to provide follow-up. Maguire has shown that at least 25 per cent of women treated for breast cancer develop significant psychological problems, and the majority of these will benefit from either simple counselling or, occasionally, more specialized psychological help (Maguire *et al.* 1978). If the general practitioner expresses continuing interest in the patient's progress, this in itself can be very supportive.

It is virtually impossible to hide her diagnosis from a woman with breast cancer, and it is therefore important to provide her with a truthful explanation of what is happening in terms which she and her family can understand. The general practitioner will be helped if informed of the details of her diagnosis, treatment, and exactly what she has been told, to enable further explanations and support to be provided as required, and future problems anticipated.

Adverse effects of treatment

(*i*) *Surgery to the breast.*   The majority of women find the loss of a breast extremely distressing, and this distress is frequently shared by their sexual partners. Mastectomy both 'confirms' the diagnosis and precipitates additional difficulties. Many women speak of feeling 'mutilated' or 'incomplete', and their self-image as a woman may be challenged. The sexual partner may also feel threatened and may fail to provide the strength and support which are needed, and the relationship may deteriorate. This can often be anticipated, and it may be helpful to discuss their anxieties with both partners, together and separately.

Mastectomy, particularly if axillary clearance has been carried out, may lead to arm oedema and stiff shoulder. Physiotherapy following surgery is essential. The general practitioner can offer very practical help here by, for example, setting the woman goals as to how far she can lift her arm each time she comes to the surgery, and guiding her in exercises to do at home. She may experience pain in the scar, and be worried by the numbness of the chest wall and medial aspect of the arm. This is very common after mastectomy, and, although it can persist for a long time, it will gradually improve. Oedema is a distressing complication, which may be symptomatically treated by elastic arm stockings or, in severe cases, with a special intermittent flow pump (the Flowtron). This should be available in physiotherapy departments and can be borrowed or bought for use at home.

A well-fitting and comfortable prosthesis is essential. The woman needs to feel free from embarrassment, and to know that she can continue to wear her ordinary clothes. The prosthesis is usually provided at the hospital, but it is important to check that it is suitable after the woman has worn it for a few weeks. Although many different varieties of prosthesis are available, not all appliance departments provide the full range, and some can be rather unsympathetic. It is important to make sure that the woman has received good and considerate care, and the general practitioner can often help if there are problems by contacting the department concerned. In addition, a few women may like to know that prostheses can be fitted and purchased (for £50–£100) in surgical appliance shops. Alternatively, some women opt for a prosthetic silastic implant. It is useful to be able to give guidance as to where to buy bras or swimsuits locally, as it is often the practical questions which, if unanswered, cause women much distress. Further help, advice, and support can be obtained from the Mastectomy Association and a booklet is also available from the Health Education Council (for addresses, see p. 104).

(ii) Radiotherapy. Lethargy and tiredness are common and may last for several months. They may be exacerbated but not caused by depression. Nausea may be helped by anti-emetics. Some skin reaction will occur during the treatment and the patient should be warned about this. The skin reddens and flakes off, sometimes leaving raw areas which can take a few weeks to heal. During the course of treatment, the skin should not be washed or covered with creams or lotions, although baby powder may be applied; a prosthesis, other than one made of light cotton-wool padding, should not be worn. If lumpectomy has occurred followed by radiotherapy, the breast can swell and become very tender; it is helpful if the woman is warned of this possibility. After treatment, zinc and castor oil cream may be applied to soothe the skin, and later, if the skin feels stiff, gentle massaging with cream may help. There may be some residual arm oedema and shoulder stiffness, and daily exercises should be encouraged. Oesophagitis (presenting as difficulty in swallowing) may occur during treatment, and later uncommon problems include radiation pneumonitis and radiation necrosis of the ribs, clavicle or humerus (presenting with local pain or tenderness).

(iii) Hormonal therapy. Tamoxifen is almost free of side effects, though occasional oedema or mild nausea may occur. Oophorectomy, or irradiation of the ovaries, may cause acute menopausal symptoms, which must not be treated by hormones. Not surprisingly, marked depression is likely to occur, for these women have had to face the diagnosis and often the loss of a breast, as well as the sudden onset of their menopause.

The management of menopausal symptoms may be difficult and may be linked to the patient's attitude towards life and her treatment in general. Drug treatment is not really indicated, except for depression. The doctor should offer encouragement, support, and reassurance. Helpful books written by women can be recommended. Occasionally, a woman is so devastated by menopausal symptoms that she is prepared to take the risk associated with hormonal therapy. In these cases, the woman's view should not be disregarded.

(*iv*) *Cytotoxic therapy*.　Most women will experience adverse effects, including nausea, vomiting, diarrhoea, mouth ulceration, hair loss, amenorrhoea (if she is pre-menopausal), cystitis, conjunctivitis, and depression. The usual regime is a monthly intravenous injection for about 12 months, and thus the distressing side effects will be experienced over a long period and with a depressing predictability. The hair loss, although temporary, will often require a wig, which the hospital should provide.

These women may spend several days not only after but also before each injection suffering from nausea and vomiting, and, not surprisingly, are at great risk of depression, especially if they have no-one at home (Maguire *et al.* 1980). The amenorrhoea may be accompanied by other symptoms associated with the menopause, but must not be treated by hormone therapy. Any woman who encouters this range of adverse effects may doubt the wisdom of continuing with the cytotoxic therapy and will require encouragement if she is to complete the course.

ADVANCED DISEASE

Breast cancer metastasises most commonly to lymph nodes, the skeleton, lungs, and liver, but spread to any organ may occur. Local infiltration or ulceration over the chest wall may occur, and is very distressing to the patient. Treatment may be local, systemic, or both and is palliative, not curative. Nevertheless, worthwhile remissions may be induced in many patients, sometimes allowing several years of normal active life.

Local treatment

Both local surgery and radiotherapy have a useful role to play in advanced disease, though appropriate systemic treatment should also be given in order to achieve maximum control of the disease. Local skin recurrences may be successfully excised; pleural effusions aspirated; intestinal obstruction relieved; pathological fractures internally fixed; laminectomy performed for spinal cord compression. These problems are not necessarily terminal events, and active intervention is often rewarding.

Radiotherapy is commonly given for painful bony lesions, providing good relief of pain, and inoperable breast disease and chest wall recurrences may be brought under control by its use. Radiotherapy also has a place in the treatment of intra-cerebral lesions.

Systemic treatment

Various methods of hormonal manipulation have long been used in the palliation of advanced disease, inducing tumour regression in 30 per cent of patients. Remissions lasting as long as 15 years have been reported. Response to treatment is correlated with the presence of the oestrogen receptor protein. Many hormonal preparations are available, including oestrogenic and androgenic compounds, progestogens, and tamoxifen. Major morbidity may occur: oestrogens may cause oedema, congestive heart failure, nausea and vomiting; androgens may have a distressing virilizing effect. Endocrine surgery is sometimes performed, including oophorectomy, adrenalectomy, or hypophysectomy. Alternatively, aminoglutethamide and prednisone can be used to block adrenal function and danazol to block pituitary function. These drugs must be given only under the supervision of an experienced clinical oncologist. With combinations of cytotoxic drugs, a 50 or 60 per cent remission rate may be expected. These remissions tend to be shorter in duration than those obtained with hormonal therapy, but are in many cases worthwhile. The side effects can be controlled, but these drug regimes should be given only at specialist clinics.

The patient with recurrent or advanced disease should not be regarded as terminal, as many forms of treatment are available which give worthwhile results. Throughout the whole management of advanced and terminal disease, the relief of pain must be given priority. There does come a time when active therapy aimed at prolongation of life should be abandoned in favour of simple palliation alone. It is sometimes difficult to define precisely when this should take place, and the general practitioner can often help in making the decision.

CONCLUSION

The general practitioner has a major role to play in the detection, treatment, and long-term care of breast disease. Women should be encouraged to check their breasts regularly and report any symptoms as quickly as possible; routine consultation can often provide on opportunity for teaching BSE and stressing the benefits of the early diagnosis and treatment of any abnormality.

When a woman presents with a breast symptom, however trivial, the general practitioner should reassure her that she was right to attend. Some women have an obvious abnormality which requires referral, others appear to have no significant change. For those women where the position is less clear, in may be best to refer for a consultant opinion, or to ensure that the patient keeps an early follow-up appointment with the general practitioner. If there is any doubt, the woman should be referred, if only to put her own mind at rest. Before referral to hospital, the general practitioner should discuss with the woman the possible diagnostic and treatment options and the more practical aspects, such as when she might expect to be seen in out-patients.

If the diagnosis proves to be breast cancer, then the general practitioner should ensure that the hospital provides prompt information about the diagnosis (including stage) the treatment and the intentions for follow-up. The primary care team can provide valuable support to the woman and her family, and may be able to alleviate some of the problems which she will face due to both the illness and the side effects of treatment. In particular, the general practitioner and community nurse may be in the best position to anticipate and help the family to cope with the psychological morbidity which often occurs.

If the disease recurs, the woman may require further surgery, radiotherapy, and/or drug therapy. She and her family may eventually need to come to terms with the fact that the disease cannot be cured, but only palliated. If the disease is incurable, it is necessary to consider the quality of the woman's remaining life. Pain relief is of prime importance, as is the need to ensure that no treatment is offered which is worse than the disease. The general practitioner, as the person who knows the woman and her family best, is involved in planning and providing terminal care together with hospital staff, and will ensure that the primary care team provides the necessary support to the family.

USEFUL ADDRESSES

Health Education Council,
178 New Oxford Street,
London WC1.

Scottish Health Education Group,
Woodburn House,
Canaan Lane,
Edinburgh 10.

Mastectomy Association,
1 Colworth Road,
Croydon,
CRO 7AD.
(Tel: 01.654.8643)

REFERENCES AND FURTHER READING

Adam, S. A., (1981). The promotion of breast self-examination in the context of the diagnosis and management of breast disease. MFCM thesis.

—— Horner, J. R., Vessey, M. P. (1980). Delay in treatment for breast cancer. *Community Med.* **2**, 195.

Bonnadonna, G., Brusamolino, E., Galagussa, P., *et al.* (1976). Combination chemotherapy as an adjuvant treatment in operable breast cancer. *New Eng. J. Med.* **294**, 405.

Brinkley, D. and Haybittle, J. L. (1975). The curability of breast cancer. *Lancet* **ii**, 95.

Bywaters, J. L. (1977). The incidence and management of female breast disease in a general practice. *J. R. Coll. Gen. Pract.* **27**, 353.

Bywaters, J. R. and Knox, E. G. (1976). The organisation of breast cancer services. *Lancet* **i**, 849.

Edinburgh Breast Screening Clinic (1978). Screening for breast cancer. *Br. med. J.* **ii**, 175.

George, W. D. Gleave, E. N., England, P. C., Wilson, M. C., Sellwood, R. A., Asbury, D., Hartley, G., Barker, P. G., Hobbs, P., and Wakefield, J (1976). Screening for breast cancer. *Br. med. J.* **ii**, 858.

Henderson, I. C. and Canellos, G. P. (1980). Cancer of the breast: the past decade. *New Engl. J. Med.* **302**, 17, 78.

Kelsey, J. L. (1979). A review of the epidemiology of human breast cancer. *Epidemiol. Rev.* **1**, 74.

Macarthur, C. and Smith, A. (1981). Delay in breast cancer and the nature of presenting symptoms. *Lancet* **i**, 601.

McKeown, T. (1968). Validation of screening procedures. In *Screening in medical care* Oxford University Press.

MacMahon, B., Cole, P. and Brown, J. (1973). Etiology of human breast cancer; a review. *J. natn. Cancer Inst.* **50**, 21.

Maguire, P., Lee, E. G. *et al.* (1978). Psychiatric problems in the first year after mastectomy. *Br. med. J.* **i**, 963.

—— Tait, A. *et al.* (1980). Psychiatric morbidity and physical toxicity associated with adjuvant chemotherapy after mastectomy. *Br. med. J.* **281**, 1179.

Nichols, S., Waters, W. E., Fraser, J. D., *et al.* (1981). Delay in the presentation of breast symptoms for consultant investigation. *Community Med.* **3**, 217.

OPCS (Office of Population Censuses and Surveys) (1980a). *Cancer statistics: registrations: cases of diagnosed cancer registered in England and Wales, 1974: series MB1 NO. 4.* HMSO, London.

—— (1980b). *Mortality statistics: cause; review of the Registrar General on deaths by cause, sex and age in England and Wales, 1979: series DH2 NO. 6.* HMSO, London.

Ray, C. (1980). Psychological aspects of early breast cancer and its treatment. In *Contribution to medical psychology* Vol. 2 (ed. Stanley Rachman). Pergamon, Oxford.

Royal College of General Practitioners, Office of Population Censuses and Surveys, Department of Health and Social Security) (1979). *Morbidity statistics from general practice 1971–2: second national study: studies on medical and population subjects No. 36.* HMSO, London.

Shapiro, S. (1977). Evidence on screening for breast cancer from a randomised trial. *Cancer* **39**, 2772.

—— Goldberg, J., Venet, L., Strax, P., *et al.* (1973). *Risk factors in breast cancer —a prospective study in host–environment interactions in the etiology of cancer in man* (ed. R. Doll and I. Vodopija). International Agency for Research on Cancer, No. 7, Lyons.

Zdeb, M. C. (1977). The probability of developing cancer. *Am. J. Epidemiol.* **106**, 6.

Further reading for patients

Baum, Michael (1981). *Breast cancer: the facts*. Oxford University Press
Faulder, Carolyn (1979). *Breast cancer*. Pan, London.
Rakusen, J. and Phillips, A. (1978). *Our bodies, ourselves*. Penguin, Harmonds-
     worth.

6 The 'ectomies'

Ann McPherson and Anne Anderson

WHY DISCUSS ECTOMIES?

The development of the idea that removing bits and pieces of the female reproductive system might have beneficial results arose from a variety of initial concepts, some of which are outlined below, and most of which no doubt seemed valid at the time. Not surprisingly, many of these in retrospect had dubious scientific basis. The reasons for including a chapter on this subject are essentially that not only is a considerable amount of a general practitioner's time spent in dealing with the symptoms which will lead to the operation's being performed, but nowadays even more time will be spent in dealing with their psychosocial consequences.

The operations we will discuss are hysterectomy, oophorectomy, and mastectomy, although it should be remembered that women are also twice as likely as men to have a cholecystectomy. We will deal in more detail with hysterectomy and oophorectomy since they are not discussed in any detail elsewhere in the book. Most of the discussion of women presenting with a breast lump is in Chapter 5 on breast cancer and benign breast disease, but we have included here a short look at psychological and social consequences of mastectomy and the role of the general practitioner in this sphere.

The general practitioner will obviously not be involved in the operation itself but by the act of referral to a consultant will make an operative procedure more likely. Signs and symptoms may necessitate referral for further investigations or surgery, or both, but often referral is for reassurance both to the doctor and the patient. Unless one indicates clearly what it is one wants from the consultant referral, some women may end up with unnecessary surgery as, once referred, the hospital machinery may take over. The consultant is inclined to think the referral is asking for surgical intervention and the general practitioner is inclined to think the patient is asking for something more to be done, but really the whole topic may never have been discussed. Perhaps as general practitioners we could have more of a role to play in this area than we think or than we do at the moment. If surgery is a likely outcome of a hospital referral, it is worth discussing it with the patient before the letter is written. Evading the issue, for example, in a woman with a breast lump, by saying 'I'm sure it's going to be all right', or 'You've got nothing to worry about', without dealing with the possible alternatives she will face when she sees the consultant can often make the patient more concerned. Another important role for the general practitioner is to see the patient after the out-patient appointment, as questions and queries often arise which will not have been dealt with either because of lack of time, or the patient's inhibitions, or because the queries have only been thought of afterwards. We have all been faced with the patient who says, 'The consultant says I need a hysterectomy—what do you think?'

STATISTICS

The figures in this section try to give some sort of numerical perspective to the whole subject of 'ectomies'. The numbers of women in a practice who will have had one of these operations will, of course, vary with the age and sex distribution of the practice. If one takes a so-called 'average' practice of 2500, then 80 women are likely to have had a hysterectomy and 20 a mastectomy (and 20 men a prostatectomy). By the age of 65, 14 per cent of women in the practice will have had a hysterectomy and 4.5 per cent a mastectomy. In 1975 in England and Wales 53 170 hysterectomies were performed, 39 580 mastectomies, 15 000 to 18 000 oophorectomies (it is difficult to obtain exact numbers because of the method of coding operations in hospital statistics), and 23 460 prostatectomies, so that each general practitioner is likely to be involved in counselling at least 2 women per year for hysterectomy, 3 women every 2 years for mastectomy, and 1 woman every 2 years for an oophorectomy (and 1 man every year for prostatectomy and rarely for orchidectomy). The reasons for doing any of the operations will, of course, be varied, particularly for hysterectomy.

If one looks in more detail at hysterectomy most are done for benign disease. For example, in 1975 in England and Wales (HIPE) only 7 per cent of hysterectomies were for malignancies of the genital tract; 33 per cent were for disorders of menstruation, 25 per cent for fibroids, 12 per cent for prolapse, and 23 per cent were unclassified. Whether differences in disease rates explain the differences across the world in hysterectomy rates (Fig. 6.1) is a matter for speculation (McPherson 1982) but it is of interest that the age-standardized hysterectomy rate is three times higher in the USA than in England and Wales. Within this country hysterectomy rates also vary widely across the regions, for example from 180 per 100 000 population at risk per annum in Mersey to about 290 per 100 000 in North-East Thames. In the Oxford region the hysterectomy rate appears to show a social class gradient, the rate being at least twice as high in the highest social class as in the others (McPherson 1982).

These differences undoubtedly have complex causes and may depend

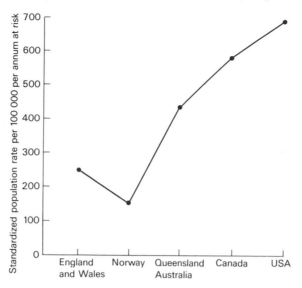

Fig. 6.1. Standardized hysterectomy rates for five countries. (From McPherson 1982, with permission.)

on factors that have little to do with disease. Women themselves may influence the rates depending on their perception about the need or otherwise for hysterectomy in their circumstances. But, again, the general practitioner may play a central role in the decision-making in terms of referral, as stated earlier in the chapter, and this would be a crucial factor in determining whether or not a woman has a hysterectomy.

HYSTERECTOMY/OOPHORECTOMY

Historical perspective

Oophorectomy was first used in the mid-1800s for treatment of ovarian cysts and tumours—these had previously been treated by recurrent tapping. Expectedly, the morbidity and mortality of the first operations were very high and within the profession there was considerable opposition to performing them. As the operation gradually became safer it was more widely performed. Although the first oophorectomies were performed for pathological disease of the ovaries, it soon became fashionable to do them for other problems. These included the treatment of epilepsy, insanity, and of nervous and psychological problems such as hysteria. It seems that people believed that women's personality was an orchestra conducted by their ovaries, and presumably any psychological problems with which women presented could be cured or controlled by performing oophorectomy. Cliteroidectomy was an operation performed by the nineteenth-century surgeons as a cure for another of women's evils—this time masturbation—which was thought to cause numerous physical disorders as well as dementia and overall moral decay. The fashion of cliteroidectomy in this country lasted for a short time and was never as popular as oophorectomy. Cliteroidectomy is however still practised in certain countries such as Africa.

Female castration was largely superseded by other operations including hysterectomy—as the womb then became seen as the seat of a woman's psychological problems. But many uteri were removed for pathology much of it related to infection. The need and outcome was affected by safer surgery, antiseptics, anaesthesia, safer childbirth, fewer pregnancies, etc. Whereas in the nineteenth century, hysterectomy and oophorectomy were performed for psychological as well as pathological reasons, by the middle of the twentieth century hysterectomy, with or without oophorectomy, was often performed with little consideration for the psychological sequelae. It was a common practice to remove the ovaries at the same time as doing the hysterectomy (a complete clean-out), a practice which has not been entirely abandoned, presumably because it was assumed that the ovaries had little function after the menopause and anyway they might become diseased in time.

Clinical perspective

The two 'ectomies' hysterectomy and oophorectomy will be considered together for two reasons. First it has been common in gynaecological practice that both the uterus and ovaries are removed together especially near or after the menopause. Secondly it is important that the general practitioner should feel able to discuss the pros and cons of oophorectomy when hysterectomy is being considered—particularly if it is being done for non-malignant reasons. Full discussion with women of exactly why hysterectomy with or without oophorectomy is required, how (by the vaginal or abdominal route) and by whom it is to be performed, and the after effects of such surgery, should take place with the gynaecologist who recommends the operation. But many women leave the hospital clinic feeling that they failed to ask the crucial questions or cannot remember clearly what was discussed in any case. These women are likely to seek further advice from their general practitioner. In turn, the general practitioner needs to know the views of their patient's gynaecologist on some of the more controversial issues concerning the operations so as to avoid the patient receiving conflicting advice.

We are not going to discuss the issues involved in performing hysterectomy and oophorectomy for malignant disease of the genital tract. By and large these are clear-cut, although it is interesting that gynaecologists are debating whether one should remove at hysterectomy the ovaries of young women with carcinoma of the cervix, recognizing that this tumour is unlikely to be 'hormone-dependent' to the extent of others such as ovarian or endometrial carcinoma.

As mentioned earlier in the chapter, most hysterectomies are being done for non-malignant reasons, in particular disorders of menstruation, fibroids, and prolapse and it is these women, especially if they are approaching the menopause, who are likely to be most concerned about their need for the operation and its long-term effects.

Gynaecologists and women themselves both vary enormously in their views. Thus some women will go to any lengths to avoid hysterectomy, even if their menstrual symptoms are severe, preferring to put up with them or control them with drug therapy for many years. Other women, even those in their twenties, almost beg the gynaecologist to remove their uterus, being unable to face endless years of menstrual problems once they have completed their family. These opposing views must be equally respected—being judgemental is not helpful and each woman must be helped to think through the problem for herself. As in most areas of medicine, if the patient can share in the decision-making, she will be less likely to regret the outcome in the long-term, especially when the treatment has implications for her sexuality.

We will now try and deal with some of the main questions that women are likely to ask concerning hysterectomy. Some gynaecological departments have in recent years prepared leaflets for women about the operation of hysterectomy and its after effects; however sadly in the days of economic stringencies within the National Health Service it has become increasingly difficult to finance these although studies have shown that they are much appreciated by women.

Anatomical

Some women may be unclear as to what will be removed at hysterectomy, in particular being concerned about whether or not their ovaries will be left and if so, whether they will continue to function after removal of the uterus. Other areas of concern may relate to whether the cervix will be removed (almost certainly—subtotal hysterectomy is very rare now) and whether the vagina will be shortened by the surgical procedure (it should not be with a straightforward operation). For many patients a picture may be worth a thousand words and a diagram of the pelvic organs be useful on these occasions.

Oophorectomy. The vexed question of whether women, especially those who are close to or beyond the menopause, should be castrated at the time of hysterectomy for non-malignant reasons has had many powerful advocates in the past. Some gynaecologists have set firm age-limits, e.g. 45 years, beyond which they would always remove the ovaries at the time of hysterectomy. The two main arguments for advocating female castration near or after the menopause have been first that the ovaries have outlived their useful function, i.e. that their role relates only to reproduction; secondly and perhaps more importantly that ovarian carcinoma is difficult to diagnose at an early stage and has, at least in the past, had a hopeless prognosis. Bilateral oophorectomy in middle-aged or older women has thus been regarded by some as a wise form of preventive surgery. It can also be argued that it does not increase the surgical risk associated with hysterectomy if the ovaries are also removed. Of course the tempting anatomical proximity of the ovaries to the uterus is likely to be one factor militating against their conservation at abdominal hysterectomy. If women kept their ovaries in a pouch outside the pelvis, as men keep their testes in the scrotum, then it is the authors' hunch that there might be far less female castration!

The argument that the ovaries have no endocrine function after the menopause is no longer tenable. In recent years it has been clearly shown that the ovaries do not cease to be hormone-producing organs at the end of reproductive life. Thus, removal of the ovaries even in post-menopausal women will deprive them of one source of both oestrogens and androgens (although of course there are others). Although these no longer have any function in relation to reproduction they might well have important implications for sexuality. Women should certainly not be told that they may as well have their ovaries removed at the time of hysterectomy in the belief that castration near or after the menopause will do them no harm. The truth is that we do not know the long-term hormonal implications in older women of bilateral oophorectomy and it seems likely that the continued production of ovarian hormones serves some purpose.

The most potent argument in favour of female castration is that one is removing a potential source of malignancy with the added problem that ovarian carcinoma is so often not diagnosed until it has reached an advanced stage. On the other hand, ovarian carcinoma is a relatively rare disease—the mortality risk in a 40 year old woman is of the order of 1.7 per 1000.

So what advice does the general practitioner give to the woman who wants to know whether or not to have her ovaries removed? As ever, there are no clear answers but at least some will welcome a frank discussion on the pros and cons as set out in this chapter. The assumption cannot be made that women want and will give informed consent to having organs removed because of their potential to develop cancer. In particular a woman who has not yet reached the menopause, or only recently so, may express the wish to conserve her ovaries more strongly than a woman several years past the menopause. The most embittered women in this respect are those who find out that they have been castrated at the time of hysterectomy only on coming round from the anaesthetic and who feel that prior discussion about oophorectomy had not been entered into either by the gynaecologist or their general practitioner. Obviously this can easily be avoided if doctors invest a little more time in advance in discussing with women what their wishes are in this respect.

The general practitioner can assure a woman opting for hysterectomy with conservation of the ovaries, that her ovaries should continue to function normally after the operation, up to the time she would naturally have reached the menopause, although in clinical practice there does seem to be anecdotal evidence that ovarian function can occasionally decline prematurely after hysterectomy alone, even in young women. The reasons may relate to a disturbance of the blood supply to the ovary, to the reasons for doing the hysterectomy in the first place, or it may have happened in any case. But the general practitioner should be aware of the possibility of premature ovarian failure in a young woman who complains of 'menopausal symptoms' often with loss of libido as a dominant feature, even if her ovaries were not removed at hysterectomy. Measurement of her FSH levels (see Chapter 4 on the menopause) will aid the diagnosis, high levels indicating ovarian failure. Appropriate hormone therapy would be indicated in that event (see Chapter 4) and both oestrogen and testosterone may be replaced.

Psychological

The psychological effects of hysterectomy are still being debated and remain unclear. Some studies have suggested that a high proportion of women experience depression after hysterectomy, others have challenged this conclusion. Probably no study is free of criticism in some aspects of its design (Meikle 1977) but there are so many variables to be considered that the perfect study may be too difficult to set up.

In a retrospective study in general practice, Richards (1973, 1974) found that 37 per cent of 200 women who had had a hysterectomy were treated for post-operative depression. Particularly vulnerable were women under 40, those with a history of depression, and those in whom there was no obvious pelvic pathology at hysterectomy. More recent prospective studies assessing the psychiatric state of the women before and after hysterectomy in hospital practice have not confirmed these findings (Gath 1980; Coppen, Bishop, Beard, Barnard, and Collins 1981). In general their conclusions were of an improvement in the psychiatric state of many patients following hysterectomy when compared with the preoperation assessment.

Because the debate about the psychological sequelae of hysterectomy continues it is difficult to know what to tell patients especially with so many conflicting data in the literature. Again, it is likely to be of importance that the woman comes to the decision herself that hysterectomy is what she wants and does not feel 'browbeaten' by the medical profession. Doctors must also be aware of the implications of loss of the uterus for some women's sexuality (see next section); open discussion about how she feels about losing her womb may help to resolve such worries. One should however remain cautious about advocating hysterectomy in the young depressed woman with no obvious gynaecological pathology.

Sexual

Many women fear that a hysterectomy will ruin their sex lives by leading to loss of libido as well as physical discomfort during intercourse. On the whole, doctors can be reassuring if the operation is uncomplicated, if the ovaries are conserved, and if there is no shortening of the vagina. Recent prospective studies support the idea that sexual activity, assessed by the frequency of intercourse and of orgasm does not decline after hysterectomy, whether or not oestrogen therapy is given (Coppen *et al.* 1981). On the other hand, the general practitioner should be sympathetic to the woman with sexual problems after hysterectomy. Vault granulations can cause pain and even bleeding during intercourse in the early weeks, and because of this and other reasons it is usually advocated to abstain from intercourse for at least a month after operation. Granulations at the vaginal vault can be treated with silver nitrate on a stick. Later complaints of a dry vagina with failure to lubricate during sexual arousal or loss of libido accompanied by menopausal symptoms should alert the general practitioner to the possibility of declining ovarian function. Clinical signs of atrophic vaginitis should be looked for and FSH levels measured if there are doubts. Local oestrogen cream or systemic hormone therapy may be required (see Chapter 4 on the menopause). In some women loss of the uterus and cervix may damp down sexual satisfaction during arousal and orgasm since according to Masters and Johnson, both these organs may participate in normal sexual function. Of course, sexual problems following hysterectomy may not relate to the operation in any way and may have been present before the operation.

Women must be given the opportunity to discuss their worries about the effect of hysterectomy on their sexual feelings both before and after the operation. They may feel too embarrassed to raise the issues, yet would welcome discussion given the opportunity. It is therefore very important that the general practitioner feels comfortable about opening up such a discussion with a woman, if that is what she wants, and be able to offer positive help and advice. This is discussed more fully in Chapter 11 on sexual problems.

Physical

Advice on when to return to full physical activity is often more readily offered by doctors than advice on other matters after hysterectomy, six to eight weeks being cited as the usual time for recovery. This must vary enormously among individuals and it probably serves no purpose to set limits. The British Medical Association's booklet *Women only*, suggests that in the early days of convalescence after hysterectomy some cooking, light dusting, or pushing the vacuum cleaner around are suitable activities for recuperating women, which might be interpreted by some as a particularly sexist view of women's daily activities! The fear that weight gain is an after-effect of hysterectomy is not upheld in recent studies.

MASTECTOMY

Mastectomy has been recognized as a therapeutic operation since the time of the ancient Greeks. Its more ancient phylogeny is probably because the pathology would be more visible and its removal more obviously feasible. Thus, since ancient times and through the ages it has been advocated with varying enthusiasm as a treatment—as well as having a vogue as a punitive measure. Renaissance times saw wide excision of breast tumours with ligatures to control bleeding and in the 1890s Halsted advocated radical mastectomy.

Most breast lumps are found by the woman herself or by her husband or lover, and more rarely on routine examination by the doctor. But sooner or later these lumps will be brought to the general practitioner. Unlike many other symptoms and signs brought to the general practitioner, the patient is more aware of the implications of having a breast lump, and the numbers coming may reflect recent publicity about breast cancer. For example, one practice showed a large increase in consultations about breast problems following the much publicized mastectomies of Mrs Ford and Mrs Rockefeller in the USA in 1974 (Bywaters 1977). Perhaps the most positive therapy to be offered by the general practitioner at this stage is a realistic picture of the likely causes and a practical picture of future management based upon the information in Chapter 5 on breast cancer and benign breast disease. Referral may be needed and, if so, avoidance of delay is important to shorten the period of extreme anxiety that is bound to follow. If the lump is found to be malignant then most women will end up having a mastectomy. Mastectomy for breast cancer will be followed by a depressive illness in between 20 to 40 per cent of women. More hospitals are involving specially trained nurse counsellors to help women who have to undergo a mastectomy, but as yet it is far from widespread. In one controlled study (Maguire, Tate, Brooke *et al.* 1980) when a specialist nurse was employed to counsel women undergoing mastectomy in the hope of reducing morbidity, it was found that she failed to prevent immediate morbidity but by its early recognition and referral for treatment, by 12–18 months after mastectomy there was much less psychiatric morbidity in the counselled group (12 per cent) than in the control group (39 per cent). The news that a woman has cancer and must lose a breast is a serious blow even when she is prepared for it. The woman has to deal with both the potentially life-threatening disease and the loss of a body part which may be important among other things to her femininity and sexuality. Whether a lumpectomy or mastectomy is medically recommended one also has to take into account the woman's own feelings. For instance, even if a lumpectomy were feasible some women might prefer a mastectomy, feeling that this would ensure more extensive removal of potentially abnormal tissue, while others would prefer the local, less disfiguring operation. Whether the disease or the operation is the main worry varies in different women but Maguire (1978) showed that much of the distress (55 per cent) experienced related to the fear of cancer. Women were questioned before and after the operation. Before the operation 18 per cent gave the loss of a breast as a main or subsidiary reason for anxiety, while after the operation this had increased to 35 per cent with special worries about the prosthesis and husbands' attitudes. The reactions experienced by women undergoing mastectomy for cancer are similar to those of bereavement, i.e. an initial phase of disbelief and often euphoria that it had been removed, followed by sadness and depression. Women often complained that they could not express their feelings to the medical staff, and follow-up studies at 3–4 months after operation showed 26 per cent had experienced at least moderate depression during this time. It does seem that patients can easily fall between two stools following the operation, with general practitioners feeling that they have little role to play and that everything is being taken care of by the hospital, and with the hospital not actually providing the support in the psychosocial areas that the patient needs. Much is written about improving the communications between surgeons and patients, but when at least 25 per cent of women who undergo mastectomy complain of a lack of opportunity to discuss their worries, the general practitioner has an important role to play in counselling before and after operation, to try and reduce psychiatric morbidity. As breast cancer can be considered a chronic disease, both the hospital and the general practitioner could consider in each individual case how the follow-up could be best managed. Some patients may get reassurance from annual hospital visits, while for others it will be a source of anxiety which might be lessened by visiting their doctor instead. In order to do this it would be beneficial to indicate clearly what examinations and investigations need doing to minimize the chance of missing a recurrence. It does not seem that the hospital has necessarily more to offer. All too often routine hospital follow-up appears to be arranged without considering what the follow-up appointment is meant to achieve. On the other hand, general practice often fails to provide routine follow-up of patients, only seeing those that present with symptoms. If general practitioners are to take on more of the follow up which is normally done at hospitals they need to organize themselves to ensure efficient and regular check ups.

REFERENCES

Bywaters, J. L. (1977). The incidence and management of female breast disease in a general practice. *J. R. Coll. Gen. Pract.* **179**, 353–7.

Coppen, A., Bishop, M., Beard, R. J., Barnard, G. J. R., and Collins, W. P. (1981). Hysterectomy, hormones and behaviour. *Lancet* i, 126–8.

Gath, D. H. (1980). Psychiatric aspects of hysterectomy. In *The social consequences of psychiatric illness* (ed. L. Robins). Brunner/Mazel, New York.

Maguire, P., Tait, A., Brooke, M. *et al.* (1980). Effect of counselling on the psychiatric morbidity associated with mastectomy. *Br. med. J.* **281**, 1454–6.

—— (1978). The psychological and social sequelae of mastectomy. In *Modern perspectives in psychiatric aspects of surgery* Chapter 19 (ed. J. G. Howells). Macmillan Press, London.

Meikle, S. (1977). The psychological effects of hysterectomy. *Can. psychol. Rev.* **18**, 128–41.

McPherson, K. (1982). Opting to operate. *Times Health Supplement* 12 March, 12–13.

Richards, D. H. (1973). Depression after hysterectomy. *Lancet* ii, 430–2.

—— (1974). A post-hysterectomy syndrome. *Lancet* ii, 983–5.

7 Contraception

Barbara Law

It is only within recent years that the subject of family planning has been included in basic medical training. This is perhaps because it has only recently been appreciated that it is important to have safe, reliable contraception over which women feel they have some control, not only for the prevention of unwanted conceptions but also for the psychological welfare of the women themselves.

In the past, many doctors found themselves ill-equipped to offer advice and most women sought help from Family Planning Association (FPA) clinics. Since a comprehensive and free service became available within the National Health Service in 1974, many more women choose to consult their own general practitioner, although some still prefer the anonymity and specialization of the FPA clinic. The important role of the general practitioner in this aspect of preventive medicine has been stressed in a recent Royal College of General Practitioners report. General practitioners are in the most favourable position to offer good advice, being already familiar with the patient's health and circumstances. They are also able to assess her special needs as well as those of her partner and her family, and may at times feel it appropriate to offer help even before it is requested.

About 95 per cent of the general practitioners of England and Wales offer a contraceptive service for their patients, but from the following figures it can be seen that many women still choose to go to a family planning clinic, and some will go to both. While there is a slight trend towards the general practitioner between 1978 and 1980 in England, there is a slight drift away in Scotland (Table 7.1).

It is clear that there is a need for both kinds of service and although at

Table 7.1 *Women obtaining family planning advice*

	1978	1979	1980
Source I England (Hansard 27.7.81)			
From general practitioners	2 118 313	1 991 193	2 033 810
From FP clinic	1 521 400	1 494 000	1 486 000
Source II Scotland			
From general practitioners	227 968	222 576	217 714
From FP clinic	135 325	137 319	141 480

either place most advice is provided by the doctor, a very important contribution is also made by the nurse. The midwife, health visitor, or other domiciliary nurse is able to motivate and guide those in need, and the trained family planning nurse can and is undertaking progressively more responsibility in providing help. Cap fitting, pill teaching, and IUCD checking are duties which can be delegated to her, as well as supervision of those who choose the muco-thermal method.

Most couples require contraception for very many years, and their needs will change over time and with altered circumstances. As already mentioned, the general practitioner is in an ideal position to cope with the subtleties and supervision which such a challenge presents. Because of this, many general practitioners have found it worthwhile to undertake the postgraduate training for the certificate of the Joint Committee on Contraception. The RCGP report (1981*b*) recommends that all vocational trainees should also take this certificate. Such training includes theoretical teaching and practical experience in all non-surgical contraceptive techniques, as well as consideration of the complicated psychological and emotional factors involved in their use.

Women are exposed to the risk of pregnancy throughout their reproductive life, potentially about 40 years between the menarche and the menopause, during which they have to face the problems of contraception. For the vast majority of women conception is easy, and controlling fertility may prove difficult. Not only are the available methods imperfect, there are also innumerable factors which influence the acceptability of both the principle and the ways and means of family planning. Psychological and emotional feelings often originating in family background, race, religion, and culture can be powerful, and increasing public anxiety concerning the risks of contraception further complicate the problems. Exaggerated press reports can cause unjustified alarm, upsetting the equanimity of some patients who are happily using a certain method and preventing others from starting it. When reassuring reports are published comment is usually brief at best. Doctors need to formulate their own assessment of the risk/benefit consideration of each method for the individual patient based on up-to-date opinion and information. This is essential, not only so that women can get the best possible advice but so that practitioners may be able to justify their actions should any litigation be involved—an event which unhappily is becoming progressively more common.

TRENDS IN CONTRACEPTIVE USAGE

The method of contraception used by couples has changed over the years and there have been changes of usage within the social classes. General

Table 7.2 *Family planning clinics in Great Britain[1]: method of contraception recommended or chosen*

	1975	1976	1977	1978	1979	1980[2]
Method of contraception recommended or chosen following first visit in the year[3] (percentages)						
Oral contraceptives	69	66	64	58	54	54
IUD	14	15	16	19	21	21
Cap/diaphragm	6	7	6	7	8	8
Sheath	6	6	7	9	10	10
Chemicals	1	1	1	1	1	1
Rhythm	–	–	–	–	–	–
Other[4]	2	2	2	2	2	2
None	3	3	4	4	5	5
Total (percentages)	100	100	100	100	100	100
(millions)	1.6	1.7	1.8	1.7	1.7	1.6

[1] Community and hospital clinics only.

[2] Figures relate to England and Wales only.

[3] For new patients to a clinic the method chosen is recorded. For other patients the method in use at the time of the first visit during the year is recorded, but if a new method is chosen this is recorded instead.

[4] Includes recommendation/choice of female sterilization and vasectomy.

Source: Department of Health and Social Security; Scottish Health Service, Common Services Agency; Welsh Office

practitioners have prescribed fewer oral contraceptives—a drop of 0.9 million from 1976 to 1979 when the number of prescriptions for oral contraceptives was 5.6 million. There is, however, some indication that this decline has stopped as the same number of prescriptions was issued in 1979 and 1980. Table 7.2 shows the method of contraception recommended or chosen in community and hospital family planning clinics for the years 1975 to 1980 (there is no similar breakdown of figures for general practice).

In 1978 there were also 90 000 women who were sterilized: 10 per cent of sterilizations being performed at the same time as an abortion, and 17 per cent at the same time as delivery.

Distinct differences have been observed in the type of contraceptive used by the different social classes, but these have diminished over the years with the growth in use of the pill. Table 7.3 shows the use of contraception by married women under 41 years of age in 1970 and 1975.

A similar pattern emerges in the use of contraception in unmarried women in 1975: 70 per cent of classes I, II, and III (non-manual), 58 per cent of class III (manual), and 33 per cent of classes IV and V used contraception.

Table 7.3 *Use of contraception by married women under 41 years of age in 1970 and 1975 by social class* (*percentages*) (*Figures in brackets refer to 1975, those without to 1970*)

	Social class (*R.G.70/A*)			
	I, II and III(N.)	III(M)	IV & V	All
Pill	28(42)	24(43)	21(39)	25(42)
IUD (coil)	6 (9)	5 (9)	4 (7)	5 (9)
Cap	10 (5)	3 (2)	4 (1)	6 (3)
Condom	38(28)	35(24)	36(24)	36(25)
Withdrawal	12 (4)	23 (8)	22(13)	19 (7)
Safe period	8 (1)	6 (1)	8 (1)	6 (1)
Abstinence	3 (2)	3 (1)	7 (1)	4 (1)
% women (or husbands) sterilized	(9)	(12)	(11)	(12)
Users of family planning services				
Current users	32(47)	24(43)	21(40)	27(44)
Ever used	62(80)	51(70)	49(65)	54(73)

Note Columns do not add up to 100 because some respondents reported using more than one, or no, method

From: Reid, Ivor (1981). *Social class differences in Britain* (2nd edn). Grant McIntyre Ltd.)

CHOICE OF METHOD

The majority of women who seek contraception are healthy and young and present fewer problems than the over-35s, teenagers, and those with intercurrent disease. Couples rarely rely on the same method throughout their reproductive life but considerable misunderstanding and ignorance still exist concerning the available varieties. There is an increasing tendency for sterilizing procedures to be demanded at a very early age. By careful discussion and explanation of alternatives it is sometimes possible to enable deferment of such an irreversible step or even avoidance of surgery altogether. Some women find difficulty in asking for advice and too often the very young do not do so until after they have actually been pregnant. Older women are often particularly unwilling to discuss this topic if they are embarrassed or doubt the propriety of sex except for procreation, or its indulgence over the age of 40.

The practitioner may feel the need to offer unsolicited advice on some occasions and needs also to assess the strength of motivation of all women who request contraception. Unless used correctly and consistently, successful use of any method is unlikely if its effectiveness depends upon the user. Condemnation of unreliable methods such as coitus interruptus does not guarantee either adoption or successful use of theoretically more effective ones. It is safe to say that 'any method is better than none, but some are better than others'. If a woman does not enjoy sex it is difficult for her to prepare for it. Her fear of pregnancy is used as a defence and she will probably find some reason why she cannot use any method, reacting badly to any one she tries. In desperation sterilization is often performed, thereby removing her main defence, and her problems remain unsolved. Religion still exerts a powerful influence concerning both the principle and practice of contraception. One Catholic girl overcame her conscience by giving up the pill for Lent. Menstrual bleeding confers restrictions for orthodox Jewish women, Muslims, and Hindus. Hence, the prolonged loss associated with the IUCD or the irregular cycles common with the progestogen-only pill weigh against the acceptability of these methods for such women.

Fashions also change. During the last 20 years the male barrier method and the pill have been the most widely used. There is an increasing demand for sterilizing procedures, while the IUCD and diaphragm are chosen by a small but varying proportion. There is a growing interest in the use of the so-called 'natural or mucothermal' method, and withdrawal is still practised by many throughout all sections of society.

The special needs, wishes, and circumstances of each individual have therefore to be considered. Identification and resolution if possible of any anxieties that she or her partner harbour will help to select the most appropriate method. Once the patient makes her choice and the presence of absolute contraindications has been excluded, then the general practitioner has the responsibility of prescribing the method correctly, teaching it carefully, and supervising the patient's progress. There are innumerable related problems which may confront the doctor. They may be physical, psychological, or psychosexual, and unless they are considered in an understanding and flexible manner, the couple may have great difficulty with the use of contraception and unwanted pregnancies may then occur. In one chapter it is possible to highlight only the more common and most important problems. Each method will be discussed in turn and then the special needs of particular types of women will be considered.

Relative reliability of contemporary methods

For the majority of women it proves very easy to conceive and much more difficult to contracept.

When selecting a method, its potential reliability is of paramount importance to most couples. To give realistic estimates, however, is not easy, because the theoretical effectiveness of each gives little indication of its likely reliability in practice, which will depend on the ability of the couple to use it correctly and consistently. Even the IUCD, which depends for its success primarily on the skill of the practitioner, involves patient effort in feeling the strings and attending for checks at appropriate intervals if it is to produce its best results.

Table 7.4

	Number of pregnancies per 100 woman years
Combined pill	< 1.0
Progestogen-only pill	0.5–4.0
IUCD	0.5–4.0
Diaphragm	1.9–7.0
Sheath	0.4–4.0
Rhythm by temperature (i.e. post ovulation intercourse only)	1.2–6.6
Rhythm by sympto thermal	1.1–37.9
Rhythm by calendar	16.0–22.0

Widely varying limits are frequently quoted because the results of any study are bound to be influenced by the motivation and sexual activity of the population concerned, and by the enthusiasm of the investigator and the degree and duration of follow-up achieved.

Table 7.4 gives a rough indication of reliability which can be quoted to those who enquire, provided the importance of correct and continuing use is stressed.

HORMONAL CONTRACEPTION

The combined pill

The chief problems encountered are connected with:
  (i) Discussion of benefit/risk considerations;
 (ii) the choice of preparation and its prescription;
(iii) supervision and follow-up.

Benefits and risks

Capable of providing virtually 100 per cent protection from unwanted pregnancy, taken at a time unconnected with sexual activity, the pill provides enormous reassurance by the associated regular, short, light, and usually painless withdrawal bleeding at the end of the 21-day pack. Inevitably, most of this section will be on possible risks and hazards associated with taking the pill, but the positive aspects should not be forgotten.

Reduction in hospital admissions for anaemia, ovarian cysts, and non-malignant breast lumps have been reported in pill-users and it has been suggested that oral contraception may afford some protection from rheumatoid arthritis, thyroid disease, duodenal ulcer, and pelvic inflammatory disease. Although some of these findings await confirmation, such good news is rarely mentioned while the suspected risks are well known, widely publicized, and often emotionally over-stressed.

Understanding of potential adverse side effects is based chiefly on the reported findings and analyses of two valuable prospective studies in this country, that of the RCGP (1977, 1981*a*) and the Oxford FPA (Vessey, McPherson, and Johnson 1977). This and other epidemiological evidence suggest an increased risk of death from cardiovascular disease in women who use the pill, compared with those who do not. Space does not allow full discussion of all the work which has been published in the 20 years during which the pill has been available in this country. Practitioners can formulate their own opinion of the risks by extensive reading, but the following points help to summarize the present medical opinion upon which contemporary prescription of the pill is based.

Cardiovascular disease.   Considerably larger quantities of both oestrogen and progestogen were used in the published studies than are customarily used today. A Swedish study (Bottiger, Bowman, Eklund, and Westerhum 1981) has demonstrated a great reduction in the incidence of venous thrombo-embolic episodes since oestrogen content of pills has been reduced.

The 1977 report of the RCGP study showed a fourfold risk of pill-takers' dying from cardiovascular disease. Reporting again in 1981 observations on larger numbers confirmed this finding but allowed clarification of the risk for certain women (Table 7.5).

From these figures it can be seen that the extra risk to non-smokers under the age of 35 is very small indeed, and that at all ages smoking considerably increases the risks. It is the fatal arterial event attributable to the use of the pill which is heavily concentrated in smokers. Venous thrombo-embolism does not appear to be related to smoking at all (Vessey 1982).

Cardiovascular deaths in the 1981 RCGP study were mostly as a result of subarachnoid haemorrhage or myocardial infarction. The death rate from subarachnoid haemorrhage in England and Wales has not increased

Table 7.5 *Circulatory disease mortality*

Age		No. of deaths reported		Ever users vs. controls		
		Ever users	Controls	Excess risk per 100 000 woman years	Relative risk	
15–24	Non-smokers	0	0		–	Non-smokers
	Smokers	1	0		–	1 : 77 000
25–34	Non-smokers	2	1	1.7	1.6	Smokers
	Smokers	6	1	10.0	3.4	1 : 10 000
35–44	Non-smokers	7	2	15.1	3.3	1 : 6700
	Smokers	18	3	48.2	4.2	1 : 2000
45+	Non-smokers	4	1	40.9	4.6	1 : 2500
	Smokers	17	2	178.8	7.4	1 : 500

From RCGP study, reported *Lancet* **1**, (approx.23 000 pill takers, 23 000 controls).

since 1959 although the pill has been available since 1961 and about 3 million women take it daily. It has been pointed out (Thorogood, Adam, and Mann 1981) that any risk is small and is probably associated with a hypertensive effect. The importance of accepting hypertension as a contraindication to the use of the pill is therefore obvious. There are many published works demonstrating a greatly increased risk of subarachnoid haemorrhage in both men and women who smoke. Thus pill users who smoke are living dangerously. The other chief cause of death was from myocardial infarction and a recent study (Adam, Thorogood, and Mann 1981) of women between the ages of 15 and 41 who died from this condition in 1978 has shown that in the absence of predisposing factors the risk for women on the pill was increased about twofold.

It is generally believed that it is the oestrogen component of the pill which is related to venous thrombo-embolism, but it is thought that the progestogen influence predisposes to the arterial problems. It has been shown that there is a dose-related reduction of high-density lipoprotein cholesterol (HDL-cholesterol) which is believed to predispose to atherosclerosis. It is important, therefore, to reduce the quantities of both components to the lowest possible levels if all cardiovascular effects are to be minimized.

The following observations from a study by Meade, Greenberg, and Thompson (1980) are reassuring:

1. The results support the large-scale move to pills with low doses of oestrogen.
2. The results support the suggestion that the risk of myocardial infarction may be less with 30 μg oestrogen pills compared with those containing 50 μg.
3. The risk of arterial disease is positively related to the progestogen dose.
4. This study concluded that there are no grounds either for alarm or for change in practice and that there is a case for minimizing the progestogen dose.

The latest report of the RCGP (1981*a*) contradicts its previous opinion concerning increased risks with duration of use, which cannot now be demonstrated.

Tumours. No medication has ever received so much scrutiny and investigation as the pill, nor has any been so widely used and tested. Fears have been expressed in connection with breast and cervical cancers, as well as pituitary and liver tumours.

To date, there is no convincing evidence of an increased risk of breast cancer and any little increased risk of cervical cancer may relate to different patterns of sexual activity in non-pill users. It is, however, not possible yet to be certain whether or not there may be late long-term consequences of previous pill use. Nor is it possible dogmatically to deny any ultimate risk of cancer.

It is hoped that the reduction in non-malignant breast lumps noted in pill users may signify some protection against cancerous ones. If it is true, however, that the late age of first pregnancy increases the risk of breast cancer, the convenience and availability of the pill might encourage delay of the first conception and might therefore be indirectly implicated.

In relation to pituitary tumours, although reports from the USA noted a high proportion of cases who gave a history of pill-taking, the RCGP study reported only five cases and were of the opinion that there was no evidence of any association but that modern technology allowed better diagnosis which might result in an apparent increased incidence in some parts of the world.

Liver tumours are rare conditions estimated to occur in between one and five women per million. A few hundred have been reported in pill users mostly in the USA, and a report on 12 cases seen at King's College Hospital, London (Williams 1981) between 1970 and 1979 has been published. These were in women between 21 and 42 years who had used 50 µg pills for between 2 and 12 years. The risk is believed to increase with duration of use, and as all cases presented with liver enlargement, abdominal palpation in long-term users would help to identify the exceedingly rare case.

Gallstones.   Gallstones were thought to occur more commonly in long-term users but this seems true only for women predisposed to gall bladder disease.

Congenital abnormalities and fertility.   There are many conflicting reports in the world literature not helped by small numbers studied and confounding factors such as smoking, alcohol, and other drugs which have not always been considered. There is no evidence of any greatly increased risk of congenital abnormality but since high doses of oestrogens and progestogens have been known to damage the developing fetus it is always wise to warn women against taking any medication if they believe themselves to be pregnant. If the general practitioner is asked the question, 'Should I come off the pill for a few months before getting pregnant?', there is no dogmatic answer. A recent report of an increased risk of neural tube defects in women who had been on the pill within 3 months prior to conception must make one err on the side of caution. But changing to use of a barrier method and spermicide may produce other hazards because of recent reports linking spermicides and congenital abnormalities.

In relation to fertility, conception may be delayed by a few months on average on stopping the pill, but there is no evidence that the pill causes

Table 7.7 *Comparative risks—estimates*

	Risk of death/100 000 at risk	Odds
Hang gliding	200	1 in 500
Coal mining	20	1 in 5000
Car driving	17	1 in 6000
Struck by a vehicle (UK)	6	1 in 17 000
Playing soccer	4	1 in 25 000
Home accidents	3	1 in 33 000
Pill: Non-smokers/under 35	1.3	1 in 77 000
Smokers/under 35	10.0	1 in 10 000
Deaths from pregnancy/childbirth: UK	10	1 in 10 000
Equador	213	1 in 470

After Guillebaud
Sources: Dinman, B. D. *J. Am. Med. Ass.* **244** (1980). *UN Demographic Year Book*, Table 21 (1979). *Lancet* **I**, 541–6 (1981).

long-term and irreversible infertility. This is discussed in more detail in Chapter 12 on infertility.

Comparative risks. From the available epidemiological evidence practitioners can have formed their own ideas on the risk/benefit ratio of oral contraception. The patient, however, wants to know what the risk is to her and would like to be able to compare it with that of pregnancy. Over the years many specialists have tried to quantify this problem and to put it into perspective in relation to other risks in life. It has been said that 'living can be hazardous to health', and in contemporary living conditions there are many dangers and any estimate must be approximate. It has been calculated that the least dangerous system of contraception is to use a barrier method and have an abortion if the occasional pregnancy occurs. As far as the pill is concerned, Table 7.7, devised by Guillebaud based on several studies, can prove very reassuring.

Choice of preparation

Having excluded those women who have absolute contraindications to the use of the pill (Table 7.8), the practitioner is faced with 28 varieties of pill on the market involving 18 different formulations from which to choose.

Table 7.8 *Absolute contraindications*

1. Presence of history of circulatory disease
2. Impaired liver function
3. Recent hydatidiform mole
4. Hypertension
5. Severe or focal migraine
6. Oestrogen-dependent tumour
7. Undiagnosed vaginal bleeding

Table 7.9 *Low dose pills*

	Levonorgestrol (μg)	*Ethinyl oestradiol* (μg)
Ovranette/Microgynon 30	150	30
Logynon/Trinordiol	6 × 50	6 × 30
	5 × 75	5 × 40
	10 × 125	10 × 30
	Norethisterone	
Brevinor/Ovysmen	500	35
Norimin	1000	35
	Ethynodiol diacetate	
Conova	2000	30
	Norethisterone acetate	
Loestrin 20	1000	20

These are listed in *Mims* and in the BNF. There are also six varieties of progestogen-only pills.

There is no simple formula for selection of the most suitable pill. Table 7.9 includes the lowest doses from which the initial choice should be made. Pills containing 50 μg oestrogen should only be selected when drug interaction is anticipated.

If the first choice proves unsatisfactory a change to a variety containing a different progestogen may prove a solution. If the cycle cannot be controlled, increasing the progestogen content is advisable. By grouping varieties of pill in a dosage ladder according to their progestogen, selection of a second choice is facilitated (Table 7.10).

New pills periodically reach the market and it is always important to check the variety and dose of the constituents to enable comparison with their predecessors. Recent additions marketed in 1981 were the first to involve a step-up dose formulation known as the 'Triphasic' (Logynon; Trinordiol). The chief advantage of this pill is the near 40 per cent reduction in monthly progestogen intake compared with Microgynon/Ovranette. Cycle control is reported to be better but time is needed to assess its reliability. Very careful teaching is essential to ensure that pills are taken in the correct order. The total monthly oestrogen intake is still less than that ingested with 35 μg oestrogen varieties. Its chief disadvantage is that it is more expensive than its predecessors. While psychologically useful to be able to offer a new dose, this variety is not suitable for those women who take 3–4 packets of pills continuously in order to avoid menstrual bleeding (tricycle system). Two new products have been recently marketed. Binovum consists of 7 tablets of the Brevinor/Ovysmen formulation followed by 14 of the Norimin dosage. A new progestagen desogestrel is contained in Marvelon in which 150 μg is combined with 30 μg ethinyl oestradiol.

Supervision and follow-up

Although each packet contains an instruction leaflet, each woman needs individual teaching. Some people may find the reading of these leaflets

Table 7.10 *System of summarizing pills according to progestogen content*

	Levonorgestrel (μg)	*Ethinyl oestradiol* (μg)
Ovran (Wyeth)	250	50
Eugynon 50 (Schering)	250	50
Eugynon 30 (Schering)	250	30
Ovran 30 (Wyeth)	250	30
Ovranette (Wyeth)	150	30
Microgynon (Schering)	150	30
Trinordiol (Wyeth) (triphasic) ⎰ 6 tablets	50	30
Logynon (Schering) (triphasic) ⎱ 5 tablets	75	40
⎩ 10 tablets	125	30
Logynon ED = Logynon + 7 inert tablets		
	Norethisterone acetate (μg)	*Ethinyl oestradiol* (μg)
Anovlar (Schering)	4000	50
Gynovlar (Schering)	3000	50
Norlestrin (Parke Davis)	2500	50
Minovlar (Schering)	1000	50
Minovlar ED (Schering)	1000 + 7 placebos	50
Orlest 21 (Parke Davis)	1000	50
Loestrin (Parke Davis)	1000	20
	Ethynodiol diacetate (μg)	*Ethinyl oestradiol* (μg)
Ovulen 50 (Searle)	1000	50
Demulen 50 (Searle)	500	50
Conova 30 (Searle)	2000	30
	Norethisterone (μg)	*Mestranol* (μg)
Norinyl-1 (Syntex)	1000	50
Norinyl 28 + 7 placebos (Syntex)	1000	50
Orthonovin 1/50 (Ortho)	1000	50
	Norethisterone (μg)	*Ethinyl oestradiol* (μg)
Norimin (Syntex)	1000	35
Ovysmen (Ortho)	500	35
Brevinor (Syntex)	500	35
Binovum (Ortho)	7 × 500	35
	14 × 1000	35
	Desogestrel (μg)	*Ethinyl oestradiol* (μg)
Marvelon (Organon)	150	30
	Lynestrenol (μg)	*Ethinyl oestradiol* (μg)
Minilyn (Organon)	2500	50

difficult while others will study them carefully and ask searching questions. If starting on day five, extra precautions are recommended for the first 14 days. This is the recommendation in all pill leaflets except Trinordiol, Logynon, Binovum and Marvelon. These follow the advice favoured nowadays of starting on day one and avoiding any extra precautions. It is important to remind the patient that pills must be taken in the correct order and the packet completed regardless of bleeding. Protection is afforded during the seven tablet-free days provided another packet is taken. If taken correctly, each new pack is started on the same weekday.

Missed pills are a recurring problem. It is probable that although the pill imposes its own cycle, the intrinsic rhythm of the hypothalamus continues in a modified manner. Follicles may at times therefore develop and missed pills at certain times could lead to ovulation. Fortunately, the endometrium is usually in a state unfavourable for nidation and so pregnancies are not very common. Nevertheless, careful warning should be given against irregular tablet taking. It is difficult to formulate a simple system of management on a scientific basis but it is customary now to advise the use of extra precautions for 14 days only if a pill is missed for more than 12 hours, regardless at which stage of the cycle. This rule should also be observed if gastro-intestinal disturbance occurs or if there is potential interaction with other medication, e.g. antibiotics. Manufacturers' leaflets recommend that extra precautions need only be used to the end of the packet.

It is important to record the patient's blood pressure before starting the pill and to check it after three months and subsequently at intervals of six months or one year as the risk of hypertension continues to be present. Although manufacturers' leaflets advise initial pelvic examination to be repeated at regular intervals, there is no scientific evidence to support the need for this in the young, healthy, gynaecologically asymptomatic woman who takes the pill. It should be performed for the purpose of smear-taking as part of routine screening, as for non-pill takers. Women should be given permission to return at any time should they experience side effects or feel the need to discuss anxieties connected with oral contraception.

General side effects

The use of contemporary low-dose pills has dramatically reduced the reporting of side effects. Nevertheless, a few women still report headache, depression, and weight gain. Such symptoms should not be treated, but managed by changing to a different variety of pill or to another method. Thus the prescription of antidepressants, antimigraine, diuretic, or hypotensive treatments should not be offered. Decreasing the dose of either or both components, changing to a different progestogen, or transferring to a progestogen-only pill could be tried. Early cycles are often associated with an increase in appetite which if indulged will lead to weight gain. Preliminary warning may help this problem. The development of headache is always worrying as the aetiology is not understood. Some women avoid it by taking the pill continuously for three or four packs, thereby also avoiding withdrawal bleeding. Trinordiol and Logynon, because of their differing doses, are not suitable for use in this 'tricycle' manner. If headache is severe, migrainous, or associated with focal symptoms such as loss of vision or speech, weakness or paraesthesia, that variety of pill should be stopped. Depression and loss of libido are more likely to be reported by those who have a depressive tendency or some psychosexual problem. Cervical erosions commonly occur in pill-takers but do not require treatment unless infected or causing troublesome discharge Monilial infections are common in all women but some feel they have more problems with it on the pill.

Cycle control

Spotting and even breakthrough bleeding commonly occur during the first two cycles on low-dose pills. The Triphasics seem to provide rather better early control. By warning women to expect these problems they will be spared much anxiety. They should be advised also to be very regular in their pill-taking as late or missed pills precipitate bleeding. If the problem proves unacceptable or persists after the second cycle, the pill should be changed. In the absence of other side effects a change to a variety with a larger progestogen dose should help. Reference to the ladders on Table 7.10 gives guidance. For example, the pill could be changed from Microgynon to Eugynon 30 or from Brevinor to Norimin.

Some women fail to bleed and do not even experience any brown discharge during the tablet-free week. If pills have been taken correctly and there has not been any gastro-intestinal upset pregnancy is unlikely. However, pregnancy is the commonest cause of absent withdrawal bleeding. It is always preferable, therefore, to identify a preparation which permits at least a little loss. The manufacturers' leaflet recommends that the woman should ask her doctor to exclude pregnancy before she starts a new pack, an impossibly difficult task at an early stage. Because of potential hazards to a developing embryo, if there is any doubt it would be preferable to advise temporary discontinuation with alternative contraception in the meanwhile. There is no simple remedy for correcting or avoiding absent withdrawal bleeding, but it is apparently less frequent with the Triphasic pill.

Drug interaction

Since low-oestrogen pills have been available, the problem of interaction with other medications leading to reduced efficacy has been reported. Impaired absorption, or induction of liver enzymes leading to enhanced metabolism has resulted in breakthrough pregnancies. Table 7.11 gives a list of drugs which have been involved. There is considerable variation between individuals, however, but it is always prudent in these circumstances to prescribe a 50 µg oestrogen pill.

Breakthrough bleeding, especially toward the end of the cycle, is a warning sign. If this cannot be overcome, progressive increase in the oestrogen dose could be tried, e.g. to 60 µg by giving two pills daily. It would probably be wiser, however, to prescribe an alternative method. Any practitioner who detects an interaction is asked to complete a yellow card

Table 7.11

Rifampicin
Phenobarbitone, phenytoin (Epanutin)
Ethosuximide (Zarontin), primidone (Mysoline)
Carbamazepine (Tegretol)
Chlorpromazine (Largactil)
Meprobamate (Equanil)
Phenacetin/amidopyrine
Ampicillin, phenoxymethyl penicillin
Chloramphenicol, neomycin, tetracycline
? Sulphonamides

on adverse reactions so that more information concerning this problem may be acquired.

Summary

The combined pill provides highly acceptable contraception for many. Individuals vary, however, and some are only suited to one formulation. Presentation of multiple side effects in spite of the prescription of low doses would indicate the need for a different method, but excessive anxiety about consequences should first be suspected and discussed. No matter how carefully those with contraindications are excluded, a few women will experience adverse effects. Supervision is essential, especially of blood pressure and weight, and it is important that the woman feels able to report back at any time. Cervical smear testing and breast examination are only necessary as screening procedures and need to be performed at the same frequency as for non-pill users. Some authorities feel that the pill should be stopped about 6 weeks before major surgery but others do not. Oral contraception is easy and a preferred method for most. If the combined pill is not suitable, the progestogen-only ('oestrogen-free', 'POP', or 'mini') pill is a good alternative.

Progestogen-only pill

There are six varieties available (Table 7.12).

This is an underused and often abused method which requires maximum motivation by both patient and doctor. Taken absolutely regularly each day within 2–3 hours, without breaks and regardless of bleeding patterns, it can provide protection from pregnancy not far short of the combined pill. The Oxford/FPA Study reported a failure rate of 1.4 per 100 woman years but it has been shown that this can be improved to 0.5 per 100 woman years.

Side effects are infrequent but cycle irregularity is common, and women require considerable support and encouragement until they get accustomed to it. Previous experience of irregular cycles helps early

Table 7.12

				Number of tablets
Noriday	(Syntex)	350 µg	Norethisterone	28
Micronor	(Ortho)	350 µg	Norethisterone	42
Femulen	(Searle)	500 µg	Ethynodiol diacetate	28
Neogest	(Schering)	75 µg	dl Norgestrel	35
Microval	(Wyeth)	30 µg	Levonorgestrel	35
Norgeston	(Schering)	30 µg	Levonorgestrel	35

(NB 75 µg dl Norgestrel is equivalent to 37.5 µg Levonorgestrel.)

acceptability, whereas familiarity with the precise timing of bleeding associated with the combined pill makes the erratic nature of periods more difficult to tolerate at first.

Careful teaching and preliminary warning help to prevent premature abandonment of the method. It is useful for those who cannot take the combined pill, for the older woman, the diabetic, the woman who is breast-feeding, and when surgery is awaited.

Problems and management

Apart from the occasional complaint of breast tenderness which is usually transient but may be recurrent and can sometimes be overcome by changing from one progestogen to another, the main problem presented is that of menstrual irregularity. It is always helpful, therefore, to ask women to keep a record chart in early months, as this quickly highlights the type of problem and usually demonstrates a gradual 'settling down'. Premenstrual tension is often relieved and climacteric symptoms sometimes eased. More than half the women will have a cycle between 25 and 35 days and with advance warning these are usually well tolerated.

Two or three days' bleeding twice a month is common, and once accustomed to this and reassured, women accept it as the loss is usually light. Even when cycles are short between 21 and 24 days, complaints are rare provided the bleeding is not too heavy. Prolonged spells of amenorrhoea occur most markedly in older women. At first this causes considerable anxiety to both patient and doctor as the method is not expected to provide 100 per cent reliability. In these cases, however, the amenorrhoea is usually the result of anovulation and is therefore highly effective. Pregnancies to women over 40 using this method have not been reported. A few women will experience prolonged and heavy bleeding and if not relieved by changing the variety of pill, another method should be selected.

Although progestogens are known to depress HDL-cholesterol, the dosage involved in this variety of pill has minimal effect in the short term. As yet, unfortunately, no long-term studies of this continuous medication have been reported. Blood pressure needs regularly to be monitored but where raised during administration of the combined pill, it usually reverts to normal when changed to this variety.

Previous ectopic pregnancy is a contraindication as there is an increased risk of ectopic pregnancy on this pill. It should also not be prescribed for a woman who has had a hydatidiform mole until HCG has become undetectable in two serum samples taken at monthly intervals. No other conditions absolutely contraindicate its use. Because it is thought not to affect blood clotting mechanisms it has been used for women who have experienced some form of thrombo-embolism. Caution must be exercised in these situations, however, as the manufacturers' leaflets recommend against its use.

The acceptability of this method depends largely on the practitioner's attitude and confidence based on experience of its use. Absolute regularity of pill-taking is essential as it has only a 24-hour action on cervical mucus, and ovulation is not usually inhibited nor the endometrium excessively modified. Pill-taking just prior to the most frequent time for intercourse is therefore obviously less than ideal.

Injectables

There are two available: Depo-Provera (medroxyprogesterone acetate) and Norigest (norethisterone oenanthate). Only the first of these need be discussed as the other is not yet marketed, although it has been approved by the Committee on Safety of Medicines. In the USA neither of these products is licensed for use. Depo-Provera has been in use for many years for the treatment of endometriosis and terminal cancer. The manufacturers have a licence to produce it for use as a contraceptive in two situations only, at the time of a rubella immunization and after vasectomy while waiting for the seminal fluid to show azoospermia.

Deep intramuscular injection of 150 mg Depo-Provera provides contraceptive protection for 3 months. In many countries the method is freely available and very popular, and considerable experience with its use has accumulated. In Britain, this method is acceptable for some women who cannot or will not use alternatives but wish and/or need to avoid pregnancy. Anxiety concerning this method has arisen from its association with the development of breast lumps in beagle bitches as a result of long-term usage in large doses.

Associated problems include irregular bleeding or amenorrhoea and in long-term users, weight gain. Preliminary warning saves anxiety about these. After long-term use there is a delay in return of fertility but studies have shown that 80 per cent of women conceive again within two years. Its action is by inhibition of ovulation and therefore the injection must be given in the post-partum period or within the first three days of the cycle if immediate effectiveness is required.

Table 7.13 *Methods of post-coital contraception*

	Pill	IUCD
Method	Eugynon 50 or Ovran Two pills stat Two pills 12 hours later	Gravigard (Copper 7) Multiload (Copper 250)
Timing after intercourse	Up to 72 hours	Up to 5 days
Efficacy	99 per cent	100 per cent (no reported cases)
Side effects	Nausea and vomiting	Pain, bleeding, infection risk
Contraindications	Ectopic pregnancy As for O.C.'s	Ectopic pregnancy As for IUCD's

Post-coital contraception

The need for an emergency measure to prevent pregnancy after an unexpected exposure to the risk is well-recognized. In cases of rape the use of large doses of oestrogen was considered effective but was usually associated with severe nausea and vomiting.

Two methods have now been shown to be very effective (Table 7.13). A high oestrogen dose (50 µg) combined pill—Eugynon 50 or Ovran—two pills stat and repeated after 12 hours will prevent implantation in 99 per cent of cases. This hormonal therapy is effective for up to 72 hours after intercourse. Nausea and vomiting may be a problem and contraindications would be a previous ectopic pregnancy or thrombosis, or risk factors for thrombosis. A withdrawal bleed may follow in a few days, the period may come at the usual time, or both may occur.

Insertion of a medicated IUCD up to 5 days, perhaps longer, after intercourse, prevents implantation in almost 100 per cent of women. There are risks of pain, bleeding, or infection as with any IUCD so that this regimen may not be acceptable for the nulliparous woman. It is also contraindicated with a previous ectopic pregnancy.

Before administration careful examination of the woman is essential and her history should be very carefully checked. Pregnancy must be excluded if possible. She should be advised against further intercourse in this cycle. Future contraception must be discussed and provided. The woman should be warned that these regimens of post-coital contraception have not been proved harmless to the fetus if they failed and pregnancy were to continue.

INTRA-UTERINE CONTRACEPTIVE DEVICE (IUCD)

This method is not 100 per cent reliable but gives about 97 per cent protection. Women who are happily suited love it, the rest hate it. Once inserted, further motivation of the woman need only be minimal and medicated devices may be left in place for two, three, or more years while the inert varieties (e.g. Lippes Loop, Saf-T-Coil) may remain as long as required.

All users will experience either longer or heavier bleeding and the acceptability and tolerance of this varies. While irregular, intermenstrual or post-coital bleeding may be associated, gynaecological causes must be excluded—especially in the older woman when genital malignancy is more common.

The effectiveness of this method depends primarily on the skill of the practitioner who inserts it. Considerable and ongoing experience is an absolute essential for good technique. Inadequately inserted devices are likely to be extruded and perforation of the uterus may occur, especially when it is soft (post-partum or post-abortion), scarred following Caesarean section or hysterotomy, or if its acutely anteverted or retroverted position is not corrected by the use of a tenaculum during insertion.

Types of device

More than 80 devices have been designed since their introduction.

Inert devices

Lippes Loop, 4 sizes (size C is most commonly used). Saf-T-Coil (recently removed from the UK market by the manufacturers).

Medicated devices

Gravigard—Copper 7 (removal recommended by manufacturers after two years, but can stay in for three years).
Orthogyne T (removal recommended after 3 years).
Multiload—Copper 250 (may be left for 3 years).
Other devices not currently on the drug tariff include:
    Antigon (inert and fitted with a small magnet);
    Minigravigard (smaller than Gravigard);
    Novagard (copper, may be left for four years);
    Progestasert (vertical arm contains progesterone—needs annual renewal.

Choice of device

Practitioners will have their own favourite device based on their own experience. Menstrual problems may occur with any, but the heavier bleeding is usually associated with larger devices. If the bleeding proves excessive and if intra-uterine contraception is preferred or badly needed, it is worthwhile removing the device and inserting another, either smaller or one of a different design. Those women who tolerate very heavy loss because of the convenience of the method must be checked for anaemia. Even with accurate insertion some women seem prone to extrusion. The

Multiload has been reported useful when others have been expelled quickly.

If a woman is keen to use an IUCD, it is worthwhile reinserting after early expulsion. Some doctors report success with the Antigon for women who have repeatedly expelled devices. It is not surprising that initial cramping pain may be experienced, but on other occasions pain should not be associated. When pain is a problem, pelvic infection or impending extrusion must be excluded.

Although this method is not usually recommended for the nulliparous woman, in those instances when it is indicated the smallest sizes should be used (Minigravigard, Gravigard, Novagard or Lippes A&B). The method for them proves less reliable, there is a greater extrusion rate, insertion is more difficult and often associated with some degree of cervical shock. Dysmenorrhoea is exacerbated and the risk of pelvic infection and subsequent fertility problems has been shown to be considerable.

For the unmotivated woman or the wanderer it may be preferable to use an inert device which may be left in indefinitely.

Infection

Although not presenting as frequently as heavy bleeding, the occurrence of pelvic infection in the presence of a device is the most serious problem. Many studies have been reported which show that there is a greater risk of pelvic inflammatory disease in IUCD users than in non-users. The relative risk has been quoted by Weström, Bengtsson, and Murdh (1976) as 3.1, and 6.9 for those who have never been pregnant. He showed that the overall risk declined slightly with age. In 1980 (Booth, Beral, and Guillebaud 1980) a worrying report from the Margaret Pyke Centre revealed that among 871 nulliparous women aged between 16 and 49 the risk was greatest for the youngest. After two years the 16–19-year-olds had an infection rate more than 10 times that of the 30–49-year-olds. It is likely that the lifestyle of these young women may have increased the likelihood of exposure to infection, and because of the risk of subsequent infertility, the method is better avoided in the young nulliparous.

Management will depend on the circumstances of each individual case. If it seems important to retain the device at all costs, the infection must be treated as quickly as possible. It is, however, preferable to remove the device as well and reinsertion should be delayed until at least six months and some authorities would say indefinitely. Full dose antibiotic therapy would be indicated, selection being modified on the result of an endocervical swab. Gonorrhoea or chlamydia are often the causative organisms. A broad spectrum antibiotic preferably a tetracycline, could be given while laboratory reports are awaited, together with metronidazole.

There have been recent reports of the presence of actinomyces-like

a temporary measure. For some, however, it is completely unacceptable. Some older men, or those who have any sexual anxiety, complain that its use may result in loss of erection. For those women who dislike the smell or messiness of semen, the sheath solves their problem.

The cap or diaphragm

Demand for this method is increasing and many women express surprise at its simplicity and complain because it had not been offered to them earlier. Some who found it unacceptable in early marriage find it much easier after experience with tampons and when sexual activity takes on a relatively regular pattern. Protecting the cervix from infection and semen, and inserted as a routine irrespective of coitus, it can be used without spoiling spontaneity. There is little reduction in physical sexual sensitivity as the clitoris and introitus are not affected and cervical pressure is still possible. The additional spermicide provides useful lubrication for the older woman and for those in the post-natal period and others who are slow to lubricate as a result of sexual arousal.

A recent report from the USA suggested that the use of spermicide might be associated with congenital abnormality of an accidentally conceived baby. Even the authors emphasize that there is little foundation for this suggestion, and laboratory investigations have failed to demonstrate any associated toxicity. Sperm is immobilized rather than destroyed by spermicidal agents and a damaged sperm is not believed to be capable of fertilization. Although many substances are well absorbed from the vagina there is no proof of harm from the use of spermicides, experience of which now spans some fifty years (see p. 126) (Volpar paste and volpar gels were withdrawn from the market ten years ago because they contained mercury. No toxicity or damage either to the woman or offspring had ever been demonstrated).

The acceptability of the cap or diaphragm depends upon the manner in which it is offered. It is capable of 98 per cent or more protection provided it is correctly and consistently used. Although the fit is important, teaching the insertion and checking the covering of the cervix is essential. The complaint of discomfort of the diaphragm implies wrong fitting.

When it is apparent that a woman has great difficulty in inserting anything into her vagina, be it tampon, pessaries, or a cap, obviously the method is not suitable. In a few instances this problem may be connected with some psychosexual difficulty and this sometimes presents during the teaching of the method. Permission to discuss associated fears and anxieties may prove helpful. Simple lack of anatomical knowledge is often the cause.

When a vaginal barrier is rejected on account of 'messiness' this also may be due to such a problem. Excessive spermicide or of an inappropriate variety is, however, the main cause. Available preparations have different active components, bases and pH values, and may be in the form of jelly, cream, or foam. The offer of alternatives may relieve the problem.

If the partner complains that he can feel the barrier during coitus it is almost certainly too small and descends from the vault and from behind the pubic symphysis. Discomfort for the woman results if the fit is too tight or a vaginal infection is present. Chronic cystitis sufferers do not usually like the method. Very occasionally a sensitivity to spermicide is apparent but rubber allergy is exceptionally rare. Additional spermicide is essential as no mechanical barrier is complete.

Diaphragms should probably be checked annually or if there is an 8 lb change in weight, gain or loss. If the size remains constant, how often a new cap is needed will vary according to amount of usage and what the cap itself looks like. A rough guide is that usually a new one can be issued annually. Some caps get misshapen, very discoloured and worn sooner than this, and some appear pristine after two years. There has also been renewed interest in cervical caps which some women find more comfortable to use than the ordinary diaphragm.

A recent report from the USA showed a high failure rate with cervical caps. But as many were shown to have been dislodged during coitus, these caps were not fitting properly.

Female barriers can be used happily and very successfully by many women, but high motivation is essential. Routine nightly insertion is practised by many, thereby allowing complete spontaneity of sexual activity. A good sense of humour helps the acceptability of this method!

Spermicides

While invaluable as adjuncts to caps and sheaths, creams, jellies, pessaries and foams by themselves are not reliable, but even used alone theoretical pregnancy rates under 10 per 100 woman years have been quoted.

MUCOTHERMAL OR 'NATURAL' METHOD

At one time the rhythm or safe period method was generally despised and only adopted by staunch Roman Catholics. It is now in increasing demand by those who prefer to use a so-called 'natural' method, even although it is necessarily restrictive. This method demands the highest possible motivation and can only result in maximum reliability if intercourse is confined to the days following a rise in temperature which has been sustained for 72 hours, until the onset of the next menstrual bleeding. Temperature estimations are difficult when some cycles are anovulatory, especially in the post-partum period, during lactation, and in the climacteric years.

The use of basal body temperature changes to establish the time of ovulation can be combined with changes in cervical mucus. The Billings method, as this is called, depends on the fact that the cervical mucus and hence the vaginal 'discharge' changes in consistency at the mid-cycle fertile time from being sticky and thick to being thin and watery. Changes in apparent vaginal 'discharge' also occur with vaginal infections and after recent intercourse, so women should be warned about these possibilities. Cervical mucus changes occur prior to the temperature rise and allow sex earlier in the cycle. Better results are obtained if both the mucus and temperature changes are used together, but one trial showed that nearly 14 per cent of women had accidental pregnancies during the first two years of use of this method.

Any who wish to use this method deserve careful explanation and teaching, and instruction leaflets are available which can be very helpful. These can be obtained from:

(i) The FPA, 27–35 Mortimer Street, London, W1N 7RJ; or
(ii) The Natural Family Planning Service, Catholic Marriage Advisory Council, 15 Lansdowne Road, London, W11 3AJ; or
(iii) The Natural Family Planning Unit, Birmingham Maternity Unit, Queen Elizabeth Medical Centre, Edgbaston, Birmingham 15.

STERILIZATION

There is a tendency nowadays for couples to expect sterilizing procedures to solve all problems and to be free of any associated risk, complications, or consequences. While providing maximum reliability, failures are occasionally reported and the rate usually quoted is 2–4 per 1000.

General anaesthetics carry their own very small risk, but modern techniques have considerably reduced the severity of the operation and the length of hospitalization required. Psychological and physical consequences have been reported of both tubal ligation and vasectomy and the need for careful preliminary discussion with both partners is absolutely essential if ultimate satisfaction is to result.

Even though modern surgical techniques can be used to reverse some sterilizations, such operations demand skill, are difficult to get, are often expensive, and are not always successful. It is still wise, therefore, to consider sterilization to be irreversible and only to proceed when both partners can accept this. While it might seem to be sensible, practical, and desirable to limit the family, couples sometimes feel differently after the passage of time. Regret is more likely if the decision is made at a time of crisis or stress, and post-partum and post-termination sterilizations should not be done as a general rule.

The psychological sequelae of sterilization have been looked at. Earlier studies showed considerably higher rates of psychiatric morbidity, psychosexual dysfunction, and regret than a recent prospective study (Cooper, Gath, Rose, and Fieldsend 1982) when women were interviewed four weeks prior to elective sterilization and followed up at eighteen months. In this latter study considerable regret was felt by 2 per cent at six months and by 4 per cent at eighteen months, and post-operative psychiatric disturbance and dissatisfaction were largely associated with pre-operative psychiatric disturbance. The poorer results in other studies may be related to several factors including that previously patients were more likely to have been sterilized in association with a termination or immediately post-partum.

Most of these studies on sequelae of sterilization were hospital-based but a small general practitioner study (Curtis 1979) identified 61 sterilized women. A control group of patients were asked similar questions about their experiences since their last pregnancy. These questions covered the area of menorrhagia, hysterectomy, libido changes, and showed little difference between the two groups. As far as patient satisfaction with the sterilization was concerned, 45 had no regrets and 16 had some regrets, but only two of these seemed to be really serious.

Although sterilization is usually undertaken as a permanent procedure, requests for reversal do occur. In a series published by Winston (1980) reporting on 103 women who requested reversal between 1975 and 1976, 87 per cent were under the age of 30; 63 per cent had been sterilized after delivery; and no less than 75 per cent had been unhappily married. He reported a 58 per cent pregnancy rate after microsurgery when the 37 per cent who had had a completely irreversible operation had been excluded. With increasing experience of such specialist surgeons and the wider use of clips and rings, it may be that reversal successes will improve. It would, however, be prudent to endeavour to exclude likely candidates in advance by sensitive counselling.

Some couples seek sterilization in the hope that it will solve their sexual difficulties. Some couples who find it impossible to use contraceptive methods may be using the fear of pregnancy as a defence against sexual activity. This defence is removed by tubal ligation or vasectomy. For most couples, however, an irreversible step is just what they want, and once this decision is reached then the most appropriate procedure needs to be identified after discussion.

Tubal ligation has the advantage of immediate sterility and the protection of the woman for ever—regardless of any change in circumstances. It usually requires a general anaesthetic, and a few days' hospitalization which disrupts a family more than the absence of the father for half a day. Vasectomy is simple in experienced hands, quick, and can be performed under local anaesthetic, but it may be several months before the semen is clear of sperm and local swelling, pain and haematoma may be associated. In the event of death of the wife, or of marriage breakdown, the man nearly always finds a new partner and may then regret his sterility. This potential needs to be faced in advance. Good counselling allows couples to face all potential consequences and to decide whether or not they are prepared to take the risk and thereby it is hoped that subsequent regrets will be few.

Later development of menstrual problems is often reported. While this may sometimes be associated with the surgical technique, it is never possible to anticipate any woman's menstrual future and indeed there are many published series which refute any connection. In a report by Newton and Gillman in 1980 of a retrospective analysis of 2122 women who had been sterilized between 1968 and 1973, 34 patients had required hysterectomy and in 18 of these this was unconnected with the sterilization. Another study that measured menstrual blood loss before and after two years showed no change.

Recent anxiety has been reported concerning auto-immunity to sperm and reabsorption leading to an increased risk of arteriosclerosis in monkeys. As yet there is no evidence in man, but vasectomy on a large scale has only been performed during the last 15 years and it is perhaps too early to discuss the remote possibility. Some authorities would advise against vasectomy if a man is already hypertensive or has a strong family history of circulatory disease.

THE OVER 35-YEAR-OLD WOMAN

Most women of this age have achieved their desired family size and/or established themselves in some form of career or working life. The combined pill was highly acceptable to many of them until the increasing hazards with age were demonstrated in 1977.

Now that there is greater understanding of the risks and doses of pills are smaller, a more flexible attitude concerning its use can be used for those who have no other complicating factors, i.e. the non-hypertensive, non-smoking, non-obese, healthy woman who needs and wants the absolute protection. The oestrogen also helps to replace her diminishing levels during the climacteric years. Scrupulously careful supervision is essential. Hormone replacement therapy is not contraceptive although involving cyclical oestrogens and progestogens. The progestogen-only pill is particularly useful for the older woman. Reliability is excellent, and the long spells of amenorrhoea are well-tolerated.

The IUCD offers its greatest reliability and acceptability in this age group. Anaemia needs to be excluded if periods are heavy and erratic episodes of bleeding investigated because of the greater risk of genital malignancy at this age. The sheath method may become uncomfortable for the menopausal woman unless additional spermicide is used, older men tire of its use and may even find it difficult.

The cap or diaphragm can be extremely reliable and acceptable, and the spermicide compensates for diminishing lubrication. The calculation of the 'natural' method becomes impossibly difficult because of cycle irregularity, anovulatory spells, and altered vaginal secretions. Sterilization solves the problems of many but surgery may often be avoided by careful prescription of alternatives.

When to stop

There is no simple answer to the question which many patients will ask— 'Have I stopped ovulating yet?' The traditional advice to use contraception for one year after the last period if over the age of 50, and for two years if under, is not based on any particular scientific evidence, and is probably overcautious, but little alternative guidance is available.

Long spells of amenorrhoea in women under 40 may indicate the arrival of a premature menopause, but may be due to other causes (see Chapter 2 on menstrual disorders). After the age of 40, particularly if the amenorrhoea is associated with hot flushes, the diagnosis of the menopause is much more likely and contraception could be abandoned. Persistently raised FSH levels would be indicative of the end of ovulation but one reading is not sufficient. While many women continue to menstruate after the age of 50, conceptions are rare and yet few continue to use contraception conscientiously. Age alone would provide medical grounds for termination of pregnancy but for those women who could not accept an abortion continuing contraception would be necessary for their peace of mind.

Total reassurance about the abandonment of contraception around the menopause, now quoted as 50 on average, is impossible. It is important to remember that many unwanted pregnancies occur in women over 40, as evidenced in Table 7.14 where, in the years 1976–8, the number of therapeutic abortions in this age-group almost equalled the number of live and still births. Although these numbers are small in comparison with other age groups, it can be safely assumed that many of these conceptions

Table 7.14 *Abortions, still and live births in residents of England and Wales, 1976–1978*

Age (years)	1976			1977			1978		
	AB	SB	LB	AB	SB	LB	AB	SB	LB
40–44	4520	154	5999	4638	107	5534	4918	119	5719
45–49	463	16	427	511	14	445	482	8	492
50+	20	2	26	18	–	9	10	2	31
Total	5003	172	6452	5167	121	5988	5410	129	6242

AB = Abortions;   SB = Still births;   LB = Live births.

would have been associated with some degree of anxiety and stress which would have been better avoided by the use of contraception.

THE WOMAN WHO HAS JUST BEEN PREGNANT

Ovulation may occur as early as 10 days after abortion and 33 days after delivery. Early contraception is therefore important.

Oestrogen may inhibit lactation and does enter the milk in small quantities, and although many women have used the combined pill satisfactorily during lactation, the progestogen-only variety is preferable. This does not interfere significantly with lactation and although traces may enter the milk the quantity would be so small that it has been equated to a baby getting the equivalent of one pill in 2–3 years and is considerably less than the progesterone level found in dried cow's milk. However, if a woman is unhappy about this type of contraception she should use an alternative method. The natural childbirth movement advise against its use.

The IUCD is easily inserted at 6 weeks post-partum but the uterus is still soft and great care is necessary. Earlier insertion is more likely to lead to extrusion. After Caesarean section or if any infection is present, insertion is better delayed.

The sheath method is useful until other methods are established. There is always a delay in the return of erotic vaginal lubrication following pregnancy, regardless of the route of delivery, and the use of additional spermicides help this problem which may otherwise cause dyspareunia and precipitate some degree of frigidity and even lead to marital disharmony. Caps and diaphragms may be refitted at 5–6 weeks and this is necessary even after Caesarean section. Calculation of the 'natural' method is very difficult at this time.

Sterilization procedures performed at abortion or in the post-partum period carry extra operative and emotional risks: surgery is now usually delayed for a few months.

THE VERY YOUNG

Although early cycles after the menarche are assumed to be anovulatory, very early conceptions are being reported. In those under 16 years old where there is a real risk of pregnancy, the combined pill usually proves the most suitable method. The IUCD, even with its increased problems in the young and nulliparous, does have a place where other methods will not be used and especially with the educationally subnormal.

Any general practitioner faced with an under-16-year-old needs to consider the many legal and emotional factors involved and to study the DHSS *Memorandum of guidance.*

WOMEN WITH INTERCURRENT DISEASE

Such women usually require maximum possible protection from pregnancy. Sterilization, however, is not always indicated and the pill may be associated with additional risks. Clearly, each has to be considered individually and discussion with the consultant in charge is often helpful.

Already, absolute contraindications to methods of contraception have been listed, but the following are a few more commonly met conditions which need special consideration.

Diabetes

The combined pill may disturb the insulin balance and is known to alter carbohydrate metabolism. The disease increases the risk of thrombo-embolism and hypertension, further contraindicating the pill. However, its use can be valuable for limited periods under careful supervision and ultimately sterilization is usually requested. This, however, carries greater operative risk. The progestogen-only pill is acceptable and very reliable because regularity of pill-taking can be guaranteed if it coincides with insulin injections. The greater risk of any infection to diabetics militates against the advisability of the IUCD and recent reports have suggested that alterations in the endometrium lead to decreased reliability. Barriers are frequently the method of choice.

Epilepsy

The possibility of decreased reliability of the pill as a result of drug interaction has already been described. There is considerable individual variation in this effect but a minimal dose of 50 µg oestrogen is recommended. The progestogen-only pill may also be affected by drug interaction and is contra-indicated. An alternative method, especially the IUCD, is preferable.

Other conditions

Hodgkin's disease, cervical carcinoma *in situ*, sickle cell disease, and multiple sclerosis do not present absolute contraindications to the use of the pill, but immobility of the latter might predispose to thrombolic complications. There is an increasing number of jejunal bypass operations currently being performed on young obese women but whether this will affect the absorption of oral contraceptives has not yet been established.

THE FUTURE

In spite of the availability of a full, comprehensive contraceptive service, the requests for termination of unwanted pregnancies continue to increase. For some women it proves very difficult to get contraceptive advice, and others seem unable to use any method successfully. Sensitive understanding of the innumerable factors which influence the acceptability of family planning is vital if women are to be helped to avoid unwanted conceptions. New pills, devices, and injectables will undoubtedly be marketed in the near future, and new varieties of vaginal barriers are already being tested. There is still a need for more understanding by the very young concerning the ease of conception and by the older woman of the persistence of fertility. Too often women conceive because they do not believe it will happen to them or because they do not intend to indulge in sexual activity but get 'swept off their feet'. Physicians in whatever field they work have a responsibility to make it easy for their patients to ask for advice and then to have the skill to help them use it happily and effectively.

REFERENCES AND FURTHER READING

Adam, S. A., Thorogood, M., and Mann, J. I. (1981). Oral contraception and myocardial infarction revisited: the effects of new preparations and prescribing patterns. *Br. J. Obs. Gynaecol.* **88**, 838–45.

British Medical Journal Leader (1981). Breast cancer and the pill—a muted reassurance. *Br. Med. J.* i, 2075.

—— (1982). Oral contraceptives and cardiovascular disease: some questions and answers. *Br. Med. J.* i, 615.

Booth, M., Beral, V., and Guillebaud, J. (1980). Effect of age on pelvic inflammatory disease in nulliparous women using a Copper 7 intrauterine contraceptive device. *Br. Med. J.* ii, 114.

Bottiger, L. E., Bowman, G., Eklund, G., and Westerholm, B. (1981). Oral contraceptives and thromboembolic disease. Effects of lowering oestrogen content. *Lancet*, i, 1097.

Curtis, D. M. (1979). The sequelae of female sterilization in one general practice. *J. R. Coll. Gen. Pract.* **29**, 366–9.

Cooper, P., Gath, D., Rose, N., and Fieldsend, R. (1982). Psychological sequence to elective sterilisation: a prospective study. *Br. Med. J.* **284**, 461–4.

Meade, T. W., Greenberg, G., and Thompson, S. G. (1980). Progestogens and cardiovascular reactions associated with oral contraceptives and a comparison of the safety of 50 μg and 30 μg oestrogen preparations. *Br. Med. J.* **1**, 1157.

Newton, J. R. and Gillman, S. (1980). A retrospective survey of female sterilisation for the years 1968–1973, analysis of morbidity and post sterilisation complications for 5 years. *Contraception* **22**, 295–312.

RCGP (Royal College of General Practitioners) (1977). *Lancet* ii, 727.

—— (1981a). *Lancet* i, 541.

—— (1981b) Report from General Practice 21. *Family planning—an exercise in preventive medicine.*

Thorogood, M., Adam, S. P., and Mann, J. I. (1981). Fatal subarachnoid haemorrhage in young women: role of oral contraceptives. *Br. Med. J.* ii, 762.

Vessey, M. P. (1982). Oral contraceptives and cardiovascular disease: some questions and answers. *Br. Med. J.* i, 615.

Vessey, M. P., McPherson, K., and Johnson, B. (1977). Mortality among women participating in the Oxford/FPA contraceptive study. *Lancet ii*, 731.

Weström, L., Bengtsson, L. P., and Mardh, P. A. (1976). The risk of pelvic inflammatory disease in women using contraceptive devices as compared with non-users. *Lancet* **ii**, 221–4.

Williams, R. and Neberger, J. (1981). Occurrence, frequency, and management of associated liver tumours. *Br. J. Fam. Planning* **7**, 35–41.

Winston, R. M. L. (1980). Reversal of tubal sterilization. *Clin. Obstet. Gynaecol.* **23**, 1261–8.

The IPPF (International Planned Parenthood Federation) produce a *Family planning handbook for doctors* and a *Directory of contraceptives* which gives names in French, English, and Spanish and lists preparations available in all countries.

Further reading for patients

Useful patient leaflets concerning all methods can be obtained form the FPA, 27 –35 Mortimer Street, London W1N 7RJ. Leaflets and pill instructions in other languages are also obtainable from the FPA and the IPPF, 18–20 Lower Regent Street, London SW17 4PW.

Manufacturers of oral contraceptives also provide instruction leaflets in other languages.

Guillebaud, John (1983). *The pill*, 2nd edn. Oxford University Press.

Law, Barbara (1982). *Contraception, choice nor chance*. Family Doctor Booklet, BMA.

Rakusen, J. and Phillips, A. (1978). *Our bodies, ourselves*. Penguin, Harmondsworth.

Smith, Michael (1980). *The woman's own birth control book*. Hamlyn.

8 Unwanted pregnancy and abortion

Judith Bury

The clinical situation of a woman who is unhappy about her pregnancy will be familiar to most general practitioners and for many it can be a particularly demanding experience. The doctor may feel uneasy at being asked to provide a service—referral for abortion—rather than being asked to exercise the classical medical skills of diagnosis or treatment. In addition, the doctor's attitude to abortion may make it difficult to respond to the woman's needs. In fact, whatever the views of the doctor, there is a great deal that can be done to help and there are useful skills that can be developed. I hope to show that the role of the general practitioner in this area can be just as rewarding as in any other medical situation. But first some background.

THE BACKGROUND

Terminology

This is not a chapter simply about abortion. To talk only about abortion would be to pre-empt the decision that the doctor and the woman with an unwanted pregnancy must make. There will however be a strong emphasis on abortion, not because it is always the most appropriate outcome for an unwanted pregnancy, but because it is the area that is most likely to involve the general practitioner rather than the social services.

I have chosen the term 'unwanted' rather than 'unplanned' or 'unintended' pregnancy. A pregnancy may have been planned and intended, yet for a number of reasons may be unwanted; on the other hand an unplanned pregnancy may yet be wanted. However, the term 'unwanted' is not without problems; in particular, it hardly does justice to the ambivalence that many women feel.

Abortion legislation

History

The 1861 Offences Against the Person Act made abortion illegal in all circumstances, although in practice an exception was made when the woman's life was in danger.

In 1938 interpretation of the law was made more liberal by Judge Macnaghten in the Bourne case when he stated that it was lawful to terminate a pregnancy not only to save a woman's life, but also 'if the doctor is of the opinion . . . that . . . the continuation of the pregnancy would make the woman a physical or mental wreck' (*Br. med. J.* 1966).

In spite of the Bourne judgement, the limits of the law remained unclear. The need for clarification was one of a number of factors that led to attempts to change the law. Firstly, there was a gradual liberalization of views on certain social issues such as homosexuality and divorce as well as on abortion. In the case of abortion this was partly due to concern about the prevalence of illegal abortion with its often dire results. During the 1950s and 60s the demand for abortion seemed to be increasing; with more effective contraception, many women were choosing to delay or limit their childbearing and take on other roles. Many women were less willing to accept an unplanned pregnancy than in the past when the opportunity to control fertility was more limited. The thalidomide tragedy in the early 1960s further underlined the need for a change in the law. Alongside these factors, the advent of new methods and the use of more effective antibiotics meant that abortion was becoming safer.

The 1967 Abortion Act

The 1967 Abortion Act was the seventh attempt to reform the law on abortion; it came into effect in April 1968. Although there have been numerous attempts to restrict this law, its provisions remain unchanged.

In 1974 the Lane Committee, which was set up to report on the working of the Abortion Act, concluded that 'the gains facilitated by the Act have much outweighed any disadvantages for which it has been criticised' (Lane 1974).

The 1967 Abortion Act did not repeal the 1861 Act but defined exceptions to that Act in which abortion would be legal. Thus, abortions not covered by the 1967 Act remain illegal.

Under the 1967 Act an abortion performed by a registered medical practitioner is legal:

if two registered medical practitioners are of the opinion, formed in good faith—
(a) that the continuance of the pregnancy would involve risk to the life of the pregnant woman, or of injury to the physical or mental health of the pregnant woman, or any existing children of her family, greater than if the pregnancy were terminated, or
(b) that there is a substantial risk that if the child were born it would suffer from such physical or mental abnormalities as to be seriously handicapped.

In determining the risk of injury to health 'account may be taken of the pregnant woman's actual or reasonably foreseeable environment.'

Late abortions

A time limit is not laid down by the 1967 Act but by the 1929 Infant Life (Preservation) Act. This states that abortion is illegal (except to save the woman's life) once the fetus has become 'capable of being born alive'. A fetus of 28 weeks or more is assumed to be so capable but it is also illegal to abort a fetus before 28 weeks if it is 'capable of being born alive'. Although the precise meaning of the phrase 'capable of being born alive' is uncertain, few gynaecologists will consider aborting a fetus of more than 24 weeks gestation.

Abortion laws in Scotland

The 1861 and 1929 Acts did not apply in Scotland. Before 1967 abortion was a common law offence but there were no prosecutions in cases of therapeutic abortion carried out without secrecy by a gynaecologist. By the 1960s a few gynaecologists were openly performing abortions on married women with many children but most gynaecologists were reluctant to test the law. When the Abortion Act passed into Scottish law in 1968, some feared it might act restrictively but this was not the case. As in England and Wales, many doctors became increasingly willing to perform abortions. Although the absence of the 1861 and 1929 Acts from the statute books does not affect the availability of abortion in Scotland, some differences between England and Scotland remain (see 'Statistics', p. 153).

Abortion laws in Northern Ireland

The 1967 Abortion Act did not extend to Northern Ireland but the 1861 Act does apply there, so abortion remains illegal except to save the woman's life. Every year more than 1000 women travel from Northern Ireland to England for a private abortion.

The changing role of the general practitioner

Before 1938, when a woman consulted her doctor about an unwanted pregnancy the doctor had little option but to persuade her to continue the pregnancy and to help her through this and through adoption if appropriate. Doctors were rarely involved in helping women to procure an abortion and when they did so they were usually acting illegally. Yet most doctors practising at that time would have been only too familiar with the sight of an ill, infected, and partially exsanguinated woman suffering the results of a backstreet or self-induced abortion.

Over the next 30 years a few women were able to obtain a more or less legal abortion but even then the general practitioner was rarely involved. The abortion was usually performed privately and the woman usually referred herself. Although the numbers began to increase during the 1960s, the availability of abortion depended above all on the woman's knowledge and her ability to pay.

Estimates of the number of illegal abortions before 1968 vary widely; inevitably we cannot know the numbers accurately as, by their very nature, illegal abortions were clandestine and usually unreported. However, there is ample evidence that illegal abortion was widespread before 1968 and has declined dramatically since (Potts, Diggory, and Peel 1977).

Since 1968 the role of the general practitioner has changed enormously. The Abortion Act leaves the decision about abortion to doctors and it gives them far more opportunity than before to help a woman decide for herself about the future of her pregnancy. Although general practitioners differ in their interpretation of the law, the vast majority support the 1967 Act and recognize the improved health that has resulted from it. However, gynaecologists also differ in their interpretation of the law with the result that the availability of National Health Service abortion varies from one part of the country to another (Table 8.3, p. 155). Thus the Abortion Act has not ensured that women can obtain help regardless of where they live and their ability to pay. But it has encouraged women to consider their situation, and to seek help, openly. The general practitioner, who will often know the woman and her family, and who can ensure adequate follow-up, is ideally placed to offer help.

Statistics

It is not easy to calculate the number of pregnancies that are unwanted. Some are terminated but some are not, so that abortion statistics do not give a true indication of the scale of unwanted pregnancy. For example, Cartwright (1978) found that 29 per cent of women having their third child and 33 per cent having their fourth child regretted their pregnancies (were 'sorry it had happened at all'). From this, and from data relating to premarital conceptions and illegitimate births, it can be estimated that more than 20 per cent of all conceptions may be unwanted.

More precise statistics are available for legal abortion (OPCS Abortion Statistics; Scottish Health Statistics). After the implementation of the Abortion Act in 1968, the number of legal abortions rose rapidly, reaching a peak in 1973. There was then a slight decline but since 1978 the numbers have risen again (Table 8.1). The abortion rates suggest that this recent rise can be partly accounted for by an increase in the number of women in the reproductive age group. Another possible cause may be the decreased use of the contraceptive pill, particularly among women over 35, since the publication in 1977 of further evidence about the risks of the pill (Bone 1982).

The abortion rate in Scotland has been consistently lower than in England and Wales (Table 8.1). This is due, at least in part, to the greater dif-

Table 8.1. *Legal abortions in Britain (resident women) numbers and rates 1969–1980**

	Abortions in England and Wales (resident women)		Abortions in Scotland†	
	Number	Rate (per 1000 women aged 15–44)	Number	Rate (per 1000 women aged 15–44)
1969	49 829	5.3	3556	3.5
1971	94 570	10.0	6856	6.2
1973	110 568	11.4	8566	7.4
1975	106 224	11.0	8354	7.1
1977	102 677	10.4	7139	7.0
1978	111 851	11.2	7453	7.0
1979	119 028	12.0	7754	7.2
1980	128 927	12.6	7855	7.3

Sources: OPCS Abortion Statistics; Scottish Health Statistics
* For clarity, alternate years only are shown from 1969 to 1977.
† Figures do not include Scottish women having abortions in England (approximately 1000 each year or 1 per 1000 Scottish women aged 15 to 44 years).

ficulty of obtaining an abortion in some parts of Scotland than in England. Thus each year nearly 1000 Scottish women travel south to obtain an abortion in England.

By 1980 approximately one in six pregnancies in England and Wales and one in ten pregnancies in Scotland ended in abortion. However, Britain still has the lowest abortion ratio (number of abortions per 1000 live births) of any country with liberal abortion legislation (see Table 8.2).

Just over half of all abortions are now performed on women who are single, nulliparous, and under 25 years of age. However, young single women are more likely to by-pass their own doctor and go direct to the

Table 8.2 *Abortion ratios—some comparisons 1978*

Country	Abortions per 1000 live births
England and Wales	188
Scotland	116
Denmark	390
Sweden	361
Norway	280
Finland	251
USA	417
Japan	295
Poland	321
Hungary	511

Source: *United Nations Demographic Yearbook* (1979).

Table 8.3.   *National Health Service provision of abortion in England and Wales 1969–1979*

	Total abortions on resident women	Abortions in NHS hospitals	NHS abortions as percentage of total abortions
1969	44 829	33 728	67
1974	109 445	56 320	51
1979	119 028	54 868	46

Source: OPCS Abortion Statistics.

private sector, so general practitioners will see a disproportionate number of older, married, parous women requesting abortion.

In most areas of Britain the National Health Service has not kept pace with the increase in the number of abortions. Whilst the *number* of National Health Service abortions has increased since 1969, the *proportion* of all abortions performed by the National Health Service has fallen, from 67 per cent in 1969 to 46 per cent in 1979 (Table 8.3); 47.5 per cent in 1981. Of the remaining 54 per cent of abortions for which women had to pay, just over half were performed by the charitable organizations, British Pregnancy Advisory Service and Pregnancy Advisory Service of London.

The provision of National Health Service abortion varies greatly from one part of the country to another (Table 8.4). This regional variation is

Table 8.4.   *Regional variation in NHS provision of abortion 1980*

Region	Percentage of abortions on women resident in that region that were performed in *National Health Service* hospitals
Northern	88
Yorkshire	39
Trent	54
East Anglian	75
North West Thames	40
North East Thames	50
South East Thames	48
South West Thames	37
Wessex	51
Oxford	51
South Western	75
West Midlands	22
Mersey	27
North Western	42
Welsh	58
England and Wales	47
Scotland	98

Source: OPCS abortion statistics.

due mainly to the difference in the attitudes of gynaecologists (Maresh 1979).

In Scotland 98 per cent of abortions are performed within the National Health Service but this is more a reflection of the lack of a private sector in Scotland than an indication of superior National Health Service resources or of a more liberal interpretation of the law.

Since 1972 approximately 80 per cent of abortions have been performed before the 12th week of pregnancy and 1 per cent or less have been performed after 20 weeks.

Methods of abortion

Although the general practitioner will not be involved in performing the abortion, a knowledge of the methods used at different stages of gestation is necessary to be able to advise a woman about the risks involved. Therefore, I have included a brief discussion on currently used methods.

Very early abortion (menstrual regulation)

Techniques for inducing abortion within two to three weeks of a missed period have been known for some years but there has been a reluctance to develop these or to make them available. Until recently it has been difficult to diagnose a pregnancy with any certainty until two weeks after a missed period, so that some women offered an early abortion would not in fact be pregnant and would be exposed to the risk of a procedure that was unnecessary. In addition, the legality of these procedures was uncertain.

In 1979 the legality of menstrual regulation was confirmed (Director of Public Prosecutions 1979). This, together with the increasing availability of accurate, early pregnancy testing by radio-immunoassay (see p. 162), may result in a development of services for very early abortion.

There are two main methods available:

Menstrual aspiration.   A narrow flexible cannula is inserted through the cervical os, usually without the need for prior dilatation. Its other end is attached to a vacuum source (e.g. a large syringe) and the uterus is emptied by suction. The procedure is simple, safe, and relatively pain-free; it can be performed under local anaesthesia or without any anaesthesia.

Prostaglandin pessaries.   Prostaglandins are hormones that have many actions. They can cause contractions of the uterus and dilatation of the cervix. In recent years analogues of prostaglandins have been developed which can be used in the form of vaginal pessaries to induce early abortion. Their use has been limited by the high failure rate (more than 10 per cent) and the high incidence of side effects such as abdominal pain, vomiting, and diarrhoea. It is hoped to develop more effective analogues with fewer side effects. By avoiding the need for surgical interference, the risk of infection is reduced. Some authors have also pointed to the potential of this method for self-administration (Mackenzie, Embrey, Davies, and Guillebaud 1978).

First trimester abortion

Vacuum aspiration (suction termination). This method has replaced D and C as the commonest method of first trimester abortion used in Britain, as it has been found to be both simple and safe.

The contents of the uterus can be evacuated by suction up to 12–14 weeks of pregnancy. The further the pregnancy is advanced, the wider the tube that must be inserted through the os and thus the greater the degree of prior dilatation that is required. Various techniques have been used to aid dilatation of the cervix and thereby reduce the risk of damage. These include prostaglandin pessaries and laminaria tents. As dilatation of the cervix is painful, vacuum aspiration is usually performed under general anaesthetic. However, local anaesthesia to the cervix can be used instead and some gynaecologists and some women prefer this.

Vacuum aspiration, at least up to 10 weeks, can easily be performed as an out-patient procedure but, in spite of recommendations in the Lane Report (Lane 1974), such a service is still not available in most areas of Britain and a hospital stay of one to two nights is entailed. However, day-care is sometimes available in the private sector; in addition, some National Health Service gynaecologists are willing to perform vacuum aspiration on a day-care basis in individual cases, especially where the general practitioner is willing to undertake the after-care.

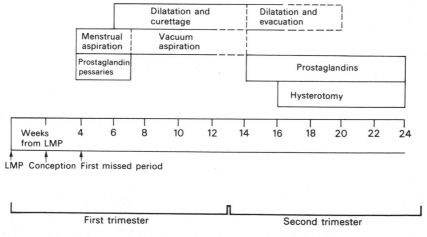

Fig. 8.1. Methods of abortion according to gestation of pregnancy.

Dilatation and curettage (D and C). This method is now used infrequently in Britain for first trimester abortion.

Second trimester abortion

Prostaglandins. This is now the commonest method of second trimester abortion in Britain. The prostaglandin may be instilled through the cervix into the *extra-amniotic* space; this approach is widely used up to about 16 weeks as the uterus will not be easily accessible abdominally. After 16 weeks it is usual to inject the prostaglandin into the amniotic cavity (*intra-amniotic*) via the abdominal wall. The uterus begins to contract within six to 12 hours and the fetus is expelled in eight to 18 hours, although oxytocin may also be required. The placenta is not expelled in 50 per cent of cases and evacuation under anaesthetic is necessary. In some centres evacuation is performed routinely to avoid the danger of retained products.

This procedure usually entails two to three days in hospital. It can be distressing to the woman and to the staff, especially after 16 weeks when the fetus may show signs of movement after expulsion. In some units this risk is avoided by instilling solutions such as urea with the prostaglandin; these also expedite the abortion.

Other substances can be introduced into the extra-amniotic space (e.g. utus paste) or into the amniotic cavity (e.g. hypertonic saline or glucose) to induce abortion. They are more dangerous than prostaglandins and are now used alone rarely in this country.

Dilatation and evacuation (D and E). This method is similar to D and C but involves the use of forceps as well as the curette. It has been claimed to be the safest method available from 12–20 weeks (Grimes, Hulka, and McCutchen, 1980), but it is still used only rarely in this country after 16 weeks. Although acceptable to women, it is unpleasant for staff and this may limit its use.

Hysterotomy. This method is now used infrequently due to the risks entailed, especially in a subsequent pregnancy. However, it may be considered when late abortion is combined with sterilization.

Risks of abortion

There is an enormous literature on this subject, much of it conflicting and difficult to interpret. Research into the long-term risks of abortion is particularly fraught with difficulties (Paterson and Savage 1981). However, there is a broad measure of agreement on certain matters.

The risks of abortion depend above all on the gestation of pregnancy when the abortion is performed. However, at any gestation, the risks also depend on the method used, the age, health, and parity of the woman, and the experience, skill, and attitude of the operator. Thus the incidence of complications will vary from one gynaecological unit to another.

First trimester abortion

First trimester abortion by vacuum aspiration is safe (Potts *et al.* 1977). Early complications (e.g. perforation of the uterus, haemorrhage, and infection) are uncommon and the mortality is very low indeed (1 per 100 000 compared to a maternal mortality of 10 per 100 000). Retained products can cause bleeding and pain some days after the procedure and this may necessitate readmission to hospital and re-evacuation of the uterus.

The main long-term risks are of infertility due to tubal damage resulting from infection, or of recurrent spontaneous abortion or prematurity due to cervical damage. The evidence suggests that these complications occur infrequently (*Br. med. J.* 1981) and the risk of infertility after vacuum aspiration is probably less than after a normal pregnancy.

Although first trimester abortion is always safer than second trimester abortion, it should be remembered that, even before 12 weeks, the earlier an abortion is performed the safer it is. In one series, an abortion at 11–12 weeks was nine times more dangerous than an abortion before eight weeks.

Second trimester abortion

The risks of second trimester abortion have been reduced by the increased use of prostaglandins (Mackenzie, Hillier, and Embrey 1974) and some people believe they may be reduced still further by the use of D and E. However, in some series, infection occurs more commonly than after vacuum aspiration, so the long-term risk of infertility (due to tubal damage) may be greater. There is also a greater risk of cervical damage: D and E requires considerable dilatation of the cervix while during a prostaglandin abortion the cervix may fail to dilate and the fetus may be expelled through a tear in the cervix. Nevertheless, a number of studies have found the incidence of such long-term complications to be low (e.g. Mackenzie and Hillier 1977).

Psychological risks

The psychological risk of abortion is small. Many women experience feelings of guilt and sadness immediately after an abortion but these feelings are usually transient and are often accompanied by a marked feeling of relief (*Br. med. J.* 1976). Although women having late abortions are more likely to find the procedure distressing, they do not seem to be at greater risk of severe psychological consequences (Brewer 1978). However, women who have been advised to have an abortion for medical reasons are more likely to experience long-term depression. Those who are psychiatrically disturbed before the abortion are also more likely to suffer serious psychological effects, but this is a likely result whatever the outcome of pregnancy. Overall, severe psychological disturbance is much less common after abortion than after childbirth (Brewer 1977*a*).

Interpreting the 1967 Abortion Act

The 1967 Abortion Act requires two doctors to decide whether a woman has grounds for abortion. However, doctors vary enormously in their interpretation of the Act and this has been a cause of much controversy. I offer here a liberal view as a basis for discussion.

A doctor who has a conscientious objection to abortion may opt out of referring a woman for abortion

> though he has a duty to assist the patient to obtain alternative medical advice . . . if she wants. (*BMA Handbook of Medical Ethics* 1981)

Any doctor who does not have a conscientious objection to abortion is required to make a *clinical* decision concerning, in most cases, the comparative risks of having an abortion or continuing the pregnancy. This decision should not be concerned with whether the woman 'deserves' an abortion or not (Aitken-Swan 1977).

From Table 8.5 it can be seen that most abortions are performed under Grounds 2 or 3, which require the doctor to make a clinical decision concerning the risk to physical or mental health of continuing the pregnancy compared to having the pregnancy terminated. If the woman has children already, how will their physical or mental health be affected if this pregnancy continues? What risks would be entailed for *her* if she continues this pregnancy? Here it is important to consider the psychological risk to the woman of having to continue with a pregnancy that is unwanted (Illsley and Hall 1976). How will the risks be affected by her circumstances, both 'actual' and 'reasonably foreseeable'?

Having assessed the risks of continuing the pregnancy, these must be compared to the risks of having an abortion. This will depend, above all, on the stage at which abortion is performed. Nine out of ten women who

Table 8.5.   *Grounds for abortion*

Grounds	Percentage of abortions for which this ground was specified (approx.)*
1. Risk to life of woman	0.5
2. Risk of injury to physical or mental health of woman	86.0
3. Risk of injury to physical or mental health of existing child(ren)	12.0
4. Substantial risk of child being born abnormal (Total abortions = 130 264 (100%)	1.5

Source: OPCS abortion statistics, 1980.

* Only approximate figures are given as more than one ground was specified in 12% of cases; e.g., ground 3 rarely specified alone.

request an abortion consult their GP by nine weeks of pregnancy (Cartwright and Lucas 1974); thus nearly all women who request an abortion will be within the first trimester. As discussed earlier, the physical and psychological risks of an abortion performed during the first trimester are very small. Taking into account the risk entailed in having a general anaesthetic, one can say that for any woman in good health the risk to her physical and mental health of an abortion during the first trimester is less than the risk of continuing with an unwanted pregnancy. Thus most women requesting an abortion will have grounds under the law (BMA 1981).

However, a few women do not consult their doctor until the second trimester. As pregnancy advances the psychological risks of abortion do not increase but by 16–18 weeks the physical risks probably outweigh those of continuing the pregnancy (see 'risks' p. 158). This will vary from unit to unit.

Later in pregnancy the decision is more difficult. However, very few women request an abortion after 20 weeks and there are usually serious reasons for the delay. The law does not make special reference to late abortions but in deciding whether or not to refer a woman for an abortion after 20 weeks, it is worth noting the BMA ethical guidelines on this matter:

The doctor should recommend or perform termination after 20 weeks only if he is convinced that the health of the woman is seriously threatened, or if there is good reason to believe that the child will be seriously handicapped. (BMA 1981)

THE ROLE OF THE GENERAL PRACTITIONER TODAY

When a woman consults her doctor about an unwanted pregnancy, the emotions felt on both sides sometimes make it difficult for the doctor to offer the help that would be appropriate.

The woman may be upset and full of self-blame; her distress may make communication difficult. Or she may appear to be irritatingly over-casual and off-hand. She may try to convince the doctor of her case for abortion or she may talk unrealistically of her plans to care for the child. The doctor may feel annoyed that the woman has conceived so unwisely, perhaps in spite of the contraceptive advice that has been given.

If the emotions on both sides can be accommodated, there is a great deal that the doctor can do to help by:

   (i) confirming the pregnancy;

   (ii) helping the woman to make a decision about the future of her pregnancy;

   (iii) carrying out the decision;

   (iv) follow-up.

I shall deal with each of these in turn.

Confirming the pregnancy

Many women who consult about an unwanted pregnancy are already certain that they are pregnant. All need to have the pregnancy confirmed and the gestation assessed but this should not be a cause of delay.

It is now possible, using radio-immunoassay techniques, to detect β subunit human chorionic gonadotrophin (HCG) in the serum or urine within a few days of conception. The test has been methodologically difficult but kits are now available so that within the next few years a number of hospital laboratories may offer this test. Other more sensitive tests are available not based on β HCG (e.g. Neo-pregnosticon, £2/test). It can be useful if a woman consults her doctor very early and is anxious to know whether she is pregnant and it may be particularly appropriate if she would want the pregnancy terminated and if there is a service for very early abortion in the area (see 'Methods of abortion' p. 156).

When there is a history of six weeks' amenorrhoea or more, conventional immunological pregnancy testing is easy and reliable. Many doctors have access to hospital pregnancy testing services; these should never take more than two days to produce a result. They usually employ a latex agglutination inhibition test to detect human chorionic gonadotrophin (HCG) in the urine. Slide tests using the same principle (e.g. Gravindex, Pregnosticon Planotest) are quick to do in the surgery, give an immediate result, rarely show false positives and are inexpensive (approximately 50p per test). Unfortunately, the testing equipment is not available on the NHS but the small outgoing may be more than compensated for by the convenience.

Although a positive test is reliable at this stage, a pelvic examination is worthwhile to check the gestation. An examination is also worthwhile if the test is negative as the test sometimes remains negative for a long time and in some cases becomes negative during the second trimester of pregnancy. An examination also helps to exclude other causes of amenorrhoea.

If the test is negative, but from the history there is a possibility of pregnancy, the woman should be asked to return for a repeat test after one or at the most two weeks rather than sent away to wait for another period.

Hormonal preparations designed to induce a withdrawal bleed should not be used to diagnose pregnancy: they are unreliable, as a withdrawal bleed not uncommonly occurs even if the woman is pregnant; they cause an unnecessary delay; and they may cause congenital abnormalities.

Sensitive do-it-yourself pregnancy tests (e.g. Discovery 2 and Neo-predictor) are now widely available and will detect pregnancy within 3 days of a missed period. It is increasingly likely that the woman who consults will already have done such a test. Although false positives are uncommon, a pelvic examination is still worthwhile to check the diagnosis and the gestation.

One pitfall for the unwary is the danger of making assumptions. It should not be assumed that a happily married woman will be pleased or that an unmarried teenager will be unhappy to be pregnant. Even before the pregnancy is confirmed it may be worthwhile to ask, 'How would you feel if you were pregnant?'

Helping the woman to make a decision

Once the pregnancy is confirmed, a decision must be made about the future of the pregnancy. Any woman who is pregnant has three possible courses of action: she may continue the pregnancy and keep the baby, she may continue the pregnancy and have the baby adopted, or she may request an abortion. Who should make this decision? This is a controversial area where the needs of the woman, the views of the doctor, and the intention of the law often become confused.

I believe it is possible to untangle these three sometimes conflicting strands by dealing with the decision-making process in two stages. Whatever the views of the doctor and whether or not the law would allow her to carry out the decision she has made, it is important for the woman to make a realistic decision for herself about what she wants. A woman will gain more self-understanding from making such a decision even when it cannot be carried out than if her decision is dictated by the views of her doctor or by the law. Once the decision has been made, she and her doctor can explore the possibility of carrying out this decision within the limits of the law or the resources available.

In practice some women seem unwilling to make this decision but seem to want it made for them. They may need positive encouragement to take responsibility for their future. The doctor may be tempted to make a decision for the woman but this should be resisted.

Despite possible initial relief, people feel ultimately demeaned if responsibility is taken from them; they also have a way of undermining decisions that they feel have been imposed on them. (Cheetham 1977)

A woman persuaded to have an abortion or to give up her baby for adoption may seem to comply readily with the arrangements made for her but then she may become pregnant again very soon afterwards. A woman who is apparently easily persuaded that she must continue with a pregnancy that she does not want may seek and obtain an abortion elsewhere.

It should be possible for any doctor to help a woman to decide the future of her pregnancy, even if the doctor's views make it difficult to pursue certain courses of action once the decision is made.

In order to decide the future of her pregnancy a woman needs:

(i) information about the alternatives available, what they entail and their risks, if any; and

(ii) an opportunity to explore the implications of these alternatives in the light of her own feelings and attitudes.

In practice, most women have made a decision, sometimes with great difficulty and often with regret, before they consult their general practitioner. Although they may need only information and support, they may also welcome the opportunity to discuss their situation further. Others consult when they are still undecided or they may feel they are being pressured into a decision by someone else. Or there may be other problems that have been brought to light by this pregnancy. Thus, although all women will need information, they will vary greatly in how much other help they need.

Helping a woman in this way is often described as 'pregnancy counselling'. (I prefer this term to 'abortion counselling' which implies that only women requesting an abortion need this help.) The need for such counselling was emphasized by the Lane Committee in its Report in 1974 and was confirmed by the Department of Health and Social Security in a circular to all health authorities in 1977 (DHSS 1977), where counselling is described as follows:

Counselling should aim to ensure that the pregnant woman has a full opportunity to make a reasoned assessment of her own wishes and circumstances, to obtain any advice she may need in reaching her own decision and to secure that any after-care facilities including social work help which she may need can be made available. In helping the woman to understand the implications of termination or the continuation of pregnancy, it is essential that counselling should be both non-judgemental and non-directional. It is in no sense a way of putting pressure on the woman either for or against abortion.

The *aims* of pregnancy counselling are:

(i) to enable the woman to reach an informed decision that she will not regret;

(ii) to lessen the risk of emotional disturbance whatever decision is reached; and

(iii) to lessen the risk of a future unwanted pregnancy.

However, counselling can sometimes achieve far more than this. The situation of crisis may help the woman to come to a better understanding of herself and her behaviour, not only about her use of contraception but also about her attitudes to her own sexuality and about difficulties she may have had with relationships. This understanding may help her to learn something from her experience and gain for the future. She may find herself not only better able to avoid a repetition of the circumstances that led to the unwanted pregnancy but also better able to plan and control other aspects of her life. Thus an unwanted pregnancy can be the trigger which leads to positive change and personal growth. Although such gains may rarely be achieved, the potential of such counselling makes it very worthwhile. Too often pregnancy counselling is seen as a barrier that a woman must pass through before she can have an abortion. To see counselling in this way is to diminish its purpose and worth.

Discussing the alternatives

However certain a woman seems of her decision, it is important to consider the alternatives with her, as this may be the only opportunity that she will have to do this. It is important to remember that most women will have discussed their situation with one (or more) other people before consulting the doctor and their opinions may be strongly influencing how the woman feels about her pregnancy. Perhaps the most important role the doctor can play is to offer information and support in an atmosphere free of pressure and free of the constraints that may have limited the woman's ability to think clearly and decide for herself.

Although this chapter is concerned mainly with abortion, I shall deal briefly with some of the factors that will need to be considered by those who wish to continue the pregnancy or at least wish to consider this option.

Keeping the baby.   Many women who consult their general practitioner about an unwanted pregnancy are married and already have children; they may have little need of factual information about pregnancy itself but may need information about child care, benefits, or even housing.

A single woman will have more questions to consider. Is she to marry or not? It may be appropriate to consider with her what likelihood there is that such a marriage would fail and the implications for her of such an outcome. If she does not intend to marry, will her partner be able to offer support? Her parents may offer help or may even offer to adopt the child. How would she feel about this? How would it work in the long term? She will need factual information about finance, housing, and child care. This is a complicated and specialized area but the doctor may wish to become acquainted with the basic information, especially as it relates to the local situation. The rules concerning benefits change rapidly and up-to-date information is best obtained from leaflets published by the DHSS, obtainable from benefit offices, social services departments, or Citizens Advice Bureaux. Information about housing is best obtained from the local housing department, social services department, or from a Shelter Housing Aid Centre. The availability of child care varies from area to area; there may be day nurseries, private nurseries, or childminders. A health visitor attached to the practice may have much of this information or it is usually obtainable from the social services department.

The National Council for One Parent Families and its Scottish counter-part, the Scottish Council for Single Parents, are excellent sources of information, support, and sometimes practical help. Gingerbread is a national self-help organization for one-parent families which has many local groups operating day care projects or drop-in information centres. In some areas there are other voluntary organizations which may have some help to offer. It may be appropriate for the general practitioner to share antenatal care with the hospital so that contact with the woman can be maintained throughout pregnancy; the health visitor should also be involved at an early stage. It is perhaps worth emphasizing the difficulties that still face single mothers today. Between one-half and three-quarters of single mothers will remain dependent on supplementary benefit and three-quarters will live with their parents (Cheetham 1977).

Adoption.   In recent years there has been a move away from adoption and, for most women, the choice now lies between abortion and caring for the child themselves. However, some women will choose adoption; often they are women who are morally opposed to abortion but are unable to care for the child themselves or occasionally are those who have opted for abortion but this has been refused. Women who wish to have their child adopted should be referred to the local social services department or to an adoption agency. Information about these agencies can be obtained from the British Agencies for Adoption and Fostering. Under the terms of the Child Care Act 1980, from the end of 1981 adoptions can only be arranged by registered adoption societies, including social services departments, except when the proposed adopter is a relative of the child.

Some women, especially young women, who are forced to leave home may need temporary accommodation during the last few months of pregnancy and for a few weeks after the baby is born. Although they are declining in number, mother-and-baby homes still exist. For example, the Life Care and Housing Trust (set up in 1977 by the anti-abortion organization, 'Life') offers accommodation to young pregnant women in over 40 areas of the country. However, this accommodation is only temporary and there may be little or no continuing support for the mother even if she decides to keep the baby.

When a woman is considering adoption it is important to remember the risk of depression in the mother, although the doctor may not feel it appropriate to warn the woman of this risk.

Abortion.   A woman who is considering an abortion should be offered information about what the operation involves and the risks entailed (see p. 158); using models or diagrams, it should be possible to do this in a few minutes. When discussing the risks, it is important to discuss their implications for the woman.

The woman should be told how long she will need to be in hospital and what kind of anaesthetic she will have (if this is known). I have found it helpful to mention the possibility that she may feel sad and weepy or even full of regrets after the abortion and that it will be worthwhile to arrange for someone close to her to be available to offer support at this time.

Exploring feelings and attitudes

Up to this point the doctor has probably adopted a fairly didactic approach. Now a change is needed. The woman needs the opportunity to explore her feelings and attitudes and to discuss any problems that this pregnancy may have brought to light. The purpose is not to offer advice, nor to try to make her change her mind, but to listen and interpret (see aims of pregnancy counselling, p.164).

When counselling a pregnant woman, it may help for the doctor to have a checklist of points to cover. Although the majority of women will have few problems, and the discussion may be quite brief, some women may have worries that they find difficult to express and a checklist may help to reveal these.

These are the main points I try to cover:

(*1*) *Why is this pregnancy unwanted?*   If this question is not asked, the wrong assumptions may be made. There may be practical difficulties that need to be resolved. Or she may have unrealistic fears—about fetal abnormalities or about pain in labour, for example. She may even be seeking reassurance about these worries so that she can continue the pregnancy.

(*2*) *Has she been able to talk to others about her predicament?*   Some women may welcome help in discussing their situation with others. For example, a young woman may wish her parents to know but may find it difficult to tell them herself; she may wish the doctor to broach the subject with them. Some women will remain unable to talk to anyone else and they may need extra support in tackling whatever they decide to do.

(*3*) *When she first suspected that she might be pregnant, what was her attitude to the pregnancy?*   Here one is concerned about the woman's own view of this pregnancy. She may reveal a degree of ambivalence about being pregnant and may need help in understanding this to avoid the danger that whatever decision she makes, she may subsequently feel that it was wrong. If the pregnancy was motivated by a need to change her environment in some way (e.g. by a need for attention or a desire to leave home) she may need help in understanding this and help to deal with her difficulties in other ways.

(*4*) *If she has talked to others, how did they react and what did they suggest she might do?* It is important to check that she is not being pressured into a decision by others. Although she may be influenced by the views of those close to her, ultimately she will need to make her own decision independently of them.

(5) *Before she found herself pregnant, what was her view of abortion, of illegitimacy, of adoption, of single parenthood—both in general and for herself?*   If she finds herself having to make a decision which does not fit in with her previous views, she may need extra help in coming to terms with her decision. For example, a woman may have strong feelings against abortion, even believing it to be murder, and yet may request an abortion.

(6) *What is the nature of the relationship she is in, if any?*   When an unwanted pregnancy occurs in a stable relationship, there may be support available from the partner. However even the most stable relationship can be threatened by an unwanted pregnancy. Sometimes the pregnancy is used to test the relationship, which is then found to be wanting. If a relationship that was previously seen to be secure has suffered as a result of the crisis, the woman may need help in dealing with this.

(7)   *What is the worst aspect of her present situation?*   It is useful to ask this at some stage. She may have worries or fears about her situation that she finds difficult to express. For a young woman it may be fear of her parents' reaction. Or she may have decided on one course of action but may have some remaining doubts. For example, she may want an abortion but may be worried about the operation or the risk of sterility afterwards. If such doubts and worries can be expressed and dealt with at this stage, they may be less likely to trouble her later.

(8) *Has this crisis come out of the blue or does she have other problems with which she needs help?*   For many women an unwanted pregnancy is a crisis which upsets an otherwise settled existence; once the crisis has been resolved she may need no further help. For other women an unwanted pregnancy may be just one more disaster in a life full of difficulties of an emotional or practical kind. Such women need on-going practical help and support after the present crisis is over.

(9) *How did this pregnancy happen and how can a further unwanted pregnancy be avoided?*   Was this pregnancy the result of contraceptive failure, risk-taking, ambivalence, or possible even a desire to be pregnant? Sometimes her motives will not be clear to the woman herself and she may need help in understanding them. Can she learn from this self-understanding for the future so that she is less likely to find herself in this situation again? Does she need to reconsider her method of contraception or her reasons for not using any? Although these questions need to be tackled at some stage, it may not be appropriate to do so in detail until

the immediate crisis has been resolved; this will depend on the woman's feelings and immediate needs. For example, she may find it difficult to consider her need for future contraception if she is not in a relationship. She should not be pressured into making a decision at this stage, particularly not a decision about sterilization (see p. 175).

Who else should be seen?   If the woman agrees to this, it is often appropriate to see others who are involved, such as the woman's husband, boyfriend, or parents. This may be helpful to the woman as it may enable her to express her feelings to them which she may have found difficult to do on her own; it may allow her to understand more clearly how these others view her situation. It may also help the others to work through their own distress about the situation or to accept the woman's decision when it is in conflict with their own views. Thus it may be useful to see the other(s) both alone and with the woman, but it is always essential to spend some of the time with the woman alone so that her own views can be aired rather than being overridden by others.

Difficulties with counselling

Although the GP is ideally placed to counsel a woman with an unwanted pregnancy, such counselling is not without difficulties.

Time.   On average, a general practitioner will see five or six women with an unwanted pregnancy in a year. For the majority of women a discussion of the alternatives is unlikely to take longer than 20–30 minutes. But sometimes this discussion reveals the need for further help which may need to be extended over two or three sessions. It is worthwhile making time for such extended counselling for the few who need it, as it may help them to cope more easily with the decision they make, as well as in the future. But a busy doctor may not be able to make time for this and referral elsewhere may be necessary.

The doctor's attitude.   It is difficult to offer help to a woman in reaching her own decision if one hopes to persuade her of one course of action rather than another. Not only can factual information be presented in a misleading way but it is also difficult to encourage a woman to explore her feelings if the doctor cannot accept them. Doctors are usually aware of their attitudes: they may be against abortion in all circumstances or they may feel it is wrong for a young girl to have a baby and care for it herself. Sometimes, however, such attitudes are less easy to recognize as they may not apply in all circumstances. One particular woman may induce a response in the doctor who may then find it difficult to offer her help. For example, a doctor may be irritated by a woman who seems very casual about her request for abortion. In fact, a casual manner often conceals considerable distress; in my experience women do not request an abortion lightly.

Although such negative feelings cannot be avoided altogether, it is important to be aware of the extent to which they affect one's ability to help. It may be profitable to discuss such cases with colleagues.

The woman's response to the doctor's role.   Some difficulties with counselling arise from the doctor's role and how the woman perceives this. When the pregnancy is confirmed the woman may feel angry with herself for what has happened and sometimes this anger will be directed at the doctor, the messenger bringing the bad news. The doctor must establish how the pregnancy occurred, an enquiry that may be perceived as criticism, and then must give factual information about the alternatives. The next stage is quite different. The doctor will try to create an atmosphere in which the woman can talk freely. But sometimes the woman's anger and the atmosphere created during the early stages of the consultation may make this difficult. It sometimes helps to make a clear change from the didactic approach involved in giving information. Or it may be appropriate to break off after giving the necessary information and arrange another appointment to discuss things further. This will also give her time to absorb the information and to talk to others who may be involved.

Another problem stems from the fact that the doctor is the final arbiter as to whether a woman may have an abortion or not and the woman usually knows this. She may feel that she needs to convince the doctor of her case and this may make it difficult for her to express any doubts that she may have (Allan 1981). If the woman is requesting an abortion, it may be appropriate to make a hospital appointment at an early stage. Once an appointment has been made 'a woman will probably be more able to look at her situation calmly, and to acknowledge any doubts she may have, without fearing that the expression of ambivalence will lead to the doctor's refusal to consider abortion any further' (Cheetham 1977). In my experience some women may be so preoccupied with the question of whether they can *get* an abortion that they are quite unable to consider whether they *want* an abortion until the first question has been resolved.

If, in spite of these precautions, a woman still finds it difficult to talk freely to the doctor yet would welcome the opportunity for further discussion, it may be appropriate to refer her elsewhere for help, especially to someone who is not required by law to make the decision (see p. 172).

Special groups

Teenagers.   Counselling a teenager with an unwanted pregnancy may present special difficulties.

1. Teenagers often present late either because they have denied the possibility of pregnancy to themselves or because they fear the reaction of their parents or the doctor.

2. Abortions, especially late abortions, in teenagers have an increased risk of causing cervical damage and thus difficulties in future pregnancies. But pregnancy and childbirth in this age group also carries substantial risks, quite apart from the difficulty that a young woman may have in coping with a child (Huntingford 1981).

3. A young woman may be quite unable to assess realistically her ability to cope with a child and she may even look forward to having a baby whom she may believe will offer her the unconditional love that she may have lacked herself.

4. She may wish to have an abortion but without her parents' knowledge. This is always a difficult situation but especially if she is under 16 years. Although it is not illegal for a termination to be performed without parental consent, such consent is always advisable (Medical Defence Union 1974) and in practice few gynaecologists will perform an abortion on a person under 16 years old without such consent. Conversely 'a termination should never be carried out in opposition to the girl's wishes even if the parents demand it' (Medical Defence Union 1974).

5. If a teenager comes with her mother it is essential to spend some time with the young woman alone to find out what *she* wants to do; she may have no opportunity to express this while her mother is there. In practice the young woman, her boyfriend, and her parents are often in agreement about the best course of action. But even here it is important that the young woman should be able to feel that she had made this decision for herself. Being given the responsibility for determining her future can then be a stage in her developing maturity rather than a confirmation of her immaturity and dependence.

6. A young woman may have difficulty in accepting her need for contraception even if she is in a stable relationship. This may be partly due to fear of parental disapproval and this should be explored.

Repeat abortion.   Women who have had a previous abortion often cause considerable concern. In fact, their numbers are small, repeat abortions accounting for only 9 out of every 100 abortions performed (OPCS 1979). In some instances it will be found that the woman has been particularly careless in her use of contraception or that she is particularly ambivalent about pregnancy and she may need help in coming to terms with this. However, such women often differ from other women with an unwanted pregnancy only in that they have more difficulties with contraception—they are often just unlucky (Brewer 1977*b*). The decision about whether a woman has grounds for abortion should depend on her present circumstances and not on whether she has already had an abortion.

Some doctors express concern that the increased availability of legal abortion has encouraged women to rely on abortion as an alternative to using contraception but there is no evidence for this.

Abortion for fetal abnormality.   Abortions performed because of a risk of handicap (ground 4 of the 1967 Act) account for only 1.5 per cent of all abortions. They present quite separate problems: the pregnancy is usually planned and wanted; the woman has often undergone an amniocentesis which is in itself often associated with anxiety: and the abortion is often performed late in pregnancy, after fetal movements have been felt. It is not surprising, therefore, that the risk of long-term depression is greater after such abortions (Donnai, Charles and Harris 1981). Such women need careful counselling, including full information, before the abortion and support afterwards. Unfortunately, the general practitioner is not always involved in the decision to abort, nor in the immediate follow-up. However, the general practitioner is in an ideal position to offer long-term support, particularly around the time that the baby would have been born and during a subsequent pregnancy.

Other counselling services

If the doctor does not feel able to counsel the woman, who else can do this? An attached health visitor may be willing to undertake this. She may need some training and, like the doctor, she would need to be aware of her attitudes, but her role in health education and her contact with mothers and young children in the community may make her a very good counsellor. Alternatively, a social worker attached to the practice, at the local gynaecology unit or social services department may be willing to offer counselling to pregnant women.

In some areas there are other sources of counselling help available; the charitable pregnancy advisory services (BPAS and PAS) have over 30 agencies throughout the country. They offer counselling for a small charge (which for women in some areas is met by the local health authority). There are also Brook Advisory Centres in some areas where pregnancy counselling may be available free of charge. Other voluntary agencies such as Marriage Counselling, although not specializing in this field, may offer counselling to pregnant women. However, some organizations (e.g. Lifeline) offer 'counselling' which may seek to persuade women to continue with their pregnancy. Therefore it is essential to find out what kind of help is offered before referring a woman.

Carrying out the decision

I have already referred to the support that is available for those women who decide to continue their pregnancy. Here I shall be concerned with those women who, after counselling, decide on abortion.

Whom to refer

If a woman feels that she wants an abortion it is necessary to consider whether she has grounds within the law. This has already been discussed in the section on interpreting the 1967 Abortion Act, above (p. 160).

If the doctor considers that the woman does not have grounds for abortion, this should be explained to her, together with the reasons for this decision. If she is still adamant that she wants an abortion, the doctor may decide to refer her to a gynaecologist for a second opinion. Such a referral should not be used as a means to delay her and she should be warned if the gynaecologist is unlikely to accept her request. Alternatively, the doctor may offer her information about other services where she can seek advice. If, on the other hand, she decides to continue the pregnancy, she may need extra help and support.

Where to refer

If the woman has grounds for an abortion, referral should be made to a gynaecologist who will consider her request sympathetically and ideally this referral will be to an National Health Service gynaecologist in a local hospital. So it is essential to know the views of the local gynaecologists. One way to ascertain this on moving to a new area is to telephone the gynaecologist about a woman who is being referred.

The likelihood of a successful NHS referral will vary very much from one region to another (see above, Table 8.3), and in any region will depend on the gestation of pregnancy. For example, some gynaecologists who adopt a fairly liberal policy during the first trimester, will perform no abortions after 12 weeks. Where National Health Service referral is unlikely to be successful, the general practitioner may feel it appropriate to refer the woman elsewhere; indeed, the woman herself may prefer this. Few NHS gynaecologists accept referrals from women outside their catchment area, so a referral to the private sector may be necessary.

Within the private sector, the non-profit-making pregnancy advisory services, BPAS and PAS, have clinics in a number of areas and between them they perform approximately 30 000 abortions each year, that is, over half of all abortions outside the National Health Service. Both organizations operate a loan and grant scheme for those who find it impossible to pay and in some areas the cost of an abortion may be met by the local health authority. Where there is no charitable clinic nearby, it is necessary to investigate the profit-making services available. Before making a referral to a private clinic, doctors should satisfy themselves about the standard of care offered. In some cases it may be preferable to travel further to obtain a better service.

How to refer

Some areas (e.g. Newcastle) operate a central referral system (Lawson,

Yare, Barron, Querido, and Phillips 1976) but in most areas appointments have to be made with individual consultants. Time can be saved by making an appointment by telephone; when a woman is close to 12 weeks or later in pregnancy direct contact with a consultant by telephone may be helpful. Appointments should always be made with a named consultant whose views are known. (The consultant with the shortest waiting list for appointments may not do abortions.)

The referral letter should indicate the woman's circumstances, the grounds for abortion, the gestation of pregnancy, and how far counselling has been pursued. If the referring doctor is supporting the request, an abortion certificate (green form in England and Wales, Certificate A in Scotland) should be signed and enclosed. If the request is not being supported, the doctor should say so. While the woman is waiting for her appointment or is awaiting admission to hospital she may welcome further support and this should always be offered.

If the request for abortion is refused, the desirability of another referral should be discussed with the woman; this will often be to the private sector. At any stage some women will change their minds and they may need help in coming to terms with their new decision.

Delays

In general, the earlier an abortion is performed the safer it is; even when a woman consults at six weeks, a delay will increase the risks. Yet women requesting an abortion are often delayed unnecessarily by the medical services (Allan 1981). Cartwright and Lucas (1974) found evidence of GPs who delayed deliberately 'in the hope that the pregnancy would be accepted or that it would be too late to get an abortion'. Most delays are not deliberate and there are many ways in which they can be avoided, while still allowing ample time for the woman to make a decision.

Follow-up

Careful follow-up is important whatever the outcome of the pregnancy. If a woman is continuing with a problem pregnancy or has had an abortion she may welcome the opportunity to talk further about her feelings. After an abortion or after giving up a child for adoption there may be a period of acute distress when much support will be needed and may not be provided by friends and family.

Although some hospitals and clinics see the woman again for a post-abortion check, some do not. It is essential that the woman be examined between two and four weeks after the abortion to confirm that the abortion has been successful and that she does not have retained products or an infection. Most women do not experience pain after an abortion. Bleeding usually becomes no more than a pink or brown loss within one to two weeks of the abortion, although this loss may continue until the first menstrual period. If the woman has previously had a regular cycle; this period usually comes within 4–5 weeks of the abortion. Further bright red bleeding with or without clots, approximately one week after an abortion and especially if associated with pain and fever, are suggestive of retained products and infection. If the uterus is enlarged, re-admission to hospital for re-evacuation is advisable; alternatively a course of antibiotics may suffice. The pregnancy test sometimes remains positive for a few days after an abortion but should always be negative by two weeks afterwards.

At follow-up it is important to consolidate the gains made during counselling. Has this crisis given her any insights into her behaviour? Does she need to make any changes in her life to avoid a repetition of the circumstances? This may be no more than a need for more efficient contraception but it may involve a more profound exploration of her attitudes and behaviour, requiring several consultations.

The follow-up appointment is often an appropriate time to establish a woman on contraception and most women will be particularly motivated to consider contraception at this time. However, some women may not accept their need for contraception and they will require particularly careful follow-up. It is sometimes appropriate to start contraception earlier than this, at the time of the abortion. An IUCD can be inserted immediately after the procedure. Insertion at this time is associated with an increased risk of infection and of expulsion but these risks may be acceptable to the woman if she is anxious to avoid any further risk of pregnancy. Alternatively, the contraceptive pill can be started on the day of the abortion or the following day and many women prefer to do this rather than wait until the first menstrual period. The time to start contraception will often depend on the woman's ability to make a firm decision about her future contraception before the abortion; she may prefer to consider this after the procedure is over. However, it is important to remember—and to emphasize to the woman—that she could conceive within a few days of having an abortion; the earliest known ovulation after an abortion was 10 days later (See Chapter 7).

A general practitioner may find it difficult to offer after-care to a woman who has referred herself for an abortion. In fact, it is quite likely that she went elsewhere for help because she did not know how the doctor would respond to her request or, for a young woman, because she feared her parents would find out. Thus the decision to by-pass the doctor may reflect the woman's uncertainty and lack of confidence rather than any criticism of the doctor.

Sterilization

Some women who have completed their family and others who do not want to have children may wish to consider sterilization. Although the unwanted pregnancy may have provoked the need to consider this option, the decision should be made quite independently of the decision about the pregnancy. They involve quite different considerations and decisions about the long-term future are not easy to make when in a crisis. It has been suggested that some gynaecologists have on occasion agreed to perform an abortion only on condition that the woman agrees to be sterilized at the same time. This is clearly unethical. Sterilization performed at the same time as abortion is far more likely to be regretted than when it is performed as an interval procedure; combining sterilization with abortion also increases the mortality from abortion sixfold (Savage 1981). There are circumstances when it may be appropriate to consider sterilization at the same time as abortion (e.g. when a woman conceives while awaiting a sterilization operation) but she should be told the risks and offered the option of having the sterilization at a later date.

Prevention of unwanted pregnancy

The general practitioner has an important role to play in the prevention of unwanted pregnancy. This requires an understanding of the causes of unwanted pregnancy as well as knowledge of contraceptive practice. These subjects are dealt with in Chapter 7.

CONCLUSION

The general practitioner is ideally placed to help a woman with an unwanted pregnancy. This can be a demanding and time-consuming task but the potential gains for the woman—and for her relationship with the doctor—make it very worthwhile.

REFERENCES AND FURTHER READING

Aitken-Swan, J. (1977). *Fertility control and the medical profession.* Croom Helm, London.
Allan, I. (1981). *Family planning, sterilisation and abortion services.* Policy Studies Institute, London.
Ashton, J. (1981). The after care of abortion patients. *Jnl. R. Coll. Gen. Pract.* **31**, 217–22.
Birth control Trust (1980). *Abortion counselling.* Proceedings of a meeting held at the Royal College of Obstetricians and Gynaecologists in 1978. (Obtainable from BCT, 27–35 Mortimer St., London W1N 7RJ, price 75p.)
Bone, M. (1982). The 'pill scare' and fertility in England and Wales. *IPPF Med. Bull.* **16**, 2–4.
Brewer, C. (1977a). Incidence of post abortion psychosis: a prospective study. *Br. med. J.* **i**, 476–7.
—— (1977b). Third time unlucky: a study of women who have three or more legal abortions. *J. biosoc. Sci.* **9**, 99–105.

—— (1978). Induced abortion after feeling foetal movements: its causes and emotional consequences. *J. biosoc. Sci.* **10**, 203–8.

BMA (British Medical Associaton) (1981). *The handbook of medical ethics.* British Medical Association, London.

Br. med. J. (1966). Report by the BMA Special Committee on Therapeutic Abortion. *Br. med. J.* **2**, 40.

—— (1976). Psychological sequelae of therapeutic abortion. *Br. med. J.* **i**, 1239.

—— (1981). Late consequences of abortion. *Br. med. J.* **i**, 1564–5.

Cartwright, A. (1978). *Recent trends in family building and contraception.* OPCS, London

Cartwright, A. and Lucas, S. (1974). *Survey of abortion patients for the Committee on the Working of the Abortion Act* (Vol. III of the Lane Report). HMSO, London.

Cheetham, J., (1977). *Unwanted pregnancy and counselling.* Routledge and Kegan Paul, London.

DHSS (Department of Health and Social Security) (1977). Arrangements for counselling of patients seeking abortion. Health Circular. HC (77) 26.

Director of Public Prosecutions (1979). Letter to Mrs Renée Short MP.

Donnai, P., Charles, N., and Harris, R. (1981). Attitudes of patients after 'genetic' termination of pregnancy. *Br. med. J.* **i**, 621–2.

Grimes, D. A., Hulka, J. F., and McCutchen, M. E. (1980). Midtrimester abortion by dilatation and evacuation versus intra-amniotic installation of prostaglandin $F_{2\alpha}$. A randomised clinical trial. *Am. J. Obstet. Gynec.* **137**, 785–90.

Huntingford, P. (1981). The medical and emotional consequences of teenage pregnancy. In *The consequences of teenage sexual activity.* Brook Advisory Centres, London.

Illsley, R. and Hall, M. (1976). Psychosocial aspects of abortion. *Bull. Wld Hlth Org.* **53**, 83–106.

International Planned Parenthood Federation (1976). *Abortion counselling—a European view.* IPPF, London.

Lafitte, F. (1975). *The abortion hurdle race.* BPAS, England. (Obtainable from BPAS, Austy Manor, Wootton Wawen, Solihull, West Midlands B95 6DA.)

Lane (1974). Report of the Committee on the Working of the Abortion Act. HMSO, London.

Lawson, J. B, Yare, D., Barron, S. L., Querido, R. M. E., and Phillips, P. R. (1976). Management of the abortion problem in an English city. *Lancet* **ii**, 1288–91.

Mackenzie, I. Z., Hillier, K., and Embrey, M. P. (1974). Prostaglandin induced abortion—assessment of operative complications and early morbidity. *Br. med. J.* **4**, 683–6.

—— and —— (1977). Prostaglandin induced abortion and outcome of subsequent pregnancies. *Br. med. J.* **2**, 1114–16.

——, Embrey, M.P., Davies, A. J., and Guillebaud, J. (1978). Very early abortion by prostaglandin. *Lancet* **i**, 1223–6.

Maresh, M. (1979). Regional variation in the provision of NHS gynaecological and abortion services. *Fertility and Contraception* **3**, 41.

Medical Defence Union (1974). *Consent to treatment.* MDU, London.

OPCS Abortion Statistics Series. AB 1–7, 1974–80.

Paterson, I. and Savage, W. The risks of abortion. *Br. J. hosp. Med.* (In press.)

Potts, M., Diggory, P., and Peel, J. (1977). *Abortion.* Cambridge University Press.

Savage, W. (1981). Abortion and sterilisation—should the operation be combined? *Br. J. Fam. Plann.* **7**, 8–12.

Scottish Health Statistics 1969–1980. HMSO, Edinburgh.

Simms, M. (1977). Report on *non-medical abortion counselling.* Birth Control Trust, London. (Obtainable from BCT, 27–35 Mortimer St., London W1N 7RJ, price 50p.)

USEFUL ADDRESSES

Pregnancy testing

Ortho Diagnostics, Denmark House, Denmark St., High Wycombe, Bucks HP11 2ER [makers of Gravindex].

Organon Laboratories, Crown House, London Rd., Morden, Surrey SM4 5DZ.

Pregnancy counselling

Brook Advisory Centres, 153a East St., London SE17 2SD. Tel: 01 708 1234.

Pregnancy counselling and abortion

British Pregnancy Advisory Service, Austy Manor, Wootton Wawen, Solihull, West Midlands B95 6DA. Tel: Henley in Arden 3225.

Pregnancy Advisory Service, 40 Margaret St., London W1N 7SB. Tel: 01 409 0281.

Single parents

National Council for One Parent Families, 255, Kentish Town Rd., London NW5 2LX. Tel: 01 267 1361.

Scottish Council for Single Parents, 44 Albany Street, Edinburgh GH 13DR Tel: 031 556 3899.

Gingerbread, 9, Poland St., London W1V 3DG. Tel: 01 734 9014.

Shelter Housing Aid Centre, 189a Old Brompton Rd., London SW5 OAR. Tel: 01 373 7276.

Adoption

British Agencies for Adoption and Fostering, 11, Southwark St., London SE1 1RQ. Tel: 01 407 8800.

9 Cervical cytology

Wendy Savage and Ann McPherson

The essential controversy about cervical screening is no longer whether or not it should be done but rather who should have it, when, and by whom it should be carried out. Screening programmes have been running for over 30 years in the USA and Canada, and 20 years in some European countries including Britain. Some regions of Scotland, North America, and Finland have all reported significant falls in mortality from cervical carcinoma. In the UK, however, there has been only a modest overall decrease in mortality due to carcinoma of the cervix and a worrying increase in younger women. The failure to reduce mortality significantly in this country may have occurred not because the current policy is wrong but because it has not been properly implemented, although it may be working more effectively than one thinks as it may have prevented an explosion of cervical cancer in the younger age group. It is the purpose of this chapter to look at the natural history and epidemiology, discuss the controversies, and provide some practical suggestions about ways of implementing screening in a practice population with a guide to the interpretation of the smear taken.

INCIDENCE

As can be seen from Table 9.1, the incidence of invasive cervical cancer varies among different countries. To try to put cancer of the cervix into some sort of perspective we need to look at the available statistics. Figure 9.1 shows the overall number of deaths from this cancer in England and Wales between 1950 and 1980. There were 2060 deaths from cancer of the cervix in 1980. They make up 3 per cent of the cancer deaths in women, while deaths from breast cancer numbered 20 167 in 1980 and make up 20 per cent of the female cancer deaths. As can be seen from Fig. 9.2, the death rate from cancer of the cervix is decreasing, while that from breast cancer is increasing. Screening is probably responsible for this decrease but there is some evidence that there was a downward trend even before widespread screening programmes were introduced. The hysterectomy rate has also increased during this time, so that there are fewer cervices at risk.

Table 9.2 shows the death rates by age and it can be seen that although

Table 9.1. *Age-standardized incidence rates for cervical cancer*

Region	Standardized rate* per 100 000 population
England and Wales (1976)	11.7
Colombia	62.8
Canada (Saskatchewan)	9.4
Israel	4.5
India	23.2
Sweden	17.7
New Zealand	
Maori	31.0
Non-Maori	9.9
USA Detroit	
White	14.0
Black	32.1
New York State	10.8

* These rates are calculated using the age distribution for a 'standard world population' described by Waterhouse *et al.* (1976), pp. 453–9. The rate for England and Wales is based on cancer registration data for 1976 (Office of Population Censuses and Surveys, 1981). The other rates are taken from Waterhouse *et al.* (1976); Office of Population Censuses and Surveys (1981); Cancer statistics: registrations (1976), series MB1, No. 7, London: HMSO.

there has been a decrease in the rates in the older woman, there has been a twofold increase in the rates in those under 35; however, the numbers in

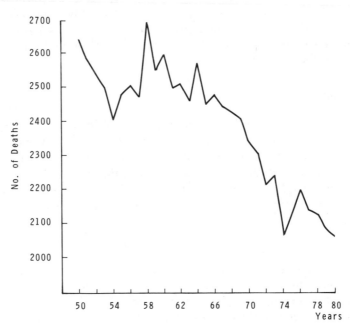

Fig. 9.1. Annual number of deaths in England and Wales from carcinoma of the cervix 1950–80.

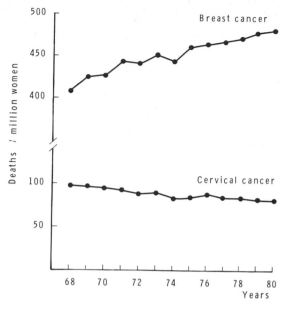

Fig. 9.2. A comparison of deaths from breast cancer and cervical cancer in England and Wales 1968–80.

the latter age group are small and still only represent one twentieth of all the deaths due to this cancer. Figure 9.3 shows age-specific mortality in a recent year, and demonstrates that the death rate increases with increasing age. Although the rates are high in the age group over 75, most of the deaths occur between the ages of 45 and 74.

In order to understand whether screening affects mortality, it is important to know how many smears are being taken, in what age group, and how many of these smears are positive. Thus, in 1965 seven hundred thousand smears were taken. In the years immediately following, there was a rapid increase in the numbers taken which subsequently levelled off so that in 1979 it was estimated that 217 million smears were taken in England and Wales. Fifty five per cent of these smears were from women aged 16 to 34—a population of seven million—while the other 45 per

Table 9.2. *OPCS mortality surveillance: age-specific death rates per million women for cancer of the cervix*

Age	1970	1971	1972	1973	1974	1975	1976	1977	1978	1979
20–24	3	1	2	4	3	5	4	1	1	3
25–29	8	6	12	8	10	12	11	10	20	16
30–34	15	22	18	17	21	30	25	31	33	31
35–75	165	163	155	157	141	146	155	148	146	141

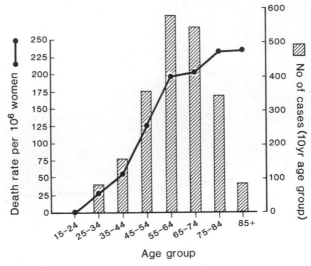

Fig. 9.3. Death rate from carcinoma of the cervix per million women and number of cases in ten-year age groups, England and Wales, 1978.

cent were from women above that age—a population of approximately thirteen million. The estimated rate of positives has averaged at around 5 per 1000, decreasing from 5.7 in 1969 to 4.3 in 1973, and thereafter increasing to 6.3 in 1979. The rate of cytologically positive smears taken from women aged less than 35 (Draper 1982) has been increasing recently so that the rate in women aged 25–34 is now higher than for that for age 35 and over.

Figure 9.4 compares the registrations for carcinoma *in situ* and invasive carcinoma of the cervix, with 1968 as the reference year. As can be seen, after an initial fall, the number of cancers *in situ* (CIS) has increased rapidly while the number of invasive cancers has fallen slightly. The increase in the rate of cancer *in situ* is in part probably due to the increase in the number of women screened, though it suggests that there may also have been a real increase in cervical neoplastic lesions. The discrepancy between the rate of CIS and invasive cancer may be due to the fact that some discovered carcinomas *in situ* do not progress or that the latent period is long.

NATURAL HISTORY

The natural history of invasive cervical cancer and carcinoma *in situ* remains uncertain, a factor which obviously has a profound influence on trying to formulate a screening policy. It is postulated that the majority of cases of invasive carcinoma of the cervix are preceded by a prolonged

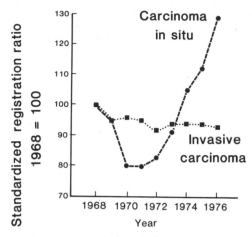

Fig. 9.4 Invasive carcinoma of the cervix and carcinoma *in situ*. Standardized ratios—cancer registrations 1968–76, England and Wales.

period of dysplastic change in the cervical epithelium which can be detected by exfoliative cytological examination.

The natural history is complicated by the fact that the investigative procedure of performing a biopsy on the cervix may itself in some cases be curative. The questions which one would theoretically like definite answers to are, what number of positive smears progress to invasive carcinoma, what number regress to normal, how long do these changes take to occur, and what factors influence these changes?

Dealing with the first question as to how many positive smears progress, the studies are conflicting and not made easy to compare by the variation in what is identified as the different stages of dysplasia as against carcinoma *in situ*. The popular theory is that there is a progression to invasive carcinoma of the cervix through various different phases, as in Fig. 9.5—though histologically all stages may be present at the same time— a fact that neither refutes nor confirms this hypothesis. Evidence to support this theory comes from several studies. One, looking at over 500 women who had three separate positive smears, concluded that a dysplasia of any degree was more likely to develop into carcinoma *in situ* (64 per cent) than remain a dysplasia (30 per cent), with 6 per cent reverting to normal (Richart and Barons 1969). Another study, in which the women were identified with a single positive smear during mild to moderate dysplasia, found that 60 per cent progressed while 31 per cent regressed, and 9 per cent were unchanged. Other investigators, who attempted to trace a group of women who had had positive smears with no clinical signs but who for two years had escaped follow-up or treatment, subsequently examined 60 of the original 101. On screening of these, 7 had clinically diagnosed carcinoma of the cervix, while further smears and biopsies done

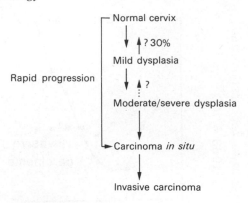

Fig. 9.5.

on the remainder showed that 30 per cent had become negative at smear, or the biopsy showed no lesion, suggesting that spontaneous regression had occurred. This regression was confined to women aged less than 40 at the time of the original smear (Kinlen and Spriggs 1978) and does not appear to be true of older women where a higher percentage progress to invasive cancer.

Most of the literature based on cytological and epidemiological evidence suggests that progression from cervical dysplasia to carcinoma *in situ* normally takes over ten years. Figure 9.6 shows that the older patient with a clinically normal cervix and a positive smear is more likely to have histological micro-invasion than the younger patient (Boyes, Worth, and Fidler 1970). Most invasive carcinomas occur in women over 40, and dysplasia in the younger age group. Recently, however, reports have appeared that in a small number of cases progression may be more rapid, but it is not known what percentage progress rapidly nor which patients they will be. Patients with apparently rapidly progressive lesions have generally only had one previous smear, whereas two satisfactory smears at a five-year interval is better evidence that no abnormality is present. Although a few

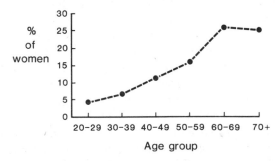

Fig. 9.6. Percentage of preclinical carcinomas which show histological invasion by age of patient. (British Columbia, Boyes *et al*, 1970.)

lesions may be rapidly invasive, in Aberdeen where a large percentage of the population have had a smear, only 2 per cent of women found to have invasive cervical carcinoma had had a negative smear within the preceding five years, while 90 per cent had never had a smear (MacGregor 1982).

RISK FACTORS

Let us assume that the risk factors are likely to be the same for mild dysplasia, severe dysplasia, carcinoma *in situ*, and invasive carcinoma. They include sexual behaviour, parity, and age of first pregnancy, contraception, occupation and social class, sexually transmitted factors, and smoking. Some are more likely to be causal, others are attributable to purely chance associations.

Sexual behaviour

Epidemiological studies of risk factors for carcinoma of the cervix have tended, until recently, to pay more attention to the sexual behaviour of women than that of men. It was not realized that not only age at first intercourse, number of sexual partners, and frequency of intercourse of the women may be important, but also the sexual habits of their consorts or husbands. Age at first intercourse was always thought to be an important risk factor, but more recently it has been shown that when adjustment was made for the number of sexual partners, there appeared to be no clear relationship with age. However, in trying to identify at-risk categories, young age at first intercourse can be included as this group of women are likely to have more partners during their lives than those starting sexual activity later in their lives, and thus be at increased risk. The number of sexual partners is a definite risk factor and there is a linear relationship between the number of partners that a woman has had and the likelihood of her developing cervical changes. Compared to having one partner, two partners increase the age standardized incidence rate by 3 and three or more partners by 5. What evidence there is does not link increased frequency of intercourse *per se* with increased cervical changes.

Evidence that the sexual behaviour of women's partners is important comes from a study of two groups of women with and without cervical pathology, all of whom had only had one sexual partner. When these partners were interviewed the number of their sexual contacts was found to be a significant risk factor in the development of cervical pathology (Buckley, Harris, Doll, and Vessey 1981).

Parity and age of first pregnancy

There appears to be no association between risk and age at menarche. Virgin women have the lowest risk of severe dysplasia and carcinoma *in situ* and women having a late pregnancy have relative risks lower than for those with an early pregnancy. An increased number of pregnancies increases the risk of cervical abnormalities but there appears to be no clear relationship once other confounding factors such as number of sexual partners is allowed for, and it is likely to be an associative rather than a causative factor. Pregnancy outside marriage, termination, and divorce have at some time all been shown to be associated with an increased risk, but it is unlikely that these will all hold up to closer scrutiny once other variables are allowed for.

Method of contraception

Certain methods of contraception may have a direct adverse effect, such as the hormonal influence of the pill, while others, such as the barrier methods, may actually have a protective effect. Long-term use of oral contraceptives has been shown to be associated with cervical abnormalities in several studies. Some of these findings have been questioned because of inadequate control for confounding factors such as age at first intercourse, number of sexual partners (both of men and of women), and inclusion of diaphragm users in the control groups. In a study (Wright, Vessey, Kenward, McPherson, and Doll 1978) in which many of these factors were taken into account, there was still a higher relative risk for people on the contraceptive pill. Another difficulty in trying to evaluate the effect of the pill is that oral contraceptives may cause eversion of the endocervix making abnormalities easier to detect. Thus, the direct importance of the oral contraceptive in the pathogenesis of cervical dysplasia and invasive carcinoma is still controversial and the issue is unlikely to be resolved until more prospective long-term studies are reported.

On the other hand, diaphragm users and users of other barrier methods appear to have a decreased risk of cervical abnormalities, as shown in several studies. But diaphragm users are less likely to have had coitus at an early age and have usually had fewer sexual partners. Even when these factors and the frequency of intercourse are allowed for, they have a much lower risk, though when looking at barrier methods the possible effect of spermicides should also be considered. But again the difficulties of interpretation are many, for although spermicides may have a direct effect, protective or otherwise, they are not applied by all users of barrier methods.

Occupation and social class

Mortality statistics for cervical cancer show a steep social class gradient. The disease is five times as common in social class V as it is in the professional classes, which may in part explain the regional variation within England: it is 40 per cent higher in the north-west than in the south-east, and it is more common in urban than rural areas. Social-class variation may also reflect women's different usage of preventive medical services. It may, of course, not be a direct effect of social class, as in one study (Harris, Brinton, Cowdell, Skegg, Smith, Vessey, and Doll 1980) that looked at the characteristics of women with dysplasia or carcinoma *in situ*, no social class influence was found once the other risk factors had been taken into account, such as earlier marriage, more pregnancies, more partners, etc. There is also the problem that within social class V housing is worse, with fewer bathrooms, and therefore it is less easy for personal hygiene to be practised.

The wives of men working in certain occupations are more likely to develop cancer of the cervix. For example, wives of miners, quarrymen, fishermen, and glass and ceramic workers have a higher incidence than expected within their socio-economic group. There may well be reasons, sexual or otherwise, to explain this, as some of these jobs involve absence from home—a situation known to be associated not only with an increased number of sexual partners but also with a higher risk of venereal disease in men—but few epidemiological studies have looked at the social and occupational risks with regard to cancer of the cervix. Nevertheless, the explanation could be a direct one such as dust under the male foreskin (Robinson 1982).

Until the beginning of the 1970s mortality data for women by their own occupation were only available for single women whose deaths from this cause were few and were more likely to be sexually inactive than married women. The only occupation that did have a significantly raised cervical cancer rate was textile workers but it is difficult to disentangle the possible effects of husbands' occupation and other risk factors until more data are collected which actually look at these possible associations.

Sexually transmitted factors

Infection passed venereally as a cause of cervical carcinoma is a popular theory. Herpes virus Type II and Papilloma virus are the two most commonly cited. There is no hard evidence to substantiate this theory, but it is the general recommendation that women who have had cervical herpes or have partners who have had it should have annual smears. Women with cervical cancer are more likely to have herpes antibodies than controls, and high titres are often found in women with cervical dysplasia. Some studies have also reported high rates of trichomonal vaginitis infection in women with positive cervical smears, while others have not. Other theories put forward in the past have been that smegma could be carcinogenic (but this is no longer thought to be so), or that protein breakdown products from sperm may induce malignant change in cervical cells at a particular stage of cell division.

Smoking

The emergence in several studies of cigarette smoking as a major risk factor for cervical neoplasia is difficult to understand as at first sight it seems unlikely that the use of tobacco has any direct effect on the cervix. It may be that smoking is reflecting some important aspect of sexual behaviour, or is indirectly linked via other social class factors. In many of these studies the sexual habits of the male partner and his occupation have not been allowed for, but where they have, smoking still comes out as a strong independent risk factor.

INTERNATIONAL EXPERIENCE OF SCREENING PROGRAMMES

Organized screening programmes in Canada, the USA, Finland, Iceland, and Aberdeen have been followed by a reduction in mortality from cervical cancer. Though the cervical cancer death rates were already starting to drop in some of these areas prior to screening, it does seem that screening is at least responsible for part of the reduction. The interpretation of these changes is fraught with the usually causality arguments when parallel changes occur over a specified period of time, for example using this method of comparing statistics it could be said that more television sets could cause more cervical cancer!

In the USA it has been shown that the incidence and mortality from invasive cervical cancer decreased by 59 per cent and 50 per cent respectively from 1947 to 1970, while the incidence of cervical carcinoma *in situ* increased over the same period. British Columbian data have also shown a significant relationship between the intensity of screening and the reduction in mortality from cervical cancer in women aged 30–64 in the period 1960/62 and 1970/72 (Miller, Lindsay, and Hill 1976). More recently updated figures from British Columbia show that the decline in mortality has continued until 1976 but does not appear to correlate so well with the intensity of screening. The reasons postulated for this include the failure of screening programmes to reach women most at risk, a recent increase in the incidence in mortality from cervical cancer in younger women because of greater exposure to risk factors, or a natural history less tractable to intervention by screening than had previously been assumed (Miller, Visentin, and Howe 1981). In Finland almost 80 per cent of the at-risk population have had smears since the introduction of screening in the early 1960s, and the incidence rates of cervical cancer have fallen from 35 per 100 000 in 1962 to 20 per 100 000 in 1970 in the age group 25–60. In Iceland, screening started in 1964 and there women are screened every two to three years with 65 per cent of women under the age of 75 having been screened at least twice by 1977. Mortality due to cervical cancer fell by 60 per cent comparing figures for 1959–70 with 1975–8. In Scotland, intensive screening programmes have been introduced in Grampian and Tayside. In Grampian the screening programme started in the early 1960s and the women were individually invited to attend for a cervical smear, with the highest proportion of women aged over 40 being screened and rescreening taking place at five-yearly intervals. There has been a fall in mortality in all age groups with most of the deaths occurring in those women who had had no previous smear.

CONTINUING CONTROVERSIES IN THE SMEAR DEBATE

Failure of the British programme

Before going on to discuss the best way to organize screening programmes in general practice in the future, it is worth considering the possible reasons for the relative failure in reducing mortality. First, it is claimed that screening has been concentrated among women who have been at low risk of dying from cervical cancer, including those of higher social class and those who are young. Secondly, many women over 35 are not even having one smear. Thirdly, it is also possible that there has been an increase in the risk of carcinoma *in situ*/invasive cervical cancer among younger women and that the screening programme, even though inadequate, has succeeded in limiting the increase which would have occurred in its absence. Lastly, as mentioned in the discussion on natural history, there is the whole problem concerning the nature of the relationship between invasive carcinoma and lesions detectable by screening.

Who should be screened and when

Accepting that cervical screening is worthwhile, one then needs the answers to certain further questions as to who should be screened and how often they should be screened. It is not a time of particular affluence and even if it were, certain cost–benefit calculations would have to be made. In general terms, in order to make the greatest impact on cervical cancer mortality, it is the older age group, i.e. those aged over 35, who need the biggest input of screening effort.

Mathematical simulations of the natural history have been used to try to devise an optimal programme (Yu Shun-Zhang, Miller, and Sherman 1982). It was shown that with a 75 per cent test sensitivity and an 80 per cent population acceptance, a programme designed to reduce mortality by 90 per cent would commence at age 25, involve either three-yearly screening to age 52 and then stop, or alternatively three-yearly to age 40 and then five-yearly to age 60, i.e. a total of ten tests in a lifetime. A repeat test at age 26 appeared to contribute nothing to mortality benefit. It was also noted that additional modifications of the natural history specifications to accommodate high-risk younger women would require a more frequent schedule of examination under the age of 35, though at a substantial 'cost' in terms of the total number of examinations required in a population.

In America, the College of Obstetricians and Gynaecologists recommends that women should be screened annually and many of them are screened even more often. In Britain and the Scandinavian countries the policy has been more conservative—screening being recommended at three- to five-yearly intervals, but in practice this has varied between one year and not at all. In 1977 the British Society for Clinical Cytology accepted recommendations (Spriggs and Husain (1977)) that (1) the age for commencement of screening be at 25 for women presenting for contraception, in pregnancy, or with venereal disease, and at age 30 if sexually active and not already tested; (2) the interval between smears should be five-yearly, or three-yearly in those over 35 if resources permitted, but a first smear in a woman over 35 years should be followed by a second smear within a year to guard against false negative error; (3) the age of cessation for screening was suggested at 70 in those previously smeared, with no upper age limit given for a first test.

The DHSS has recently received a report of the Working Party looking at cytology and screening services. In formulating their policy they took into account the fact that the majority of deaths occurred in older women and that even one negative cytological examination, preferably around the age of 35 to 40 years, appeared to be associated with a considerable degree of protection. Their recommendations are:

1. There should be an immediate publicity campaign designed to ensure that all women aged 35 or more who have never been screened should have a smear. This is seen as a short-term intensive screening campaign.

2. For a long-term policy, screening should continue to be offered to all women over the age of 35, smears being taken every five years. For women with at least two negative smears, screening should cease after the age of 65.

3. Although the main screening efforts should be concentrated on the older age group, a limited number of smears should be obtained from women attending family planning and antenatal clinics as there is some evidence that cervical cancer is becoming more common in younger women, as outlined in the section on incidence.

This would also provide an opportunity for encouraging a habit of routine attendance for smears to be taken at the scheduled ages. They suggested that:

(1) a smear should be taken early in the course of care for each pregnancy;

(2) all women attending for family planning advice and who had not previously been screened should have a first smear at age 22 or at the next visit after this;

(3) for women attending these clinics a further smear should be taken at around age 30 if five years or more had elapsed; and

(4) all women aged between 22 and 35 who were or had been sexually active should be screened at least once.

Cervical screening will not prevent every case of squamous carcinoma of the cervix, and rapid progression of lesions after normal recent smears will occur from time to time. Because of the latter factor it might seem sensible to accept that three-yearly smears should be the maximum interval, to reduce the incidence of the few cases where there is more rapid progression. Even the above recommendations may have to be reviewed in the light of changes in sexual practice. Recent surveys in the USA and to a lesser extent in the UK of women now in their teens may invalidate the age recommended to start screening.

A suggested screening programme for a practice

(1) *Age at first smear.* If sexually active and presents for consultation about pregnancy, contraception, or gynaecological problems, a smear should be taken regardless of age, although it is not necessary at the first consultation for contraception in a young woman. Alternatively, a woman could be offered this test at age 25 if she is sexually active.

(2) *Frequency of smears.* If two negative smears, then smear every five years until age 60, after which screening is no longer necessary if all smears have been negative. In a woman presenting at age 35 or later, the second smear should be performed within one year to pick up false negatives, and then she should have five-yearly smears. If abnormal smears have occurred, screening should be carried out more frequently— six-monthly or annually, depending on the advice of the local cytology service.

(3) *High-risk women.* This group should include those women with a previous abnormal smear; those who commenced having intercourse under the age of 17 and with multiple partners; those who have had herpes genital infections and possible genital warts (and that very small group of women whose husbands develop carcinoma of the penis). High-risk women should probably have annual smears. Using the knowledge of the risk factors already outlined, such as sexual behaviour, high parity, young age of first intercourse, multiple partners, occupation and social class, and geographical location, general practitioners are in an ideal position to

judge whether certain of their women patients are in need of more frequent surveillance.

It could be argued that in an ideal programme it would possibly be reasonable to advocate that there should initially be two negative smears taken at a year's interval with three-yearly screening thereafter. The resource implications that such a programme would pose do not make this feasible at the present time and even with such a programme it is still likely that some cases would be missed.

How should screening be organized?

Since 1971 a national recall system based on the National Health Service central register at Southport has informed Family Practitioner Committees of women due to have follow-up smears. The system has been criticized in that it is not cost effective, since less than 20 per cent of names generated from Southport have repeat smears taken (DHSS 1981). To get on to the Southport register a woman must have had a smear taken, but it is those who have never had a smear who are, of course, at most risk. At the end of 1981 the Southport system was abandoned and each Family Practitioner Committee was encouraged to set up alternative recall systems. Such a breakdown in a national recall system reverts responsibilities to the local general practitioner, possibly linked with other areas of their health care work and other parts of the health service. However, at present it does not appear that the family doctor in all areas is meeting this challenge (RCGP 1982), partly because of the complexities of the different set-ups available. Thus, identification of women could be from electoral roll, general practitioner lists, age–sex registries, or special computer lists. Screening can be carried out by general practitioners, community health family planning clinics, sexually transmitted diseases clinics, gynaecological clinics in hospitals, etc., and smears can be taken by nurses, clinical medical officers, other doctors, etc. Sensitive co-operation among interested parties is essential and examples as to how this might be done are:

1. General practitioners themselves could identify the female populations at risk on their list and organize a screening service.

2. General practitioners could act in conjunction with local health authority. For example, in a study in Oxfordshire a group of general practitioners was provided with lists, organized by a community physician (Jackson 1979), of women aged 40–70 from their own practices. After one year there was a small increase in the total number of women in this age-group being smeared, but little change in the number of women having first smears. There seemed considerable variation in the methods of presenting information to patients and the extent to which they were helped by having these tests.

3. District nurses could be used to take smears, and their potential increased by using them as a domiciliary service to high-risk non-attending groups. In one area where this was tried there was a resulting 50 per cent increase in the number of smears taken from women in social classes IV and V.

4. Screening could be based at one's place of work and there is evidence that screening in an industrial setting might be rewarding in getting to 'high-risk' groups.

5. Health education could be used more effectively, though again such programmes need careful evaluation.

SETTING UP A CERVICAL SCREENING SERVICE IN GENERAL PRACTICE

Many general practitioners are involved in screening programmes for several diseases and broadly the same principles apply to all of them. These are:

1. The disease being sought should be reasonably common within the population being screened, and should cause significant morbidity and mortality which would be reduced by earlier detection.

2. The screening techniques should be simple, cheap, reliable, and acceptable to those being screened.

3. The false negative rate must be low, and management of the false positive case should not result in the production of serious morbidity.

4. There must be methods and facilities for treating cases of the disease picked up on screening.

5. In addition, a long natural history of the disease allowing periodic screening and the identification of risk factors in order to pinpoint a high-risk group allows concentration of resources when planning such a programme.

Squamous carcinoma of the cervix is a disease which fulfils these criteria.

Opportunistic screening costs nothing to the general practitioner and would reveal to busy general practitioners to what extent their female patients had been tested. A simple question as to whether or not a woman had had a cervical smear within the last five years, asked of every woman presenting with a complaint or when bringing her children, or what may be even more important, her aging relative, should identify women who had not been screened. So, by simply taking smears from all the appropriately aged women when seen in the practice for other problems, 70 per cent of the population at risk will be screened in one year as 70 per cent of a practice population see their doctor in one year. There are obvious problems about the practicalities of this and therefore additional methods of case identification are necessary, but a notice in the waiting-room alert-ing women to the opportunity to have smears taken, combined with post-ers and literature produced by the Women's Cancer Control Campaign or the local health education unit, would improve patient education in this area and their awareness of the services available. Films on cervical can-cer screening are also available for hire and can be shown to patient groups, health visitors, and midwives.

It might seem that the National Health Service lost a golden opportu-nity to improve health care and awareness by not including a 'medicard' with the card which is issued to people registering with a doctor. This identity card could be used to record the person's height, standard weight, actual weight at five or ten-year intervals, baseline and repeat blood pressure, blood group, haemoglobinopathies if relevant, immuniz-ation status including tetanus and rubella, chest X-rays and any known allergies, and in the case of women, cervical smear results. All these could be recorded inside, and on the outside important episodes of illness could be added on one side and on the other the details of medication in the case of diabetics or others on long-term therapy. Failing this, a card which recorded the woman's cervical smear test results and which could be completed by the general practitioner, hospital, or family planning cli-nic would increase efficiency and enable the woman to check on her own health. Patient-held records are known to be feasible, and it is clear that most people keep very carefully all the documents relating to health and social security, even the most recent immigrants who cannot read English.

The use of age–sex registers and computers are the most obvious choices for the future. Although the initial outlay for an age–sex register in terms of clerical time is fairly high, once set up, this register, using different coloured index cards for the two sexes, filed in date rather than alphabetical order, can be used for the basis of all sorts of preventive measures. By systematically working through women in the various age groups, checking from their notes whether or not they have had a recent smear and then sending those who have not had one, an appointment to attend a special session, good coverage of the practice can be obtained without any sophisticated means.

Obviously, with the increasing computerization within practices and at the Family Practitioner Committee administration, identification of women needing a first smear and their follow-up is likely to become easier in the near future.

As well as effort going towards general screening of the female popu-lation, special effort should perhaps be made for specific groups. Spenser in 1967 identified the typical non-attender as 'a woman in her late forties or fifties, of lower social class, relatively inarticulate, more likely to be a member of a small household and going out to work, and less likely to be a frequent attender at the doctor's surgery unless for psychiatric symptoms of some severity'. This portrait is probably still true today, but there are other women likely to be missed. Earlier studies of women sterilized pointed out the higher risk of cervical carcinoma, presumably related to the social characteristics of these women in the days when sterilization was rarely done at the woman's request, but now that sterilization is being done earlier in a woman's life it is important to remind her of the need for repeat smear tests. While they are receiving contraception from their general practitioners or the community services women are likely to receive fairly regular reminders about the need for cervical smears, but as they approach the menopause and cease to need contraception—at a time when the risks of cervical cancer increase—increased efforts will be needed to contact them.

The other consideration is the question of money, as it is said that fee for service incentives for general practitioners are effective. The general practitioner cannot recover the cost of doing a smear test until the woman is 35, and is only paid for doing tests every five years. However, it would be fair to point out that as 50 per cent of all smears taken are in women aged less than 35, and the general practitioner does not receive payment for these, much of the screening service is being provided 'free' as part of general health care. It can certainly be argued that there is little difference between regular checks on blood pressure and doing a cervical smear.

TECHNIQUE OF CERVICAL CYTOLOGY AND FOLLOW-UP

The technique of cervical cytology depends on the study of single cells from the cervix which are either aspirated from the posterior fornix, or scraped from the surface of the cervix by means of a spatula and aspirated from the cervical canal as described by Ayre (1947).

Papanicolau first described the aspiration technique and developed the stain which bears his name, but better specimens are obtained by the scraping technique. Richart considers that Ayre's original technique gives the best results of all. The cells are then spread on to a glass slide, and fixed rapidly by immersion in 95 per cent alcohol or by spraying with a carbowax fixative if transmitting to the laboratory by post. If the clinician suspects malignancy, aspiration of the cervical canal or obtaining cells with a moist cotton-tipped swab or a special brush after taking the cervical smear may reduce the false negative rate, especially in invasive lesions, where necrosis, infection, and haemorrhage may obscure the diagnosis.

The study of exfoliated cells depends on the fact that the rate of exfoliation of body cells is constant in health, and the cells mirror the tissue of origin. In neoplastic tissue, the rate of exfoliation increases and because the orderly rate of change from basal through intermediate to superficial squamous cells is distorted, the relative proportions of these cells change, as well as the cells themselves showing abnormal features.

Taking the smear

Using an unlubricated Cusco's speculum (inserted with its screw upwards if the woman is in the dorsal position), the asymmetrically curved end of the Ayre's spatula is inserted, with the longer end placed inside the cervical canal so that there is a snug fit between the spatula and the cervix encompassing the squamo-columnar junction as well as the two types of epithelium adjacent to this area. If there is a copious amount of ovulatory or infected mucus obscuring the cervix, it is better to wipe this away gently with a piece of dry cotton wool held in a sponge holder.

The spatula is rotated through 360 degrees, removed, and spread on a clean glass slide with a single stroke from each side of the spatula from one end of the slide to the other. Rapid fixation is essential to prevent air drying and subsequent distortion of the cells, which make cytological interpretation difficult.

If the vagina is dry, which only occurs if the woman has just removed a tampon or has atrophic changes without vaginitis, water may be used as a lubricant, but many cytologists dislike the lubricants in common use (and even water), which we have never found necessary except in the circumstances mentioned. Dr Fay Hutchinson of the Brook Advisory Centres has found that many women are glad to be offered the chance of inserting the speculum themselves, and exposure of the cervix is usually adequate.

Sometimes when the blades of the Cusco speculum are opened there is no sign of the cervix, and then it is usually in the posterior fornix and withdrawal of the closed blades and redirection in a superior direction usually reveals the cervix. If not, a bimanual examination in which one takes care not to touch the cervical os but locates the uterus with fingers on either side of the cervix, thus not removing the surface epithelium prior to taking the smear, is preferable to lengthy manipulations of the speculum within the vagina. If asked, some women can tell the examining doctor whether the cervix is being pushed down or up by the speculum, and this can then be re-positioned.

If any cervicitis or vaginitis is present, smears for culture should be taken, and if the smear is being taken for screening rather than because of symptoms, it may be preferable to treat trichomonas infections and take the smear one month later to avoid wasting the cytologist's time. However, this is a point which it is worth discussing with your local cytology laboratory.

When in the menstrual cycle to take the smear

There are changes in the cervical epithelium during the menstrual cycle, although these do not reflect the hormonal changes as accurately as do the changes in the vaginal epithelium. Taking smears during menstruation is not a practice welcomed by most cytologists as erythrocytes, leucocytes, endometrial cells, and blood pigments obscure the field. However, in high-risk women any chance should be seized as they may not present again, and a note made to this effect on the request form. Following menstruation and after ovulation, i.e. days 10–20 of the 28-day cycle, is probably the best time to take a smear as there are few polymorphs and the cells are mature. Histiocytes may be seen up to the 12th day of the cycle. In the latter part of the cycle, days 21–28, there is an increase in leucocytes which gives a dirty background to the smear. However, while in planning screening midcycle smears are ideal, rarely should a woman needing a smear (especially if high risk) be asked to return at another time.

Interpretation of smear

Cervical smear reports and their significance

The early Pap (Papanicolau) smear results were classed as 1 to 4. Class 1 smears were those where no malignant cells were seen, Class 2 inflammatory, Class 3 suspicious, and Class 4 malignant. This simple classification was overtaken by more interpretive reports in most parts of the UK in the last decade. Smears were reported as showing dyskaryosis or dysplasia, inflammatory cells, or cells originating in carcinoma *in situ*, as well as invasive carcinoma as cytologists gained experience. In some laboratories cytologists may suggest what action the clinician should take, i.e. repeat smear in three months, repeat after treatment or, more recently, colposcopy and biopsy being indicated. It is essential that the clinician is aware of the bias of the local laboratory which may be towards under- or over-reporting of abnormal smears, and it is ideal if the doctors concerned can meet on a regular basis and discuss cases together. General practitioners often do not feel able to go into hospitals and seek out their colleagues, but in our experience cytologists are usually delighted to meet those who send them smears, and will make helpful suggestions about improving the quality of the slides if this is a problem.

With the advent of the colposcope a new system of reporting has come into use in some areas. This was first suggested by Richart in 1966 and the 'CIN' or cervical intra-epithelial neoplasia classification is used by most colposcopists though not all cytologists (see Table 9.3).

If the national form is used there is a space for the cytologist to record whether or not endocervical cells are present, thought by some workers to be an indication that adequate sampling of the squamo-columnar junction has been made, thus allowing general practitioners to keep an eye on their own performance. Air-dried smears may make interpretation difficult, and smears reported as 'inadequate for diagnosis' should be repeated.

Table 9.3 *Cytological classification*

New' system	Old' system
Inadequate for diagnosis	
Essentially normal findings	Class 1
Atypical cells present suggestive of	Class 2
Cytological findings consistent with:	
CIN Grade 1 (mild dysplasia) ⎫	
CIN Grade 2 (moderate dysplasia) ⎬	Class 3
CIN Grade 3 (severe dysplasia to ⎫	
carcinoma-in-situ) ⎪	
Invasive squamous cell ⎬	Class 4
Endometrial carcinoma ⎪	
Other cancer ⎭	

Class II or inflammatory smears

Those smear reports in which inflammatory changes or atypias are present should also be repeated 4–6 weeks after treatment with the appropriate agent. If neither candida nor trichomonas has been found, using appropriate tests, we suggest that the woman asks her partner to have a check for non-specific genital infection. These tests can be done in a clinic specializing in sexually transmitted diseases, as can those for the woman if the doctor suspects herpes or gonorrhoea on clinical grounds. Despite the greater freedom in discussing sexual matters, patients of both sexes still regard the possibility of sexually transmitted disease with fear and embarrassment, and a fairly long explanation about non-specific genital infection is usually needed. The use of the two-glass test in the general practitioner's surgery might be a useful screening procedure, and a letter to the clinic explaining why the man has been asked to attend prevents further embarrassment for him. Cultures for chlamydia are now available in some sexually transmitted diseases clinics, and over one-third of men with NSU and their consorts have been found to have positive cultures. If NSU is present in the man, treatment of his partner with tetracycline or erythromycin will be followed in the majority of cases by the removal of inflammatory cells from the cervical smear. In the absence of pathology in the male partner, hydrargaphen (Penotrane) pessaries are often effective in achieving the same result. The chronic cervicitis which was seen so commonly 25 years ago is rare today, but may continue to contribute inflammatory cells to the smear so making interpretation difficult. Chlamydial cervicitis may be unrecognized by many gynaecologists and in the past may have been treated by cauterization, although colposcopists can distinguish this from malignancy.

Class III or dysplastic smears (CIN lesions)

If the cervix had looked normal when the smear was taken and did not bleed afterwards, it is reasonable to repeat the smear at the interval indicated by the cytologist. However, if there was any suspicion of malignancy on looking at the cervix initially, the woman should be referred urgently to the gynaecologist without waiting for the result of the cervical smear.

In an older woman, referral as soon as an abnormal smear result is received would seem the best course. If the gynaecologist is satisfied that there is only mild dysplasia further follow-up smears could be done by the general practitioner. In a younger woman, infection should be sought for and treated, and the smear repeated after this or in three months; a second abnormal smear result should prompt the general practitioner to refer the woman.

Obviously, individual gynaecologists will have their own protocol for management and policy for referral, and if this is unknown to the general practitioner it would be sensible to meet and discuss this point or in the city to write and ask the local gynaecologists for their thoughts, so that you can then choose the service which you prefer for your patients.

In remote areas, where referral is difficult or in underdeveloped countries the use of Schiller's or Lugol's iodine to delineate the abnormal tissue and allow a punch biopsy to be taken for diagnosis (using local anaesthesia with paracervical block) could be justified.

Technical problems

There are two main reasons why one gets false negative smears. They are errors in taking the smear and errors in reading the smear. Overall, it has been estimated that there can be up to a 20 per cent 'false' negative rate. All those people involved in taking smears need to be adequately trained. If many smears are coming back reported on as 'insufficient material' or with other problems indicating poor technique, it would be worth asking for some further assistance in training. In certain studies that have looked at this issue, up to 30 per cent of small *in situ* lesions have been missed by missing the squamous–columnar junction or sending an inadequate number of cells for diagnosis. At the laboratory end, the volume of work going through a laboratory appears to be important. The suggestion has been made that laboratories examining less than 25 000 slides per year will have insufficient positives to maintain both the skills of technicians and an adequate teaching service.

Explanation of the result

As most women know the purpose of having a cervical smear and may have presented themselves to the general practitioner because of a worrying symptom, they are anxious to know the result as soon as possible. The usual system is that women are not told the result but are told that the test is normal unless 'you hear from us in two or three weeks'. Most women accept this situation but a few become very anxious, and all women are anxious if they are recalled for another smear, so careful explanation is necessary.

The general practitioner is in the best position to know the personality of the woman and what language to choose in explaining the result. Our own policy is always to tell the woman the truth and try and explain what dysplasia or CIS means, emphasizing the 100 per cent cure rate if these lesions are confirmed. We find it helpful for many women to draw diagrams both to explain the diagnosis and the treatment which may be offered to them. It probably confuses the woman to talk about infection when one means dysplasia, and most women even when anxious can understand the difference between abnormal cells which may over the years go on to become cancer cells, and the concept of an *in situ* lesion.

If the woman is young and has not completed her family, it is as well for the general practitioner to discuss the effect of treatment on her future fertility, as when she goes to hospital the unfamiliar surroundings and inadequate time available in most gynaecology clinics may not allow her to voice her fears if cone-biopsy is suggested. The general practitioner must know what is likely to be offered to the woman in terms of colposcopic assessment, or biopsy as an in-patient procedure, and also have some idea of the waiting list so that one can emphasize that these precursor lesions do not become invasive cancer overnight. Questions about contraception and its effect in producing the abnormal result are frequently asked, and the IUCD is often associated by the woman with the abnormal result, although there is no evidence linking IUCDs with cervical dysplasia.

If the smear is reported as having malignant cells or carcinoma *in situ*, confirmation of the cytology report requires cervical biopsy. By arranging this quickly, the doctor can relieve the patient's anxiety about the extent of the disease as soon as possible. If the cervix looks malignant clinically, then it is best to prepare the woman for hearing this in hospital and possibly suggest that she is accompanied there by her partner or a friend. If the cervix is clinically normal on examination by the naked eye, then the question of frank malignancy need not be raised and one should prepare her for colposcopy and/or biopsy.

Hospital management

When a woman is referred to hospital with a positive smear, it is usual to repeat the smear test as laboratory errors may occur in labelling or reporting. Depending on the presence or absence of symptoms, infection or lesions of the cervix seen with the naked eye, the woman will either be followed by repeated smears or have the cervix assessed by colposcopy. Depending on the appearance of the cervix under the colposcope, directed biopsies may be done usually combined with endocervical curettage. Treatment using cryo-cautery or laser beam therapy is available in a few units. Some gynaecologists in the UK, however, do not have access to a colposcope, and while this may be a disadvantage in treating mild dysplasias in young women, for those with severe dysplasia or carcinoma *in situ* cone biopsy is still considered by some to be the treatment of choice.

At the present time, although in the hands of experts colposcopy can save in-patient beds and operating time for the National Health Service and surgery for the woman, in less experienced hands, or where the number of cases seen by an individual is small, the use of Schiller's iodine, endocervical curettage, and punch biopsy in younger women, and cone biopsy in older women, would seem the safest alternative. Laser beam therapy is very expensive because of the initial cost of the equipment, and there have been worries that it does not reach lesions deep in the glands; similar problems were encountered when diathermy was used. This may mean that except for very minor lesions (which are removed by punch biopsy anyway), the recurrence rate will be unacceptable. The treatment of early cancer is a fast-changing field with new techniques still being assessed.

REFERENCES AND FURTHER READING

Ayre, J. E. (1947). Selective cytology smear for the diagnosis of carcinoma. *Am. J. Obstet. Gynecol.* **53**, 609.

Buckley, J. D., Harris, R. W. C., Doll, R., and Vessey, M. P. (1981). Case control study of husbands of women with dysplasia or carcinoma of the cervix uteri. *Lancet* **ii**, 1010–14.

DHSS (Department of Health and Social Security) (1981). Cervical cytology. New recall schemes for screening of women. Press release. 81/101.

Draper, C. J. (1982). Screening for cervical cancer—revised policy. The recommendations of DHSS Committee on Gynaecology, Cytology. *Hlth Trends* **14**, 37–40.

Harris, R. W. C., Brinton, L. A., Cowdell, R. H., Skegg, D. C. G., Smith, P. G. Vessey, M. P., and Doll, R. (1980). Characteristics of women with dysplasia or cancer *in situ* of the cervix uteri. *Br. J. Cancer* **42**, 359–69.

Jackson, J. (1979). Screening in general practice. Cervical cytology for higher risk women. *Publ Hlth, Lond.* **93**, 300–5.

Kinlen, L. and Spriggs, A. I. (1978). Women with positive smears but without surgical intervention. *Lancet* **ii**, 463–5.

MacGregor, E. (1982). Leader. *Br. med. J.* **284**, 441–2.

Miller, A. B., Lindsay, J., and Hill, G. B. (1976). Mortality from cancer of the uterus in Canada and its relationship to screening for cancer of the cervix. *Int. J. Cancer* **27**, 651–7.

—— Visentin, T., and Howe, C. R. (1981). The effect of hysterectomies and screening on mortality from cancer of the uterus in Canada. *Int. J. Cancer* **25**, 651–7.

RCGP (Royal College of General Practitioners) (1982). Cervical cancer—the challenge to general practice. Editorial. *Jnl R. Coll. Gen. Pract.* **235**, 69–70.

Richart, R. (1966). Influence of diagnostic and therapeutic practices on the distribution of CIN. *Cancer* **19**, 165.

—— and Barons, B. A. (1969). A follow-up study of patients with cervical dysplasia. *Am. J. Obstet. Gynecol.* **105**, 386–93.

Robinson, J. (1982). Cancer of the cervix—occupational risks of husbands and wives and possible preventive strategies. *Preclinical neoplasia of the cervix* (eds. J. Jordan, F. Sharp, and A. Singer). RCOG pp. 11–22.

Spenser, J. T. (1967). A survey of cervical smear screening in general practice. *The Practitioner* **198**, 274–82.

Spriggs, A. I. and Husain, O. A. N. (1977). Cervical smears. A policy document for the British Society for Clinical Cytology. *Br. med. J.* **i**, 1516–18.

Waterhouse, J., Muir, C., Correa, P., and Powell, J. (1976). *Cancer incidence in five continents* Vol. III. IREAC Scientific Publications, No. 15, Lyon: International Agency for Research on Cancer.

Wright, N. H., Vessey, M. P., Kenward, B., McPherson, K., and Doll, R. (1978). Neoplasia and dysplasia of the cervix uteri and contraception: A possible protective effect of diaphragms. *Br. J. Cancer* **38**, 273–9.

Yu-Shun-Zhang, A., Miller, B., and Sherman, C. J. (1982). Optimising the age, number of tests, and test interval for cervical screening in Canada. *J. Epidemiol. Comm. Hlth* **36**, 1–10.

10 Depression

Judy Greenwood

Psychiatric training for general practitioners has traditionally centred on the diagnosis and management of major psychiatric illnesses— schizophrenia, manic depressive illness, and organic brain disease— within a psychiatric hospital patient population. Yet in general practice, such illnesses are rarely encountered. By contrast, minor psychiatric disorders (emotional or mood disorders) are highly prevalent, with women afflicted at least twice as often as men. Although such cases form a significant proportion of the caseload, in many cases the general practitioner will have received little or no training in the management of such patients. With whom the responsibility for this training should rest is open to question, but undoubtedly both psychiatrists and general practitioners have an urgent need to rethink the whole area of training and service provision for minor psychiatric disorders within the NHS. In this chapter, it is intended to examine some of the aspects of presentation, aetiology, assessment, and management of depression and anxiety in women in a primary care setting.

PREVALENCE

Although depression and anxiety are universally experienced mood states, it is possible to arrange people along a hypothetical continuum with cheerful, relaxed individuals at one end and frankly depressed (ill) patients at the other end, and those experiencing minor mood disorders (anxiety or depression) somewhere in the middle. It is far from clear at what point along this hypothetical line a person 'should be deemed a patient or a case' or a set of symptoms should be labelled an illness. Nevertheless, Professor David Goldberg (Goldberg and Huxley 1980) using his General Health Questionnaire to detect psychiatric symptoms and their somatic manifestations in the general population, has attempted to assess the prevalence of psychiatric symptoms in samples from both the general public and from general practice. Using an arbitrarily agreed cut-off point to differentiate those with symptoms sufficient to cause discomfort or inconvenience and to be clinically recognizable, he found that 25 per cent of the general population had significant psychiatric symptoms, mainly anxiety and depression (95 per cent), although less than 5 per cent of these

Table 10.1 *One-year period prevalence of psychiatric disorders in community and health settings per 1000 population*

General population	GP attendances	GP identified	Psychiatric out-patients	Psychiatric in-patients
250	230	140	17	6

displayed recognizable syndromes of major psychiatric illness—see Table 10.1.

Women were twice as likely as men to have psychiatric symptoms. His findings also demonstrated that, despite the fact that most of those with symptoms attended their family doctors, at least one third of cases were not recognized as psychiatric by their general practitioner. The bulk of psychiatric disorders can be seen to be supported and treated in the community by the general practitioner and/or the patient's family and local community and voluntary services with only a minority of selected cases referred to psychiatric hospital care. Further evidence of the extent of depression in women comes from George Brown's Camberwell Surveys (1975) which showed that 15 per cent of women had significant depressive symptoms. A recent Oxfordshire study of general practitioners' prescriptions (Skegg *et al.* 1977) showed that over 20 per cent of women between 25 and 40 were on psychotropic medication (antidepressants or anxiolytics).

As discussed in the first chapter of this book, women attend their general practitioner much more often than men for many reasons: this is also true in the area of psychiatric problems. Although they are both more likely to experience psychiatric symptoms and more willing to express their symptoms, they are proportionately less likely to be referred on to psychiatric services than men, so that hospital referrals ultimately reflect about the same sex ratio distribution seen in the community.

IDENTIFICATION OF PSYCHIATRIC SYMPTOMS

A breakdown of patients' problems in a typical general practice surgery is given in Table 10.2.

It can be seen that, although 24 per cent of the caseload has significant

Table 10.2 *Distribution of psychiatric symptoms in general practice*

54% physical symptoms only
22% miscellaneous (immunization, relatives, etc.)
 8% entirely psychiatric symptoms
16% psychiatric + physical symptoms (either associated or unrelated)

psychiatric symptoms, in two-thirds of these cases physical symptoms could divert the patient or the doctor from the psychiatric condition. The ability of a doctor to identify psychiatric symptoms depends on many factors. These include the doctor's sensitivity and bias towards psychiatric diagnosis, the patient's inability or reluctance to identify non-specific symptoms as psychological, and the assumption that a doctor would be more receptive to somatic symptoms and might see psychological symptoms as being a waste of medical time. It should be remembered that psychologically induced somatic symptoms can in fact make a patient feel just as miserable as physical conditions, and that the doctor's skill is needed both to defuse anxiety about the physical condition and to recognize the underlying emotional disorders.

Goldberg's studies of general practitioners suggested that factors associated with the accurate detection of psychiatric cases included not only the doctor's personality and academic ability, but also interviewing style. Certain doctors were more able to detect with accuracy the cases which had underlying psychiatric problems. Doctors who did well showed frequent eye contact, clarified the presenting complaint by using open questions (for example: 'How are you feeling?' 'Tell me more about it'), used directive questions for physical problems, were frequently empathic and sensitive to verbal and non-verbal cues, did not read notes during interviews, and could deal with over-talkative patients, asked fewer questions about the past (i.e. did not take refuge in fact-finding), and asked more questions about the patient's current home life and relationships.

PRESENTATION AND CLASSIFICATION OF ANXIETY AND DEPRESSION

Although anxiety and depression are extremely common mood disorders, their impact on a woman's daily coping and behaviour will vary enormously with her lifestyle, social class and intelligence, her work role, the quality of her friendships, her personality, her past experiences, and the current support systems available to her in the community. The impact will also vary according to the intensity of her symptoms.

With so many factors affecting the form of presentation, neat classification of depression into syndromes becomes almost impossible. Most authors, however, would agree with a rough division into those syndromes associated with the problem of coping with stress. In this chapter I shall deal with minor psychiatric disorders, also called neurotic depressions, reactive depressions, anxiety neuroses, situational reactions, minor psychiatric disorder, and so on, and those recognizable as major true depressive illness and also called manic depressive illness or depressive psychosis, endogenous depression, bipolar or unipolar.

Minor psychiatric disorders

The majority of psychiatric cases in primary care will come under this heading, i.e. the patient is not suffering from a major depressive illness but is impaired by psychiatric symptoms and possibly associated behavioural changes. It must be remembered that despite the label minor psychiatric disorders, such individuals may feel just as disturbed or distressed as those with major psychiatric illness. Typical complaints may include in descending order of frequency:

- feeling depressed;
- feeling anxious, tense, and worried;
- feeling fatigued and despondent;
- somatic symptoms—palpitations, headaches, backache, feeling out of sorts, weak, etc;
- sleep disturbance—difficulty getting off to sleep or interrupted sleep;
- irritability and aggression—emotional or physical, towards spouse, children, or parents;
- reduced sexual interest, often associated with poor self-image or body image;
- poor concentration and function—failing to cope with normal work, normal domestic work, or financial budgeting;
- obsessions about housework, etc.—over-attentiveness and fussiness;
- phobias—particularly agrophobia; increased difficulty in leaving home, panic attacks if out, etc.

Less commonly described in the literature but commonly experienced in the community are women whose main manifestation is of behavioural changes that may even mask the underlying emotional disorder, for example:

- increased drug use and dependence on tranquillizers, sleeping tablets, etc.
- compulsive overeating—with or without vomiting;
- shoplifting—often of a compulsive nature for unnecessary items;
- alcohol abuse;
- self-poisoning (or parasuicide).

Alcoholism has become an increasing problem since the 1960s. Drink is more readily available and the social stigma of women drinking is now less strong. However, the stigma attached to female drunkenness (particularly a woman with young children) persists both in the view of society and in the estimation of the woman herself so that a downward spiral of self-esteem tends to perpetuate the drinking behaviour. Depression is often an important reason for women turning to drink. They are more likely to be secret drinkers, which may explain the reported increased vulnerability to liver cirrhosis and women are less likely to be identified by their general practitioner as having an alcohol problem.

Self-poisoning

This is considered here under minor psychiatric disorders but is a good example of the difficulty in attempting a classification into minor and major disorders. Actual suicide is not common in women. Those who seriously attempt to die are usually older, have serious depressive illness, and often leave a suicide note. If they recover they are in urgent need of psychiatric treatment as they continue to be a high suicidal risk.

Attempted suicide, however, is extremely common (over 100 000 per year in Britain). It is twice as common in women than men, usually the younger age group (18–30), social classes IV and V, who live in cities and use anxiolytic or antidepressant drugs previously prescribed by their general practitioner. Most (63 per cent) will have visited their doctor during the month preceding the self-poisoning attempt. 10–20 per cent will eventually die by suicide and 58 per cent will have had a previous attempt at self-poisoning. 15 per cent repeat within the same year (Hawton and Blackstock 1975). Less than 20 per cent of self-poisoning patients have an identifiable psychiatric illness, but many are suffering from symptoms of anxiety and depression as described above for which they may already be receiving medication. In most cases the precipitating event prior to the overdose will be conflict within an intimate relationship (spouse, boyfriend, child, parent, etc).

In general, individuals suffering from problems of living or reactive depression are more likely to have chronic personality problems, although this is not invariably the case. Often they will have experienced a series of stresses or life events prior to the onset of symptoms. The course of minor psychiatric disorders tends to be more variable and unpredictable than major illnesses with episodes of feeling well, interspersed among the tension and depression.

Typical case examples

Bridie, a 28-year-old single parent with two children (12 and 10), who compulsively shoplifts and overeats, and has sought help because she is due for a court appearance. She is in financial difficulties and chronically depressed, bored, and lonely. She has few social outlets and eats to relieve her boredom, but her increased weight makes it difficult for her to face mixing with other people. She has, on occasions, bouts of heavy drinking. She describes depressed feelings, low self-esteem, and a feeling of helplessness about her current condition.

Helen, an 18-year-old girl who married two years earlier when pregnant (aged 16) and now lives in a high-rise flat with her baby and husband. Three months ago she found her husband in bed with her girlfriend, since when she has become increasingly depressed, has gained weight, and lost all interest in sex and going out.

Jean, a 36-year-old woman whose marriage broke up a year ago. Her 12-year-old son has started stealing money from her, and she is feeling anxious and desperate about what to do. She is sleeping poorly and feeling increasingly irritable with all the children, and at times feels like running away and leaving them all.

Major depressive illness

Although much less commonly encountered, the general practitioner must be able to differentiate those patients suffering from major depressive illness. Classical symptoms include:

- diurnal mood variation—feelings of depression, despair, and hopelessness, worse in the mornings, often associated with weeping, feelings of low self-worth, depersonalization, feeling detached from self;
- disordered thought processes—preoccupation with difficulties and worthlessness, hypochondriacal feelings, impaired concentration—inability to watch TV, etc.;
- guilt feelings—becoming delusional on occasions;
- biological concomitants—early morning wakening, loss of libido, appetite, and weight, retardation, slowing down of thoughts, speech, and movements, poverty of facial expression;
- suicidal thoughts (such patients are a high suicidal risk);
- possible agitation or irritability, which may mask depressed mood.

In general, such patients often have a good premorbid personality. There may be no apparent precipitating causes, although an increased number of life events are often reported prior to the breakdown. In a substantial number of cases there is a family history of depressive illness. Depressive illness may be unipolar—with a past history of previous depressive episodes, which is twice as common in women, or bipolar—with past episodes of over-excitement (hypomania), which occurs equally in men and women.

Typical case cameo of depressive illness

A 48-year-old woman with one previous admission to psychiatric hospital fifteen years ago who, in the last four weeks since her last daughter's wedding, has become increasingly preoccupied with obsessions about housework at home. She feels the house is permanently dirty and even may have germs which will affect her grandchildren, yet she feels unable to get on with the cleaning as she would wish. She is constantly preoccupied by depressed thoughts about herself, about the future, and about the dirt in the home. Although getting off to sleep all right, she wakes around 3 a.m. each morning and cannot get back to sleep, finding herself coming downstairs attempting to start housework but always failing to carry it through. She has lost her appetite and lost interest in people and friends around her. She frequently cries and feels life is not worth living.

In summary, although major depressive illness is most common in middle-aged women, it can occur at any age and general practitioners should remain alert for variations in presentation, for example:

– childhood and teenage depression—which may manifest themselves by behavioural changes such as school refusal or antisocial behaviour, or by a regression to a more infantile stage of development with eneuresis, failure to thrive, or signs of emotional disturbance, for example, phobias sleep disturbance, eating disorders, etc.

– puerperal psychosis—a severe and acute psychotic depression often with florid symptoms, marked agitation, and delusions.

– agitated depression in elderly women, often with paranoid delusions and obsessional ruminations.

Hypomania

Bipolar depressive illness is less common in women than men. Hypomanic mood swings can be seriously disabling, both to the individual and to her family. Symptoms include over-activity, restlessness, excitability and agitation, over-talkativeness, over-spending, and other manifestations of impaired personal judgement such as promiscuity and loss of social inhibitions, sleeplessness, weight loss, etc.

Grief

Grief should also be discussed since, although not a depressive illness in the accepted sense of the word, the acute loss of someone or something held dear produces a recognizable set of psychological reactions in normal individuals. A woman's reaction to grief is no different from a man's. Typical symptoms are as follows:

- somatic symptoms—sighing, crying;
- disbelief and unreality;
- anger and guilt;
- restlessness and disruption of normal life pattern;
- preoccupation and identification with the lost person;
- possible pseudo-hallucinations (the illusion of seeing the lost person in the room).

AETIOLOGY

One of the fundamental questions that affect our clinical approach to the management of depression and anxiety is why women are so much more vulnerable to these conditions than men. Weissman and Klerman (1977) have looked at this subject in some detail. They questioned whether women show different psychological reactions and have different inner feelings from men, but decided that women and men showed no different reactions to bereavement or the stress of major life events and that, if depressed, men are rather more likely to kill themselves by suicide. Nevertheless, women are more willing to express depressed feelings and perhaps turn for medical help, whereas a depressed man may maintain a 'stiff upper lip' or use alcohol to mask his depression. They asked could there be a biological susceptibility, genetic or hormonal, to depression in women? A genetic link to the female sex remains unproven and hormone influences such as the menstrual cycle have yet to be proved to be correlated with true depressive illness. The greatest risk of severe post-partum depression is in the first two months after childbirth when hormonal variables obviously occur, but definite links with specific hormone changes have not been established. The picture is further confounded by the effect on women's hormones, of methods of feeding, the natural variation in return to normal cyclical ovarian function, and many other factors. Even the menopause has not been shown statistically to increase the risk of depressive illness but rather the life events that occur around the same time. In fact, it is social factors and social stresses that have been shown by Weissman and Klerman and by many other authors to be highly significantly related to the increased tendency of women to experience depression.

Historically, women have held for generations a disadvantaged social status. The feminine role has emphasized passivity, helplessness, and dependency, with less 'mastery' over their lives and any hope of self-realization being centred mainly on the home and close personal relationships. It has been postulated that such a role causes women to be more vulnerable to low self-esteem and feelings of depression. Some authors argue that because the mother is usually the key parent in childrearing, daughters are subtly disadvantaged throughout childhood by the rivalry of the same sex parent, whereas sons tend to be favoured by the male/female relationship with their mother. A young woman's self-esteem and self-image are further eroded by the socio-culturally learned conflicts between her desire to be sexually attractive and her need for intellectual achievements. These two forces tend to oppose each other, whereas in a man they enhance each other and cause less personal conflict. This is more marked after marriage, when a man can more readily combine marriage, fatherhood, and a career, whereas a woman finds herself pulled in several directions (wife, mother, worker, or possibly daughter), usually with guilt feelings that she is not giving of her best in any role. Perhaps because of her lower self-esteem, or her biological need to be a caretaker, she tends to put the needs of others before herself and becomes increasingly less self-assertive, or more prone to depression, as time passes. Brown and Harris (1978) has shown a statistical correlation between an increased vulnerability to depressive illness in women and has identified several social variables which are vulnerability factors. These are: loss of mother before the age of 11, being working class, having three or more children under the age of 14, being unemployed, and lacking a confiding intimate relationship with her spouse.

Table 10.3

Vulnerability factors + precipitating stresses
→ Depressive illness
→ Minor mood disorders (problems of living)

RELEVANCE OF AETIOLOGY TO CLINICAL PRACTICE

At a practical level, the general practitioner must decide what are the relevant factors possibly responsible for the precipitation of the current depression in the patient, in order to assess both the form of treatment and where the particular emphasis on counselling should lie. Table 10.3 suggests a rough guide of possible problem areas leading to an individual's psychiatric disturbance. It must be emphasized that for some women vulnerability factors will be so powerful that even the slightest stress may precipitate a depressive reaction, whereas for others with little or no vulnerability it may take a series of major stresses or massive life events to tip them into a similar depressive reaction.

Vulnerability factors

1. Female (socio-cultural expectations leading to low self-image).
2. Genetic history.
3. Developmental problems
   - constitutional trait (personality problems)
   - loss of mother before age 11
   - emotionally disorganized childhood
4. Social factors
   - working class
   - poor housing and environment
   - overcrowding
   - three children under 14
   - unemployment
   - lack of intimate relationship with spouse

Precipitating stresses

1. *Interpersonal conflicts.* Women appear more dependent than men on their emotional relationships. Conflict or breakdown in personal relationships are the commonest form of stress in a woman's life. One in four marriages end in divorce, often leaving young women as single parents to face further interpersonal stress with adolescent children and/or their own parents. Other stresses include relationships at work or difficulties with neighbours, etc.

2. *Personal changes or losses.*
   - loss of employment and associated self-image;

- loss of health or impaired self-image through surgery, etc.;
- transitional life stage, adolescence, adjustment to marriage, parenthood, menopause, retirement, etc.;
- loss of close relative by death or separation, children leaving home, moving house, etc.

From our current understanding of depressive illness, it remains unclear whether there is a natural progression from minor psychiatric disturbances associated with problems of living to the more classical illness syndrome of an acute depressive illness. It is likely that the two conditions are quite distinct, especially when in many cases of major depressive illness, fewer precipitating stresses can be elicited, and genetic links are clear. It is possible that biochemical changes in cerebral pathways are more consistently present with major depressive illness rather than the minor mood changes, and there is little doubt that major depressive illnesses show a more predictable response to biochemical treatment. It may be, however, that stress reactions will be shown to be mediated via the same biochemical pathways as genetically induced depressions, as some reactive depressions are improved by antidepressant medication too. For completeness I must conclude this section by suggesting that the outcome of psychiatric disorders, both major and minor, appears to be dependent on the same social processes that produced the vulnerability factors in the first place. Hence continued social pressures or problems appear to prolong psychiatric disorders either by decreasing the likelihood of remission or increasing the likelihood of relapse.

CLINICAL MANAGEMENT IN GENERAL PRACTICE

Surveys of general practitioners' treatment methods have shown that the majority of women with depressive symptoms are given a short interview and prescription for tranquillizers or antidepressants, increasingly so with age. Few cases receive psychotherapy or counselling. Only 15 per cent of patients acknowledged that they had received personal help from their doctor, and 59 per cent had defaulted from taking the medication within twenty-one days of attending the surgery. Most who were given medication received it inappropriately or in inadequate dosage.

General practitioners themselves report finding psychiatric work irksome by comparison with other medical work. It takes time and has an uncertain response, and general practitioners may feel anxious lest a sympathetic approach might increase the number of chronic cases on their list. Yet general practitioner studies have shown that of the psychiatric morbidity within a typical practice, three-quarters of such cases will be chronic and will be already recognized by the general practitioners. It is the *newer* cases, which form approximately a quarter of the psychiatric caseload, that tend to be missed. These are likely to be most in need of short-term support, and have a 70 per cent turnover rate, i.e. they do not go on to become chronic cases. A recent Royal College of General Practitioners Working Party (1981) has advocated that appropriate primary care of minor psychiatric disorders should include: '*The ability to listen* with understanding and consideration to the patient's difficulties and *offer* a sympathetic explanation, reassurance, advice and support within the intimacy of the doctor/patient relationship.'

There seem to be certain critical decisions and processes that must be undertaken if a general practitioner is to be able to cope realistically and effectively with the psychiatric morbidity among the patient population. These can be listed as follows:

recognition of psychiatric and emotional problems;
clarification of the problem;
differential diagnosis;
general practitioner management of depression;
alternative settings for management of each patient;
medication.

It is important that we look at these issues in more detail.

Recognition of psychiatric and emotional problems

General practitioners should examine their own bias and resistance to identifying psychiatric problems within their patients. Perhaps they should take a calculated risk that by acknowledging and allowing more discussion of emotional problems they may in the long run decrease their workload by the more effective management of their patient's symptoms and their underlying psychological stresses. Changes in interviewing technique may be needed to alter this bias (see p. 205).

Clarification of the problem

In a setting of trust, genuine interest, acceptance, and empathy, general practitioners should be able to conduct an interview in such a way that they can clarify the patient's symptoms, their effect on herself and her family, and possible reasons why she is experiencing them. They will need to have checked for significant problems in her immediate close relationships, her work role (if any), and her domestic environment. Also of relevance will be her current self-image and physical health and any relevant recent and distant past events. Specific queries about sexual problems, alcohol consumption, and financial problems may need to be made as such problems are rarely volunteered. It may be necessary to stress the confidentiality of the doctor–patient relationship when discussing this.

In the course of this initial assessment, 'cathartic ventilation' of the patient's emotional tension may occur as she graphically expresses her depression, anxiety, or anger. This is an important part of the counselling process, yet is often inhibited by a well-meaning general practitioner, whose own comfort is disturbed by tears or angry outbursts.

Differential diagnosis

The general practitioner must metaphorically step back from the patient and make a responsible medical choice between labelling the patient ill or not; i.e. to determine whether she is currently too distressed to take responsibility for tackling the causes of her distress, or whether she is incapacitated with the symptoms of a major depression. In either of these cases, she will need a medical approach, i.e. to be called ill and to be treated accordingly, with loss of responsibility for normal function and the relief of pressures wherever possible by mobilizing external supports. Most importantly, any suicidal risk, or risk to others, especially young children, must be evaluated (Bancroft 1979). The alternative option is to determine that she is indeed suffering from an emotional or psychiatric problem, but not of sufficient severity or quality to be deemed an illness. In her terms, this is an understandable reaction to life stresses, and as such is causing sufficient distress to require counsel and support while the patient maintains personal responsibility for change. Such reactions are by far the commonest psychiatric problems seen in general practice, and therefore their management will be considered in detail.

Management of depression by the general practitioner

This may take two forms:

(i) patients with major depressive illness will require antidepressant medication and regular follow-up and support from family members (see p. 219);

(ii) patients with depressive symptoms requiring counselling by the general practitioner with or without medication.

Simple counselling can be carried out in a variety of settings by many varied groups. Nevertheless, general practitioners should possess these skills themselves, and should be able to use them when appropriate in a medical practice. Because the general practitioner has the additional authority and ability to relieve anxiety about somatic symptoms, patients often choose a medical setting for counselling in preference to other services. If general practitioners are overwhelmed by requests for such help they should be encouraged to educate their patients towards a pattern of shared care within the particular community.

General principles of counselling

The general practitioner should act as a mirror, encouraging the patient to see her problems more clearly and find new ways of tackling them. Important steps in the process are:

(i) establishing an adult relationship with the patient, avoiding a patriarchal (medical) approach, with the general practitioner showing interest, acceptance, and sympathy for the patient, preserving her dignity and self-respect;

(ii) eliciting appropriate history of problems, their effect and possible background causes;

(iii) allowing 'cathartic ventilation' of the patient's pent-up emotions during the interview;

(iv) redefining and clarifying the problems with the patient;

(v) reducing anxiety by reassurance, education, and by offering hope for change; possibly medication is indicated here;

(vi) attempting to boost the patient's self-esteem by reminding her of past examples of her coping with stress, by showing non-judgemental acceptance and empathy with her current plight, and if possible by drawing attention to aspects of her life that continue to go well;

(vii) making a therapeutic contract for agreed limited objectives and fixed number of sessions, to ensure that neither the patient nor the doctor feels a failure after aiming too high, preferably aiming to avoid an interminable relationship which is debilitating both to the doctor and to the patient;

(viii) producing an agreed problem list together with possible solutions such as alternative methods of coping or additional support;

(ix) negotiating small behavioural changes with the patient in a step-by-step fashion;

(x) showing continued interest in the progress and problems encountered *en route*.

The general practitioner may need to be quite directive in suggesting possible changes in behaviour with the patient. Often a tangible goal can be more valuable than simple discussion of problems, but the patient must maintain responsibility for deciding which changes she wishes to make. If the problem is primarily interpersonal, the general practitioner should attempt to interview both parties either individually or, better still, together. A family interview gives the fullest picture of all, and general practitioners are in a good position to arrange these on a domiciliary visit.

Marital problems are common and may require counselling. If both partners attend, the following counselling objectives should be sought:

1. Outline a mutual problem list—common problems centre on power struggle between the sexes, rearing children, finance, housework, hobbies, going to the pub, interference from relatives.

2. Facilitate communication—teach each of the pair to self-assert 'I like'. and self-protect 'I feel hurt when . . .', and encourage each of the pair to *listen* to their partner. Only in this way can they air past griev-

ances, clarify each other's current needs, and arbitrate a suitable settlement of what changes need to be made.

3. Encourage positive reinforcements between the couple, i.e. getting each to notice something nice their partner does each day rather than concentrating on criticism and nagging.

4. Ensure time together for at least fifteen minutes a day without interruptions from children or television, for simple communication and shared feelings and thoughts without aggression.

If only the woman is available for counselling:

1. Examine what ways *she* can alter her behaviour to improve the situation.

2. Clarify the patient's expectations and aspirations about marriage, and question their appropriateness.

3. Alter focus away from marriage by encouraging other activities, for example, work role, social hobbies, more interest in children.

4. Encourage referral to Women's Aid or AA (Alcoholics Anonymous) if particular problems of aggression or alcohol exist with the spouse.

5. Seek legal advice about rights re separation.

6. Suggest possible temporary separation from partner to 'clear the air' and clarify feelings.

7. Encourage them both to attend marriage counselling.

If individual problems of low self-esteem and anxiety predominate, the doctor should encourage the patient to test out:

(i) new personal hobbies—example, night school or increased reading, reporting back to the general practitioner of changes made;

(ii) possible assertiveness training—to re-establish sense of self;

(iii) changes in personal behaviour—slimming course, taking more exercise, reducing alcohol, etc., writing down changes in diary for the general practitioner to check at subsequent interview;

(iv) new employment or voluntary work, perhaps helping others less able than herself, for example the handicapped, animals, or small children;

(v) joining women's groups, church, or clubs, perhaps with supportive hand from volunteer to encourage the patient to attend initially;

(vi) increased exposure to feared situations, e.g. programmed leaving home for agoraphobic, perhaps with voluntary helper at first.

Follow-up of progress is essential, with the general practitioner showing continued interest in changes made. Improvements in the patient's mood and interaction during the interview should be noted.

External problems may be the main underlying cause of the depression and then the patient should be encouraged to mobilize supports and services for herself which may be essential in tackling such problems. Agencies may need to be contacted by the general practitioner, for example, housing department, DHSS, fuel boards, school and educational services, and social work departments, patient's employer, etc. Often the 'medical authority' of a practitioner's letter may be sufficient to persuade a relevant agency to alter its decisions about a client whose main symptoms may be directly related to social or financial factors, and so on. The issue of confidentiality is often mooted as a reason against such contacts. In the author's view, it is perfectly possible to maintain confidentiality about private personal matters while at the same time sharing one's concern and support for a patient with emotional distress, and this shared approach should be actively encouraged by the general practitioner's becoming familiar with these other agencies in the area so that referral is facilitated and shared care becomes an accepted part of community medicine.

Alternative setting for treatment and/or counselling

The general practitioner has an important role in evaluating which setting is appropriate for the particular patient, aiming for a balance between the biological, psychological, and social elements of patient care. It must be determined whether medication is essential, in which case the bias will be towards a more medicalized setting, or whether a counselling approach is more relevant with scope for settings other than medical. For simplicity, the following list can be drawn up, showing the different alternatives of patient care that the general practitioner should contemplate:

Psychiatric in-patient care.   Determining factors will include severity of symptoms, danger and disturbance to self or others in family, suicidal risk, lack of family support system, homelessness, complicating physical factors, lack of compliance with medication, availability of appropriate hospital beds, and the general practitioner's relationship with psychiatrist.

Psychiatric out-patient referral.   Possible reasons for referral will include the general practitioner's need for an expert opinion or diagnosis, the need for specialist treatment (for example, lithium or out-patient ECT), the need to share the burden of responsibility for patients with reinforcements from outside. Surveys of general practitioners have shown this to be the commonest reason for referral (Williams 1979).

Day centre referral.   Various types of day care facilities exist, particularly for older people, some with a more medical bias, others with more social support. In many cases such centres can provide valuable care for those with anxiety and depression. Social contacts, a sympathetic ear, and a feeling of belonging may be all that is needed to restore the self-esteem and emotional wellbeing of many patients with symptoms of anxiety and depression. Such centres are of particular relevance if community-based and local, and the author would urge general practitioners to consider setting up such a centre on an *ad hoc* basis using volunteers where possible. Crucial to the success of such ventures would be continued support and interest in the centre and ease and availability of professional help when needed to support the voluntary counsellors.

Referral to community groups and self-help organizations.   General practitioners can encourage and educate patients to use self-help and voluntary agencies, at the same time maintaining their interest and support both of the patient and possibly the voluntary agency. Many such agencies exist. General practitioners should be familiar with them and if possible have direct contact so that they can facilitate the patient's referral, for example, Marriage Guidance Council, Women's Aid, Alcoholics Anonymous, phobic groups, post-natal depression groups, Gingerbread (single parents), CRUSE (widowhood), women's groups including Housewives' Register, Weight Watchers, local community groups, church groups, and other agencies too numerous to mention, some of which will be specific for the local community. Peer group support is often very useful and most effective for those with low self-esteem and feelings of helplessness. By moving outside the professional and medical model, an individual is likely to be more self-sufficient and self-reliant and may in time become an active, assertive member of the community once again. The transition from patient to individual may be one that requires subtle handling by the general practitioner and in my view it is appropriate that the general practitioner and voluntary agency maintain a shared interest in the individual's outcome (Greenwood 1982).

Other treatment strategies.   Relaxation groups, psychotherapy groups, individual psychotherapy, social skills groups, assertiveness training groups, are often organized in local psychology or psychiatric clinics and some may be privately arranged. Patients with young children have especial needs and although health visitors take an interest in such families until the child is two or more, sometimes the general practitioner could facilitate an infant's referral to day nursery or playgroup or to mother and toddlers clubs which often provide a very important support system for a lonely, isolated young mother. Home help systems are highly effective in alleviating the distress and boredom of elderly patients and wherever possible the general practitioner should attempt to meet regular home helps to acknowledge the importance of their role in primary care.

Samaritans, agony columnists, radio/telephone counselling, and self-poisoning units tend to see people in acute distress, often unknown to the general practitioner. There is little doubt that such agencies do valuable work and should receive as much support as possible from primary care teams.

Medication

The majority of patients with major depressive illness respond predictably to antidepressant medication provided it is given in adequate dosage and over sufficient time. Care must be taken, however, not to neglect social and interpersonal problems that may be concurrent with the depressive illness and which may themselves need tackling at a later stage when the patient's emotional state has improved sufficiently for her to face such problems. Those with minor psychiatric disorders may also require temporary medication—a hypnotic if in crisis or a high state of arousal, or antidepressants if a consistently low mood is described. Long-term medication, however, is very seldom indicated for such cases, and benzodiazepines (Librium, Valium, etc.) should be avoided. For brevity, the author does not propose to go into medication in detail but urges general practitioners to familiarize themselves with a few well-known psychotropic drugs taken from the following range:

Tricyclic antidepressants. Most may be given in a single dose at bedtime, some are more sedative than others, e.g. amitriptyline, some have less anticholinergic side effects than others and are thought to be safer in patients with heart disease and prostatic problems, e.g. doxepin, mianserin. Most tricyclic antidepressants are ineffective for at least ten days after commencement of therapy and this must be indicated clearly to the patient who may experience disturbing side effects in the first week with little sign of improvement in her mental state. The general practitioner should be clearly familiar with all side effects, drowsiness, dry mouth, blurred vision, constipation, urinary retention, and cardiac arrhythmias, and also ensure that an adequate dosage is given for a minimum of four to six weeks. Such drugs are dangerous in overdosage and great care must be taken in dispensing small quantities to those who are a suicidal risk.

Monoamine oxidase inhibitors. These are more dangerous preparations because of their serious interaction with tyramine-containing products. Caution is needed in the use of such drugs and the general practitioner must ensure the patient has a clearly written list of contraindicated foods, drinks, and drugs during such therapy. Some workers have reported that these preparations have a beneficial effect for those with 'neurotic depression', but there is a danger of patient-dependence on such drugs, especially tranylcypromine.

Tryptophan. This is a natural amino-acid, a precursor of 5-HT and in some drug trials in general practice setting it has been shown to be as effective with some individuals as tricyclic antidepressant treatment. It is totally safe in overdosage and may be used in combination with tricyclics. It has few side effects and has been shown to be significantly better than placebo in a recent study.

Lithium salts.   These are said to have a prophylactic effect in lengthening the time of remission for manic-depressive illness. Such medication needs careful and regular monitoring of blood lithium levels, to ensure that a therapeutic range is being reached and that the patient is not in danger of toxic side effects. The side effects of lithium salts can be considerable: on regular dosage they include hypothyroidism, weight gain, and polyuria; in overdosage they include vomiting, dysarthria, tremor, ataxia, and coma. In the author's opinion such medication should only be instituted by hospital services who can do the appropriate monitoring and long-term follow-up, unless the general practitioner has easy access to adequate laboratory facilities. For many cases, remarkable improvements have occurred with such prophylactic treatment which is more effective for bipolar depressive illness than unipolar depression.

Anxiolytics and hypnotics.   A large variety of such compounds exist and it is a good idea to get to know one or two regular preparations rather than experimenting with the vast range of newer and more expensive drugs. One should particularly avoid the use of combined drugs which cause nothing but therapeutic confusion. The regular use of hypnotics should be discouraged as much as possible, and the use of addicting drugs such as barbiturates totally abandoned as they are lethal in overdose. Anxiolytics should rarely be used as they increase impulsive outbursts to the detriment of family relationships though they may be of short-term use to alleviate a patient's withdrawal from alcohol abuse.

Withdrawal from long-term benzodiazepine treatment can be problematical as the drugs cause dependence. One double-blind controlled trial (Petursson and Lader 1981) showed that all patients experienced some form of withdrawal reaction ranging from anxiety and dysphoria to moderate affective and perceptual changes. Other features included loss of weight and sleep and appetite disturbances. The symptoms lasted from 2 to 4 weeks. As the withdrawal symptoms can be confused with the reason the patients are put on the drugs, patients should be warned of the dangers of long-term use and the symptoms they are likely to experience on their withdrawal.

EVALUATION OF TREATMENTS AND PREVENTION OF DEPRESSION

Because of the diverse nature of depressive disorders and the diverse nature of possible treatment approaches, both in general practice and other settings, it is difficult to do any rigorous and controlled studies of outcome. Most studies have concentrated on traditional psychotropic medication which has usually shown that patients do better with medication than placebo. Nevertheless, studies have repeatedly indicated that social and interpersonal factors have an important effect on outcome of depressive illness. Therefore it is naive to assume that by simply giving appropriate medical treatment we have effectively treated the patient. For most psychiatric disorders and medical problems in general there should be a holistic approach to the patient. The general practitioner has a vital part to play in maintaining the appropriate balance between the biological, the psychological, and the social aspects of such patient care. In time it is hoped that more research will be done in this area of psychiatric medicine.

The Royal College of General Practitioners has recently published a report (1981) which addresses itself to this crucial yet neglected problem of prevention of psychiatric disorders. It suggests that general practitioners have an important role in primary psychiatric prevention as well as treating those with early symptoms (secondary prevention) or those with full psychiatric illness (tertiary prevention). Among other recommendations it stresses that general practitioners:

(i) should recognize crucial periods in an individual's life, for example, bereavement, early marriage, parenting, adolescence;

(ii) should offer anticipatory guidance and education or supportive intervention and early treatment when indicated.

(iii) should work along with psychiatrists, psychologists, social workers, GPs, health visitors, and counsellors together in the community in a team approach;

(iv) should show a more positive approach to patient self-help groups and community care;

(v) should in their training have more emphasis on psychiatric treatment and counselling in primary care and the community setting.

The author heartily agrees with all these recommendations and hopes that this chapter will at least have encouraged a few family practitioners to cast off the protective armour of their metaphorical 'white coats' and join forces with other agencies in the community to alter the traditional medical assumption that only doctors can cure psychiatric problems.

REFERENCES AND FURTHER READING

Bancroft, J. (1979). Crisis intervention. In *An introduction to the psychotherapies* (ed. Sidney Bloch). Oxford University Press.

Brown, G. (1975). Social class and psychiatric disturbance in women. *Sociology* **9**, 225–54.

—— and Harris, Tirril (1978). *Social origins of depression—a study of psychiatric disorder in women.* Tavistock Publications, London.

Goldberg, D. and Huxley, Peter (1980). *Mental illness in the community.* Tavistock Publications, London.

Greenwood, Judy (1982). Community psychiatry in Edinburgh. *Psychiatry in practice.* **1**.

Hawton, Keith and Blackstock, E. (1976). General practice aspects of self-poisoning and self-injury. *Psychol. Med.* **6**, 571–5.

Petursson, H. and Lader, M. H. (1981). Withdrawal from long term benzodiazepine treatment. *Br. med. J.* **283**, 643–5.

RCGP (Royal College of General Practitioners) (1981). *Prevention of psychiatric disorders in general practice.* Report No. 20. Royal College of General Practitioners, London.

Skegg, D. C. G., Doll, R., and Perry, J. (1977). Use of medicines in general practice. *Br. med. J.* **1**, 1561–3.

Weissman, M. and Klerman. G. L. (1977) Sex differences and the epidemiology of depression. *Archs Gen. Psychiat.* **34**, 98–111.

Williams, P. (1979). *Interface between psychiatry and general practice.* SKF Publication, Vol. 2, No. 7.

Further reading for patients

Stanway, Andrew (1981). *Overcoming depression.* Hamlyn, London.

Hauck, Paul (1979). *Depression—why it happens and how to overcome it.* Sheldon Press, London.

Winokur, G. (1981). *Depression: the facts* Oxford University Press

SELF-HELP GROUPS

Depressives Anonymous,
Self-Help Centre,
83 Derby Road,
Nottingham
NG1 5BB.

National Association for Mental Health (MIND),
22 Harley Street,
London
WIN 2ED.
Tel: 01–637 0741

Relatives of the Depressed,
c/o Doreen Phillips,
27 Strickland Street,
London SE8.

Al-Anon Family Groups (UK and Eire),
61 Great Dover Street,
London
SE1 4YK.
Tel: 01–403 0888

Alcoholics Anonymous,
PO Box 514,
11 Redcliffe Gardens,
London
SW10 9BG.
(See local phone book for details of local groups)

The Association for Post-Natal Illness,
7 Gowan Avenue,
London SW6.

Depressives Associated,
c/o Janet Stevenson,
19 Merley Ways,
Wimborne Minster,
Dorset.

The Samaritans,
17 Uxbridge Road,
Slough,
SL1 1SN.
(For local Samaritans see local telephone book)

Relatives of the Mentally Ill,
7 Sclwyn Road,
Cambridge,
CB3 9EA.

(If you have been widowed:)
CRUSE
Cruse House,
126 Sheen Road,
Richmond,
Surrey
TW9 1UR.
Tel: 01-940 4818

Scottish Council on Alcoholism,
49 York Place,
Edinburgh,
EH1 3JD.
Tel: 031-556 0459

Meet-a-Mum Association,
Mary Whitlock,
26A Cumnor Hill,
Oxford.

Gingerbread,
9 Poland St.,
London.
WIV 3DG

11 Sexual problems

Keith Hawton and Catherine Oppenheimer

This chapter is addressed in particular to those doctors who would like to offer help to their patients with sexual problems, but who feel they need further information in order to be able to help more effectively.

The main emphasis will be on the sexual difficulties of women, but the difficulties of men will also be discussed as it is almost invariable for a problem in one partner in a sexual relationship to be associated with some difficulty in the other partner, whether as a secondary effect or as a partial cause of the presenting problem. Most attention will be devoted to sexual dysfunction (such as lack of libido, vaginismus, and erectile impotence) arising in a heterosexual relationship, but we shall also mention female homosexuality and male sexual variations because these may come to the attention of the general practitioner and can be related to sexual dysfunction.

HOW COMMON ARE SEXUAL PROBLEMS?

The incidence of sexual dysfunction in the general population is unknown. Masters and Johnson (1970) made the surprising claim that as many as 50 per cent of marriages in the USA are troubled by sexual dysfunction at some time, and their estimate received support in 1978 from a small interview survey carried out in the USA. No equivalent information is yet available from the UK, but it is known that approximately one in ten women who attend family planning clinics have sexual problems, and most would like help with them.

Just as little is known about the numbers of female homosexuals in the general population, or about the proportion of those who would like help. It has been estimated that in England approximately one in 45 women will be exclusively homosexual, so that the average general practitioner with a list size of 2500 patients can expect to have 20–30 women in the practice whose sexual interest is exclusively homosexual, and more who have experienced homosexual interest at some time. However, only a small proportion of these will regard their homosexuality as a problem.

THE EFFECTS OF SEXUAL PROBLEMS ON PEOPLE'S LIVES

All those, whatever their profession, who work with couples or families will know how commonly sexual problems are linked with marital disharmony, or with actual breakdown of a marriage, and will know also how in the absence of a happy sexual relationship one vital channel for the resolution of disharmony is removed from the partnership. Unfortunately, no statistics are available to confirm this clinical impression. It is impossible in a brief account to do justice either to the complexities of cause and effect between sexual difficulty and general tension in a relationship, or to the depth of unhappiness that such difficulties may cause. However, the following case illustrates some of the effects:

Mary and Arthur married when he was 24 and she was 20. They knew at the time that he had a problem with premature ejaculation, dating back to his first hasty intercourse at the age of 16 in the back of a car after a party. Mary had been involved in several unhappy relationships before she met Arthur, and found that she was very slow to become aroused during lovemaking. They hoped that the problems would resolve once they were married, but they did not, and by the second year of their marriage they were on the verge of separating. They tried to make a fresh start and Mary became pregnant. During the pregnancy Mary felt very keen on sex, but Arthur found her unattractive, and when after delivery his interest in her returned, she felt sore and began to be repelled by the idea of sex. On the few occasions that they did try to make love, Arthur ejaculated so quickly that he began to feel 'a complete failure', and acquiesced in Mary's avoidance of sex. By the time they went to their doctor they had not had sex for eight months, and the subject had become unmentionable. They were still determined to stay together for the sake of the child. Mary said 'I want to sort things out but I feel it's impossible'.

Sexual dysfunction also may cause a woman to avoid forming further relationships, especially if a previous sexual encounter was unsuccessful. Such avoidance may lead to further unhappiness and lack of confidence, which in turn can add to the woman's conviction that she is 'sexually inadequate'.

HOW SEXUAL PROBLEMS MAY PRESENT TO DOCTORS

In spite of the drastic changes in public attitudes to sexuality that have occurred over recent years, people still find it embarrassing to talk honestly about sexuality, especially their own, and a very important part of the help that a doctor can give is in making it easier for patients to overcome this hurdle. Doctors need to be sensitive to clues that a patient has a problem that she (or he) wants to discuss, and be able to convey their willingness to enter into the discussion. Often patients have heard, through the press and elsewhere, of the availability and effectiveness of treatment for sexual problems, and such patients may come to the doctor with *direct requests for help.*

Other patients may be too shy to express their worry directly, or may not even realize that there is a sexual cause to the difficulty that they experience, and in these cases the doctor must be aware of the possible *covert presentation* of sexual problems. On the whole such covert presentations take the form either of emotional or psychological symptoms (such as depression, marital disharmony, poor sleep), or gynaecological complaints (such as requests for a change of contraceptive pill, or the report of a vaginal discharge). The following case illustrates such a presentation.

Alicia was 35 and had been married for 9 years when she attended a cervical screening session at her doctor's surgery. The doctor found it almost impossible to take the smear and it then came to light that Alicia's marriage had never been consummated. For 9 years she had allowed her husband to stroke her but not to approach her genitals, while she had masturbated him. She had been too ashamed of her inability to have sex ever to confide in anyone else. Her doctor referred her for sex therapy but she cancelled the appointment; however a few months later she asked to be re-referred.

A gynaecological examination can provide a surprisingly helpful setting in which to enquire into a patient's sexual anxieties, and in which reassurance (e.g. about the normality of the genitals) can be given. Another common presentation is for the patient to complain of the partner's sexual dysfunction. This sometimes may be because the partner is unwilling to attend, but often it is because the patient has not recognized that the problem is primarily her or his own.

NORMAL SEXUAL FUNCTION

Understanding of the different types of sexual problems is facilitated by a knowledge of normal sexual behaviour, and particularly of the events that occur during the various stages of sexual desire and response. Only a brief summary of such information can be provided here. For further details the reader is referred to Masters and Johnson's (1966) book, *Human sexual response*. (We have not, however, adhered exactly to the phases of sexual response suggested by Masters and Johnson.)

Normal sexual behaviour can be divided into four phases:

(i) *Interest or desire*. This includes the background level of interest in sexuality, willingness to seek opportunities for sexual contact, and occurrence of sexual thoughts or fantasies outside as well as within times of actual sexual contact.

(ii) *Arousal or excitement*. This refers to the initial physiological responses to sexually stimulating activity or thought. This phase includes:

(a) the *vascular* changes that produce genital engorgement and lubrication in the female, erection in the male, together with flushing of the face and body; (b) *neuromuscular* changes such as ballooning of the interior of the vagina and retraction of the clitoris in the female, elevation of the testes and tightening of the scrotum in the male. During this phase of arousal, thoughts and feelings also become increasingly focused on the sexual experience. It is normal for the subjective experience of arousal to intensify not gradually, but by a series of waves of arousal of increasing intensity.

(iii) *Orgasm.* This includes both the observable events of pubococcygeus contractions in the female or ejaculation in the male, and the subjective experience of orgasm. The male response may be divided into two phases: the first in which seminal and prostatic fluid enters the urethral bulb, and the second, beginning from the point at which the process becomes inevitable and irreversible, in which the seminal fluid is ejected from the urethra.

(iv) *Resolution.* During this phase the physiological events of arousal are gradually reversed. Descent of the uterus and resolution of vascular engorgement occur in women. In men a moderate immediate loss of erection is followed by a slower complete reversal to the flaccid state. In both sexes these changes are accompanied by subjective sensations of relaxation and langour. For the male this phase includes a *refractory period* of variable length (from 15 to 30 minutes for a 15 year old, to 24 hours or more for an 80 year old) before full sexual arousal can recommence; for the female there is no corresponding physiological refractory period, and some women experience a series of orgasms in close succession.

These four phases normally follow each other in sequence. It is said however that for many women there seems to be less 'need for orgasm' than for many men: whether this is physiologically or culturally determined is not clear. In any case, many woman enjoy sexual arousal, intercourse, and the ebbing of arousal without necessarily experiencing an orgasm on each occasion, or regretting its absence (see Jehu (1979) for further discussion of this).

The role of hormones in sexual behaviour has not been defined very accurately. Although *androgens* are essential for the development of full sexual functioning in men, their withdrawal, as occurs following castration, often does not cause loss of a man's ability to respond to sexual stimulation with erection, but the ability to ejaculate may be impaired. Androgens do appear to be important with respect to a woman's sexual drive, although much lower levels of androgens are necessary in females than males to have this effect. In women, *oestrogens* appear to be important in facilitating normal vaginal response to sexual stimulation; whether they play any part in maintaining sexual drive is uncertain. The role of *progesterone* in female sexual response is unknown.

Table 11.1 *Sexual dysfunction of females and males*

Phase of sexual response	Sexual dysfunction	
	Female	Male
Interest or desire	Inhibited or impaired sexual desire	Inhibited or impaired sexual desire
Arousal or excitement	Lack or impairment of arousal	Erectile impotence
Orgasm	Orgasmic dysfunction	Premature ejaculation Retarded ejaculation Pain on ejaculation
Other types of dysfunction	Vaginismus Dyspareunia Sexual phobias	Sexual phobias

TYPES OF SEXUAL PROBLEMS

Sexual dysfunction

In general terms a sexual dysfunction refers to a failure or impairment of sexual interest or response. The types of sexual dysfunction of women and men are listed in Table 11.1. The classification is based on the first three phases of sexual response; that is, sexual interest or desire, arousal or excitement, and orgasm. However, vaginismus and sexual phobias do not usually correspond to a particular response phase.

All the problems listed may be either *primary* or *secondary*. A *primary problem* is one that has been present since the onset of sexual activity. A *secondary problem* is one which occurs after a period of normal sexual function. The types of sexual dysfunction which occur in women and men will be described separately.

Sexual dysfunction in women

The general term 'frigidity' was in common use at one time to describe any female sexual dysfunction. The term is non-specific, incorrectly suggests an association with lack of emotional warmth, and has a pejorative tone, so it should be avoided.

Inhibited or impaired sexual drive

This is the most common sexual problem for which women seek help. The effect that impaired sexual interest will have on a woman's life will depend on the degree of the impairment and on other circumstances. Some women who experience no spontaneous interest in sex may choose to avoid sexual activity; but many others will choose to enter relationships in which they are expected to engage in sexual activity. In this latter category will be some women who also suffer from difficulties during the phases of arousal and orgasm, while others will find that, although they lack spontaneous interest in sex, they can respond to the partner's interest and experience orgasm during sexual activity. Primary inhibition of sexual drive is often related to an upbringing in which sexuality was regarded as unmentionable, dirty, or wicked, while secondary inhibition is more usually related to general difficulties in the relationship, or to an important event such as childbirth, or to depression.

Impairment of arousal

Problems of the excitement phase are characterized by failure of the normal physiological responses which occur during arousal, especially vaginal swelling and lubrication, and by lack of the sensations usually associated with sexual excitement. Such problems are relatively uncommon in women with unimpaired sexual drive, except during later life when hormonal changes may cause impairment of the normal vaginal response so that intercourse becomes uncomfortable and willingness to engage in it is reduced.

Orgasmic dysfunction

We have already noted that enjoyment of sexual activity without reaching orgasm does not necessarily constitute a 'problem'; the extent to which a woman feels she has a problem concerning orgasm will depend in part on her or her partner's expectations. These can change with time and because of information picked up from the media, and sometimes such information can set up unreasonable expectations.

Orgasmic dysfunction can be *total*, which means that orgasm is never experienced during sexual activity of any kind, or it can be *situational*, which means that orgasm can be achieved under some circumstances but not others, such as masturbation but not with a partner, or with one partner and not with another. It is important to establish which type of orgasmic dysfunction is present, because the choice of treatment will depend on the nature of the problem.

Vaginismus

This refers to spasm of the pubo-coccygeus muscles surrounding the entrance to the vagina, which makes sexual intercourse impossible or difficult and painful. Vaginismus is a major cause of non-consummation of marriage. It mostly presents as a primary problem although it can occur following vaginal trauma such as an episiotomy especially if this has not been satisfactorily repaired.

Dyspareunia

This refers to pain occurring during sexual intercourse. The pain may be localized to the entrance to the vagina (in which case it is usually related to mild vaginismus or a vaginal infection), or the pain may occur on deep penetration. Although this deep pain occasionally has a psychological basis, it much more is likely to be due to pelvic pathology, such as chronic salpingitis or endometriosis.

Sexual phobias

Some women are repelled by certain aspects of sexuality. These might be very specific, such as aversion to kissing, or to seminal fluid, or more generalized, such as aversion to foreplay. A sexual phobia need not necessarily inhibit a woman's enjoyment of the rest of sexual activity, but in many cases the phobia prevents arousal altogether. Sexual phobias are occasionally related to a past traumatic experience such as rape or incest.

Sexual dysfunction in men

Inhibited or impaired sexual desire

Although it is probably common for men to feel lessened sexual desire at some time, it is rare for them to complain of this symptom to their doctors, other than as an aspect of another disorder, such as depression. Possibly the widely held myth that men are always ready and able to have sex makes it difficult for a man to acknowledge that his desire for sex is lacking.

Erectile impotence

Whereas impairment of arousal in women is not very common, erectile impotence is probably the male sexual dysfunction most commonly encountered in clinical practice. The erectile response is extremely vulnerable to psychological influences, especially anxiety, and may also be affected by several organic disorders, such as diabetes and multiple sclerosis.

Erectile impotence is often a secondary phenomenon and is particularly likely to occur in middle aged and older men. Where it is due to psychological factors it is usually situational, in that the man is able to get an erection on his own through masturbation or wakes with an erection at night, but fails to get an erection with his partner or easily loses it—especially when he wishes to penetrate. Sometimes the failure is complete, so that no erection occurs; in other cases a partial erection may be obtained.

Premature ejaculation

This is an extremely common problem among young men, and may be viewed as a relatively 'normal' phenomenon in many males having their first sexual relationships. There is no satisfactory definition of premature ejaculation. Probably the best guide is the extent to which a man himself feels that his ejaculatory control is sufficient to allow intercourse satisfactory to him and his partner. In its most severe form it includes failure to prevent ejaculation before vaginal penetration. More often the man ejaculates within a few seconds of the start of sexual intercourse or immediately he begins to thrust.

Retarded ejaculation

This disorder of ejaculation is relatively uncommon. It includes total failure of ejaculation under any circumstances, partial failure where ejaculation is not possible with a partner but does occur through masturbation, and difficulty in ejaculating where sexual stimulation or intercourse must be continued for an excessively long time for ejaculation to occur. It is sometimes associated with a sexual variation such as fetishism when the man is unable to ejaculate unless the fetishistic object (e.g. female clothing) is present.

Pain on ejaculation

This is rarely encountered in clinical practice. However, some men do complain of acute pain in the perineum and penis during or following ejaculation. This is usually asssociated with an infection, although in some cases it may be related to spasm of the perineal muscles.

Sexual phobias

Men rarely present complaining of aversion to specific aspects of sexual behaviour. However, phobias sometimes appear to be part of another sexual dysfunction. Thus among men with erectile impotence will be found some who experience aversion to extreme sexual excitement in their partners, and others who are particularly averse to vaginal penetration.

Sexual variations

The term 'sexual variation' refers to sexual interest or behaviour which varies from that experienced predominantly by the majority of the population, and in women it refers principally to homosexuality, transsexualism, and sadomasochism. 'Sexual variation' (or its alternative, 'sexual deviation') is a better term than 'sexual perversion', which has a pejorative tone.

Female homosexuality

As in men, homosexual interest may range from simple feelings of attraction towards another woman, to full sexual activity with a female partner. Some women are exclusively homosexual, but many more experience sexual feelings towards both sexes, and some degree of attraction to other women appears to be extremely common.

Occasionally, unacknowledged homosexuality turns out to underlie a complaint of sexual dysfunction such as inhibited sexual desire (for a heterosexual partner). Therefore the doctor should routinely ask an appropriate question about homosexual interest during the course of a full assessment of a sexual problem, and be receptive to any sign that the patient wishes to discuss the issue further.

Other sexual variations

A *transsexual* is a person who feels that his or her gender is really that of the opposite sex. This leads in many cases to a wish to adopt the style of dress of the opposite sex and to undergo hormonal and surgical treatments in order to bring about appropriate anatomical changes. The greater general acceptance of masculine styles of dress for women than feminine styles for men may allow many female transsexuals to go relatively unnoticed. Occasionally a female transsexual will seek specialist help to obtain hormonal treatment and surgery. The latter can include mastectomy, hysterectomy, and genital reconstruction, although the last of these is unlikely to be successful.

    Sado-masochism is the only other sexual variation likely to be found in women. Sadistic behaviour includes infliction of pain or restriction of the partner's mobility ('bondage'), while 'masochism' refers to the wish to be the recipient of such activities. It has been argued that a mild degree of sadomasochistic behaviour should be regarded as abnormal only when it consistently provides the main focus of a sexual relationship, and where sex cannot be enjoyed in its absence. It is unequivocally a problem either when one partner does not wish to take part, or where the sadistic or masochistic activities become dangerous.

Male sexual variations

Not uncommonly a woman will present to her doctor complaining directly or indirectly about her partner's sexual behaviour or desires because in her opinion these are abnormal. The behaviour may be of a kind which many couples ordinarily include in their lovemaking, such as orogenital sex, or anal intercourse, but sometimes the source of concern will be a sexual variation such as fetishism, sadomasochism, or homosexuality. Where this is so, it is crucial to try to see the partner and discuss this with him, not moralistically, but with the intention of helping the couple come to an arrangement that suits them both. Sometimes the woman can be helped, if she wishes, to accept the practice; in other cases it may be possible to encourage the man to restrict his interest in the variation to masturbatory activity or to fantasy alone. Sometimes the sexual variation seems to be maintained because of a sexual dysfunction in one or other partner and therefore this should be the focus of treatment.

CAUSES OF SEXUAL DYSFUNCTION

In most cases there are multiple causes for sexual dysfunction. The range of possible causes is very wide but may be separated into *psychological and physical factors*.

Psychological factors

Factors which may lead to sexual dysfunction can usefully be divided into: (a) *remote factors*; (b) *precipitants*; and (c) *maintaining factors*. These will be considered separately and are summarized in Table 11.2.

Table 11.2. *Psychological causes of sexual dysfunction*

(a) *Remote factors*
Family attitudes to sexuality
Inadequate sex education
Traumatic sexual experiences
(b) *Precipitants*
Psychiatric illness
Childbirth
Infidelity
Dysfunction in the partner
Problem in the general relationship
(c) *Maintaining factors*
Anxiety
Poor communication
Lack of foreplay
Depression
Dysfunction in the partner
Poor sexual information
Problem in the general relationship

(a) *Remote factors*

These are factors arising out of experiences early in life which either made a person vulnerable to developing a sexual problem at a later date or actually caused a sexual dysfunction to develop at that stage. Remote factors usually operate by leading to vulnerability rather than directly causing a sexual dysfunction. Such factors typically occur in three areas of early experience: family attitudes to sexuality, sex education, and traumatic sexual experiences.

Family attitudes to sexuality. The attitudes to which a person is exposed during early development can have a profound effect on later sexual adjustment. In many families, sex is never discussed and to the children this can imply that sex is a taboo subject and must be in some way wrong or shameful. In other families, negative attitudes towards sex may be expressed openly. For example a mother may tell her daughter that sex is a chore that must be undertaken in order to please her partner. Either type of experience is likely to make a young woman feel guilty about her sexual desires or enjoyment, and may contribute to the development of sexual dysfunction. Attitudes which suggest that sex is dirty or shameful are likely to lead to difficulties in arousal or orgasm difficulties. Those which suggest that lovemaking is painful may contribute to the development of vaginismus.

The following case is an example of a mother's adverse attitudes that may have been important in causing a subsequent problem for her daughter:

Helen's parents had frequent rows and separated when she was in her early teens. She lived with her mother, a tense, nagging woman who had instructed Helen carefully from an early age in the 'facts of life', while conveying an idea of sex as something joyless and mechanical. When Helen began to go out with boys she repeatedly warned her to 'be careful', and a few years later Helen got engaged and allowed her fiancé to persuade her to make love, it was her mother who first detected Helen's pregnancy. Helen had enjoyed lovemaking before marriage, but after the baby was born (after a difficult delivery), she enjoyed it no longer; she came easily to climax but was overcome by guilt afterwards. She enjoyed foreplay with her husband but would rarely agree to go on to intercourse.

Inadequate sex education.   Inadequate or poor information about sexuality is a very important factor in the development of sexual dysfunction. For many people, especially those now of middle or older age, sex education has been either woefully inadequate or entirely lacking. Such information as they possess is likely to be based instead on 'dirty' jokes heard during childhood and adolescence, or discussion with other children whose information may have been equally inadequate. This can lead to serious misinformation, and particularly to those incorrect beliefs which have been termed *sexual myths*. Some examples of these are given in Table 11.3. Belief in such myths can lead to false expectations concern-

Table 11.3. *Some common sexual myths*

1. A man always wants and is always ready to have sex
2. Sex must only occur at the instigation of the man
3. Any woman who initiates sex is immoral
4. Masturbation by either sex is dirty or harmful.
5. Sex equals intercourse: anything else does not really count
6. When a man gets an erection it is bad for him not to use it to get an orgasm very soon
7. Sex should always be natural and spontaneous: thinking or talking about it spoils it
8. All physical contact must lead to intercourse
9. Men should not express their feelings
10. Any man ought to know how to give pleasure to any woman
11. Sex is really good only when partners have orgasms simultaneously
12. If people love each other they will know how to enjoy sex together
13. Partners in a sexual relationship instinctively know what the other partner thinks or wants
14. Married partners with a good sexual relationship never masturbate.
15. If a man loses his erection it means he does not find his partner attractive
16. It is wrong to have fantasies during intercourse

ing sexuality and therefore may cause dysfunction because of the anxiety that results. Lack of knowledge about sexual anatomy (e.g. the position of the clitoris, or even that it exists) can likewise lead to sexual dysfunction. Knowledge of sexuality is likely to be particularly poor with regard that of the opposite sex. This may mean that a person does not know how to provide a partner with adequate stimulation.

Traumatic sexual experiences. Although there seems little doubt that unpleasant sexual experiences can make a woman vulnerable to developing a sexual problem, the frequency of this occurrence is uncertain. Some sexual experiences, such as incest, are relatively common, and, although often reported in the histories of patients who suffer dysfunction, seem likely also to have been experienced by many people who subsequently develop very satisfactory sexual relationships. Experiences probably more likely to lead to problems later on are those involving force or pain (especially sexual assault and rape), and those which, out of innocence, have been enjoyed at the time but lead to guilt later on when the girl realizes that the activity was taboo (e.g father–daughter incest).

As with the other remote factors, the extent to which such experiences lead to sexual dysfunction will often depend upon events which occur later, and particularly upon the type of relationships which are established. Some women have very adverse early experiences in terms of family attitudes, sex education, or early sexual relations, yet enjoy highly satisfactory sexual relationships in adulthood.

(b) Precipitants

These are numerous and only some of the more common ones (listed in Table 11.2) will be dealt with here. Psychiatric disorder, as well as physical illness and medication, which can be particularly important precipitants, are discussed later.

Childbirth. Sexual problems in women are particularly likely to develop after childbirth, especially after the birth of a second or subsequent baby. Most women experience a decline in sexual interest and activity in the later stages of pregnancy and during the early puerperium. A number of factors may then inhibit the return of sexual interest which normally occurs during the three months after childbirth (p. 253).

Infidelity. Discovery of her partner's infidelity may cause a woman to lose interest in continuing a sexual relationship with him, or infidelity on her own part may cause loss of interest because of anxiety resulting from guilt, or simply because her other sexual relationship is more rewarding. Sometimes a woman first discovers that she has a sexual problem, or that she has one only with her current partner, when she encounters a new partner who is perhaps more knowledgeable or sensitive than her regular one. This is illustrated in the following case example:

Sally and George had difficulties from the beginning of their marriage, mainly because of his premature ejaculation and her lack of enjoyment of sex. In the fourth year of the marriage they began to attend an infertility clinic where it was discovered that George had a moderately low sperm count. The sexual difficulty was not picked up then, nor when Sally became depressed and went into a psychiatric hospital for a month. After this they separated, and Sally had an affair with an older man. With him she discovered that she enjoyed sex and was orgasmic. A year later she and George decided to live together again, and at this point she came to her doctor to ask for help with their sexual difficulties.

Dysfunction in the partner.   Clearly where the male partner either already has, or develops, a sexual problem this may cause the woman herself to suffer sexual dysfunction. For example, failure of orgasm or loss of interest in sex in a woman are often associated with premature ejaculation or erectile impotence in her partner. In such cases it is important to determine which dysfunction developed first because that should usually be the initial focus of treatment.

Problems in the general relationship.   Deterioration in the general relationship between a woman and man often, although by no means always, leads to problems in their sexual relationship. Where the partners' affection for each other has declined or disappeared then the sexual relationship is almost certain to be disrupted. Distinguishing between a sexual dysfunction which has resulted in general relationship difficulties and one which is symptomatic of problems in the general relationship is one of the most important tasks in the assessment of sexual dysfunction.

(c) Maintaining factors

It is the factors perpetuating a sexual problem which are most important for treatment purposes because only these perpetuating or maintaining factors are directly amenable to modification. Recognition of the remote factors and precipitants can provide the doctor with an understanding of the disorder, and explanations to the patient on this basis may be therapeutic in the sense of helping the patient see that the problem is explicable. However, one cannot change events that have already occurred; one can only try to deal with the consequences of such events. The following are some of the more common maintaining factors (listed in Table 11.2).

Anxiety.   This is the main factor underlying most sexual problems. Anxiety may be due to a wide range of causes, including sexual inhibitions, poor self-image, fear of failure, fear of pain, a specific phobia concerning vaginal penetration, and ignorance. Whatever the cause of the anxiety, it can affect sexual function by leading to avoidance, by causing lack of drive, by inhibiting arousal, or by preventing orgasm. Some women clearly recognize that they become anxious during sex. Others may notice a sense of detachment from the sexual activity, almost as if the woman had become an uninvolved observer. This experience has been termed 'spectatoring' by Masters and Johnson (1970).

Poor communication. If a woman fails to let her partner know about her sexual needs and anxieties it is very likely that difficulties will result. In addition, partners often become less communicative about sex once a problem begins, thus making the situation very much worse. This is illustrated in the following case example:

Andrew and Jackie were in their 50s when they came for help. They had married in their 20s, having known each other for a while before that. Sex was always enjoyable for Andrew; for Jackie it was less good at first, but improved as the years went by. Neither had ever read any books about sex, or discussed sex at all with friends; their lovemaking was simple and straightforward. About four years before they presented, Andrew came under a lot of stress at work. He became very tired, and on a couple of occasions he lost his erection. Jackie was upset but did not know how to help him, and Andrew refused to talk about it. On holiday things improved a little, but gradually Andrew's interest in sex declined and he found his erections becoming more transient. He became irritable if Jackie made tentative advances to him, and began to cut off all affectionate physical contact with her. Jackie felt very hurt and rejected, and dealt with this, as she had done with similar feelings in her rather neglected childhood, by withdrawing into silence.

When communication is impaired there is a danger that each partner will try to guess what the other is thinking, and this is likely to lead to further problems due to incorrect guesses. Two 'sexual myths' are likely to aggravate this situation. The first myth assumes that men should know all about sex and especially should know 'how to handle a woman', the implication being, that if the man does not, he is not a proper man. The second myth assumes that people who love each other, instinctively know what the other thinks and feels. On the basis of this myth, where communication is already hampered, people may begin to think 'He (or she) doesn't understand what I feel, he doesn't say what I need to hear; it must be because he doesn't want to, because he doesn't love me'.

Lack of foreplay. A sexual problem, such as impaired sexual arousal, orgasmic dysfunction, or vaginismus, may well be caused and also persist because there is little or no foreplay by the man. This may of course be due to ignorance on the partner's part, especially about the longer amount of foreplay required by many women (although not at all times) in order to become aroused compared with men. In addition, where a problem has developed it is very common for the amount of foreplay to decline because one or other partner encourages this. Thus a woman who has lost interest in sex may hurry her partner through the sexual act because she knows it is not going to be enjoyable for her and so she would prefer to get it over with quickly.

Depression. Loss of interest in sex is usually found in patients who develop depression, and may bring additional distress to the patient through the guilt she feels over the loss of affectionate feelings towards her partner. It is important to reassure such a patient that these are normal symptoms of depression, and that her interest in sex will return as her depression lifts, although libido is often one of the last things to be restored to normal.

Other factors mentioned already, as remote antecedants or precipitants, can also, if they persist, help to maintain the dysfunction.

Physical factors

Physical disorders and medication can have very profound effects on sexual function. They may directly interfere with physiological or anatomical mechanisms involved in sexual response, or cause secondary psychological reactions leading to sexual dysfunction, or, and not uncommonly, they may disrupt sexual function due to a combination of direct and psychological effects. Thus a woman who initially finds sexual intercourse very uncomfortable after a gynaecological operation may subsequently lack interest in sex because of secondary fear, in spite of complete healing at the surgical site.

The physical disorders and surgical procedures which may lead to sexual problems are listed in Table 11.4 and briefly discussed in the text. The reader who wishes to obtain more detailed information is referred to Kolodny, Masters, and Johnson (1979).

Table 11.4. *Some medical disorders and surgical procedures which may cause sexual dysfunction*

(a) *Medical disorders*	
Endocrine	diabetes
	hyperthyroidism; myxoedema
	Addison's disease
Cardiovascular	myocardial infarction
	angina pectoris
Respiratory	chronic obstructive airways disease; asthma
Arthritic	osteoarthritis
	rheumatoid arthritis
	Sjögren's syndrome
Neurological	pelvic autonomic neuropathy
	spinal cord disease or trauma
Renal	dialysis
Gynaecological	vaginitis
	pelvic infections
	endometriosis
(b) *Surgical procedures*	
Mastectomy	
Colostomy and ileostomy	
Gynaecological	oophorectomy
	episiotomy
	vaginal repair of prolapse
Amputation	

(a) Medical disorders

Endocrine. Much is known about the effects of *diabetes* on male sexual function, but very little about the corresponding effects on female sexuality. What evidence is available suggests that diabetes may lead to failure of orgasm in some women, and difficulty in vaginal lubrication in others. In addition, recurrent vaginal infections may also complicate diabetes and interfere with sexual activity. Nevertheless, it is probable (in men at least) that psychological factors are at least as important as physical factors in the sexual dysfunction associated with diabetes, and since psychological factors are amenable to treatment, there is no need to approach such problems in a defeatist spirit.

Both *hyperthyroidism* and *myxoedema* may affect sexual function, the former because of anxiety and irritability, and the latter because of tiredness and menorrhagia. Reduced activity of the *adrenal glands*, as in Addison's disease, often affects sexual interest and performance, presumably due to impairment of androgen production.

Cardiovascular. At present there is a scarcity of information about the effects of *myocardial infarction* on female sexuality. However, it seems that many women reduce the frequency of their sexual activity after a heart attack. As with men who have had heart attacks, this may be because of an unfounded fear of precipitating further attacks. Depression, poor self-esteem, and medication may be other factors. Sexual difficulties, including erectile impotence or fear of resuming sexual activity, commonly occur in men after heart attacks. This is likely to cause sexual problems for their partners, who in addition may feel guilty about continuing to experience sexual desire. *Angina pectoris* may also limit sexual enjoyment if chest pain or palpitations occur during sexual activity. Prophylactic use of a nitrate preparation or a beta-blocking agent can help prevent these symptoms.

Respiratory. Severe chronic respiratory disease is likely to inhibit sexual activity because of limitations on sexual positions which can be tolerated, especially the 'missionary' position. Occasionally patients with *asthma* repeatedly experience asthmatic episodes during sex.

Arthritic. Joint pain, especially if this arises in the hip joints, may severely limit a woman's ability to enjoy or even participate in sexual activity. Chronic pain is likely to lead to tiredness and loss of interest in sex. In *Sjögren's syndrome* there may be impairment of vaginal lubrication.

Neurological. As sexual response is mediated largely through neural pathways it is obvious that disruption of such pathways will affect sexual performance. Thus damage to the pelvic autonomic nerves (e.g. through neuropathy, malignant disease, or surgery), or the spinal cord, is likely to interfere with genital swelling and lubrication, and orgasm. Further discussion of the effects of spinal cord damage occurs later (p. 255).

Renal.   Difficulties in becoming sexually aroused are found in some women on *renal dialysis*. This may in part be due to tiredness and depression, and also to electrolyte and hormonal disturbances.

Gynaecological.   Obviously many gynaecological disorders may be associated with sexual problems. Examples include *vaginitis*, due to infection (e.g. thrush) or oestrogen deficiency, which may cause soreness during sexual intercourse, and *pelvic inflammatory disease or endometriosis* which can cause pain on deep penile thrusting.

(b) Surgical procedures

Several surgical procedures in women are likely to affect sexual function (Table 11.4); some because they interfere directly with organs and structures involved in sexual activity and response; others because of their psychological effects.

Examples of surgical procedures which may cause organic damage are gynaecological operations such as *oophorectomy*, following which reduction in circulating oestrogens will impair vaginal lubrication, and *episiotomy* and *vaginal repair of prolapse*. Episiotomy, if poorly sutured, may cause tenderness or tightness of the introitus, and vaginal repair may have a similar effect if the repair is unsatisfactory. Finally, *amputation*, especially if a leg has been removed, can cause considerable mechanical difficulties during sexual activity.

Several surgical procedures are likely to have psychological consequences which may profoundly affect a woman's ability to enjoy her sex life. A common psychological sequel is an altered self-image leading to a decreased sense of sexual attractiveness. This is particularly likely after mastectomy. At least one-third of women who have had a breast removed suffer severe long-standing deterioration in their sexual relationships, and in many cases sex is abandoned altogether. Part of the problem may be revulsion experienced by the woman's partner. Similar impairment of self-image may occur following amputation, or after colostomy or ileostomy, where, in addition, concern about possible odour or fear that discomfort or damage might result from sexual intercourse are likely to complicate the picture. Although hysterectomy has been regarded as being associated with a high incidence of sexual problems, in a recent systematic prospective study this was not found to be so. Indeed, some of the women studied experienced an improvement in their sexual relations. Depression, which commonly occurs following some operations (e.g. mastectomy), is likely to be an added factor contributing to impairment of sexual function following surgery.

Table 11.5. *Some drugs which may affect female sexuality*

Anticholinergics (e.g. probanthine)
Anticonvulsants (phenytoin; carbamazepine; phenobarbitone)
Antihypertensives and diuretics (methyldopa; beta-blockers; bendrofluazide)
Anti-inflammatory drugs (indomethacin)
Hormones (oral contraception; steroids)
Hypnotics and sedatives (barbiturates; benzodiazepines)
Major tranquillizers (especially thioridazine)
Alcohol
Opiates

Effects of medication

Unfortunately there is a paucity of information concerning the effects of medication on female sexuality. Largely by extrapolation from what is known about the effects in men, it seems that several types of medication may have important consequences for sexual interest and performance in women and that one should always enquire about medication when a woman presents complaining of impaired sexual desire or arousal, or difficulty in achieving orgasm.

The drugs which may affect female sexuality are listed in Table 11.5. *Anticholinergic agents* may interfere with vaginal engorgement and lubrication. It is possible that *anticonvulsants* may in some cases have an adverse effect on a woman's sexual interest because of their induction of hormone-binding globulin which binds testosterone and therefore leads to a reduction in circulating free testosterone. Although not proven, it is worth considering as a cause of impaired libido where the decline in interest has developed after a long period of anticonvulsant therapy. *Antihypertensives* which act centrally (e.g. methyldopa) can reduce sexual desire in men, though the effect on women is uncertain. The same applies to *anti-inflammatory agents* such as indomethacin. Other drugs used to treat hypertension, such as beta-blockers (e.g. propranolol) and diuretics (bendrofluazide) are known to have erectile impotence as a major side effect.

Considerable controversy has surrounded the possible role of *oral contraception* in causing sexual dysfunction. A higher incidence of reduced sexual drive was found in contraceptive pill users than non-users in the Royal College of General Practitioners (1974) study. Sometimes this reduced libido may be secondary to depression occurring as a side effect of the pill. In some cases, psychological reactions to using contraception (e.g. unacknowledged wish for pregnancy) might also be relevant. It is worth emphasizing that most women using oral contraception experience no significant changes in their libido, and some report enhancement of their enjoyment of sex.

The chronic use of *barbiturates* may impair sexual interest. Because the *major tranquillizers*, especially thioridazine, can have profound effects on male sexual performance, this suggests that they may also interfere with female sexual response. Although *benzodiazepines* (e.g. diazepam) are sometimes prescribed as treatment for sexual problems related to anxiety, it seems likely that they may have an adverse effect in some patients because of their tendency to cause drowsiness. While *alcohol* is likely to enhance sexual desire and reduce inhibitions when used in moderation, chronic alcohol abuse often leads to loss of interest in sex because of its depressant effects, and to erectile difficulties associated with autonomic neuropathy. *Opiate* abuse often causes sexual dysfunction in both men and women.

If it is thought that a particular drug is having a deleterious effect on a woman's sexual interest then it will be necessary to weigh up the pros and cons of stopping or changing the medication and the likely effect on the physical or psychological condition for which drug has been prescribed. Where an effective alternative drug is available this might be tried. However, it is most important to be alert to the fact that changes in sexual interest or enjoyment are often blamed on medication when other factors, especially those of an interpersonal nature, are the real cause.

Some forms of medication can improve sexuality. *Androgens* administered for medical conditions can enhance sexual interest, and some attempt has been made to incorporate these drugs in the treatment of women with impaired sexual desire, though results of studies are equivocal. *Oestrogens* administered for menopausal symptoms may improve sexual arousability because of their beneficial effects on the post-menopausal vaginal mucosa.

HOW TO ASSESS PATIENTS WITH SEXUAL PROBLEMS

Help or advice should *never* be offered to anyone presenting with a sexual problem without first making a careful assessment and coming to a clear understanding about what the problem is. Often the problem is very different from that suggested by the initial complaint. Sometimes the woman may believe that it is she who has the problem when in fact it is primarily her partner's, so that, for example, a woman whose husband has premature ejaculation may complain to her doctor of inability to achieve orgasm during intercourse.

Assessment of a sexual problem has in itself a very important therapeutic function:

1. It can begin to clarify and make intelligible a problem that, in the patient's mind, is obscure and associated with much shame, bewilderment, and suffering.

2. It demonstrates that it is both respectable and feasible to talk effec-

tively about sex, and that it may therefore be possible for the woman to talk to her partner about it too.

3. It demonstrates that sexual difficulty is regarded by doctors as a legitimate worry, and one that they are trained to deal with. The doctor can make it clear that the problem is neither extraordinary nor blame-worthy, and that it can be helped.

4. It offers an opportunity for mistaken fears and beliefs to be dis-pelled. Much anxiety and self-blame is based on half truths, muddled information, and 'sexual myths' (see Table 11.3).

Unfortunately many doctors have not received training in taking a sex-ual history. Two general points are important here. First, it is essential for the doctor to feel comfortable about the procedure, in order to concen-trate on dispelling the patient's embarrassment and anxiety, and also so that accurate information can be obtained without the doctor feeling obliged to side-step any issues because of her or his own embarrassment. Secondly, there is a difficulty about the words used to discuss the prob-lem. Doctors feel comfortable using medical terminology, but many patients will not comprehend words like lubrication, ejaculation, and so on; on the other hand, colloquial words do not always have a precise enough meaning, and also they may seem shocking or inappropriate to the patient when spoken in a medical consultation. Often the only remedy to this problem is to discuss the difficulty openly with the patient, and then to come to a gradual agreement on the terms to be used in the interview, by translating frequently between the technical and the colloquial terms, and allowing the patient to select and to become accustomed to using the words that she prefers. For example, the doctor might say 'ejaculation is the technical word for the moment when the seminal fluid comes out of the end of the penis. In ordinary speech people often call that "coming", and they may call the seminal fluid "spunk". Do you know what I mean by that? Which words would you like us to use? . . . All right, now you were telling me that when your husband ejaculates, he . . .'.

There are other considerations, applicable to interviewing in general, that can help to make the interview less stressful for the patient, and more productive of information. Thus, it is often a good idea to proceed from 'less painful' to 'more painful' topics, and to switch temporarily to less painful topics if the patient needs to recover herself at any time later in the interview. Examples of 'less painful' areas are: simple factual in-formation (times, places, events); information about other people; and happy or successful aspects of the patient's life. Examples of 'more pain-ful' areas may be: details of the sexual difficulty; the patient's own feel-ings, and any discussion of marital or family tension. It is worth trying to use a judicious mixture of 'open-ended' questions that allow the patient to tell her story in her own words, uncontaminated by the doctor's presup-positions, and more 'closed', detailed questions that allow precise in-

formation to be established while relieving the patient of some of the burden of naming embarrassing things. Examples of open-ended questions
are 'Tell me more about the problem' and 'How did you feel when that
happened?' A closed question might be: 'I think you are telling me that
you feel that your vagina doesn't become wet enough, so that it feels uncomfortable when your husband wants to put his penis in. Is that what
you mean? Or did you mean something different?'

It is particularly helpful to ask the patient to recall a *specific* occasion,
as recent as possible, on which the sexual difficulty arose. If the patient
can describe such an occasion, she can be asked to give a minute-by-
minute account, which should include an idea of how her partner responded to anything she did, of her response to his actions, of her
thoughts and what she imagined he was thinking at the time. Such a detailed account of a single episode, which is probably best obtained later in
the interview when the patient is more relaxed, is much more informative
than any general statements about the nature of the problem that the
patient may have worked out for herself. Having established a picture of
one occasion, the doctor should then ask whether other occasions have
followed the same pattern, or, if not, how they have differed.

When a patient appears embarrassed it can be helpful if the doctor ac-
knowledges this and then explains that she will get more confident with
time. It is crucial not to side-step issues because they are embarrassing;
they may be central to the problem.

If the woman has a partner and he is relevant to her difficulty it is important to try to see him. Apart from the possible necessity of involving
him in subsequent treatment, the information obtained from him may
cast a very different light on the problem. When a woman says she doubts
if her husband will attend, the doctor might consider dropping him a note
to encourage him, provided the patient gives her permission.

History taking

The main points to be covered in carrying out a detailed assessment of a
patient with a sexual problem are contained in the Appendix to this chapter (p. 258). A systematic assessment of this kind will take at least three-
quarters of an hour and therefore might be spread over two or three
interviews. Certainly a detailed assessment is required if the doctor is considering treating the patient with some form of sex therapy. For other
purposes a briefer assessment might be sufficient. If the doctor is short of
time on the day when a woman first mentions that she has a sexual problem, she could be asked to return for a longer and more leisurely interview later. However, every effort should be made to ensure that at the
first interview she has said enough and has received enough encouragement for her to want to attend for a second longer interview.

In making a *brief assessment* the doctor should cover the following points: (i) what is the precise nature of the problem?; (ii) what is the effect of the problem on the woman and her partner?; (iii) is there a major problem in the couple's general relationship?; (iv) has the patient had a satisfactory sexual relationship in the past?; (v) is the patient adequately informed about sex?; (vi) is there any medical or psychiatric condition which might contribute to, or cause the problem?; (vii) is the patient on any medication and what is her level of alcohol consumption?; (viii) what changes would the patient like to achieve in her sexual adjustment?

It will be clear that even a brief assessment must be far from cursory if the doctor is to obtain sufficient information to decide what help to provide, including whether or not to refer for specialist treatment.

MANAGEMENT OF SEXUAL PROBLEMS

The variety of approaches available for dealing with sexual problems can be separated conveniently into two categories, distinguished by the intensity and scope of treatment. These are (a) *brief counselling*, and (b) *sex therapy*. The first category, which includes the provision of simple advice and information, should be within the scope of all general practitioners. Some general practitioners will also want to practise sex therapy, in which a detailed step-by-step programme is used to help an individual or couple. However, this requires special training and is fairly time-consuming so that the majority of general practitioners may not wish to carry this out themselves.

The important therapeutic function of the assessment interview must be re-emphasized here. Often a patient or couple will experience a great deal of relief from simply having the opportunity to talk about the problem and from the reassurance that the doctor can provide during the assessment. It is not always necessary to provide advice at this stage; often it is better to ask the patient(s) to return a few days later, when the doctor will have had time to think further about the problem and the best means of tackling it, and the patient(s) will have had time to discover whether they need any further help.

In this section we consider the two categories of management in relation to couples with sexual dysfunction. We then discuss treatment-of the individual woman without a partner, the management of problems related to sexual variations, and the referral of patients for specialist treatment. Finally, management of problems associated with rape and incest are described.

Treatment of couples with sexual dysfunction

(a) *Brief counselling*
This is most appropriate for those problems that arise from inadequate or muddled information, and for those which involve anxieties about sexual

behaviour of a particular kind (e.g. oral sex) or at a particular time (e.g. pregnancy; after the menopause). Usually such problems can be managed over the course of only a few consultations. Sometimes only one consultation will be necessary, although the doctor should always try to assess subsequently whether the counselling has been effective.

Brief counselling can include the following strategies:

(i) *Provision of information.*   As ignorance or misinformation are often shared by a couple, both partners should, if possible, be present when information is to be given by the doctor, so that they can both question it at the time, and discuss it together afterwards. The doctor can provide accurate information on sexual anatomy (especially using pictures), can describe what happens during sexual arousal in either sex, can convey an idea of the range of normal biological variation in anatomy and physiology, and the frequency (and therefore 'normality') of different types of sexual behaviour, such as oral sex or homosexual contacts during adolescence. The patient might also be recommended suitable reading material (David Delvin's (1974) *Book of love* being an excellent example).

(ii) *Advice.*   For example the doctor may give advice on the following: how to engage in more enjoyable foreplay, suitable positions for sexual intercourse during pregnancy or recovery from a physical illness, and means whereby a couple can come to a compromise over their differing levels of sexual drive. Advice should only be given after careful appraisal of what is likely to be acceptable for the couple.

(iii) *Permission-giving.*   Sometimes a patient feels needlessly guilty about some aspect of sexual behaviour (such as masturbation or the occurrence of sexual fantasy). Where such feelings are the legacy of repressive parental attitudes, they can be countered by the doctor adopting a different parental role; helping the patient to accept that the activity in question is not harmful or wicked and is shared by most other ordinary people. However, this must be done with caution and respect, to avoid putting pressure on patients to accept a value system that is alien to them.

(b) Sex therapy

Masters and Johnson (1970) revolutionized the treatment of couples with sexual problems when they introduced their brief but intensive approach to sex therapy. This is based on the rationale that although sexual problems may arise from a wide range of causes, some of which are rooted in the past, nevertheless the problems are maintained by factors which operate in the present, and therefore are amenable to modification by techniques focused on present occurrences and feelings.

The methods of Masters and Johnson have proved very effective, with some modifications, within the setting of the National Health Service.

This modified approach will be summarized here; anyone wishing to use the method will need to consult a fuller account (e.g. Jehu 1979) and obtain appropriate training.

After full assessment of each partner individually, the couple is presented with a *formulation* of the problem, setting out its nature, the remote antecedents, precipitants, and maintaining factors that have contributed to it. The purpose of the formulation is to provide the couple with a better understanding of their problem and to provide a rationale for the treatment approach. The principal components of the treatment are (i) a graduated behavioural approach; (ii) counselling; (iii) education.

(i) Graduated behavioural programme. This programme has two purposes. The first is to provide a method by means of which couples can establish or re-establish the confidence and freedom in their sexual contact with each other that will allow unhindered sexual response to occur. The second is to assist the therapist and the couple to identify precisely the factors that are contributing to maintenance of the problem. In essence the programme consists of a graduated series of clearly defined tasks in touching and being touched by each other in specific ways, so that the difficulty is broken down into manageable steps, in which room is made for discussion of obstacles arising at any stage. Where appropriate, additional specific techniques are used to tackle particular kinds of dysfunction.

The couple is first asked to agree to undertake the programme which includes an initial ban both on sexual intercourse and on touching of the genital areas and the woman's breasts. Instructions for *sensate focus* are then provided. The partners are asked to find a suitable time when they can concentrate on this exercise in a relaxed fashion. The exercise consists of each partner taking turns at caressing the other over all areas of the body, apart from the 'no-go' areas already mentioned. The purpose of this is for each to learn to accept pleasure from the other, for each to find out how and where the partner likes being caressed, and to help the partners feel relaxed and comfortable with each other without striving towards arousal. Through this they can begin to learn to communicate on sexual matters, and advice specifically addressed to this issue will also be given by the therapist.

When this stage is satisfactorily established, the couple is asked to progress to *genital sensate focus*, during which both the genitals and breasts are included in caressing, but the emphasis is still on discovery of each other and on improving communication. Subsequently the couple moves from individual caressing, turn and turn about, to simultaneous mutual pleasuring. The next stage is a gradual progression to sexual intercourse via an intermediate stage of *vaginal containment* in which penetration occurs but there is no movement.

Specific techniques are used for particular types of dysfunction, only some of which can be mentioned here. Finger exploration of the vagina in a series of graded steps by both partners is suggested where the woman has vaginismus. Masturbation exercises are often advised where the woman is unable to achieve orgasm. Kegel's vaginal muscle exercises (as advised for women following childbirth) are useful for both vaginismus and orgasmic dysfunction. The 'stop-start' or 'squeeze' techniques may be suggested where the man has premature ejaculation. In both of these the woman provides her partner with intermittent penile stimulation according to his level of sexual arousal. In the squeeze technique she also applies firm pressure with her fingers to the base of the glans penis when her partner feels he is near to ejaculation. Masturbation exercises are also suggested in the treatment of ejaculatory failure.

(*ii*) *Counselling.*   As the couple move through the graduated programme, discussion at each stage enables both the therapist and the couple to get a clearer idea of the factors maintaining the problem. In addition, at some stage almost every couple encounters a block to progress, which yields further valuable information. In order to help modify the factors maintaining the sexual problem and particularly to overcome blocks to progress, a considerable amount of counselling will be necessary. The components of such counselling include the following:

(a) helping the partners re-consider *attitudes* they hold and perhaps have never questioned (e.g. that sexual activity should always be the responsibility of the male partner, with the woman playing a passive role). As discussed in relation to brief counselling, the therapist should avoid imposing values on patients, but should help them to look at attitudes which clearly obstruct their progress towards the goals they have chosen for themselves.

(b) *confronting* patients when there appears to be a discrepancy between their stated aims and what they are actually doing in practice. Quite often a couple say that they are keen to improve their sexual relationship but in fact fail to carry out the therapist's instructions.

(c) identifying and discussing *feelings* originating from other areas of the relationship but finding expression through the sexual relationship.

(d) *permission-giving*, as when a therapist encourages the partners to carry out sexual activity which they had not thought of, or regarded as taboo (such as masturbation) but which is likely to help overcome their problem.

(e) providing *reassurance*.

(*iii*) *Education.*   The educational aspects of sex therapy are similar to those involved in brief counselling. It is often advisable to devote part of an early treatment session to providing simple information about sexual anatomy and response.

The duration of sex therapy will vary from couple to couple but on average approximately 12 sessions of treatment are required. Although Masters and Johnson use male and female co-therapists to treat couples, it seems that one therapist is just as effective.

The results of sex therapy originally reported by Masters and Johnson (1970) have proved to be far superior to those obtained by other workers. However, results obtained elsewhere are far from disappointing. Thus, in clinical practice in this country (Bancroft and Coles 1976; Hawton 1982) it appears that two-thirds of couples derive considerable benefits from treatment. Vaginismus and premature ejaculation respond particularly well. At present there is a dearth of information regarding long-term outcome of sex therapy.

Treatment of women without partners

It may happen that a woman will present asking for help, but have no partner, or be unwilling to involve her current partner in treatment. Fortunately there is much that can be done to help such women, especially those with vaginismus or orgasmic dysfunction. For some such women brief advice can be given, e.g. concerning the use of a vibrator. For others, more detailed graduated programmes will be necessary.

A woman with vaginismus may first be asked to become familiar with her vaginal anatomy, perhaps while in the bath. Subsequently, after a vaginal examination by the doctor, the woman will be encouraged to explore her vagina with a finger in order to become more comfortable with vaginal penetration. She can also be taught the Kegel exercises.

In orgasmic dysfunction, the woman will be encouraged to learn to masturbate. During the course of such treatment she may require help to modify her attitudes to masturbation. She will also need advice on ways of subsequently showing a partner how to stimulate her appropriately. The results of such treatment of orgasmic problems are usually very good.

Treatment of problems related to sexual variations

It will be rare for the general practitioner to be called upon to counsel a woman with established homosexual interest. Most such women do not feel they need help. However, a general practitioner who is asked for help by a homosexual woman who wishes to come to terms with her sexual interest might be best advised to refer her to an organization such as Campaign for Homosexual Equality (CHE) which has its own counselling service.

The female transsexual who asks for help will invariably require referal to a specialist.

When a woman complains about her husband's deviant sexual interest it will be most important to try to see the husband and to find out whether he is concerned about his sexual interest and whether he wishes to do anything about it. If he does, specialist referral will usually be necessary.

Referral of patients for specialist treatment

Only a rough guide can be given as to which patients with sexual problems should be referred for specialist attention. This will depend in part on how well-equipped the general practitioner feels to deal with the problem. Assuming the general practitioner does not wish to undertake sex therapy, referral will be indicated for women who present with a sexual problem that appears to be the result of significant early experiences and where simple advice and reassurance do not have any effect. This applies to any type of sexual dysfunction. It is also particularly worth trying to arrange treatment where the man has premature ejaculation, because the results of appropriate treatment are very good.

Before initiating referral the partner should be seen if possible to assess his attitudes to the problem and particularly whether he is willing to do anything about it. A brief assessment, along the lines suggested earlier, should be made for both partners before making the referral. A physical examination should be carried out where indicated. This applies particularly to vaginismus and erectile impotence. Advice on what is likely to happen when the couple see the specialist may help to reassure them.

Sometimes a couple may say they would prefer not to be referred at present. They may already have been helped by their discussion of the problem with their doctor and therefore referral might be delayed a while to see whether this was enough to allow them to make further progress unaided.

The general practitioner will need to know who runs the nearest sexual dysfunction clinic. Unfortunately the availability of such clinics varies greatly from area to area. Some Marriage Guidance counsellors are now specially trained in sex therapy; likewise a number of family planning doctors undertake such training; and some sex therapy clinics are based in psychiatric hospitals. The doctor might enquire from any of these agencies in the area.

Rape

The main possible *physical* after-effects of rape are: damage to pelvic organs and to the rest of the body; venereal infection; and pregnancy. Examination of a raped woman by a police surgeon for forensic purposes may not necessarily deal with these aspects. Therefore the woman may need the help of her general practitioner in detecting and dealing with possible infection or pregnancy.

Many cases of rape do not come to the notice of the police. However, a woman who wishes to report that she has been raped can be given useful advice by her general practitioner on how best to go about this. She should expect to be seen by a police surgeon and examined if medical evidence is needed in Court. She should not wash or change her clothing, nor have a drink or take any medication, until she has been seen by a police surgeon. As she may be asked to leave her clothes behind at the police station she should take a change of clothing with her. She may be helped if she is accompanied by a supportive friend, especially if this friend saw her soon after the incident and can give evidence to the police. Finally, she should be advised to make a note of details of the sequence of events associated with the rape to help her in making her statement to the police.

The *psychological* violation experienced by a raped woman is unfortunately often compounded by attitudes of suspicion or contempt that she may meet at medical, legal, or police hands. These attitudes, and some of the woman's own responses to the assault, arise partly as defences to the very powerful feelings aroused by the thought of rape, and partly from the myths that surround the subject. Such myths include the belief that a woman can always resist rape if she really wants to, that women lead men on and falsely cry rape afterwards, that respectable girls do not get raped, and that a woman with sexual experience is not bothered by being raped. The truth is very different, as research (chiefly in America) has shown.

The most immediate psychological need of a raped woman is for sympathetic, informed, and gentle handling. Early support is thought to be very important in preventing long-term psychological damage, and it should be offered in a way that fosters the woman's sense of autonomy and her freedom to choose what help she wishes, so as to counter the feeling of enforced helplessness induced by rape. It is useful if those providing the initial help to the raped woman can at that early stage involve a suitable person close to her, who can then continue the support through the weeks to follow. Professional help in the long term should also be available as necessary.

The initial emotional responses to rape include severe anxiety, disruption of normal coping strategies, sleep disturbance, somatic symptoms, guilt, anger, fear of further attack, and feelings of isolation and worthlessness. There may follow a phase of superficial adjustment coupled with denial of feelings. The long-term consequences include depression, phobic anxiety, and a range of sexual problems from vaginismus to orgasmic failure. However, the incidence of such difficulties following rape is unknown. The woman is also likely to have to cope with the feelings of those around her, and particularly of her sexual partner, who may succeed in being supportive but who may be overwhelmed by his own feelings of rage, helplessness, or revulsion. These feelings may result in sexual problems (especially erectile difficulty) for the partner.

In some areas, self-help groups for the victims of rape have been formed, with the object of providing emotional support, information on medical and legal matters, companionship at court hearings or other stressful times, and often with the additional and wider aim of educating the general public and encouraging a change in attitudes. (For further information concerning rape see Kolodny, Masters, and Johnson (1979), Chapter 16.)

Incest

Incest probably occurs far more often than seems likely from official statistics based on cases reported to the police. Sibling and father–daughter relationships are the most usual forms of incest, the latter being that which most commonly comes to light. Many factors may contribute to the development of a father–daughter incestuous relationship including personality disorder and alcohol abuse in the father, marital disharmony between the parents, and collusion of the girl's mother. Often a girl is drawn into an incestuous relationship when she is too young to appreciate its implications. Only when older might she come to experience guilt and remorse about the relationship and this may have implications for her subsequent sexual adjustment.

Sometimes disclosure of the relationship and the ensuing sequelae, especially punishment of the father, appear to cause more damage to the girl than the relationship itself; her position in the family may become untenable, especially where there was collusion by the mother. Therefore the doctor who discovers such an incestuous relationship must proceed with caution. It may be possible to discuss it with the father and to warn him of his position in law (father–daughter incest is prohibited by law, whatever the girl's age). In many cases the father may be as disturbed by the existence of the relationship as is his daughter and may be willing to accept help for his own problems. In other cases, where direct intervention by the doctor has had no effect, and the girl is thought to be at serious risk, it may be appropriate for the local Social Services Department to be informed. It is the duty of a Social Services Department to investigate all cases where incest is suspected if it is thought that a child may be in moral danger and the circumstances might justify legal proceedings to protect her. The Department has a duty to inform the police, although in practice discretion is exercised in some cases. Unless there are strong indications to the contrary, the best management of incest is probably through working with the family because incest is often symptomatic of family pathology.

SEXUALITY AND SEXUAL PROBLEMS AT SPECIAL TIMES IN A WOMAN'S LIFE

There are certain times in a woman's life when sexuality is particularly likely to undergo change and these are times when sexual problems commonly occur. The most significant of these times are pregnancy and childbirth, the menopause, and older age.

(a) Pregnancy and childbirth

Although there is some variation in the findings from different studies of the changes in sexual activity during pregnancy, all studies agree that most women's sexual interest declines during the third trimester, with a consequent decline in the frequency of sexual intercourse. Reduced frequency of intercourse may also be due to physical discomfort, awkwardness, sense of loss of attractiveness and recommendations from doctors to avoid sex.

Although only limited information is available about the effects of intercourse during pregnancy, it appears that there are no specific complications of, or contraindications to, intercourse at any stage in normal pregnancy. Thus there is no evidence that coitus will cause physical damage to the fetus, or rupture the membranes, nor that orgasm might induce premature labour. Some clinicians may advise against sexual intercourse if there is a history of miscarriage, ante-partum bleeding, or pain during intercourse. Under such circumstances the doctor might recommend non-coital sex but female orgasm need not be avoided. However, orgasm should probably be avoided where there is either a history of premature deliveries or any evidence of premature labour. At present there is little scientific basis for the variety of advice that women may be given about sexual intercourse during pregnancy.

Apart from providing reassurance to the woman who is concerned about her loss of sexual interest during pregnancy, the doctor might also advise a woman about positions for sexual intercourse that are likely to be comfortable for her. These include the side-by-side and rear-entry positions.

Following childbirth, most women experience a reduction in their interest in sex, which may last for up to three months or even longer. In addition, soreness of an episiotomy scar and post-partum vaginal dryness associated with reduced levels of circulating oestrogens, particularly in breast-feeding mothers, may make intercourse uncomfortable and therefore lead to avoidance or reduced interest. The stress for both partners in adapting to their new roles as parents, the husband's possible sense of partial exclusion, and puerperal depression may all contribute to sexual difficulties. In addition, a nursing mother may feel guilty about sexual arousal that can occur with breast-feeding. Finally, previous sexual maladjustment often manifests itself as frank sexual dysfunction following childbirth.

The general practitioner can forewarn women about some of these problems and give appropriate advice if they actually occur. If post-partum vaginal dryness occurs the patient can be given an explanation and recommended to use a lubricant (such as K-Y jelly) during inter-course. Where soreness of an episiotomy scar prevents intercourse, a gradual return to non-coital sexual activity might first be recommended. It is important to reassure both women and their partners that loss of interest in sex is normal after childbirth and that it will gradually return. It is es-pecially important to encourage the partners to maintain physical contact with each other over this period. Some couples may only want a loving cuddle; in other partnerships, the wife may wish to continue caressing her husband, though not yet wishing to be caressed by him.

(b) Menopause

The onset of the menopause can provide a profound sense of liberation for some women and this may lead to enhanced interest in sex. However, in others there is a decline in libido. Whether or not the latter is hor-monally determined is uncertain. A number of other factors are likely to be operating at this time. For example, children may be about to leave home, the woman may worry that she is unattractive (especially by com-parison with an attractive daughter), the risk of developing depression is increased, and her husband may be experiencing a decline in sexual per-formance. Many post-menopausal women experience vaginal dryness due to reduction in circulating oestrogens and this may cause discomfort dur-ing intercourse.

Hormone replacement therapy, or vaginal application of hormonal cream, will benefit the vaginal dryness. Oestrogen and progestogen ther-apy do not appear to have much effect on impaired libido. There is some suggestion that testosterone administration will help restore libido in post-menopausal women but this requires further investigation. In ad-dition to hormone administration the general practitioner may be able to provide counselling, along the lines suggested earlier, which will assist the woman who is experiencing sexual difficulties. Whenever possible the partner should be included in such consultation. The management of problems of the menopause is discussed in more detail in Chapter 4.

(c) Older age

Several studies have demonstrated that the majority of women and men remain sexually active beyond the age of 60, and, depending on the availability of a partner, as many as one in five are active at 80. For women in particular, it is very often the loss of the spouse that determines the end of sexual activity.

'Sexual myths' affect the attitudes of both young and old towards sexuality in later life. These myths include the following: (i) because procreation is not possible after the menopause sexual activity should therefore cease; (ii) sex is the prerogative of the young and attractive person; (iii) sexual performance declines rapidly after middle age; (iv) the problems associated with aging preclude any interest in sexual activity. Belief in such myths may cause guilt in people who find that their sexual interest does not suddenly decline after middle age, and may contribute directly to problems such as loss of interest and impaired performance.

A number of physical and other psychological difficulties may affect the sexual life of older women. First, the physical changes which occur with normal aging, such as atrophic vaginitis, a decline in the vaginal response during sexual arousal, sagging breasts, impaired mobility and weight gain, may impair the sexual interest and performance of both the woman and her partner. In addition, those physical illnesses which are likely to impair sexual function become more common in old age. These include cerebrovascular disease, especially strokes, degenerative joint disorders, maturity-onset diabetes, thyroid dysfunction, Parkinsonism, malignant disease, especially of the breast and bowel, and amputations. In parallel with the increase in physical disorders, the numbers of women receiving medication, and the range of medication used, steadily increase with age. Some of the drugs used may have profound effects on sexuality (p. 241). Finally, psychiatric disorders, especially depression, anxiety, and dementia become more common, and all three, together with drugs used to treat them, are likely to be associated with impaired sexual interest and function.

Some of these difficulties will be amenable to brief counselling, particularly if the doctor has an understanding of sexuality during older age and is able to discuss the topic without embarrassment. Sexual dysfunction in older persons is often very amenable to sex therapy, provided the therapist is sensitive to the sexual value systems of older patients, which may be considerably more restricted than those of some younger people. Particular attention should be paid to physical aspects of therapy, including hormone replacement and the use of physical aids.

SEXUAL PROBLEMS ASSOCIATED WITH DISABLEMENT

Only in recent years have the sexual problems encountered by physically and mentally handicapped people begun to receive appropriate attention. Several factors seem to have contributed to this neglect. Firstly, some people responsible for the care of the disabled have maintained the illusion that disabled persons somehow lack sexuality. Not only is this obviously untrue but it is also apparent that as many as three-quarters of persons who are disabled encounter problems in fulfilling their sexuality. Probably this attitude stems partly from the fact that both disablement and sex are found by many people to be sensitive and difficult topics; the combination of the two therefore tends to provoke extreme discomfort which is dealt with by denial. This is reinforced by a general notion that to be sexy one must be able-bodied and attractive.

We can consider the problems of disablement in terms of (a) the woman who is disabled; (b) the woman with a disabled partner; and (c) management of sexual problems associated with disablement.

(a) Sexual problems of the disabled woman

Although most of our information about sexual problems and physical disability concerns men, it is clear that disabled women are likely to suffer just as many problems as disabled men. Several aspects of a woman's sexuality can be affected. First, her image of herself as a physically desirable individual is likely to be precarious. Secondly, her awareness of the stigma attached to sexuality of the disabled may limit her interest in sex. Thirdly, the debilitating effects of the disorder from which she suffers, or of the medication she receives for it, may impair her drive. This particularly applies to chronic painful conditions. Fourthly, the condition may interfere with her mobility; thus, for example, severe arthritis or a spinal cord lesion may make coitus difficult or impossible. Fifthly, her capacity to receive the sensory input necessary for sexual satisfaction may be limited: this is particularly likely with neurological disorders. Finally, if she is being cared for by others (whether by relatives or in an institution) it is their attitude which will determine whether she has any opportunities for sexual activity, alone or with a partner.

Some of the conditions which may cause disability and affect sexuality have already been considered (p. 238). Others deserve mention in this context. Many neurological conditions, such as multiple sclerosis and cerebral palsy, are associated with sexual problems. The woman with a complete spinal cord transection will be unable to achieve an orgasm through genital stimulation, though she may well still be capable of pregnancy. She is also likely to have problems of urinary and bowel control. Often the woman with a spinal cord lesion develops new erogenous zones, especially at the level of the lesion. A woman who is blind may face taboos concerning learning about sexuality through touch, may be concerned about odour associated with sexual activity, embarrassed about nudity, frustrated due to the extra dependency she must have on her partner, and will lack completely the visual components of sexuality. Social isolation and difficulties in communication are likely to lead to poor sexual information for the woman who is deaf. Finally, mental retardation is associated with a whole range of further problems, particularly those arising from the attitudes of staff responsible for the woman's care, and especially from their concern about the woman's vulnerability to sexual exploitation and risk of pregnancy.

(b) Sexual problems for the spouse of the disabled man

The woman whose partner is physically disabled is likely to face numerous difficulties concerning their sexual relationship. First and foremost there are the problems that arise because other people often are unable to accept a sexual relationship between an able-bodied woman and a disabled man. In addition, there are the problems arising out of role reversals that may be necessary in the general relationship, the concern the woman may have about hurting her partner, impairment of fertility (especially when the partner has a spinal cord lesion), difficulties the man may have in accepting his wife in a more sexually active role, and the attitude both partners have to non-coital sexual activity where sexual intercourse is impossible. The man may suffer considerable jealousy about the wife's ability to enjoy sex more than he does, and about the risk that she may develop another relationship. Furthermore, the woman may have great difficulty in accepting a role that combines the tasks of nurse (especially where excretory functions need to be looked after) and the feelings of a sexual partner.

(c) Management of sexual problems of the disabled

Many of the sexual difficulties discussed here are straightforward and ideally could be dealt with by those who care for the disabled in the course of their everyday work, if only they received more education and support than they mostly do at present. Many other sexual problems associated with disability however are of a special nature, and will need referral for expert counselling. Until recently there were few people experienced in this type of work, but in some areas in the UK special clinics offering expert counselling have now been established and should receive every encouragement. The voluntary organization called SPOD (Sexual Problems of Disabled People) can offer advice and assistance to the disabled themselves, their partners and families, and also to those who care for the disabled. The address of this organization is supplied at the end of this chapter (p. 260). The general practitioner who wishes to learn more about sexual problems of the disabled and their management is recommended to read Heslinga's (1974) book, *Not made of stone*.

CONCLUSION

General practitioners are in the front line for presentation of most of the sexual difficulties we have discussed in this chapter. They should be able both to detect and assess patients with sexual difficulties, and provide counselling for at least the more straightforward cases. Teaching of human sexuality in medical schools should provide the necessary background knowledge for such work, but this needs to be supplemented by opportunities through general practice training schemes, for experience in managing sexual problems. Most sexual dysfunction clinics can arrange further training for those who wish to improve their counselling skills in this area and some may be able to offer supervision to those who wish to treat their own patients with difficult or complicated sexual problems. For the patient the most critical moment is when she first hints to her general practitioner that she has a problem, and it is the general practitioner's response which will determine whether she ever discusses this fully and receives appropriate help.

APPENDIX

ASSESSMENT OF A PATIENT WITH A SEXUAL PROBLEM. MAIN POINTS TO BE COVERED

1. *The problem.*   Clarify in detail the nature of the sexual problem, its duration, any precipitants, and the way it has developed including any factors that have made it worse and any that have led to improvement.
2. *Partner's response.*   What has been the partner's response to the problem? Does he/she have a sexual problem? Are the couple able to discuss the problem, or talk about sex in general?
3. *Family history.*   Parents ages and occupations; nature of their relationship; nature of patient's relationships with both parents and with siblings; was sex discussed in the home?—if so, in what context and what impression did this have on the patient? Is there any important family history of physical or psychiatric disorders?
4. *Early development.*   Was patient happy during childhood? Did she encounter any problems in developing her sense of femaleness? What age did menarche occur, whether informed beforehand, and what was her reaction? What age did puberty (development of breasts, pubic hair, etc.) occur and what was patient's reaction?
5. *Sexual information.*   How did patient acquire her knowledge about sex; does she feel she has adequate knowledge? (One should check on the patient's knowledge about sexuality throughout the interview.)
6. *Early sexual experiences.*   Age at which sexual interest developed; masturbation (ask 'when did you find out about masturbation?') and reactions to it if has masturbated; nature of early relationships with boyfriends including sexual experience; any homosexual interests or behaviour?
7. *Current relationship.*   Duration; how relationship developed; nature of general relationship, especially interests, friends, communication and

friction; nature of sexual relationship; (if married) effect of marriage on sexual and general relationships; effect of pregnancy and childbirth on sexual relationship; relationships with children and attitudes to their sexuality.

8. *Schooling and occupations.*

9. *Religious beliefs.*

10. *Medical history.* Including menstruation, contraception, and medication.

11. *Psychiatric history.* Including medication.

12. *Use of alcohol and drugs.*

13. *Mental state examination.* In particular is the patient suffering from depression or anxiety?

14. *Physical examination and investigations.* If appropriate (e.g. vaginal examination should be carried out, with care, if a woman complains of vaginismus).

15. *Goals of treatment.* What would the patient consider a satisfactory sexual relationship, and what would she like to change in her relationship? (i.e. what might be the aim of treatment?)

ACKNOWLEDGEMENTS

We thank Drs Simon Street and Helen McBeath who provided helpful comments when this chapter was being planned.

REFERENCES AND FURTHER READING

Bancroft, J. and Coles, L. (1976). Three years' experience in a sexual problems clinic. *Br. med. J.* i, 1575–7.

Felstein, M. (1980). *Sexual medicine. Clins Obstet. Gynaecol.* **7**, No. 2. (Excellent reviews of several aspects of sexual medicine, including sexual physiology, endocrinology, disablement, female homosexuality, effects of illness, older age and the use of physical aids.)

Greengross, W. (1976). *Entitled to love: The sexual and emotional needs of the handicapped.* Mallaby Press and National Marriage Guidance Council, in association with National Fund for Research into Crippling Diseases. (For patients and professionals: very sensitive account with more emphasis on emotional and social aspects than on practical details of sex.)

Hawton, K. (1982). The behavioural treatment of sexual dysfunction. *Br. J. Psychiat.* **140**, 94–101.

Heslinga, K. (1974). *Not made of stone.* Charles Thomas, Illinois. (A clinical approach to the management of sexual problems of the disabled.)

Jehu, D. (1979). *Sexual dysfunction: A behavioural approach to causation, assessment and treatment.* John Wiley, Chichester. (An excellent account of behavioural treatments of sexual problems.)

Kaplan, H. S. (1974). *The new sex therapy.* Ballière Tindall, London. (A detailed account of an eclectic approach to sex therapy, with more attention to emotional aspects than Masters and Johnson provide.)

Kolodney, R. C., Masters, W. H., and Johnson, V. E. (1979). *Textbook of sexual medicine*. Little, Brown, Boston. (An excellent comprehensive review of the effects on sexual function of physical disorders and their treatments.)

Masters, W. H. and Johnson V. E. (1966). *Human sexual response*. Little, Brown, Boston. (A very detailed account of research concerning physiological and anatomical aspects of sexual response.)

—— and —— (1970). *Human Sexual Inadequacy*. Churchill, London. (The original description of intensive sex therapy.)

RCGP (Royal College of General Practitioners) (1974). *Oral contraceptives and health*. Pitman Medical, London.

Further reading for patients

Barbach, L. G. (1976). *For yourself: The fulfilment of female sexuality*. Signet, New York. (A self-help guide for the non-orgasmic woman.)

Delvin, D. (1974). *The book of love*. New English Library, London. (Very useful for recommending to patients: covers all important aspects of sexuality in a pleasantly simple and direct manner.)

Felstein, I. (1980). *Sex in later life*. Granada, London. (A general discussion of sexuality and sexual problems for older people.)

Heiman, J., LoPiccolo, L., and LoPiccolo, J. (1976). *Becoming orgasmic: A sexual growth program for women*. Prentice-Hall, New Jersey. (Another self-help book for the non-orgasmic woman.)

Books on sex education for young people

Claesson, B. H. (1980). *Boy, Girl, Man, Woman*. Penguin, Harmandsworth.

Kaplan H. S. (1979). *Making sense of sex*. Quartet Books Ltd., London. (A detailed account of sexuality for the sophisticated teenager.)

USEFUL ADDRESSES

Association of Sexual and Marital Therapists,
P.O. Box 62,
Sheffield S10 3TS
(Will give advice on sex therapists available in different parts of the UK.)

CHE (Campaign for Homosexual Equality),
P.O. Box 427,
Manchester M60 2EL.

SPOD (Sexual Problems of the Disabled),
The Dirama,
14 Peto Place,
London NW1 4DT.

12 Infertility

Mark Charnock

There are many different complex and deep-rooted reasons why a couple may want to have children, and in many cases these are not consciously considered by the couple. Should a desired conception be delayed or thwarted, either one or both of the couple will seek advice, usually initially from their general practitioner. While help may be requested as a simple expressed desire to conceive, there may be a wide variety of other less easily articulated and recognized dimensions to the problem, some of which will reflect attitudes within the family and others of the society to which the couple belong. Without contraception about 50 per cent of 25-year-old women will conceive in four months, and 70 per cent within eight months. However, about 15 per cent of all couples will experience a delay of greater than one year and as a result 10 per cent of all couples will seek advice about this delay.

As the problem essentially concerns both members of the couple they should be interviewed together if possible and investigations should then commence simultaneously. Therefore, although this is a book about women's health, some aspects of male as well as female infertility will be discussed in this chapter. The range of investigation and forms of management, some of doubtful value, that can be offered to the couple is vast and will depend on the interest and enthusiasm of the general practitioner. This chapter highlights those areas in which the general practitioner can contribute, while also covering areas that are better dealt with in specialist clinics but about which opinions may be sought from the general practitioner. While the general practitioner cannot participate directly in the more dramatic forms of treatment such as extra-corporeal fertilization, microsurgery, and artificial insemination, there is much that can be offered to the far greater number of couples in the practice who will not require or benefit from these techniques.

There are several areas in which general practitioners can make major contributions towards the care of sub-fertile or infertile couples, as they are in a unique position to evaluate the effect on the couple of the delay in conception. A careful, sympathetic, and thorough medical, social, and psychological assessment of the difficulty with conception will be of benefit to understanding the couple's problems. The knowledge of their background will permit a decision as to whether some initial investigations and treatment should be instituted by the general practitioner or whether referral of the couple directly to a specialist clinic would be more appropriate.

Early on, an outline can be given of the likely directions that investigation and treatment may follow. Although many couples will eventually require assistance from doctors specially interested in the field of infertility, they will need support, encouragement, advice, and explanation from their general practitioners while management is carried out by the hospital clinic, as many clinics unfortunately lack a personal element even when attempts are made to achieve one. The general practitioner also has an important role in the prevention of infertility—for example, prompt investigation and treatment of women with suspected pelvic inflammation is beneficial, as would be the referral of a boy at the appropriate time for orchidopexy for an undescended testicle.

Although female and male problems are, of course, often intertwined, for practical purposes I have dealt with each separately and then tried to discuss their interaction.

ASSESSMENT OF THE WOMAN IN GENERAL PRACTICE: HISTORY AND EXAMINATION

The initial assessment by the general practitioner will use the history and examination to try to pinpoint what the problem is and its likeliest reason. Table 12.1 gives a brief outline of the main features that need to be covered in the history.

The history may not only reveal possible explanations for the delay in conception but in addition factors which may influence the outcome of any future pregnancy, or which may make it unwise for the patient to conceive.

The main points of the examination are covered by Table 12.2.

Having taken a careful history and examined the patient, the cause of the infertility may become clear or, more likely, further investigation may be necessary to unravel the problem. The commonest reasons for female infertility are problems with ovulation, which can also affect the quality of the cervical mucus, problems with the Fallopian tubes so that passage of the ovum is prevented or impeded, and problems with intercourse so that the timing does not coincide with ovulation, or because of psychosexual difficulties. Sometimes several factors contribute. Ovulation, tubal problems, and sexual and marital difficulties are the three main divisions which have therefore been chosen for the purposes of this chapter, perhaps artificially, to help the doctor identify the likeliest reasons for the infertility.

Table 12.1 *History: female*

Age	*Past medical history*
Delay in conception	Serious illnesses
Duration	Pelvic inflammation
Previous investigations	Venereal disease
Effect on their life	Peritonitis
	Pelvic operations
Menstrual history	Ovarian cystectomy
Menarche	Caesarean section
Menstrual cycle—length, regularity	Tubal pregnancy
Dysmenorrhoea	Appendicectomy
Premenstrual symptoms	*Drug therapy*
Symptoms related to	*Endocrinological*
ovulation—mittelschmerz, mucus cascade,	Weight change
ovulation bleeding	Galactorrhoea
	Hirsuties
Reproductive history	Acne
Previous pregnancies	
Same or different partners	*Social history*
Time taken to conceive	Occupation and intentions
Outcome—termination	Marital relationship
—spontaneous abortion	Domestic circumstances
—ectopic	Diet
—preterm or term delivery	Smoking
—mode of delivery	Alcohol
	Stress
Sexual history	Exercise
Intercourse	
Frequency	*Psychological history*
Enjoyment	Reasons for wishing conception
Technique	Conflict concerning conception
Dyspareunia	Depression
Lubricants	Previous psychiatric problems
Difficulties	
Past contraceptive history	
Oral contraception	
Duration	
Time of cessation	
Resumption of menses	
Galactorrhoea	
Hypertension	
IUCD	
Symptoms of infection	
Sympto-thermal methods	

Ovulation problems

If the woman has not been keeping a basal body temperature chart (see p. 269), then the features of the history suggestive of *ovulation* would be regular menstrual cycles, primary dysmenorrhoea, severe premenstrual syndrome, mid-cycle symptoms such as pain (mittelschmerz), bleeding, or an increase in cervical mucus with a change in its character. Features suggestive of *anovulation* are amenorrhoea (although pregnancy must always be excluded), oligomenorrhoea, and extremely irregular and/or prolonged cycles.

Table 12.2. *Examination: female*

General	Cervix (see later)
Fitness	Score
Height	Cervicitis
Weight	*Uterus*
Blood pressure	Size
Endocrine features	Position
Goitre	Regularity
Hirsuties	Mobility
Acne	Tenderness
Breast—size	*Adnexae*
—galactorrhoea	Masses
Abdomen	Tenderness
Scars—laparoscopy	Thickening
—lower abdomen	Nodules
Masses	*Rectal*
Tenderness	Nodules in uterosacral ligaments
Pelvic	
Vulva and vagina	
Vaginismus	
Virgo intacta	
Oestrogenization	
Cliteromegaly	
Vaginitis	
Discharge	

Certain drugs can influence ovulation. Oral contraception can delay conception in a small number of women. However, this effect disappears after about 27 months in parous women and 48 months in nulliparous women when pregnancy rates in these groups equal those achieved by women discontinuing other methods of contraception. Five per cent of parous and 12 per cent of nulliparous women are affected at 18 months and 6 per cent of nulliparous women at 30 months. Even those women who develop post-pill amenorrhoea have normal pregnancy rates following treatment and the patient should be reassured about this. Some drugs raise prolactin levels and thus may inhibit ovulation, for example phenothiazines, cimetidine, and methyldopa. Excessive smoking or alcohol consumption may interfere with normal ovulation. Weight loss or severe depression may be the explanation for anovulation and amenorrhoea.

Factors on examination which may indicate an ovulatory problem include low weight for height (anorexia nervosa) and failure of development of secondary sexual characteristics. Galactorrhoea may be a sign of hyperprolactinaemia; obesity, acne, and hirsutism may suggest polycystic ovarian disease and there may be clinical features of thyroid dysfunction. Atrophic changes in the vagina and poor quality of the cervical mucus at mid-cycle will also point to an ovulatory problem.

Tubal and uterine problems

The previous medical and reproductive history may give clues that there may be a specific tubal or uterine problem. Tubal damage may have been sustained during peritonitis or an attack of gonorrhoea. Pelvic adhesions may develop after operations such as ovarian cystectomy, appendicectomy, and Caesarean section, particularly if these were complicated. A history of tuberculosis should be noted. Secondary dysmenorrhoea and deep dyspareunia may be associated with endometriosis and pelvic adhesions. Symptoms such as pain, fever, or prolonged bleeding after delivery or abortion may suggest pelvic sepsis with potential tubal damage. Users of the intrauterine device have an increased risk of pelvic inflammatory disease, a condition which may not have been diagnosed at the time. Lower abdominal pain and discharge may suggest the possibility (appropriate swabs for bacteriological examination should be taken from any abnormal discharge). Pelvic fibrosis following chronic pelvic sepsis or endometriosis may be suggested by loss of mobility of the tissues, fixed retroversion of the uterus, nodules in the fornices or thickening of the utero-sacral ligaments often accompanied by pelvic tenderness. Rectal examination may be helpful.

A uterine factor is rarely the sole explanation for infertility. Fibroids are the commonest and may be felt on pelvic examination.

Sexual and marital problems

The sexual relationship should be discreetly explored as this may be the underlying problem rather than the infertility but only come to light when the question of fertility is raised. Rarely, non-consummation of marriage may manifest itself as a delay in conception. Problems with intercourse may also reflect the strains and tensions imposed on the relationship by the failure to achieve a pregnancy. This may become more pronounced as the time passes without success but may not be admitted by the couple. Premature ejaculation and other specific sexual problems with their management are dealt with in Chapter 11 on sexual problems, and while not wanting to minimize the importance of such problems, this chapter deals mainly with the physical problems involved. The frequency of intercourse may be insufficient or excessive, or it may not be occurring at mid-cycle. Superficial dyspareunia raises various possibilities including vaginismus which may be noted on physical examination.

ASSESSMENT OF THE MAN: HISTORY AND EXAMINATION

Whereas a full history is usually taken from the woman before she is examined and before laboratory tests are arranged, in practice the reverse frequently applies to the male, and it is only after an abnormal semen sample is obtained that a history is taken from him and an examination performed. Certainly at the first interview only a brief history from the male is necessary, reserving fuller assessment for those males from whom samples are found to be abnormal. The more severe the semen abnormality the more likely will clinical abnormalities be, but even in patients with less than 5 million sperm per millilitre only 50 per cent have an obvious cause. In fact, in the majority of infertile men, the history is not particularly helpful. An outline of aspects that may be covered is included in Table 12.3.

The psychological evaluation is important, especially as many males feel their virility is threatened if their semen sample is found to be abnormal. Stress in work or in the marriage may be unearthed and anxieties and sexual difficulties uncovered.

Table 12.3. *History: male*

Age
Sexual history
  Puberty
  Erection
  Ejaculation—premature, retrograde, painful
  Potency
Reproductive history
  Fathered previous pregnancy
Past medical history
  Torsion
  Trauma
  Adult mumps, especially with orchitis
  Venereal disease
  Tuberculosis
  Acute illness
  Chronic illness—renal, hepatic
  Operations
    Orchidopexy
    Hernia repair
    Bladder neck surgery
  Radiation
  Drug therapy—methotrexate, cyclophosphamide, furadantin and sulphasalazine can
                produce oligospermia
              —antihypertensive therapy can produce retrograde ejaculation
  Endocrinological
    Gynaecomastia
    Hair growth
Social history
  Occupation—especially exposure to drugs, chemicals; extreme heat may cause reduced
                spermatogenesis
  Smoking
  Alcohol
  Stress
  Psychological factors
  Diet

Careful examination may reveal clues to the diagnosis, but in half there will be no abnormality. Absent or poorly developed secondary sexual characteristics, together with eunuchoidism, may suggest deficiency of gonadotrophin secretion. The genitalia are best examined both with the patient standing and lying. The penis and prepuce should be carefully examined noting its size, the presence of phimosis, the site of the urethral opening, and the presence of any skin lesions or urethral discharge. The cords should be carefully palpated to confirm the presence of the vas deferens on each side and to exclude a varicocoele. A small varicocoele may only be demonstrable with the Valsalva manoeuvre but can be found in about 10 per cent of normal fertile men. The testicular volume should be estimated, if necessary reference can be made to a set of graded ovoids—the orchidometer. Normal testicular volume is 15–25 ml. Normal testes measure 3.5 to 5.5 cm in length, and 2.1 to 3.2 cm in width. Their consistency and site should also be noted. Small testicular size with severe oligo- or azoospermia suggests loss or absence of spermatogenesis, while normal testes would make clinical obstruction more likely. Careful palpation of the epididymes may reveal features suggestive of previous infection such as thickening, tenderness, or nodules.

WHO TO REFER AND MANAGEMENT BY THE GENERAL PRACTITIONER

The general practitioner will need to consider carefully when to refer the couple for specialist advice. The decision will only be reached after careful individual assessment, although women in their late thirties with, for example, secondary amenorrhoea or likely tubal pathology should be referred sooner rather than later. The duration of the attempt to conceive is most important. As about 90 per cent of couples will conceive within one year and 95 per cent within two years, couples should be considered for investigation after a delay of between 12 and 24 months and should be reassured until then. Age may be an important consideration and it may be wise to refer a couple early with primary infertility when the woman is over 35 years. It may be appropriate for the interested general practitioner to assess ovulation, semen quality, a cervical factor, and problems with intercourse, and to offer advice as discussed above, but referral will be necessary for many other problems. Should these problems either be suspected or confirmed, the couple should be offered a specialist opinion.

The couple will value a careful explanation of the rationale of any investigation and an outline of what this involves, especially as confusion may arise or persist after a visit to the specialist clinic despite attempts there to devote sufficient time to discussion and clarification of the problems.

After referral, regular contact with the couple may help them to understand any uncertainties that develop; and in addition it will allow the general practitioner the opportunity of assessing the psychological effects of the investigation and treatment and of discussing the prospects of success, or the alternatives should it seem likely or certain the couple will remain infertile.

Some clinics may rely to a great extent on this continuing support from the general practitioner, an aspect of the patient's management that is to be strongly encouraged. The general practitioner should expect full communication from the hospital and in turn the specialist should welcome any further information from the general practitioner.

Sympathy and concern for the plight of the couple must be present at all times. It is essential for the general practitioner to understand the stresses imposed on each of them, not only by the delay in conception but also by the investigations, by the treatment, by their family and friends, and by the possibility or eventual certainty that they will be unsuccessful. Advice can be offered about how to improve their fertility, and also some specific advice about the optimal timing and other aspects of intercourse, about disorders of ovulation and about oligospermia, whereas problems concerning tubal, uterine, or cervical function should be referred to specialist assessment. If a decision for hospital referral is made it will be helpful for the general practitioner's continued dealings with the couple to know what the likely investigations and treatment will involve, and what the likelihood of success will be with the various forms of therapy. While a realistic assessment of their prospects is welcomed by most couples, an optimistic approach is important where possible.

General advice

The couple can be given an outline of the basic anatomy and physiology of reproduction which is often clarified by the use of a diagram. It should be explained that an assessment will be made of the different complex steps involved in conception and the maintenance of the early pregnancy in so far as these steps are understood and are able to be evaluated by clinical methods. It should be emphasized that not only are not all the steps fully understood but that not all those that are understood can be tested in practice and that remedies are not available for some of those found to be inadequate. However, the purpose of the assessment will be to try to find out how treatment may either restore fertility or reduce the time until conception occurs. The atmosphere of the interviews should always be such to ensure that questions about investigations or recommended treatment will be welcome and answered fully.

The general practitioner should always consider the risks of the investigations and treatment in the light of the fact that most of the couples involved are in perfect physical health, although many would be prepared even to undergo the risks involved in major surgery to achieve pregnancy.

It should be explained that at no time would the doctor feel aggrieved if advice was not followed nor if a halt in the proceedings was wished. The general practitioner should be aware of some of the more sensational methods of treatment to which great publicity is often given, despite their not necessarily having been proven to be effective. A note of caution should be sounded, should the couple wish to embark on such treatment, particularly as it is often not relevant to their circumstances. It should also be appreciated that treatment which is of doubtful efficacy may be suggested in the specialist centre.

General health

Advice about the general health of the couple may be appropriate both in order to speed conception but also to ensure the optimal outcome for any pregnancy achieved. Recommendations may be made about weight, exercise, smoking, and alcohol intake. Suggestions about altering their lifestyle in a more far-reaching way may be important. Rubella vaccination should be offered to mothers without immunity. The concern of certain couples about the delay in conception may be associated with the need for advice about whether conception should occur. While reassurance about the effects of maternal age may be all that is necessary, in other couples an opinion about risks should be sought from the appropriate source, often a physician or a genetic counsellor. Examples include women with diabetes or severe renal disease or couples with a family history of a hereditary disorder such as thalassaemia or haemophilia.

Specific investigation of the woman

A summary of investigations which one might need to undertake is included in Table 12.5.

Ovulation

The tests involved in assessing ovulation are temperature charts, assessment of the quality of the cervical mucus at mid-cycle, and measurement of progesterone levels in the second half or luteal phase of the cycle. For the cycle to be potentially fertile, not only must ovulation occur but adequate function of the corpus luteum must follow. Abnormalities of these two aspects are the major explanation for the delay in conception in about one-third of couples. Of these, 40 per cent of patients have amenorrhoea, a further 40 per cent oligomenorrhoea, and 20 per cent have luteal phase inadequacy.

Temperature chart. One way to assess ovulation is to ask the woman to keep a daily record of her basal body temperature. This should always be done in women who menstruate regularly. In amenorrhoea or oligomenorrhoea the assumption can be made that ovulation is not occurring, and temperature charts are only necessary to assess the response to treatment unless other anatomical causes exist for amenorrhoea. The basal body temperature is recorded carefully each day by the woman before she rises after at least three to five hours' uninterrupted sleep. Although the rectal temperature may be more accurate, the oral route is usually recommended. A specially calibrated basal thermometer may be easier to read. The temperature shift following ovulation is only slight—about 0.2 °C to 0.4 °C (0.4 °F to 0.8 °F). This shift can occur in a variety of ways—abruptly, gradually, preceded by a sharp drop, in stepwise or, less often, in sawtooth patterns. The illustrative diagram on many available charts usually shows a preceding drop followed by a sharp rise— the patient should be told not to expect this invariably as the only pattern with ovulation. Interpretation, even by experts, is often not easy and may be impossible. Various other factors can alter basal temperatures including illness and emotional tension. The elevation usually begins one or two days after ovulation but it may occur before or it may not rise at all despite other evidence of ovulation.

As the maximal thermal response is produced by only a relatively small rise in serum progesterone, the chart provides no quantitative idea of progesterone production in the luteal phase and therefore has disadvantages in the diagnosis of luteal phase inadequacy. Although much valuable information is gained from carefully maintained charts, many women find it distressing to continue them for a considerable length of time. Should the potential fertility of three cycles be clearly shown it is often advisable to discontinue them. However, should treatment for inadequate ovulation be commenced, they form a useful means of monitoring the effectiveness of the treatment. In addition, they provide some guidance regarding the timing of intercourse.

Serum progesterone levels. Ideally, the level should be measured at the peak of the progesterone concentration in the mid-luteal phase which is above five to ten days before the next period. The temperature chart is helpful in indicating when blood should be sent. A single sample can be sent on about the twentieth day in regular 28-day cycles, or serial samples at three- to five-day intervals in order to ensure the correct time in irregular cycles. A level greater than 15 nmol/l is usually accepted as confirmatory of ovulation although it may be that a level of greater than 30 nmol/l (10 ng/ml) would be a more accurate guide to the overall fertility of the cycle.

Cervical factor

Many aspects of the investigation of the important role that the cervix and its mucus play are still controversial. Some authorities do not emphasize it in their fertility assessment, whereas others attribute to it major significance, a view which is becoming more dominant. Some perform the tests prior to semen analysis, reserving the latter for patients with poor results. An improved understanding has developed of the role of the cervix in regulating entrance of sperm into the genital tract and in being a major site of antibody formation and concentration. Currently performed tests indicate not only coital adequacy but also evaluate semen quality, immunological factors, and the hormonal effect on cervical mucus. It is suggested that abnormal cervical function is responsible in 10–15 per cent infertile couples.

Post-coital test.   Many elements of the test are controversial. An essential element for the correct interpretation of this test is that it is performed in the immediate pre-ovulatory phase of the cycle which is usually the thirteenth or fourteenth day. The general practitioner often has an advantage over the specialist clinic, which is usually held weekly, in that a negative test can more easily be repeated daily if necessary, especially in slightly irregular cycles when it can be related to the temperature chart. In some fertile women the test may only be positive for two days during the cycle.

Relation to intercourse.   The recommended interval between intercourse and the test has varied greatly without much scientific basis. As sperm can survive for many days in cervical mucus, a convenient time is between 6 and 24 hours as this enables intercourse to take place the night before.

Abstinence.   Unless repeated tests are being performed, two days' abstinence is usually advised.

Cervical mucus assessment and cervical score.   By scoring the features of the cervical mucus as shown in Table 12.4, an index is provided of its abil-

Table 12.4. *Cervical score*

Parameter	0	1	2	3
Amount	None	Scant	Dribble	Cascade
Spinnbarkeit	None	Slight—can be drawn a quarter distance from external os to vulva	Moderate—can be drawn half way	Pronounced—can be drawn to vulva
Ferning	None	Linear—ferning in parts with no side branches	Partial—in part good ferning with side branches	Complete—good ferning throughout slide
Cervix	Tightly closed	Closed	Partially open	Gaping

ity to facilitate sperm passage. Some authorities feel that the important criteria are the amount, cellularity, and *Spinnbarkeit* of the mucus, and ignore the other criteria.

Collection of the sample and its examination.   Many instruments have been recommended for collection of the sample from the endocervix. This can be difficult because of the viscosity and *Spinnbarkeit* of the mucus. Artery forceps or a 1 ml tuberculin syringe with a Luer lock will obtain a sample in the most difficult cases, but pipettes, bacteriological loops, and catheters have all been suggested.

Examination and interpretation.   The specimen is transferred to a microscope slide, covered with a cover slip and examined under high power, between 50 and 400 ×. The interpretation is controversial but many feel that 10–20 sperm per high-powered field with at least 50 per cent motility is a good result which excludes a cervical factor as an explanation for the infertility. In addition it implies that intercourse has been satisfactory, that there are an adequate number of good quality sperm, and that the production of cervical mucus is being influenced by the appropriate hormonal stimulus. The couple can be shown the microscopic findings which is often reassuring to them.

The interpretation of a negative or poor test is less easy. It should certainly be repeated with care to achieve optimal timing and semen analysis arranged if it has not already been performed. Should normal mucus and a normal sperm count be associated with repeated negative post-coital tests in the absence of faulty coital technique, a problem with sperm invasion of mucus is a strong probability which should be investigated further in a specialist centre.

Tubal function

Assessment of tubal function remains sadly inadequate and is best done in a specialist centre. The question of when to test tubal patency in a woman with no symptoms or signs to suggest tubal problems, and which method to use, provokes considerable discussion. In the absence of such features, treatment of other causes for the delay, particularly anovulation, for some months is justifiable in a young couple before referring to a specialist centre where hysterosalpingography or laparoscopy will be arranged as appropriate by the gynaecologist.

Anovulation

If the tests described so far suggest that most of the cycles are anovulatory, it is necessary to consider the cause. The following hormone measurements can be made.

Table 12.5. *Specific investigations*

FEMALE	MALE
General	Semen analysis
Haemoglobin	Repeated abnormal semen analysis
Rubella antibodies	LH
VDRL	FSH
(Cervical smear)	Testosterone
(Chest X-ray)	Prolactin
	Thyroid function
Related to fertility	
Ovulation and corpus luteum function	
Basal temperature chart	
Serum progesterone level	
Cervical function—cervical score	
—post-coital test	
Amenorrhoea or anovulation	
Prolactin	
Gonadotrophins—LH	
—FSH	
Thyroid function	
Tubal function	
Hysterosalpingography	

Hormonal factors

Prolactin. Hyperprolactinaemia is rarely found in regularly menstruating women and need not necessarily be associated with galactorrhoea. A high level should be confirmed with a repeated measurement and the possibility of stress be considered as a cause. The upper limit of normal is usually 600 u/l. Women with high levels should be referred for specialist advice because of the possibility of a prolactin secreting pituitary adenoma, although the general practitioner should reassure the patient that there are numerous other causes (see later).

Gonadotrophins. Apart from their value in determining the cause of amenorrhoea, measurement of luteinizing hormone (LH) and follicle stimulating hormone (FSH) levels help confirm the diagnosis of polycystic ovary syndrome (PCO) suggested by oligomenorrhoea, obesity, and hirsuties. In this syndrome the LH level is often elevated and the FSH concentration low or normal. A raised testosterone level may also be found in this syndrome. High levels of FSH are associated with premature ovarian failure which may present as oligomenorrhoea before amenorrhoea develops (see Chapter 4).

Thyroid function. About 1–2 per cent of patients with an ovulatory disorder have thyroid dysfunction which is usually accompanied by symptoms. The most useful measurements are the free thyroxin index, serum tri-iodo-thyronine and TSH levels.

Specific investigation of the man

Seminal fluid analysis

Most authorities recommend this as an essential step in the evaluation of all couples seeking advice about a delay in conception. Some suggest it can be omitted if a good result is obtained in a post-coital test.

Collection of the sample.   A period of two to three days' abstinence is usually recommended. Each day's abstinence can increase the count by 13 million/per ml and the volume by 0.4 ml, but not indefinitely! The specimen should be produced by masturbation and collected in a wide-mouthed container. It should be delivered to the hospital from home within two hours, having been kept warm in transit. Coitus interruptus is not recommended for production of the sample as the first portion of the ejaculation which has the densest sperm concentration may be lost. Remember to tell the man that condoms should not be used as their spermicide content may adversely affect motility.

Interpretation.   A suggested set of criteria for defining an abnormal sperm sample is given in Table 12.6. An abnormal result requires repeating on at least two further occasions because of the great variability in the results. While repeated azoospermia indicates infertility, it is only with counts of less than 20 million per ml that sperm density is related to infertility. However, conception can occur with counts below 5 million per ml. A very low volume may suggest absence of the vas or severe inflammation of the accessory glands as the seminal vesicles produce 65 per cent and the prostate 30 per cent of the ejaculation. Explanations such as cooling of the specimen, delay in examination, or collection in a condom should be excluded when low motility is reported. Assessment of morphology is difficult as opinion varies as to the criteria for normal appearances of sperm.

Marked oligospermia or azoospermia usually warrants referral to a specialist centre. Although in most cases no endocrinological abnormality will be detected, some investigations may be arranged especially if impotence is associated. An elevated FSH level is of grave prognostic value in the presence of oligospermia and small testes as it suggests irreversible end-stage damage to germ-cells associated with abnormal inhibin production. Low gonadotrophin levels (FSH, LH) in association with a low tes-

Table 12.6. *Criteria for abnormal sperm sample*

Volume:	Less than 1 ml
	Greater than 6 ml
Sperm concentration:	Less than 20 million per ml
Sperm motility:	Less than 40% progressive motility
Sperm morphology:	Less than 60% normal oval forms

tosterone concentration suggest the rare possibility of gonadotrophin deficiency which responds well to treatment. While a raised prolactin level may occasionally explain oligospermia and associated impotence it should be interpreted with care. Assessment of thyroid and adrenocortical function may be suggested by clinical features.

TREATMENT AND ADVICE BY THE GENERAL PRACTITIONER

The treatment must obviously be appropriate to the cause, as determined above. The initial treatment for and advice on some infertility problems can be readily undertaken by the general practitioner; in particular disorders of timing of intercourse, psychological problems, and disorders of ovulation. For example, it is useless to deal with problems of ovulation if intercourse is the main stumbling block. Also included here is a section on pelvic inflammatory disease as this is becoming an increasingly common problem and needs early and appropriate diagnosis and treatment by the general practitioner.

1. Timing of intercourse

No study has evaluated the effectiveness of advice about timing of coitus in relation to the fertile period. The couple should be encouraged not to become obsessed by timing intercourse to coincide with the fertile period, as the feeling of having intercourse to order can strain the sexual relationship. There is also no evidence at present to confirm the suggestion that it is possible in practice to influence the sex of the offspring by precise timing of intercourse in relation to ovulation. The length of the period of fertility in an ovulatory cycle is uncertain owing to ignorance as to when ovulation will occur and as to the fertile lifespan of the ovum and sperm. That of the ovum is generally felt to be about 12 to 24 hours, whereas the sperm retain their ability to fertilize the egg for at least 48 hours and possibly for as long as seven to nine days. Although the temperature chart may indicate ovulation by the fall in temperature which occurs before the rise, this is often not helpful as this pattern may well not develop and a fall may occur without a subsequent rise. It may offer a rough guide, however, and be a justification for continuing the charts for more than three cycles. In addition, about two-thirds of women have cycles which vary by more than eight days. Should the woman have noted the changes in mucus in the pre-ovulatory phase, this may be a guide, or if not she could be given advice on how to record the changes.

2. Sexual and marital problems

In some couples it would appear that intercourse is too frequent and advice to abstain for two days prior to ovulation may be beneficial. In others the use of lubricants may be contributing and it should be advised that their use be discontinued near ovulation. The general practitioner will often be able to assess which form of treatment or help will be most suitable for sexual or marital problems. The amount of direct help which can be provided by the general practitioner will depend on experience and training. The severity of sexual dysfunction will determine the most appropriate therapy. In some, a brief course such as that proposed by Masters and Johnson will suffice, whereas others may require prolonged courses of psychotherapy which can only be provided by a specialist in the field.

3. Ovulation problems

Psychological problems and weight loss

A careful history is essential to the diagnosis. The weight loss is usually in the past and may have been largely restored. The typical features of chronic anorexia nervosa may not be readily divulged by the patient and the psychological features must be sought carefully. Depression may be associated. The patient should be encouraged to gain weight until she is the average weight for her height, but it may prove difficult to achieve this although the patient usually understands the rationale for it (see Chapter 17). Clomiphene may be successful once a set target is reached even though the patient may be below the optimal weight required.

Clomiphene citrate

Since this is the commonest drug used in treatment of ovulatory problems it will be discussed in detail as general practitioners could consider using this for inducing ovulation in oestrogenized patients.

Pharmacology.   Clomiphene is a weak oestrogen related to diethylstilboestrol. In oestrogenized women it acts, however, as an anti-oestrogen by competing with oestrogen at oestrogen-binding sites. The hypothalamic–pituitary unit is released from the negative feedback effect of oestrogen thus increasing the output of gonadotrophins. However, for its effect clomiphene depends on some oestrogen production being present initially.

Dosage.   The usual initial dose is 50 mg daily for five days early in the cycle, although it may be wiser to use 25 mg daily for patients with polycystic ovary syndrome who may be hypersensitive to the drug. This can be increased up to 200 mg daily for five days should an inadequate response be produced. However, particularly as the evidence is uncertain that doses in excess of 100 mg are of value, this should probably be the maximum dose used by a general practitioner before considering referral.

Many recommend starting the course on the fifth day of the cycle, while others maintain that by starting on the second day a better effect is obtained. In patients with oligomenorrhoea a five-day course of medroxy-progesterone acetate 5 mg daily can be used to cause a withdrawal bleed. Clomiphene can commence a week after the end of the progestogen therapy.

Table 12.7. *Clomiphene citrate: side effects*

Hot flushes
Nausea and vomiting
Breast discomfort
Mild visual disturbances
Skin reaction
Reversible hair loss
Multiple pregnancy
Hyperstimulation syndrome

Side effects (see Table 12.7). These are usually mild and are infrequent but should be mentioned to the patient. They are more common with higher doses. The hot flushes do not respond to oestrogen treatment. The visual disturbances are particularly distressing if the patient does not know they may occur. They are described as blurring or spots and flashes, and will disappear within days or weeks after discontinuation of the therapy. Further courses of clomiphene should not be prescribed to such patients. The multiple pregnancy rate is increased about six times but the large majority of these are twins. Severe hyperstimulation is rare with the current short course of clomiphene. However, mild forms should be considered a possibility should abdominal pain develop and a careful pelvic examination performed to assess ovarian size. Should ovarian enlargement be detected it will usually settle within a few weeks and it is advisable not to use clomiphene in the next cycle.

Monitoring and duration of therapy. The temperature chart, cervical mucus and serum progesterone levels are all used to check that ovulation is occurring. Pelvic examination each month is not warranted, but should be performed if abdominal pain occurs. Should ovulation be occurring, the treatment can be continued for 12 to 24 months but general practitioners should probably consider referral to a specialist clinic after about six months for a full review including investigation of tubal patency.

If conception does not follow treatment with this drug alone, various combinations of therapy have been proposed as worth trying before considering more powerful ovulation induction drugs such as gonadotrophin therapy. These should only be used in specialist clinics. The addition of human chorionic gonadotrophin (HCG) at mid-cycle may trigger ovulation and boost function of the corpus luteum but in general its use has been disappointing. The addition of mid-cycle oestrogen has been advocated in an attempt to overcome the adverse anti-oestrogenic effect of clomiphene on the quality of cervical mucus. Its effect has been uncertain.

Results. The ovulation rate will depend on the underlying condition with the best results being achieved in those patients with oligomenorrhoea. It will vary between 30 per cent and 80 per cent. However, the pregnancy rate will be only half this for reasons that remain largely obscure. It will be best in patients with amenorrhoea. The abortion rate of 15–20 per cent is probably no different from that of other infertile couples achieving pregnancy nor probably from that of the normal population. The congenital malformation rate is not increased unless the drug is given in early pregnancy when an incidence of 5 per cent has been reported compared with one of 2–3 per cent in the normal population.

4. Pelvic inflammatory disease

The tubal disorder which accounts for the infertility of about 20 per cent of couples is due to pelvic infection in the vast majority. Apart from gonorrhoea, a wide range of organisms can be responsible, including bacteroides, coliforms, haemolytic and anaerobic streptococci, gardnerella, tuberculosis, mycoplasma, chlamydia, and viruses.

Typical symptoms may occur, such as lower abdominal pain or purulent discharge and fever, but the general practitioner should be alert to the earliest symptoms and signs, particularly in a woman who has not completed her family, who has recently been pregnant, or who has an intrauterine device as the symptoms and signs can be unreliable (see Table 12.8).

During the examination of the pelvis swabs and smears may be taken from the cervix, vagina, urethra, and possibly the rectum. Appropriate media should be used and satisfactory arrangements for transport made. Blood could be taken for serology.

Unfortunately, in many cases accurate guidance as to the most suitable antibiotic regimes is not provided by the culture result. In view of its increasing resistance to penicillin it is probably wise to discuss the management of patients with gonorrhoea with the specialist clinic. In practice, initial therapy is normally blind. The drugs may be used orally or parenter-

Table 12.8. *Patients with proven pelvic inflammation*

16% no pain
40% no raised ESR
40% no fever
50% no tenderness or mass

ally in various regimes. Currently popular are those combining metronidazole with tetracycline or erythromycin for chlamydia or with amoxycillin, co-trimoxarole-trimethoprin or a cephalosporin. Adequate dosage must be ensured and the course continued for at least seven days while monitoring the response. Investigation and treatment of the patient should always be considered.

Patients with severe disease, with an uncertain diagnosis, with a poor response to therapy, or with recurrent attacks should be referred for a specialist opinion. Laparoscopy has enabled greater accuracy of diagnosis, which without it is often incorrect (see Table 12.9).

The patient's anxiety concerning tubal function and occlusion is unfortunately often justified (see Table 12.10), but they should be reassured strongly, especially after a single, mild attack.

Table 12.9. *Laparoscopy with suspected pelvic inflammation*

60% confirmed with swollen, inflamed tubes
25% no pathology found
10% other pathology

Table 12.10. *Tubal occlusion after pelvic inflammation*

1 attack	12.1%
2 attacks	35.5%
3 attacks	75.0%.
Mild attack	2.6%
Moderate attack	13.1%
Severe attack	26.0%

Oligospermia

Many men will feel their virility is being questioned should a repeated low sperm count be found. The general practitioner should do all that is possible to reassure the man while at the same time trying to help the couple adopt a realistic approach to their prognosis. Much debate surrounds the value of methods to try to reduce scrotal temperature. While the use of loose boxer trunks as underwear and twice-daily cold scrotal douches are still widely recommended, some authorities feel their efficacy is doubtful. Attempts to improve the general fitness of the man will be important in many cases. Reduction of weight, smoking, and alcohol intake should be encouraged, as well as trying to avoid stress from overwork. The man should be reassured that the sperm count may improve should he recently have had an acute viral illness.

Any drug therapy should be reviewed and any medical condition such as diabetes or hypertension controlled. In patients where chronic infection may play a role, as suggested by the association of oligospermia with symptoms such as dysuria, painful ejaculation, or lower back pain, with an abnormal prostate, or with increased leucocytes in the seminal plasma, or in those men with isolated disorders of sperm motility only, appropriate therapy may be recommended. Culture of semen, midstream specimens of urine, or expressed prostate secretions may be obtained in such patients to guide therapy, but agents used should be from amongst those concentrated in the genital tract secretions. These include erythromycin, demethylchlotetracycline, and trimethoprim-sulphamethoxazole combinations which should be used for prolonged periods of up to three months. Most cases, having had the abnormal findings confirmed in repeated semen analysis, should be referred for specialist advice.

MANAGEMENT BY SPECIALIST

It is not the function of this chapter to deal in detail with the complexities of investigation and treatment of infertility in the hospital clinic. Rather, some of the more recent or controversial aspects have been picked out for discussion. It is hoped in this way that the general practitioner will be able to discuss with the couple the alternatives for treatment and the likelihood of their success.

Hyperprolactinaemia

The assessment of the cause of high serum prolactin levels needs expertise. As the level can be elevated by the stress of a consultation or a venepuncture, further investigation and treatment should follow only after high levels have been confirmed in several samples obtained under basal conditions and after cessation of any drug therapy, if possible. Thyroid dysfunction must be excluded. Hyperprolactinaemia should probably be ignored in the presence of normal ovulatory cycles. Should high levels be confirmed, the pituitary gland can be examined by a variety of means including X-rays, tomograms, or CAT scans. An endocrinologist and a neurosurgeon's opinion will be sought regarding the possibility of a prolactinoma being present which may require excision or destruction with radiotherapy before pregnancy is safe. The ideal treatment of a prolactinoma is still to be fully clarified.

Bromocriptine

This ergot derivative suppresses prolactin production by its dopamine agonist effect. It may be used as the sole treatment for a small prolactinoma, or after excision or destruction of a larger lesion has failed to be followed by ovulation. It may be used to control the expansion of a prolactinoma should this occur during pregnancy. A dosage of 5–10 mg is usually sufficient but up to 40 mg can be required. The most common side effects of mild nausea and postural hypotension can be avoided by starting the course with small doses in the evening with meals, preferably while lying down, and then gradually increasing it. If the woman has amenorrhoea, menstruation should return within six weeks of commencing treatment, although it may be delayed for up to three months. Ovulation can be confirmed thereafter in the usual way and will occur in 95 per cent of patients. The drug is usually continued until pregnancy is suspected or confirmed. There is, however, no evidence of teratogenesis. Neither the abortion nor the multiple pregnancy rates are increased.

Gonadotrophin therapy

Therapy with gonadotrophins provide the most powerful form of ovulation induction as it bypasses the role of the hypothalamic–pituitary unit. Following stimulation of the ovarian follicle with FSH, ovulation is triggered using a dose of HCG which has an effect similar to LH. The source of FSH is usually human menopausal urine (HMG). It is especially indicated in patients with low oestrogen levels associated with normal concentrations of prolactin and FSH, particularly if they have failed to respond to a course of clomiphene. However, consideration should first be given to dealing with any psychological causes of hypothalamic–pituitary dysfunction especially in patients with weight loss. It may also be indicated should conception not follow reversal of hyperprolactinaemia with bromocriptine or should ovulation not occur after clomiphene in oestrogenized patients. The incidence of hyperstimulation and multiple pregnancies following its use can only be kept to a minimum by careful monitoring of its effects by doctors skilled and experienced in this form of treatment. Repeated clinical assessment by cervical mucus scoring and ovarian palpation must be accompanied by measurement of serum or urinary oestrogen levels, performed daily if possible. Recently the use of ultrasound to assess the number of ovarian follicles responding and the growth of the follicle has been recommended to reduce further the incidence of multiple pregnancies. The expense of the therapy demands that it is only embarked upon after careful review of the problem. Should the general practitioner be involved in the provision or monitoring of the treatment, precise instructions should be issued by the clinic.

Results. These will depend on the underlying condition requiring treatment. A 90 per cent conception rate in oestrogen-deficient amenorrhoeic women seems possible, provided treatment is continued for six months, while only 50 per cent conception rate in oestrogenized amenorrhoeic or menstruating women would follow similar duration of treatment. The multiple pregnancy rate can be as high as 28 per cent but the spontaneous abortion and malformation rates do not seem increased.

Tubal problems

Tubal problems will be the cause of infertility in about 10–35 per cent of couples depending on the population studied. The history and examination may suggest this possibility, but assessment of tubal function must be made either early on in the investigation of the couple or later should, for example, success not follow induction of ovulation. Investigation of tubal function can be by hysterosalpingography or laparoscopy. Controversy and discussion still surround which should be done first, and occasionally the full answer will only be provided by laparotomy.

Hysterosalpingography

In this procedure a radiopaque dye is injected through the cervix to outline the uterus and tubes which are examined by fluoroscopic screening. Water-soluble media are widely used. Tubal patency is assessed by observing the flow of dye into the peritoneal cavity. The test should not be performed either during or shortly after an acute attack of pelvic infection, nor if there is an adnexal mass. Ideally, it should be performed within ten days of the first day of the last menstrual period to avoid any possibility of irradiating a newly-formed conceptus. While many gynaecologists recommend it to be performed only under general anaesthesia, it is often done as an out-patient procedure. Various abnormalities within the uterus or the tubes can be detected but it is important to realize that tubal spasm can account for the failure of the dye to pass through the tubes. In addition, the tubes can be blocked and yet dye flow into the peritoneal cavity through a perforation. Complications include pain, vasovagal attacks, perforation of the uterus, and pelvic infection.

Laparoscopy

In addition to providing a means of assessing tubal patency, this provides much valuable information about the structure and function of the pelvic organs. However, gynaecologists differ greatly as to when to recommend it during the assessment of the couple owing to its associated risks (see Table 12.11). It is usually performed under general anaesthetic with an in-patient stay of 12–24 hours. Usually the patients will experience only mild abdominal discomfort, shoulder-tip pain, and after-effects of anaesthesia, but a considerable range of complications can occur with a morbidity rate of 3 per cent. The patient should be able to return to full activity within a few days. In addition to assessing tubal patency by hydrotubation with a dye such as methylene blue, laparoscopy can detect the site of any blockage or previous tubal damage by noting thickening or thinning, peritubal or periovarian adhesions, and endometriosis. If the test is performed in the second half of the cycle the presence of a corpus luteum or the recently described unruptured luteinizing follicle can be sought. It may be

Table 12.11. *Some complications of laparoscopy*

Death	0.01%
Morbidity	3.00%
Failed procedure	10.0%
Anaesthetic complications	
Direct trauma:	
Bowel	
Urinary tract	
Pelvic organs	
Haemorrhage:	
Abdominal wall	
Pelvic blood-vessels	
Tubal mesentery	
Bowel mesentery	
Infection:	
Abdominal	
Pelvic	
Chest	
Urinary	
Pulmonary emboli	
Deep vein thrombosis	

advisable to use contraception if laparoscopy is performed during the luteal phase. An endometrial biopsy can be performed and submitted for histology and, if necessary, for culture for tuberculosis.

Therapy

This may be of supportive value in patients with tubal factors contributing to their infertility but it will rarely reverse tubal damage. For example, antibiotics are important in patients with past infection either before or after surgery. Various hormonal preparations may be used for mild endometriosis. The prospects for success following tubal *surgery* are very difficult to quantify accurately. They vary from almost nil with major tubal damage associated with dense and extensive pelvic adhesions to about 70 per cent when only mild salpingolysis or fimbriolysis is required. The total disorder of tubal function is impossible to define precisely and other factors need to be considered such as the fertility of the male and the quality of the other elements in the female's fertility. Current developments in surgical technique including the use of microsurgery offer hope for some improvement but highly skilled expertise is not available in all centres. Despite these problems, in discussing the option of surgery as accurate an idea as possible should be given of the prognosis with or without surgery. Most conceptions will occur within 18–24 months. An assessment of the psychological state may help foretell how the couple will react should it prove unsuccessful. A discussion about the precise nature of the possible forms of surgery is beyond the scope of this chapter and the patients should discuss details with the surgeon involved.

In vitro fertilization and embryo transfer

This exciting technique has been developed only recently and many aspects are still being assessed. It is only available in a very few centres. It offers some hope for couples whose infertility arises from severe disease or loss of the Fallopian tubes. At present the success rate of clinical pregnancies per laparoscopy may be 15–20 per cent with about a 4 per cent liveborn rate. It is hoped that eventually about 30 per cent of patients having embryo transfer will deliver babies. Many ethical and legal questions need resolution and the final assessment will need information about the incidence of malformations. The local specialist clinic should be able to advise about the current position and about where facilities may be available, but the general practitioner may need to advise as to whether to choose this option as opposed to doing nothing further or considering adoption. Apart from the physical risks, the inconvenience, and the cost, the likely response of the couple to the small chance of success and to failure should be discussed before a decision is reached.

Cervical factors

An abnormality of cervical function may be responsible for infertility in 5–15 per cent of couples. *In vitro* tests have been devised to assess the ability of sperm to penetrate the pre-ovulatory cervical mucus. Should inadequate penetration be confirmed, various possibilities exist. Many patients will, however, have antisperm antibodies in either the mucus or the seminal plasma suggesting the possibility of some immunological disturbance. This has led to many ingenious methods of therapy with little convincing evidence to confirm their efficacy. Since treatment has not been convincingly shown to be better than placebo therapy, the prognosis for a couple with a persistently negative post-coital test without obvious explanation must remain guarded.

Abnormal seminal fluid

This is another area where, for the most part, recommended forms of treatment are of unproven benefit. In about 50 per cent of infertile males there is no explanation for the abnormal semen analysis. A wide range of forms of therapy from cooling of the scrotum to gonadotrophin therapy have been recommended with varying enthusiasm. Few have had controlled trials to assess their efficacy, leaving many unanswered questions about their role. However, despite the lack of scientific justification for their use, therapy is often suggested rather than telling the patient that nothing can be done and is often willingly accepted by him on this understanding. All should be tried for at least three months. Antioestrogens such as clomiphene citrate and tamoxifen have been recommended. Long-acting androgens such as mesterolone have been used while it has been hoped by others that a rebound improvement in spermatogenesis will follow cessation of long-term treatment with high doses of testosterone. *In vitro* fertilization has recently been suggested as a form of treatment to be considered for severe oligospermia as only 100 000 to 200 000 sperm are required for this technique.

Azoospermia has an extremely poor prognosis whatever the cause. If no therapy can be offered these patients should be informed in a sympathetic manner of their very slight chance of conception, and a discussion opened concerning the option of adoption, AID, or acceptance of the position without further action.

Artificial insemination

Numerous aspects of artificial insemination provoke discussion, including moral, ethical, and legal questions. Developing techniques in storage and treatment of sperm may improve the prospects for some infertile couples with factors which are at present untreatable.

Artificial insemination with donor semen (AID)

Recent years have seen a great increase in the demand for and the supply of AID semen. The general practitioner can play a considerable role in the selection of suitable couples. It must be reasonably certain that the male cannot or should not initiate a pregnancy. A clear indication is azoospermia; there is less certainty regarding severe oligospermia or repeated negative post-coital tests. With the latter group a considerable period without success should elapse before they are considered. More precise may be genetic reasons for the male not fathering a pregnancy— for example, Huntington's chorea. It should at the same time be reasonably certain that the female is able to conceive. Opinion varies as to how thoroughly the female should be assessed, especially with regard to tubal function. It is much more difficult to assess the general suitability of the couple to undergo the procedure. While the general practitioner's views are often of considerable help, it may be necessary to seek guidance from a psychiatrist or social worker regarding the stability of the partnership, the response to their infertility, their reasons for choosing this option, and their attitude to the religious, ethical, and legal dimensions of AID. The possible response to failure should be considered.

Regimes and results.   Either stored, frozen, or fresh semen is used for two inseminations each cycle. There would seem to be no reason why a limit should be set to the number of cycles treated as, while about 70–80 per cent of patients will conceive in twelve months, half of the remainder will do so in a further twelve months. This success rate is strongly influenced by the age of the female. Studies suggest that the marriage is not more likely to end in divorce as a result of AID and that the offspring have a normal development. Possibly up to a third of all pregnancies related to treatment for infertile couples should eventually result from this relatively inexpensive but effective form of therapy. About 20 000 births each year world-wide are due to the technique but the United Kingdom is greatly lacking facilities at present.

Artificial insemination with husband's semen (AIH)

In contrast, considerable uncertainty surrounds the benefit conferred by using AIH for the many conditions for which it has been recommended. Intrauterine AIH has not been as generally successful as had been hoped in couples with antisperm antibodies. It may be more promising if the female has antibodies. Its use for oligospermia or poor semen quality is doubtful, although better results may be obtained by using the first portion of a split ejaculate. Although tried in patients with retrograde ejaculation or with cervical mucus hostility not due to immunological problems, it has been of uncertain value. Psychosexual problems leading to infertility should not be treated with AIH unless supported by a psychiatrist's opinion. Anatomical reasons accounting for failure to deposit semen in the vagina form a group of indications including such conditions as epispadias and vaginal anomalies. It would be of undoubted advantage for a man due to undergo vasectomy or radiotherapy or cytotoxic therapy for testicular tumours or lymphoma. The semen could be frozen and used later but facilities are lacking.

ADJUSTMENT TO INFERTILITY

Although it should always be given with caution and tact by the specialist, a final verdict that the couple are infertile will release in them a wide range of traumatic emotional experiences. This may be aggravated by information being given at a time of marital difficulty and of emotional tension following investigations. It may require several months for the couple to recover from the emotional reaction and during this time it may be unwise for them to rush into a decision concerning the alternatives for parenthood. Shock, confusion, numbness, loneliness, anger, guilt, a loss of identity and hopes and grief are among the emotions described. Sexual dysfunction may result for some months, particularly if the fertile partner resents the other being infertile. The emotions which are similar to those in bereavement may be suppressed only to emerge later. The general practitioner should understand these feelings and provide support during this time.

When these have subsided can a choice be made from the options available to them? Some couples will prefer to remain childless, others to adopt, and others to foster children. Should the man be infertile, AID may be chosen while *in vitro* fertilization and embryo transfer may be arranged for women with blocked tubes and, possibly, couples with idiopathic infertility. The long-term success of these options will depend on the ability of the couple to resolve their feelings about infertility. Even when strictly only one partner is infertile, both have to recognize and accept each other as an infertile couple. Should these conflicts persist, for example, the adopted child or the marriage may suffer greatly. The most appropriate person to help with these difficult psychological processes and decisions is not necessarily the general practitioner or even a doctor. Social workers, psychiatrists, adoption agencies, or self-help groups all have much to offer and careful communication between them and the patient is essential.

Adoption

The number of children placed for adoption has fallen dramatically in the United Kingdom since the 1960s. This means many couples will be unable to adopt a normal child as a result. The process has become long and frustrating and certainly not one to be embarked upon until the above crises have been resolved. A list of agencies can be offered to a suitable couple and an outline given of the various policy guidelines used by each. The need for the agencies to be thorough in their assessment should be explained as the detailed investigation usually involved can otherwise be upsetting.

Fostering

An increased interest in fostering has occurred in recent years, encouraged by more flexible schemes, better training of foster parents, and careful selection of parents and help and support afterwards. More agencies are now offering children to childless couples. The local schemes available can be discussed with the parents and they can be put in touch with the agencies.

Remaining without children

Some couples will, after careful reassessment of their options, decide to remain childless. This may lead to a reorganization of their life in a very positive way—an approach which should be encouraged. Some couples will wish to avoid all exposure to children, while others seek contact through, for examples, working in a school.

Prognosis

The couple will be eager to have an idea of their chances of success after completion of the investigations. Current policies tend to favour assessing the overall fertility in general terms in a relatively short time, whereas in the past a deliberate attitude of procrastination was sometimes adopted in the knowledge that many pregnancies would occur spontaneously. Many difficulties surround attempts to give the couple accurate information about their chances without treatment, particularly when multiple factors are involved, and about how treatment would improve them. As indicated, the medical profession itself is often uncertain. Where possible, a realistic picture should be described, and the natural inclination to continue active management for its own sake and not because of proven worth be resisted. This particularly applies to couples with unexplained infertility. Life table analysis has been used to present data on this subject but the information remains vague as yet for many factors discussed above. The general practitioner should try to obtain an idea of the outlook from the specialist involved. The decision to persist with active management should be reviewed regularly with the patients.

General practitioners have much to offer couples with infertility, and can contribute directly to many dimensions of the problem even when much of the active management is being supervised in specialist clinics. The care in specialist clinics will only be optimal when close communication is maintained in both directions with the general practitioner.

FURTHER READING

Pepperall, R. J., Hudson, B., and Wood, C., (ed.) (1981). *The infertile couple.* Churchill Livingstone, New York.
Hull, M., (ed.) (1981). Developments in infertility practice. *Clinics in obstetrics and gynaecology.* W. B. Saunders, Eastbourne.
Lunenfeld, B. and Iusler, V. (1978). *Infertility.* Grosse Verlag, Berlin.

Further reading for patients

Stanway, A. (1980). *Why us?* Granada, London.
Decker, A. and Loebl, S. (1980). *We want to have a baby*: Penguin, Harmondsworth.

USEFUL ADDRESSES

National Association for the Childless,
Birmingham Settlement,
318 Summer Lane,
Birmingham.
B19 3RL

13 Vaginal discharge

David Barlow

Vaginal discharge is one of the more common complaints of women attending the general practitioner surgery, and it seems that women with a vaginal discharge see the general practitioner as the appropriate person to consult, whereas men with a urethral discharge are more likely to attend Sexually Transmitted Disease (STD) clinics. Of those women with such a discharge investigated by the general practitioner there will be no demonstrable organism in approximately 50 per cent of cases, although a higher rate of specific diagnosis is made in women attending STD clinics. This may be for several reasons, including the self-selected type of population going to STD clinics and the thoroughness of the investigations.

It is all too easy to make a quick diagnosis on the history and symptoms and all too easy to get the diagnosis wrong. Most doctors would accept that a white discharge with pruritis might be likely to be due to a vaginal infection with *Candida albicans* and that an appropriate antifungal preparation would clear up the trouble. This was the case in one general practitioner series where 48 per cent of non-pregnant women presenting with vaginal discharge and/or pruritis were found to have monilia. However, balanced against this is the fact that 40 per cent of women with gonorrhoea (and no other coincidental infection) present with vaginal discharge and 9 per cent present with pruritus as their main complaint. Nevertheless, Fry (1979) found that he only diagnosed one case of gonorrhoea in his practice every five years. But of course the incidence will vary according to the type of practice.

The 'classical' descriptions of the more common vaginal infections are well known and a thick, curd-like white discharge which is itchy yet not offensive, would quite rightly make most doctors think of thrush. However, such a presentation, as with other 'classical' appearances, may well be the exception rather than the rule. Candidal infection is often found in conjunction with other infective causes of vaginal discharge and the resultant combined discharge may well be both difficult to diagnose clinically and resistant to simple anti-candidal treatment.

There are many different causes of an increase or alteration in vaginal discharge, some of them infective and some of them secondary to other disease processes or changes in normal physiological function. The possibility of a psychosexual reason for consultation, particularly if the discharge is normal, should also be remembered. Assessing the degree of abnormality of a vaginal discharge is not easy but a history of soiled underwear or the need to use tampons or towels to cope with the increased flow is always significant. Discharges are difficult to assess clinically during the menstrual period (although laboratory samples can be taken) and a patient should be advised to return for re-examination several days after the period has finished. Finally, it should be remembered that it is impossible to distinguish between vaginal and cervical discharges by examination of the vulva and introitus. A well-lit speculum examination is vital.

BACTERIAL CAUSES OF VAGINAL DISCHARGE

Candida albicans

Patients with vaginal or vulval symptoms secondary to infection with *Candida albicans* make up the largest group of patients presenting with discharge.

Symptoms

The predominant symptoms are of discharge and pruritus or soreness. These symptoms by no means always go together, the patient's reaction to the infection determining which seems to be the most important. The reason for this is that *Candida* is a potent allergenic agent and, as with infestation by *Sarcoptes scabei*, it is a hypersensitivity which causes the intense itching. Thus one woman may have a quantity of candidal discharge which is apparent to her doctor and herself and yet feel no irritation, while another may present with no discharge at all but have a marked vulvo-vaginitis. In many cases, of course, both symptoms are present. Superficial dyspareunia occurs, sometimes manifesting itself as a post-coital feeling of genital 'heat'.

The first indication of vaginal infection with candida may be the development of an itchy, inflamed balano-posthitis in the male sexual partner. Not infrequently, it is impossible to isolate any fungus from the male as his reaction is of the allergic type. Candida often also infects the perineum, perianal region, and the natal cleft and all or any of these sites may serve as a source of reinfection if they are not treated.

Signs

The discharge in 'pure' candidal infection is white, may be profuse, and is sometimes described as having the consistency and appearance of cottage cheese. Certainly candida may have that appearance but it need not, and the lack of such a classical look does not exclude the diagnosis. When there is infection of the surrounding skin, it may take on a waxy appearance with occasional longitudinal fissures up to 5 mm in length. These thin red streaks are by turns itchy or slightly painful and, if present, are a more reliable diagnostic criterion than the nature of the discharge. Similar fissures are seen on the foreskin in some cases of candidal balanitis and give rise to much anxiety in the patient and confusion in the examining doctor.

Diagnosis

A confirmed rather than an assumed diagnosis is always preferable, if sometimes inconvenient, particularly in recalcitrant cases. It is an all too common story of the patient with recurrent 'thrush' who is repeatedly treated with the full gamut of antifungal agents while the true cause of the discharge remains stubbornly, but naturally, resistant to such treatment. The counsel of perfection is to examine a sample of discharge microscopically, suspended in a drop of normal saline or, preferably, Gram-stained when the typical oval spores or strings of mycelium can be identified. At very least, a sample should be sent to the local laboratory. Although there are special culture media available such as Sabouraud's, the fungus will survive perfectly well in Stuart's medium. The organism can be readily diagnosed on a Papanicolau-stained cervical smear but the local cytology service may rightly cavil at its use for this purpose.

Treatment

There is a large and lucrative market for antifungal agents and the pharmaceutical companies who spend a great deal of time and money on advertising and promotion are well aware of this. There are two main groups of antifungal compounds in general use, nystatins and the imidazole derivatives. Neither griseofulvin nor amphotericin B are suitably formulated for the treatment of vulvo-vaginal candidiasis. Painting with gentian violet is messy, time-consuming, and of dubious advantage. It is very difficult to assess the relative merits of the various treatments available and it is suggested that the two prime considerations should be patient acceptability and cost. There is conflicting evidence about the antifungal activity of the different imidazoles—little of it of any scientific merit.

The first principle in treatment is to deliver the antifungal agent to the infected site. There will be scant hope of eradicating vaginal infection if only pessaries are used when there is a concomitant perineal candidiasis. Whether an attempt should be made to clear the intestine of commensal candida with oral nystatin (which is not absorbed) is not agreed. Such evidence as exists shows little difference in overall cure or relapse rates when oral treatment is used.

Patient compliance is of great importance although most patients with recurrent thrush are sufficiently motivated to complete a course of treatment. Pessaries should always be prescribed in conjunction with a cream or ointment for local use. This local treatment may need to be continued for longer than the vaginal applications since the skin may take many weeks to become free from infection.

Reinfection by a similarly infected sexual partner is probably less common than has been suspected in the past, but it may well be worth suggesting that the cream be used on the penis, particularly if it is uncircumcised. While sexual transmission of *Candida albicans* undoubtedly occurs, it is perhaps more common for sexual intercourse to provoke symptoms from an already present infection.

Predisposing factors which make eradication of candida more difficult include treatment with broad-spectrum antibiotics, the oral contraceptive, glycosuria, and steroid tablets and creams. It is also found commonly in immuno-compromised patients. Some patients have many recurrent attacks and for these, intermittent treatment over a period of months (for instance, one nystatin pessary at night, three times weekly) often succeeds where other attempts have failed. A useful adjunct to this is the recommendation that some antifungal cream be used on every occasion of sexual intercourse, a small amount being put around the introitus before the act. This not only ensures good distribution of the antifungal and treatment of any penile infection, but also adds an element of lubrication to what has often become a tense and dry vagina. I do not believe that recurrent candidal infection is an indication for stopping the oral contraceptive.

Nystatin pessaries are usually given, two at night, for fourteen days. They are quite messy and compliance is probably less good than with the shorter course treatments. However, they are as effective as the more modern preparations and are much cheaper if used (see above) for a prolonged, intermittent treatment. They should always be prescribed with cream or ointment.

There are three imidazole derivatives on the market for local use, clotrimazole, econazole, and miconazole. For all the claims of therapeutic superiority there is no significant difference between them apart from the question of cost. Treatment varies between 6 days and 1 day which is an advantage in the first-attack patient. Some preparations are solid pessaries, some on the end of a tampon, others vaginal creams with an applicator. As with nystatin, a cream should also be prescribed. There has recently been released an oral, absorbed antifungal called ketoconazole. It is, no doubt, the first of a whole generation of such products and time alone will show whether they hold any advantages over local treatment. They may certainly be more acceptable to the patient. Ketoconazole should not be prescribed for pregnant women or those at risk of pregnancy.

Trichomonas vaginalis (TV)

Trichomonas vaginalis is a sexually transmitted infection. The causative motile protozoon is frequently found in association with other infections and some authorities believe that the patient with TV should *always* be screened for other sexually transmitted conditions. Between 30 and 40 per cent of women with gonorrhoea also have TV and, depending on which population is screened, 10 to 30 per cent of women with trichomonas have gonorrhoea.

Symptoms

The symptoms are mainly due to the irritant discharge which is produced. There may be considerable vulval and introital discomfort, a typical fishy smell, and in some cases an 'external' dysuria. Sexual intercourse can be extremely uncomfortable, if not impossible, and the underwear is often soiled. Some women are rapidly aware of their infection, while others put up with the increase in discharge, regarding it as part of normal variation. Others are truly asymptomatic.

Signs

Classically, the discharge of TV is thin, profuse, bubbly, and off-white. As with *Candida albicans* one does see the 'classical' appearance from time to time but as often as not the discharge, perhaps because it is mixed with other pathogens, differs from pure infection both in colour and consistency. The offensive smell is probably the most constant feature. There may be a marked vulvo-vaginitis and, particularly in fatter women, a soggy, uncomfortable intertrigo may spread down the inner thighs. There may be a degree of vulval oedema and the epithelium looks red and raw. There are few, if any, signs or symptoms in the male partner although a mild urethritis may be present.

Diagnosis

The easiest method of diagnosis is to take a drop of discharge with a cotton wool-tipped swab and suspend it in a drop of normal saline on a slide. This, with a cover-slip on top, can be examined under the microscope with a low-power (×40) lens. The trichomonads may be seen moving around the field with a typical 'whirring' movement of their flagellae, the whole examination needing to take less than three minutes. Unfortunately, other than in departments of genito-urinary medicine, microscopes seem very thin on the ground and it would be well worthwhile resurrecting or investing in a cheap microscope as it is also of great use in the immediate diagnosis of *Gardnerella vaginalis*. Although specialized culture and transport media exist for TV, it will survive very well in Stuart's medium and, if no microscope is available, it is vital that the putative diagnosis be confirmed in the laboratory. The important differential diagnosis is with *Gardnerella* (see below).

Treatment

Until the late 1950s, there was no satisfactory treatment of TV and a wide variety of ineffective local preparations was used. The introduction of metronidazole literally revolutionized treatment. A dose of 400 mg twice daily for five days will give a cure rate of over 90 per cent, although 200 mg three times daily for seven days is a more common alternative. A single dose of 2 g orally has recently been shown to be as effective. An alternative preparation, nimorazole, has also had therapeutic success in a dosage of 1 g twelve-hourly for three doses or 2 g in a single dose. There seems to be little to choose between these two preparations.

Prescription of these drugs should be avoided during the first trimester although no teratogenic effects have been reported. Side effects are rare but there is an interaction with alcohol, which can produce a severe headache and vomiting, about which all patients should be carefully warned.

There are several reasons for apparent treatment failure, of which the most common is reinfection by the sexual partner. As mentioned above, the male is frequently asymptomatic and, much as it may conflict with the philosophy of diagnosis before treatment, it is advisable to treat the male partner anyway in situations where his attendance is difficult or inappropriate with the proviso that one or other must be tested for other sexually transmitted diseases. It is often easier to exclude other infection in the male and he should be encouraged to attend a special department for screening. True metronidazole resistance is exceedingly rare other than in the laboratory and treatment failure which is not due to reinfection may result from poor absorption from the gut and inactivation of metronidazole by other bacteria in the vagina. In the difficult cases where these two causes are a possibility, May and Baker, the manufacturers of Flagyl (metronidazole) can be contacted to analyse serum levels of the drug and look for metronidazole-splitting vaginal flora.

Gardnerella vaginalis (Haemophilus vaginalis, Corynebacterium vaginale)

This Gram-variable, facultative anaerobe is associated with non-specific vaginitis (not to be confused with non-specific urethritis or non-specific genital infection), and, after *Candida albicans*, is the most common cause of vaginal discharge in women of reproductive years. Non-specific vaginitis is itself a misnomer since the condition is not characterized by any inflammation of the vaginal wall and the prime symptom is of vaginal discharge and genital odour. It has only recently been generally recognized that *Gardnerella*, with its almost invariable accompanying Gram-negative anaerobic infection, is of such clinical importance and its uncertain taxonomy, pleomorphism, and variable nutritional requirements in the laboratory make it a microbiologist's nightmare. For all that, it is fairly easy to diagnose in the clinic and is also readily treatable.

The role played by the coincidental anaerobic infection is uncertain and it is quite possible that the bulk of the discharge and the offensive smell associated with this organism are not due to *Gardnerella* but to the other organisms present. It is interesting to speculate that *Gardnerella vaginalis*, with its symptoms and discharge similar to those of *Trichomonas vaginalis*, may well have been treated for years as Trichomonas with the correct antibiotic but for the wrong reasons, metronidazole being effective in both conditions. There is increasing evidence that this organism is sexually transmitted and, although it is early days in the evolution of management of these cases, it may well be important to treat the sexual partners of infected women in spite of difficulty in isolating the bacterium in male subjects.

Symptoms

The symptoms are of vaginal discharge and/or offensive genital odour. This latter symptom is a not uncommon complaint amongst women attending STD clinics, and a recent survey (Blackwell 1982) from St. Thomas' Hospital, London showed 34 per cent of unselected patients to have this problem. Blackwell has also pointed out that they may only recognize that an abnormal odour was present after treatment. She advocates sniffing the vaginal speculum after insertion, a method first suggested by Gardner and Dukes in their original article on the subject in 1955. In experienced hands, the clinician's assessment of the odour correlates very well with laboratory findings. The discharge may sometimes be enough to soil the underwear but in some cases, although obvious to the examining doctor, it is not thought troublesome by the patient.

Signs

The odour has already been mentioned. It is described most commonly as a fishy smell or like rotting flesh. The similarity between the odour found in TV and *Gardnerella* is probably due to their both being associated with anaerobic infection. The vaginal discharge is off-white, often grey, profuse and runny. It would take a confident clinician to distinguish this from a trichomonal discharge in the majority of cases.

Diagnosis

Although not often done in general practice, the on-the-spot diagnosis of *Gardnerella vaginalis* is comparatively easy and fairly accurate. If a microscope is available a drop of discharge suspended in saline will reveal 'clue' cells. These are vaginal epithelial cells to which bacteria are adherent. They may be seen as a speckling on the surface of a cell and a slight protuberant irregularity on the edge of the cells due to bacteria. This appearance should not be confused with the stippling which is seen in normal cells due to the granular intracellular contents. In the most obvious cases there are sheets of bacteria overlying the cells. The microscopic differentiation between *Gardnerella* and *Trichomonas* is thus very easy although, of course, both infections may coincide. The pH of the vaginal discharge is always greater than 5 and this can be checked with pH paper. If a microscope is not available, a drop of discharge can be placed on a slide and admixed with a drop of 10 per cent potassium hydroxide. Transiently (the mixing should be done under the nose) there is release of an ammoniacal smell and the results of such a positive 'amine test' correlate very well with the subsequent culture of *G. vaginalis*, and may be preferable to sniffing the speculum. A sample taken in Stuart's medium may give culture confirmation of the infection with the proviso that not all bacteriologists agree on the diagnostic criteria for this organism.

Treatment

Somewhat to most investigators' surprise, it was found that gardnerella infection responds best to metronidazole *in vivo* while the *in vitro* sensitivity to this antibiotic is not very great. There are two possible explanations for this. It may be that the invariable anaerobic organisms are responsible for all the signs and symptoms and that their elimination enables recolonization of the vagina by lactobacilli to take place. Alternatively, there is some evidence that a breakdown metabolite of metronidazole is much more active than the parent drug.

A five- or seven-day course of metronidazole in the dosage used against trichomonas is effective in the majority of cases. As yet there is little information on a single-dose treatment although it might be expected to be effective. In our own clinic a high proportion of male contacts of women with this infection are found also to have a non-specific urethritis (although *G. vaginalis* is not an accepted cause of NSU) and it is likely that patients with gardnerella will be shown to need screening for other sexually transmitted diseases. Information on this point is at present scanty.

Other bacterial causes of vaginal discharge

Neisseria gonorrhoeae

If it is the only infection present, gonorrhoea produces a vaginal discharge in about 40 per cent of women. Contrary to the textbook descriptions, there is no characteristic appearance to this discharge and it is unhelpful as a pointer to the possibility of gonococcal infection. Nor, incidentally, are urinary symptoms common in cases of female gonorrhoea today. Whether a woman should be screened for gonorrhoea depends very much on the circumstances. Thus some 15 per cent of women attending our clinic at St. Thomas' Hospital have gonorrhoea whereas less than 0.3 per cent of antenatal patients are infected. In a family planning clinic the figure might vary between 0.5 and 2 per cent depending on the district. There are no reliable figures for the numbers presenting to a general practice surgery with gonorrhoea but they are unlikely to be high nor justify routine screening. However, the finding of *Trichomonas vaginalis* should alert the examining doctor to the possibility of an associated neisserian infection and such patients might constitute a high-risk group in whom gonorrhoea should be excluded. There is *no place* for the high vaginal swab (HVS) in the diagnosis or exclusion of gonorrhoea in women since it is simply not sensitive enough. Likewise, the GCFT is neither sensitive nor selective enough to be of any use. Samples should be taken from the sites most likely to be infected (cervix 90 per cent, urethra 75 per cent, and rectum 40 per cent) remembering that 5 per cent of infections occur only in the urethra and 5 per cent only in the rectum. A charcoal swab taken from the relevant sites and put into Stuart's medium will survive up to 48 hours if kept at 4 °C in a 'fridge.

Penicillin is still the treatment of choice for gonorrhoea but increased resistance of the organism to this and other antibiotics continues to pose problems. The ideal treatment is a single dose either orally or parenterally which can be seen to be taken at the time of prescription. Two grams of ampicillin combined with one gram of probenecid, both orally, gives a cure rate of over 95 per cent in the UK, although in areas of high antibiotic resistance such as the Far East or the USA larger doses will be needed. There has recently been noted an increase in the number of truly pencillin-resistant organisms, the so-called β-lactamase producing gonococci. At the present time the majority of such infections are imported from abroad and do not pose any great numerical problem although there is always the risk that, with the indiscriminate use of penicillin in the treatment of undiagnosed urethritis in the male, they will become more widespread. Some of the more modern cephalosporins (such as cefotaxime, 500 mg intramuscularly) are effective against the β-lactamase-producing strains.

Many other antibiotics are capable of eradicating gonorrhoea including tetracyclines and co-trimoxazole. This latter, in a dose of five tablets twelve-hourly to a total of fifteen tablets, is effective in cases of penicillin hypersensitivity.

Where gonorrhoea is complicated by salpingitis the single-dose treatment is inadequate and antibiotics should be given for at least ten days preferably combined with bed-rest although this is rarely practiced. Although the gonococcus may be the organism isolated from the cervix uteri in a case of salpingitis, it is not necessarily responsible for the pelvic infection. (One recent study from Scandinavia showed that only 13 per cent of such cases had the gonococcus in the tubes.) It may be better practice to give an antibiotic known to be effective not only against the gonococcus but also against chlamydia and mycoplasma. In these circumstances tetracycline, two grams daily in divided doses, is probably preferable although some authorities recommend penicillin and metronidazole. It is most important, when treatment for gonorrhoea is given outside the 'special' clinic, that adequate tests of cure are taken from all the potentially infected sites and that efficient contact-tracing takes place to ensure that all possible contacts are examined for infection.

Chlamydia trachomatis

This odd bacterium is more common than the gonococcus but, because of difficulty in laboratory culture, is not readily diagnosable in many areas. Chlamydia is responsible for the majority of cases of non-gonococcal urethritis but does not produce any specific signs or symptoms in women although, as with gonorrhoea, an alteration in vaginal discharge is noticed in 45 per cent of women (Oriel, Johnson, Barlow, Thomas, Nayyar and Reeve 1978). If the local laboratory is able to culture *Chlamydia*, special culture medium is required but the problems involved in sample handling make it advisable that this infection should be excluded in a special clinic.

It is likely that chlamydial infection is more common in general practice than gonorrhoea with a prevalence of perhaps 2 or 3 per cent amongst those attending for contraceptive advice or with genital problems (compared to a figure of 20 per cent of those attending a special clinic).

Unlike gonorrhoea, chlamydial infection cannot be eradicated with a simple single dose treatment and a minimum of ten days is needed to ensure success. Tetracycline or erythromycin (one gram of either daily in divided doses) are the only commonly available antibiotics which are effective against *Chlamydia*. Chlamydial conjunctivitis which is seen in both adults and neonates (in whom it is a much more common cause of 'sticky eye' than gonorrhoea) should be treated with a tetracycline ointment. It sometimes happens that a male partner attends a clinic and, having been diagnosed as having a non-specific urethritis, is asked to bring his wife or girlfriend for examination and treatment. If circumstances prevent her attendance at the clinic it is reasonable for the general practitioner to prescribe the appropriate antibiotic, but it is important that *Trichomonas vaginalis* (which may masquerade as NSU in the man) is first excluded.

Group B streptococci

These bacteria are a not uncommon finding in vaginal secretions and may be mentioned in the report on a high vaginal swab, but it is not clear whether they are a significant cause of vaginal discharge. They are of obvious importance if present in the genital tract in pregnancy or at the time of childbirth, since they may not only be the cause of serious puerperal infection in the mother but are an important cause of overwhelming and lethal infection in the newborn. There is therefore increasing awareness of this finding in pregnancy and that treatment, usually penicillin, should be given. It is debatable as to whether they should be treated in the otherwise asymptomatic, non-pregnant woman. If other symptoms are associated, for example, cystitis, it is probably reasonable to give treatment.

VIRAL CAUSES

Many viruses may be responsible for an alteration in vaginal discharge and the appearance of a discharge coinciding with an attack of measles may be put down to the same cause. Some women notice an increase in discharge when they have a cold.

Herpes simplex

This virus (with its two sub-types, type II predominantly causing genital infection and type I causing facial infection) is now the most common cause of genital ulceration in the UK, and although the obvious infections involve the vulva, there may be involvement of the cervix too in a proportion of cases. In some instances the infection is restricted to the cervix. The resultant discharge, which to the patient will appear as 'vaginal', is mucoid or muco-purulent and will be difficult to diagnose without a speculum examination. Although there is a great deal of anxiety about the possibility of a link between cervical herpes and later development of carcinoma of the cervix, the evidence for this is circumstantial and a large 15-year study has so far failed to reveal any cases of post-herpetic carcinoma, nor has there been any significant increase in the expected small number who have developed a degree of mild dysplasia.

There is no reliable treatment for herpes simplex genital infection although the antiviral compound, idoxuridine, is prescribed by many people in the hope of damping down or shortening an attack. This may be used in an ointment base or, more often, dissolved in di-methyl sulphoxide (DMSO) which aids epithelial penetration. DMSO tends to sting when in contact with the raw, painful ulcers and many patients find the ointment more soothing. The primary attack of genital herpes in the adult may be a very traumatic event with excruciating vulval pain and marked external dysuria. Some patients go into acute retention partly due to the exquisite discomfort on urination, and in some cases because of a sacral myelitis. Catheterization should be avoided if possible and the patient encouraged to pass water in a warm bath. Local application of an anaesthetic such as xylocaine ointment may make urination bearable. A new antiviral compound, acyclovir, seems to be effective in reducing the pain and duration of attacks but is not yet released for general use.

Cytomegalovirus

This is a genital pathogen for which the evidence of sexual transmission is increasing. It is not known whether it is responsible for production of a significant vaginal discharge but it is certainly true that the virus can be isolated from vaginal secretions for several months after the initial infection. Like herpes, genital CMV may present with dysuria.

FOREIGN BODIES

The most common unwanted foreign body today is the retained tampon (see toxic shock syndrome, p. 39). It is productive of the foulest and most evil-smelling of discharges and is also the most easy to treat. Other foreign bodies usually reveal themselves easily unless they have penetrated the wall of the vagina and moved on. Foreign bodies are less easy to diagnose in pre-pubertal girls and it may be necessary to examine the youngster under anaesthetic to exclude this as a cause of vaginal discharge, particularly in the very young from whom no reliable history may be obtainable. Removal of the foreign body is usually treatment enough and antibiotic treatment is not required.

Other foreign bodies are made up of contraceptive aids. A condom is sometimes found high in the vagina and, although it would be unlikely that a cap could be left *in situ* and forgotten, the spermicidal creams and jellies used in conjunction with the cap may be the reason for a complaint of increased discharge. The intrauterine contraceptive device is not uncommonly associated with an increase in vaginal discharge although its origin is not, strictly speaking, the vagina. There is an increased incidence of pelvic inflammatory disease in those with IUCDs and the increase in discharge may originate in the uterus or reflect increased secretion from the endocervix. It is unusual to get positive microbiological reports from patients whose increase in discharge is simply due to the IUCD but the presence of gonococci or chlamydiae greatly increases the chances of salpingitis developing (see Chapter 7, on contraception).

EROSION AND CERVICITIS

Cervical erosion is sometimes offered as the explanation for an increased discharge and many gynaecologists will treat the erosion by cautery or freezing. Although theoretically the increased number of secretory endocervical cells present with an erosion will produce added discharge, the nature of this ought to be mucous and not of itself greatly symptom-producing. Cervicitis is an ill-defined term difficult of accurate description; indeed, the differentiation between 'erosion' (strictly speaking a histological diagnosis) and 'cervicitis', an inflammatory or infective condition, may be clinically impossible, particularly as elements of both may co-exist.

Infections that involve the cervix, including gonorrhoea and chlamydia, may be associated with an abnormal appearance of the cervix and *Trichomonas vaginalis*, a largely vaginal infection, not only gives a 'cervicitis' but may also increase the degree of inflammation on the Papanicolau-stained cervical smear, necessitating repeat six weeks after treatment.

VAGINAL DISCHARGE IN YOUNG GIRLS

Vaginal discharge and/or vulvitis is not uncommon among young pre-pubertal girls. Most of the causes seen in adults are also seen in youngsters, with an emphasis on foreign bodies and threadworm in the very young. Little girls may not complain of symptoms but their underwear may be stained as a result of the discharge.

Gonorrhoea should not be forgotten as a cause of vulvo-vaginitis for perhaps 5 per cent of daughters of women with gonorrhoea can be shown to have the infection. It seems that transmission via infected fomites such as towels or shared flannels is the usual explanation and sharing the parental bed also carries a high risk. Delicate enquiry may have to be made as to the possibility of sexual transmission, although this is uncommon in the UK.

OTHER SEXUALLY TRANSMITTED INFECTIONS

Although this is primarily a chapter on vaginal discharge, some mention should be made of one or two other infections that are commonly found in conjunction with discharge. Genital or venereal warts thrive in a warm, moist environment and in a majority of cases there is some treatable cause of discharge, the eradication of which will facilitate treatment of the warts. *Condylomata acuminata*, like plain skin warts, are caused by a virus but have a more frond-like appearance. They spread very quickly and may involve the perineum and anus. Local application of podophylline in a strength of 5 to 25 per cent is usually effective, although cautery may be needed in recalcitrant cases. Sexual partners must be screened for infection lest they act as a source of reinfection. *Phthirus pubis*, the 'crab' louse, is almost invariably sexually transmitted and its diagnosis must be followed by vaginal examination and exclusion of other infection. *Molluscum contagiosum*, if found on the genitalia or lower abdomen, is usually sexually transmitted and is an indication for further screening. These small orange/pink umbilicated papules are not, as was previously thought, confined to public school children and all-in wrestlers, and can be treated by piercing the shiny opalescent top with an orange stick dipped in phenol.

REFERENCES AND FURTHER READING

Blackwell, A. L. Non-specific vaginitis. In *A textbook of genito-urinary medicine* (ed. D. Barlow and I. Phillips). Oxford University Press. (In press.)

Fry, John (1979). *Common diseases*. MTP Press, Lancaster.

Gardner, H. L. and Dukes, C. D. (1955). Haemophilus vaginitis. A newly defined specific infection—previously classified "non-specific vaginitis". *Am. J. Obstet. Gynecol.* **69**, 962–76.

Oriel, J. D., Johnson, A. L., Barlow, D., Thomas, B. J., Nayyar, K. C., and Reeve, P. (1978). Infection of the uterine cervix with *Chlamydia trachomatis*. *J. infect. Dis.* **137**, 443–51.

Further reading for patients

Barlow, David (1980). *Sexually transmitted diseases: the facts*. Oxford University Press.

Catterall, Duncan. *Sexually transmitted disease and venereal disease*. BMA Family Doctor booklet. British Medical Association, London.

14 Cystitis

Shirley Elliott and Richard Mayon-White

Most women know what cystitis is, and many will experience it in their lifetime. They will therefore often come to the general practitioner with the diagnosis already made by themselves. Unlike many diseases which have lay synonyms, women use the medical terminology for cystitis. There are hints that the incidence of cystitis in women may be increasing, just as there seems to be an increased incidence in men with non-specific urethritis.

On average 25 women per 1000 people per year will consult their general practitioner with symptoms of cystitis, and many more will have symptoms and treat themselves. A recent survey questioned 3000 women between the ages of 20 and 60 years. Twenty per cent had experienced dysuria in the previous year and of these only ten per cent had consulted their general practitioner. Nearly 50 per cent had experienced dysuria at some time in their lives. Attacks of cystitis occur most commonly in the 25 to 34 age group. First attacks are most common in women aged 15 to 24 years but do occur in older women.

DEFINITIONS

There has been a lot of confusion about what is meant by different terms used in cystitis and urinary tract infections. Although it may seem tedious to go through these terms, we need to define clearly what we mean if we are to understand the problems.

Cystitis is a common complaint in which symptoms of burning pain on micturition (dysuria) and increased frequency of micturition are the principal features. The syndrome is well known to be associated with urinary tract infection, but two-thirds of patients with cystitis do not have significant bacteriuria and many women may have bacteriuria without symptoms of cystitis. The definition of *urinary tract infection* as the presence of micro-organisms in the urinary tract pre-supposes that it is normally sterile. While this is generally true, it is conceivable that bacteria ascend the urethra only to be washed down and out before infection is established. *Bacteriuria* is the presence of bacteria in bladder urine. Because voided urine may be contaminated by organisms from the vaginal labia and introitus, the quantitative criterion of more than 10^5 bacteria per ml of voided urine is generally accepted. These criteria were developed for epidemiological studies in which tests could be repeated to reach a specified degree of certainty that a person did have bacteriuria. The significance of a single result with more than 10^5 bacteriuria per ml will depend on a number of factors which will be discussed in more detail in the section on diagnosis. At this point it is sufficient to say that bacteriuria is present at any one time in about 1 per cent of girls aged 5–10 years, and that this prevalence in women increases with age at the rate of 1 per cent per decade. Many of the women with bacteriuria do not have specific symptoms at the time that the bacteriuria is detected, hence the expression *asymptomatic bacteriuria*. However, a number may have had cystitis in the past or present with other symptoms, so the preferred phrase is *covert bacteriuria*. The term *abacterial cystitis* is used to describe the syndrome of frequency and dysuria without bacteriuria as defined above. This has also been called the *urethral syndrome* but this term does not satisfactorily embrace all the signs and symptoms associated with cystitis, so the preferred term is abacterial cystitis. A proportion of these patients have faecal organisms, particularly *Escherichia coli* (*E. coli*) colonizing the vaginal introitus, and some have evidence of bacteria in the urethra and not the bladder. Thus, there may be an intermediate stage between bacterial cystitis and the absence of infection implied by the term abacterial cystitis.

The major complication of cystitis is acute bacterial *pyelonephritis* and subsequent renal scarring. Acute pyelonephritis is really a clinical diagnosis for a combination of loin pain, fever, and cystitis with supporting evidence from positive urine cultures and occasionally blood cultures. Focal renal scarring with pyelonephritis is partly due to concurrent vesicoureteric reflux which may be the primary abnormality. Another complication is chronic interstitial nephritis with more diffuse nephritis. This has many causes including analgesics and bacterial infections. In clinical practice, cystitis by itself is rarely associated with progressive renal damage. In contrast to the high incidence of cystitis, chronic renal failure due to pyelonephritis is uncommon, about 20 people per million per year. Moreover, many of the women presenting with the effects of pyelonephritis do not have histories of symptomatic urinary tract infections.

NATURAL HISTORY

Until fairly recently there were few epidemiological data about the natural history of urinary tract infections. It is now becoming clear that they represent a continuous spectrum of disorders varying in clinical severity and prognosis. Women with cystitis do not always suffer from the same kind of attack. Symptomatic bacteriuria is not infrequently followed by asymptomatic episodes of bacteriuria and symptomatic patients without bacteriuria may subsequently develop bacteriuria.

Urinary tract infections can be broadly divided into three main groups: covert bacteriuria, cystitis, and pyelonephritis. Covert bacteriuria is not a static condition but shows a constant turnover. As mentioned above, it has been found in screening programmes that 1 per cent of schoolgirls have covert bacteriuria at any one time. By the age of ten, 3 per cent of all girls have had at least one symptomatic urinary tract infection. The prevalence of covert bacteriuria increases at one per cent per decade, so approximately 5 per cent of the adult female population has covert bacteriuria at any one time. The prevalence is constant despite the fact that approximately 25 per cent of the infected population spontaneously lose their infection each year. This finding is confined to non-pregnant women with normal urinary tracts. Antimicrobial treatment of covert bacteriuria in non-pregnant women does not appear to diminish the frequency of symptomatic urinary infections. In one year, approximately 30 per cent of women with symptomless infections go on to develop an attack of cystitis, whereas less than 2 per cent of women with covert bacteriuria develop acute pyelonephritis. The relationship between covert bacteriuria and chronic pyelonephritis with renal scarring is a controversial subject. Until recently it was thought that untreated lower urinary tract infections progressed slowly and often silently to renal scarring, hypertension, and renal failure. Several long-term follow-up studies have suggested that in adults such progression is rare and that, in the absence of complicating factors such as diabetes or obstructive uropathy, lower urinary tract infection is a benign condition. The exceptions to this are infections in pregnant women and those women whose history of urinary tract infections could be traced back to childhood. However, a more recent study by Evans, Kass, Hennèkens, Rosner, Miao, Kendrick, Miall, and Stuart (1982) has shown a positive association between bacteriuria and mortality in women. Further long-term studies are needed to clarify the situation.

It seems probable that renal damage due to infection has its origins in childhood. In studies of children with urinary tract infections 25 per cent had grossly scarred kidneys. About one-third of children with urinary infections show vesico-ureteric reflux which appears to be closely related to the severity of renal scarring.

The situation in pregnant women is quite different. The incidence of covert bacteriuria in the first trimester is between 2 per cent and 6 per cent but the high spontaneous remission rate seen in non-pregnant women does not occur. The reasons for this are poorly understood but hormonal changes leading to dilatation of the pelvi-ureteric system and consequent stasis of urine, together with pressure from the gravid uterus, are thought to be contributory factors which disturb the normal protective mechanism ensured by complete emptying of the bladder. Between 20 and 40 per cent of women with covert bacteriuria in pregnancy go on to develop pyelonephritis of pregnancy. Associated with this is an increased incidence of abortion, prematurity, and small-for-dates babies. Effective anti-microbial treatment of covert bacteriuria in the first trimester lowers the incidence of acute pyelonephritis by 80–90 per cent. Doctors should ensure that all pregnant women are screened for covert bacteriuria at their first antenatal visit. In contrast to the relatively benign course of lower urinary tract infections in non-pregnant women, studies suggest that there is a higher incidence of abnormal urinary tracts in women presenting with covert bacteriuria and/or acute pyelonephritis of pregnancy. There is also a risk of subsequent renal impairment in these two groups.

CAUSES

Although there are several causes of cystitis, there is but one pathology which is inflammatory change in the urethra and bladder.

Infection

(a) Bacteria

Infection with bacteria is the most commonly recognized form of cystitis, where a cause is found, and is characterized by large numbers of bacteria in the urine, greater than 10^5 organisms per ml, and pyuria. It is generally accepted that infection ascends from the perineum along the short female urethra, perhaps during sexual intercourse, with the introduction of a tampon, whilst wiping after defaecation, or through retrograde flow while bathing. This hypothesis is, however, insufficient to explain the pathogenesis of urinary tract infection. The normal flora of the vestibule and urethra consists of lactobacilli, Staphylococcus epidermidis, diphtheroids, and streptococci, and these organisms do not commonly cause cystitis. For infection to ascend, the vestibule needs to be colonized by pathogenic coliforms from the stool and women who have recurrent cystitis are particularly vulnerable to such colonization. The factors predisposing to this are not fully understood but it is thought that the pathogenic bacteria have an enhanced ability to attach themselves to uro-epithelial cells lining the urinary tract. *E. coli* is the commonest bacterial organism found, responsible for 80–90 per cent of bacterial cystitis. *Staph. saprophyticus* accounts for a further 10 per cent and *Neisseria gonorrhoea*, *Klebsiella*, *Proteus*, and *Pseudomonas* make up the remainder. These last three organisms are commonly responsible for urinary tract infections complicated by other factors including obstructive uropathy, e.g. stones, diabetes, or catheterization. Recently it has been easier to culture more fastidious organisms in the laboratory. It is now clear that microaerophilic and anaerobic organisms are a more common cause of bacterial cystitis than previously recognized.

(b) Chlamydia

Recent work suggests that as many as 20 per cent of cases of cystitis may in fact be caused by chlamydial infections. The syndrome may be analogous to non-specific urethritis (NSU) in males, where chlamydial infections are responsible for 40 per cent of cases of non-gonococcal NSU. It is more common where there has been a new sexual partner or where there are several sexual partners.

(c) Other agents

Vulvo-vaginitis needs to be distinguished from cystitis as a cause of dysuria. Infection with *Trichomonas, Candida albicans*, or any organism causing vulvo-vaginitis may give rise to symptoms which mimic cystitis.

Sexual intercourse

The incidence of cystitis is highest among sexually active women although this is by no means the whole story as virgins (from a study on nuns) still have a much higher incidence of cystitis than young men. The incidence of cystitis also rises with parity, which is not necessarily related to the frequency of intercourse. As prevalence of significant bacteriuria increases at a rate of 1 per cent per decade of life in adult females and persists well beyond the peak of sexual activity, this suggests that age as well as increasing parity is a predisposing factor. It is thought that sexual intercourse 'milks' bacteria from the heavily colonized introitus into the sterile urine of the bladder, and any mucosal damage sustained during intercourse acts as a portal of entry for bacteria. However, it may be just coincidental that the peak incidence of cystitis occurs with sexual maturity as 50 per cent of girls with covert bacteriuria had symptomatic urinary tract infections just before embarking on sexual activity. This would support the idea of a susceptible group of women who are more prone to cystitis and in whom intercourse is a trigger.

Contraceptive methods

There is no consensus of opinion whether oral contraceptive use is associated with an increased incidence of cystitis. There is a positive correlation between oral contraceptive use and frequency of intercourse which in itself would predispose to an increased prevalence of cystitis. The peak age of the use of oral contraceptives also coincides with the peak incidence of cystitis. There is anecdotal evidence of increased incidence of cystitis with the contraceptive diaphragm which may be due to the mechanical pressure on the urethra preventing the complete voiding of urine.

Other hormones

There is a further peak in the incidence of cystitis after the menopause. This is related to atrophic urethritis secondary to oestrogen deficiency (see Chapter 4). Anecdotal evidence suggests that hormonal fluctuations in younger women may also contribute to recurrent cystitis, as some women complain of it at a well-defined time during the menstrual cycle.

Chemical factors

Allergy to rubber in contraceptives, foams, and jellies may trigger off attacks of 'chemical cystitis', as can bath salts, soaps, and vaginal deodorants.

Diet

Some patients give a history of dietary-induced symptoms related to foods, e.g. asparagus, which acidify the urine; alcohol is also sometimes implicated. It is thought that chemical changes which alter the pH of the urine interfere with the normal protective mechanism of the normally slightly acid urine which is usually voided in large amounts.

GENERAL MANAGEMENT

It is known that general practitioners see only the tip of the iceberg in terms of all complaints and illnesses. Community studies have shown that less than 20 per cent of women with dysuria and frequency consult their doctor. Management is a complex balance between home-based self-management, treatment initiated by the GP, and, rarely, hospital management.

The reasons which bring women with cystitis to their GP are complex. In a first attack, anxiety about the diagnosis and pain are common reasons for attending the surgery. In recurrent attacks, a woman knows only too well what she has, and her previous experience will usually dictate her course of action. Many patients will have been treated with a course of antimicrobials even if they have abacterial cystitis, and will believe in the efficacy of drug treatment. Others will have discovered that self-treatment with a high fluid intake will often cut short an attack of cystitis, and prefer to treat themselves. A few will opt for self-treatment even if previous attacks have been treated with antimicrobials because of drug-related problems such as thrush or diarrhoea. It is important to remember that recurrent attacks of cystitis may be caused by bacteria and at present the evidence is that they need anti-microbial treatment. Conversely, women who have abacterial cystitis should not be given the impression that there is nothing wrong simply because an obvious cause has not been identified.

In the following sections we will try to outline some strategies for 'self help' as well as the more conventional antimicrobial treatment.

Clinical history and examination

In both the single attack and in recurrent attacks of cystitis, the history is generally more helpful than examination. The symptoms of dysuria, frequency, suprapubic tenderness, and occasionally haematuria are common to the two groups. A careful history may elicit factors predisposing to cystitis such as sexual intercourse or allergy to contraceptive foams. Most women will have noticed if their cystitis is related to sex, but may not volunteer the information unless asked directly about it. Both abacterial and bacterial cystitis can relate to sex but the bacterial type seems to start relatively earlier than abacterial cystitis which may not present for up to 36 hours after intercourse. A full sexual history will reveal whether there is adequate lubrication during intercourse and whether the choice of contraception is a relevant factor.

A distinction should be made between dysuria caused by vulvo-vaginitis and that caused by cystitis. Direct questioning as to whether the burning is on the 'outside' of the labia or 'lips' (vulvo-vaginitis) or on the 'inside' of the urethra (cystitis) may help to distinguish these two conditions. One should ask about vaginal discharge and penile discharge in partners as sexually transmitted diseases such as trichomonas infection can cause dysuria. If there is a history of several sexual partners or a recent change of partner, *Chlamydia* may be the cause.

Examination should include palpation of the loin area to exclude acute pyelonephritis. A pelvic examination may reveal atrophic vaginitis, prolapse, urethral caruncle, or constipation which may cause incomplete emptying of the bladder; in practice this is only done if the clinical history gives some indication that this is necessary.

INITIAL INVESTIGATION

The question of whether a patient's cystitis is due to bacteria or not can only be resolved by bacteriological tests. However, it is generally accepted that it is not always feasible to arrange these tests or to delay therapeutic decisions until results are available.

Collection of urine specimen

Clearly, to test whether there are bacteria in the bladder urine one needs to collect a specimen with little or no contamination from the urethra or vulva. Patients should be given clear instructions for the collection of midstream specimen. Written instructions are helpful and several drug companies print leaflets. Involvement of the practice nurse in the collection of specimens may also be useful. As a general guide, women should be given the following instructions in a readily comprehensible form.

1. If there is vaginal discharge or menstruation, place a tampon in the vagina.
2. Spread the vulva with one hand.
3. With the other hand, wipe the vulval area with cotton wool, gauze or tissues moistened with warm water and soap. Wipe from front to back.
4. Repeat this 2 or 3 times with fresh pieces of cotton wool without soap. Finally wipe dry.
5. Take the specimen container in one hand and start to pass urine into the pan. Catch some of the middle part of the stream in the bottle, then continue into the pan.
6. Replace the lid on the container or transfer to a container with a lid. It is often easier to collect in a wide-mouthed container.
7. On no account should disinfectant solutions be used for cleaning the perineum or containers as traces may remain and kill the bacteria in the specimen.

But in practice many patients give adequate specimens without any prior cleansing. However, greater care should be taken when collecting critical specimens, for example, collecting a repeat specimen from a pregnant woman whose previous specimen was contaminated. Rarely it is necessary to resort to suprapubic aspiration of urine to obtain a diagnostic specimen. This technique is generally reserved for children, and occasionally during pregnancy and in situations where it is impossible to obtain an MSU.

Transport of urine specimen

Every transport method has problems, whether administrative, financial, or technical. A major problem is the speed with which specimens have to reach the laboratory to get meaningful bacteriological results. Transit time should be less than two hours, but this is feasible only when patients can take their own specimens to the laboratory; it would clearly be impossible in rural areas.

The bacterial population of a urine specimen can be kept stable during transit by keeping the specimen at 4 °C (ordinary refrigerator temperature) or with boric acid which acts as a preservative. Both methods have the advantage of preserving the cells in urine. Another solution to the transit problem is the urine dipslide. The principle is to inoculate a bacterial medium with a standard volume of urine by immersing an agar-coated slide or spoon in freshly collected urine. Bacterial growth can then occur during transit without distorting the final bacterial count, which is measured by the density of bacterial colonies on the agar surface. Another advantage is that the dipslide can be incubated and read in the surgery without more technical procedures. The disadvantages of the dipslides are less readily perceived. They are difficult to inoculate with small amounts of urine (less than 10 ml); they can become dried out or contaminated before use; it is less easy to examine the bacterial colonies for mixed growths than the conventional bacteriology petri dish; and the agar does not always adhere to the slide, making the culture difficult to read. Dipslides also require some care on the patient's part; not to touch the agar surface; to immerse the slide fully; to drain the excess fluid off the slide. Some patients leave the urine in the dipslide container, so invalidating the test. The ease of use within the surgery also leads to disadvantages: lack of quality control and a temptation to test for antibiotic sensitivity with a non-standard method sometimes against only a second line antimicrobial agent. These disadvantages can be minimized provided that the facility for sending whole urine specimens to the laboratory is retained. The advantages of the whole urine specimen are important. The microscopic evidence of pyuria or haematuria indicate organic urinary tract disease when the results of culture are equivocal.

One difficulty with dipslides has been administrative. Laboratory budgets are related to the number of specimens received, and microbiologists may be reluctant to provide dipslides which will be read in the surgeries and will not be credited to their departments. Most laboratories can prepare media for less than the cost of dipslides (15–20p in 1981) and so have little incentive to provide general practitioners with dipslides. On the other hand, most general practitioners have been unwilling to buy dipslides on the practice accounts.

Laboratory methods

The typical laboratory test for urinary tract infection is a semiquantitative culture on one or more bacteriology media. The media are chosen to assist the identification of the common urinary pathogens, and may not support the growth of more fastidious organisms, like anaerobes, which are not regarded as common causes of cystitis. Urine specimens are a major part of the microbiology laboratory workload and methods must be kept simple. Some laboratories screen urine specimens by a simple culture technique that divides them into those that are essentially normal and those that require further investigation. While this approach is suitable for screening for covert bacteriuria, it is rather insensitive for the clinical diagnostic specimen.

All present cultural methods have the disadvantage of taking 18–24 hours. Unfortunately, the chemical methods which can give a rapid diagnosis are relatively insensitive. But newer chemical methods are being developed, with the object of automating the technical procedures and giving a rapid screening test. These methods will be laboratory based, and will not solve the practical problems of the general practitioner.

Simple light microscopy on a centrifuged sample of urine (400 r.p.m. for 10 minutes) is a useful adjunct to culturing specimens. The technique requires practice, but can be used in a surgery. The finding of more than 20 pus cells per high power field suggests inflammation of the urinary tract. A purulent vaginal discharge can produce an apparent pyuria, but vaginal epithelial cells should also be seen. Cell counts can be made more accurately with a microscopic counting chamber: 100 pus cells per cc mm of uncentrifuged urine is strong evidence for infection, and more than 10 per cc mm is abnormal. Squamous cells come from the vaginal or vulval epithelium and indicate a degree of contamination. Proteinuria is a very insensitive indicator of bacteriuria.

INTERPRETATION OF BACTERIOLOGY RESULTS

Trying to interpret bacteriology results can be confusing and we will try and find a way through the maze. There are four common types of results from the bacteriological tests on urine from symptomatic patients (see Table 14.1).

Table 14.1 *Interpretation of urine bacteriology*

Bacterial count (ml)	Culture	wbc more than 100/mm^3	Interpretation
10^3 or less	Few or no colonies	No	No infection
		Yes	On antimicrobials? If repeated, unusual organism?
about 10^4	Mixed	Yes or no	Probable contamination; repeat if possible
	Single organism	No	
		Yes	Probable infection but repeat if asymptomatic
10^5 and above	Single organism	Yes or no	
	Mixed	Yes or no	Probable contaminants; repeat if possible

1. No (significant) bacterial growth

If the urine contains fewer than 10^3 bacteria per ml, the woman either has abacterial cystitis or has a falsely negative culture. A common cause of false negative results is antimicrobial drugs taken before the specimen. Rarer causes are slow-growing or fastidious microorganisms which are missed by ordinary laboratory methods. Renal tuberculosis, viruses, chlamydias, and anaerobes are examples of the latter. Pyuria without bacterial growth should be checked with a second specimen collected when the woman is not taking antimicrobial drugs.

2. Significant bacteriuria

If the urine has been cleanly collected, suitably transported, and contains more than 10^5 per ml of a likely urinary pathogen, a diagnosis of bacteriuria is straightforward. In such cases, the bacterial count is much higher than 10^5 per ml, and this finding is supported by pyuria. The likely pathogens are *Escherichia coli*, Proteus species, *Staphylococcus saprophyticus* (also called *Staph. albus, Staph. epidermidis*, or micrococci), other types of enterobacteria (sometimes labelled 'coliforms', or identified as Klebsiella or Enterobacter species), and faecal streptococci. The main question left by such a result is the choice of treatment which will be discussed under a separate heading below.

High bacterial counts without pyuria in specimens which have been in transit for more than four hours without refrigeration or boric acid, must be suspected as false positives. This is particularly so if faecal streptococci are found, because these bacteria multiply rapidly in urine.

3. Intermediate bacterial counts

Bacterial counts in the range of 10^4 to 10^5 per ml can be difficult to interpret. Some women with urinary tract infections have specimens with counts in this range; a repeat specimen taken a few hours later may have higher counts. A pure culture from a fresh specimen with pyuria can therefore be taken as evidence of infection. On the other hand, these results should be treated with suspicion, and classified as probable contaminants if there is more than one organism, no pyuria, or if the specimen has been delayed more than two hours in transit.

4. High mixed counts

Urinary tract infections with more than one strain of bacterium are unusual in the uncatheterized person. Therefore mixed cultures, and different organisms from repeated specimens, are regarded as evidence of contamination. There is a tendency to treat a contaminated specimen as a negative result. There is little else that one can do with a unique specimen, like the pre-treatment specimen from a single episode of cystitis. However, a contaminated specimen really gives no result at all. Another specimen should be collected with as much care as possible if there is still a need to determine whether the patient has bacteriuria. There is one exception to the uselessness of the contaminated specimen. If the contaminating organisms include large numbers of beta-haemolytic streptococcus group A, the patient probably has vulvo-vaginitis due to this organism and the diagnosis is made.

APPLICATION OF BACTERIOLOGY RESULTS

A logical procedure for the management of cystitis would be to await the result of the test for bacteriuria before deciding on treatment. Three factors militate against this logic: one is the difficulty of collecting and transporting specimens satisfactorily; the second is the delay of at least one day in obtaining a definite result; the third is a general belief in the efficacy of antimicrobial drugs in relieving the symptoms within one or two days. So the choice of treatment is often decided at the first consultation. Yet urine specimens collected from women in the acute phase of cystitis continue to be a major part of a microbiologist's workload. What purpose is there in these specimens? One purpose is to have the results of antibiotic sensitivity testing, in case the patient does have bacteriuria and does not respond to the initial therapy. However, such changes in therapy are infrequent in practice. A second reason is to make the diagnosis of one illness as complete as possible, because an attack of cystitis may be part of a repeated process. Thirdly, one may wish to follow up the bacteriuric episodes with specimens to test clearance or with other investigations. As a general rule, women with recurrent attacks of cystitis or with signs of pyelonephritis should have urine cultures to make the diagnosis as definite as possible, and to assess the effects of treatment.

The educational value of specimens is less easy to define. An intelligent interest in the results may help the general practitioner to distinguish subgroups with the broad syndrome of cystitis. Such features are likely to be subtle and not demonstrable in a clinical trial. The accumulation of knowledge about antibiotic resistance depends on a supply of clinical specimens. However, there have been few attempts to collect this information in a systematic way from representative samples of the population. When conclusions are drawn from laboratory results it is assumed that general practitioners are fairly consistent in their patterns of clinical investigation. Perhaps doctors with easy access to laboratories should have definite policies for urine cultures from their female patients to provide the basis for these conclusions.

FURTHER INVESTIGATIONS AND FOLLOW-UP

Attitudes on investigation and follow-up of women with proven urinary tract infections have changed in recent years. An awareness of the high incidence of bacterial cystitis and covert bacteriuria compared with the low incidence of complications has tempered the enthusiasm for numerous post-treatment checks and radiology.

Further investigation of a patient with abacterial cystitis is limited. If the attacks are repeated, it is worth culturing the first 5 ml of voided urine in addition to the midstream urine in the acute stage. This first urine washes out the urethral contents. Pus cells and numerous bacteria of one species indicate a urethritis antecedent to bladder infection. It is therefore reasonable to use anti-microbial drugs to treat such episodes. At present, a search for more unusual microbial causes of cystitis, e.g. viruses and anaerobic bacteria, has no established place in the management of such patients. If a woman has repeated attacks of bacterial cystitis within weeks or months of each other, urine cultures at 3 days and 5–6 weeks after the end of treatment will help to define whether the recurrences are a reinfection, i.e. a new organism starting a fresh infection or relapse with the re-emergence of an incompletely treated infection. The distinction is not sharp, but re-infection should be managed by a preventative regime whereas relapses need longer courses of treatment. The length of these courses depends on what has been tried before. There are no golden rules, 7–14 days instead of 2–7 days. Rather than extending full dosage treatment beyond 14 days, a half or quarter dosage daily continued for three months can control frequent relapses or re-infections. It is worth discussing these patients with the microbiologist for advice on anti-microbial drugs and help in distinguishing relapses from reinfections.

Attempts to distinguish upper from lower urinary tract infections using methods such as antibody coated bacteria in urine specimens have not gained wide acceptance. This particular test promised to be a useful non-invasive method, but it is not sufficiently specific or sensitive for routine use in most laboratories. Bladder wash-out methods and ureteric catheterization are outside the scope of general practice and are usually used as research methods.

Indications for radiological investigation

The clearest indication for radiological investigation is clinical pyelonephritis. There is an increased incidence of structural abnormalities in women with covert bacteriuria of pregnancy so any patient with covert bacteriuria or pyelonephritis of pregnancy should have an IVP and post-voiding films after delivery.

There is no consensus of opinion about radiological investigations in non-pregnant adult women, but children should be investigated by IVP and micturating cystogram in reverse relation to age, i.e. the younger the child the more important it is to exclude a structural abnormality of the urinary tract. Smellie and Normand (1968) have shown that infections in children in the presence of vesico-ureteric reflux can lead to renal scarring and impairment of kidney growth. However, less than 5 per cent of children investigated needed surgery. With increase in age the likelihood of having a structural lesion diminishes and indications for radiology in teenagers are poorly defined.

Our present understanding is that if the patient has no underlying abnormality of the urinary tract or other disorder such as diabetes, and if there is an easily identifiable trigger, such as sexual intercourse, radiological investigation is unlikely to reveal any abnormality. There are two exceptions. First, those women whose history of urinary tract infections dates back to childhood are more likely to have a structural abnormality and to develop renal impairment and so merit further investigation. Secondly, infections due to unusual or resistant organisms such as proteus are more likely to be associated with urinary calculi and should be further investigated. Investigations such as cystoscopy and cysto-urethrography will depend on the results of the IVP.

TREATMENT

High fluid intake and anti-microbial agents have been the mainstay of treatment, but which of these is the more important is not known. Nor is it known how long the treatment should last or what the dosage of drugs should be.

Fluids

The urinary tract is usually kept sterile by regular voiding of large volumes of slightly acid urine. These natural defences can be usefully employed in treating cystitis. It is known that bacteria do not multiply as rapidly in very dilute urine, so increasing fluid intake to stimulate a diuresis helps to flush out bacteria and decrease the number of bacteria in bladder urine. Bacterial growth is also inhibited in urine which is either more acid or more alkaline than normal. Agents which are commonly used to make urine more alkaline are lemon barley water and Mist. Pot. Cit. Some authorities advise raising the urinary pH by taking one teaspoon of sodium bicarbonate every two hours which also seems to help the symptoms of dysuria. Various herbal remedies have been used throughout the ages. Although their efficacy has never been scientifically evaluated, they appear to work empirically. 'Bladder' tea made of Buchu leaves, flax seed, and bearberry is a remedy which should not be used for more than two weeks. Juniper berries have a diuretic and antiseptic action and a tea can be prepared from the berries. It should not be used during pregnancy as juniper is an abortifacient agent. Nor should it be used over prolonged periods. Dandelion leaves, garlic, and goosegrass form the basis of other herbal remedies. It is not known whether it is the herbs or the large volume of fluid taken with them that relieves the symptoms.

Antimicrobial drugs

The antimicrobial treatment of cystitis is dominated by two agents— amoxycillin (and ampicillin) and co-trimoxazole. They are as safe as other antimicrobials and are active against most bacterial species causing cystitis. Both are used for other infections seen in general practice, so are well known and well tried. Outside hospital, bacterial resistance to ampicillin and to the sulphonamide and trimethoprim components of co-trimoxazole has not developed into a major problem. Although both drugs can cause rashes and gastro-intestinal upsets, most patients can tolerate one or other. The variety of preparations of both drugs add to their attractions.

Nine out of every ten patients with bacterial cystitis will have clinical and bacteriological cures following treatment with either agent. A seven-day course is as effective as longer courses, and has become standard therapy. More recently, shorter courses have been shown to be equally good: two large (3 g) doses of amoxycillin 12 hours apart is perhaps the best known. Other agents given for one or two days are probably as effective as seven-day courses, because of the tendency of symptomatic and covert bacteriuria to spontaneous remission. Even when seven days of treatment are prescribed, patients will often stop taking tablets when the symptoms remit.

Co-trimoxazole is used for long-term treatment, particularly in children. A single tablet daily which is the paediatric formulation for girls aged less than 12 years can be taken for three months without causing folate deficiency, and with effective control of bacteriuria. The potential for causing folate deficiency is the main reason why co-trimoxazole and trimethoprim alone should not be given to pregnant women. There is a problem of which antimicrobial to use for a woman who is pregnant or trying to become pregnant and is allergic to penicillins (and maybe cephalosporins due to a cross reaction). A sulphonamide such as sulphamethizole may be used or alternatively nitrofurantoin. The use of the latter may be limited in early pregnancy by its side effect of nausea. At present, trimethoprim alone is a reasonable alternative to co-trimoxazole for treating urinary infections in general practice. Resistance to trimethoprim may become common; this possibility was one reason for originally marketing the drug in combination with a sulphonamide, as co-trimoxazole. Sulphonamide resistance is more common than trimethoprim resistance, and there are advantages in avoiding the risks of sulphonamide hypersensitivity by using trimethoprim alone. In past clinical trials, sulphonamides have been nearly as effective as ampicillin and co-trimoxazole, and remain a cheap alternative.

Nitrofurantoin and nalidixic acid have been used as urinary antimicrobials for many years. Both have a similar disadvantage in that some bacteria are intrinsically resistant to them: *Staphylococcus saprophyticus* to nalidixic acid, and *Proteus mirabilis* to nitrofurantoin. Nitrofurantoin has had a special place as prophylactic treatment for cystitis, one tablet (100 mg) taken each morning or after intercourse. If full therapeutic dosage (100 mg qds) is used, nitrofurantoin may cause nausea, but both drugs are useful second choices for treating sensitive bacterial infections.

The advantages of newer antibiotics may not be sufficient to counter the familiarity of amoxicillin and co-trimoxazole. Pivmecillinam is more active *in vitro* than ampicillin against Gram-negative bacteria like *E. coli*, but it is difficult to demonstrate a significant clinical advantage since amoxycillin is so effective. It is less effective against Gram-positive organisms like staphylococci. Both amoxycillin and pivmecillinam are inactivated by penicillinase produced by resistant bacteria. A combination of amoxycillin with clavulanic acid (Augmentin) is effective against penicil-linase-producing bacteria that occasionally cause urinary tract infection. However, this sort of problem with resistant bacteria is best resolved with advice on individual patients from the local microbiologist. Pseudomonas infections are notoriously difficult to treat, but carbenicillin and related compounds like carfecillin are specific therapies for this type of urinary infection.

The oral cephalosporins have come into use for urinary infections in general practice and in hospital. A proportion of ampicillin-resistant organisms are sensitive to the cephalosporins, but once again the differ-ence in bacteriocidal activity seen in the laboratory will make little clinical difference in uncomplicated cystitis in general practice. There are impor-tant differences in safety, and cephalosporins should not be given to peo-ple with hypersensitivity to penicillin.

There is a case for keeping the more potent antibiotics in reserve for patients who develop repeated resistant infections or pyelonephritis.

The management of chronic infections with low doses of co-trimoxazole and nitrofurantoin has already been described. Another drug is hexamine mandelate, which has a disinfectant rather than antibiotic action when metabolized and excreted in the urine. The choice between these should depend on the patient's preference because compliance with an unpalat-able drug will be poor. Only a small minority of women with cystitis have such chronic symptoms that long-term drug therapy is justified. Renal damage plus proven recurrent infection is the main indication. For other patients, a different approach is preferred, aimed at preventing the illness without antimicrobial drugs.

FURTHER HELPFUL HINTS

The woman suffering from recurrent attacks of abacterial cystitis requires a different approach; not least in importance is sympathy and understand-ing for what may be a very disabling condition. Angela Kilmartin has helped countless women suffering from cystitis by forming 'U and I' clubs for sufferers and by writing *Understanding cystitis* or more recently *Cysti-tis: a complete self-help guide*. The Health Education Council have pub-lished a leaflet, *Cystitis, what you should know about it* which contains some suggestions, some of which are discussed below.

Bladder habits

A recent study has shown that women with recurrent cystitis were more likely than a control group to give a history of voluntarily delaying mic-turition. It appears that by distending the bladder the normal emptying mechanism is disturbed. This habit often begins in childhood and thus steps to enable children to empty their bladders when they want to, may prevent disturbance of the sphincter mechanisms. It is suggested that women urinate at least four-hourly.

Hygiene

Many studies have shown that women who are prone to recurrent cystitis have an altered bacterial flora in the vaginal introitus consisting mainly of enterobacteria. The reasons for this are not entirely clear. Various authors have suggested that children should be taught to wipe from 'front to back' which soft lavatory paper after defaecation, to minimize contamination of the introitus with faecal organisms. Similarly, adult women have been advised to wash after defaecation with a flannel especially kept for this purpose, and unperfumed soap. The perineal and anal areas should be washed, morning and evening, and the flannel should be boiled frequently. Underwear should preferably be made of cotton and changed frequently. Strong biological powders unless properly rinsed out can be irritating to the perineal skin. It is suggested that tight constricting clothes such as tights and jeans should be avoided, as should vaginal deodorants, bath salts, and talcum powders. Regular, gentle vaginal douching with cool water may be helpful. All the suggestions have never been validated scientifically but in clinical practice are certainly worth suggesting as they are the remedies least likely to do harm.

Sex

Much suffering has been attributed to 'honeymoon cystitis'. The picture is far from clear to what extent sex is a contributory factor. There is no doubt that for many women cystitis is sexually related and some simple guidelines may considerably reduce the frequency of attacks.

1. Wash the genital areas of both partners before intercourse: this is particularly advisable in uncircumcised men.
2. Void urine immediately before intercourse and as soon after as is practicable. This 'flushes out' any bacteria which have been 'milked' into the urethra from the introitus during intercourse. It is advisable not to have intercourse with a full rectum as this tends to put pressure on the urethra. In particularly troublesome cases a single dose of an antimicrobial, e.g. sulphadimidine, may be taken after intercourse. This presumably rapidly reaches the bladder in concentrations high enough to kill any bacteria. If this approach is found to be helpful, medication may be given nightly on a long-term basis. In addition, a high intake of fluid immediately after intercourse may be suggested.
3. Advice on sexual techniques may be helpful in some cases, particularly where lubrication is inadequate and intercourse causes stretching and maybe tearing of urethral tissues. Use of K–Y jelly as a lubricant may be

useful, especially in post-menopausal women suffering from atrophic vaginitis. Sexual positions which cause pressure on the urethra may predispose to cystitis and a simple change to the lateral or female superior position may help.

4. The role of various contraceptives has already been discussed. It is often worth trying a different method of contraception to see if this helps.

Hormones

Oestrogen deficiency is mostly seen after the menopause or following hysterectomy with oophorectomy, when it causes changes in the bladder and urethra resulting in atrophic cystitis and urethritis as well as atrophic vaginitis. These changes may also be seen in younger women with relative oestrogen lack and respond well to treatment with oestrogen. If associated with menopausal symptoms such as flushing, oral oestrogen therapy may be considered on a short-term basis, but most women respond well to treatment with local oestrogen creams.

Diet

Some women find that particular foods will precipitate cystitis. Coffee, tea, and alcohol are common offenders. There has been little work done on the treatment of cystitis with diet, although there is some evidence that a low roughage diet reduces the number of uropathogenic faecal organisms. Most people find this diet unpalatable but 'replacement' of these organisms with lactobacilli found in natural yoghurt has been suggested as an alternative.

In conclusion, the evidence which has accumulated over the last decade has shown that cystitis is a relatively benign condition in terms of subsequent renal impairment, yet it still causes a great deal of misery. There is plenty of scope for further elucidation of causes and natural history. General practitioners are in an ideal position to carry out such research and it is hoped that the next decade will bring further developments in management which will not necessarily mean reaching for our prescription pads.

REFERENCES AND FURTHER READING

Asscher, A. W. (1981). Urinary tract infection. *J. R. Coll. Phys.* **15**, 232.

Brumfitt, W. and Asscher, A. W. (1973). *National symposium on urinary tract infection* (2nd edn). Oxford University Press.

Evans, D., Kass, E., Hennekens, C., Rosner, B., Miao, L., Kendrick, M., Miall, W., and Stuart, K. (1982). *Lancet* **i**, 156–8.

Fry, J., Byrne, P. S., and Johnson, S. (1976). The kidney and urinogenital tract. In *A textbook of medical practice*. MTP Press, Lancaster.

Health Education Council. *Cystitis*. (Leaflet obtainable from Health Education Council, 78 New Oxford Street, London WC1A 1AH).

Kilmartin, Angela (1973). *Understanding cystitis*. Pan Books, London.
—— (1980). *Cystitis: a complete self-help guide*. Hamlyn, London.
O'Grady, F. and Brumfitt, W. (ed.) (1968). *National symposium on urinary tract infection*. Oxford University Press.
Smellie, J. and Normand, I. (1968). In *Urinary tract infection* (ed. F. O'Grady and W. Brumfitt), p. 123. Oxford University Press.
Stamm, W., Wagner, K., Amsel, R., Alexander, E., Turck, M., Counts, G., and Holmes, K. (1980). *New Engl. J. Med.* **303**, 409.

15 Migraine

Katharine Peet

DEFINITION AND DIAGNOSIS

It occasions unseemly and dreadful symptoms—nausea, vomiting of bilious matter; collapse of the sufferer; there is much torpor, heaviness of the head, anxiety, and life becomes a burden. . . The patients are weary of life and wish to die.

This translation of a second-century description of migraine holds good today, though it is oddly unemphatic about the headache, nor does it mention headache on only one side of the head. Migraine is called classical if the headache is unilateral and preceded by neurological symptoms (the aura), and common if the headache is generalized and without an aura. This division is not important clinically and the word migraine is here used to include both varieties.

The prodromal or aura symptoms present in many different ways, usually develop over 10–20 minutes and fade away during 20–60 minutes. Visual symptoms are commonest and vary from simple blurring of vision to complete homonymous hemianopia, coloured or moving patterns in part of the visual field, multiple blind spots (scotomata) and photophobia may be prominent. The aura may also present as paraesthesiae and/or weakness in one or both limbs on the same side, or in both hands and around the mouth, speech difficulties especially word-finding, confusion, and even stupor. The diversity of symptoms from person to person, and from one time to another in the same individual, indicates that the area of the brain affected is unlikely to have a fixed anatomical location. A rare form of migraine, tending to occur in several generations of the same family, gives rise to marked hemiplegic signs which may outlast the headache; these signs are generally similar from attack to attack though varying in severity.

Migraine is twice as common in women as in men. Estimates of the prevalence of migraine have ranged from 5 per cent to 25 per cent of the population. A realistic figure probably lies in the 12–15 per cent range. In a large Welsh community migraine occurred in 19 per cent of the women of whom nearly half had never consulted a doctor about it. As with many recurrent complaints it is the tip of the iceberg that is seen in the surgery, those in whom it is severe or its frequency causes a problem: The frequency varies from once in a lifetime to attacks every week for several decades. We still do not know its cause, why it often runs in families, nor why it may spontaneously remit. There is no laboratory test for migraine, which remains a clinical diagnosis.

Guidelines to diagnosis are five characteristics, the diagnosis being allowable if any three of the following are present together: unilateral headache; nausea and vomiting; symptoms of neurological dysfunction; a family history of migraine; and episodicity of attacks. Thus, episodic attacks of nausea and vomiting where there is a family history of these or of migraine can qualify as migraine. This is sometimes designated as a migraine 'equivalent' and is a common presentation in children. The episodic nature is fundamental and a daily headache is *not* migraine. An attack can occur at any time of day or night though morning is the commonest time; if a person wakes with the headache already established it is often more severe and less responsive to medication than usual. In women; migraine is twice as frequent in the premenstrual and menstrual period as at other times in the month. Despite a frequently expressed belief that migraineurs have higher psychoneuroticism scores than non-migraineurs, the evidence for this is shaky and migraineurs have lower scores than sufferers from tension headaches. Much has been written about the 'migraine personality', in particular about obsessional and perfectionist traits, but without any definite conclusions.

MECHANISM OF THE MIGRAINE ATTACK

All the evidence indicates that the migraine attack is a cerebrovascular disturbance, the aura phase reflecting cerebral vasoconstriction. Cerebral angiograms made during the fortuitous onset of a migraine attack do not show *arterial* constriction (except in one unique case) but *arterioles* are too small to be visualized and it is thought that these are the vessels that become constricted.

Recent studies have shown that in the preheadache aura stage there is a substantial reduction of bloodflow through both cerebral hemispheres. The decrease in flow is patchy and is always more marked in the hemisphere on the side of the subsequent unilateral headache. The areas of most reduced flow usually, but not always, correlate with the neurological symptoms present at that time.

When the headache starts the cerebral bloodflow increases dramatically, to above normal rates, and this hyperperfusion outlasts the headache for one or two days. Those brain areas where flow is most reduced may remain relatively ischaemic for a time, perhaps explaining the occasional persistence of aura symptoms into the headache stage.

The extracranial (external carotid) bloodflow also increases by 50 per cent or more coincident with headache onset. Despite this the face is often pale, associated with a drop in skin temperature on the painful side. There is a shut-down at the arteriolar-capillary junction. The capillary bed is starved and all the blood is forced to flow through a diminished vascular territory, with consequent arterial and large-vessel distension. Not surprisingly in view of the tissue hypoxia produced there is leakage from blood-vessels, and some migraine subjects will develop visible lumps in the forehead, scalp, or around the eyes. These swellings contain fluid rich in kinins. Kinins stimulate pain fibres, especially when the fibres are 'primed' by local prostaglandin production; this, together with the lowering of the pain threshold by hypoxia, probably accounts for the intensity of the pain felt.

It used to be thought that the cerebral blood-vessels had no nervous innervation and responded only to changes in pO_2, pCO_2 and pH. However, noradrenergic fibres penetrate deeply into the brain substance and noradrenaline has been visualized in the intima of arterioles. Noradrenergic neurones are found in dense concentration in a locus in the midbrain where, in monkeys, stimulation causes profound generalized cerebral vasoconstriction. Furthermore, this area lies outside the blood–brain barrier and could respond to alterations in blood constituents. Some changes in the blood relating to different phases of the attack and the attack-free interval are now known, though our knowledge is incomplete.

The most striking of these changes concerns 5-hydroxytryptamine (5-HT; serotonin) and there are several indications that 5-HT has a central role in the genesis of the migraine attack. The 5-HT in blood is almost all contained in platelets, from which it can be released when platelets aggregate strongly and undergo the platelet release reaction. In between attacks, migraine patients have greater numbers of circulating platelet micro-aggregates, and increased platelet vulnerability to aggregating agents, than controls. At the onset of the headache there is a precipitous fall in blood 5-HT levels and that this is the result of platelet aggregation and release is confirmed by the appearance in the serum of the platelet release specific protein. The products of 5-HT metabolism appear in increased quantities in the urine as the headache develops. It is conceivable that the loss of 5-HT allows dilatation of the external carotid (of which it is a constrictor) and initiation of the headache sequence.

Whether the observed changes in 5-HT levels are primary, or reflect a platelet disorder, or are due to the presence of a circulating aggregating agent, is by no means clear. The nub of the problem is identifying the prime mover in what may be a cascade phenomenon. This is a very active field of research at present.

TRIGGER FACTORS

General

Migraine is thought to be a stress-related illness but the stress involved may not be capable of detection or correction. Many stress events cannot be anticipated—bereavement, financial worries, illness—and these patients need support as well as treatment of their migraine. But stress is by no means the whole explanation. Television, strobe lights, some types of fluorescent lighting, and word processors can be incriminated. Certain foods may trigger attacks, red wine, chocolate, pork, cheese, citrus fruits, etc., but in my personal experience only in about 10 per cent of subjects. Tyramine, a vasoactive amine present in some of the foods mentioned, has been shown to precipitate a migraine attack in some patients. The oxidizing enzyme for tyramine, monoamine oxidase B, shows decreased activity in the platelets of some migraineurs during an attack, but tyramine has not proved a reliable agent to precipitate migraine for experimental purposes. There has been a fashion for elimination diets to exclude possible food factors, undertaken by some patients to extreme and drear degrees and it is sad to find so many of them still suffering their headaches despite the diet. It is nevertheless worthwhile in long-standing resistant migraine looking for some basic food allergy such as wheat, maize, or dairy products.

Some migraine sufferers appear to have carbohydrate handling abnormalities. It is well known that going without a meal may precipitate migraine or the subject may be voraciously hungry before an attack. A glucose load after an overnight fast will often initiate an attack in those in whom fasting is a precipitant. In one of the rare studies made in the course of attacks of migraine, insulin and glucagon levels were significantly reduced as compared with levels between attacks in the same individuals. Hypoglycaemia unresponsiveness was found in some migraine patients after injection of insulin. In another group, who showed relative hypoglycaemia in the later stages of the glucose tolerance test, small frequent meals and restriction of sucrose in the diet resulted in significant improvement in their migraine. I have found this regime helpful to a small proportion of patients who specifically identify hunger as a trigger. The weight gain caused by certain prophylactic drugs for migraine should be controlled by eliminating sucrose from the diet rather than by calorie control of other types of food, including more complex carbohydrates. What part the liver plays in all this has not been elucidated and further investigations of carbohydrate metabolism in migraine are needed.

An increase in positive ionization of the air as in thundery weather or the hot dry winds of the Middle East or southern Mediterranean is attended by an increase in frequency of migraine attacks. It is possible to

buy a negative ionizer for personal atmosphere control, but the effectiveness of these machines is not known to the medical profession, perhaps
because the patients find them effective and do not return!

I myself conceive of a trigger factor in terms of being the last straw that
breaks the camel's back, but giving us no information about the number
and kind of straws in the rest of the load.

Hormonal

Because women get migraine so much more commonly than men, interest
has been aroused in the role of women's hormones in this disorder.
Studies on the relationship between headaches, migraine, and hormones
have often seemed contradictory and bewildering, not least because the
strictness of definition of headache type has been very variable, making
comparisons of series difficult.

It is evident that the female sex hormones may act as a trigger for
migraine. The onset of migraine, or its worsening or improvement, is often
noticed at times in a woman's life when these hormones are fluctuating—
menarche, menstruation, pregnancy and the puerperium, menopause,
and during hormone therapy such as oral contraception.

The anterior pituitary hormone prolactin has been implicated in the
genesis of a migraine attack but plasma levels of prolactin have not been
found to be different in women with migraine compared to controls. In
addition, treatment with the dopamine agonist bromocriptine which lowers prolactin levels has failed to improve migraine. Our own pilot study of
bromocriptine therapy in a few women with menstrual migraine was not
encouraging enough to continue to a full trial.

Menarche

Surveys of schoolchildren, several involving very large numbers, have
confirmed that in prepubertal children migraine occurs with equal frequency in boys and girls. Schoolgirls who develop migraine tend to do so
at, or just before, the menarche (Fig. 15.1). The 1:1 ratio of migraine in
boys and girls changes gradually after puberty till in the third and fourth
decades women outnumber men by more than two to one.

Menstruation

Migraine is more common in the premenstrual and menstrual period. Premenstrual water retention is not the initiator of the migraine since artificially induced water retention does not provoke migraine nor, usually,
can diuretics prevent it. Migraine occurring solely in relation to menstruation and not at other times is relatively uncommon. My own search of
more than 200 migraine patients threw up only 12 in whom the menstru-
ation-only relationship was maintained over an eight-month study. One
concludes that while strictly menstrual migraine does occur, it would

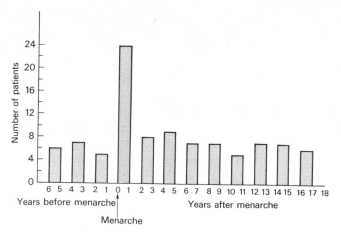

Fig. 15.1. Age of onset of migraine in relation to menarche, showing interval in years between the first attack of migraine and onset of migraine. (After Epstein, Hockaday, and Hockaday 1975.)

seem to differ from the more usual presentation in being monofactorial. Clinical experience is that this type of migraine may be particularly difficult to prevent, though no more difficult to treat when the attack occurs.

Increased frequency of migraine at menstruation focused attention on alteration in hormone levels around this time. In particular, the role of the fall in oestrogen and progesterone levels before menstruation has been investigated. In a group of women who had migraine only, and regularly, at menstruation, Somerville (1972) failed to prevent the headache by keeping the progesterone level artificially high, although the onset of bleeding was delayed. If the oestrogen level was maintained the headache did not come until the oestrogen level was allowed to fall, although bleeding had started at the normal time. The falling oestrogen level before menstruation may thus be implicated in this type of migraine. But measurement of oestrogen and progesterone throughout the cycle showed significantly higher levels in a migraine group compared to controls, particularly in the premenstrual period (Epstein *et al.* 1975). No particular hormonal changes could be identified in connection with the migraine attacks, whether they were menstrually related or not. This lack of hormonal difference suggests that some factor other than pituitary or ovarian hormones must produce the menstrual link. It is difficult to draw firm conclusions.

Pregnancy

Improvement of migraine in pregnancy happens in the majority of women who have migraine, and many are completely free of attacks. The remainder do not improve, or worsen. A small number of women develop migraine for the first time in pregnancy, usually in the first trimester. No connection between oestrogen or progesterone levels in pregnancy and the occurrence of migraine, or its disappearance, has ever been shown. Severe migraine in pregnancy poses a difficult therapeutic problem.

Menopause

At the menopause migraine can cease or much improve, stay the same, worsen, or occur for the first time. There is no consistency in individual response to declining ovarian function. Oestrogen and vasoactive amine (5-HT, catecholamines) production are intricately connected and post-menopausal oestrogen deficiency may by this means alter vascular reactivity. What the alteration will be is unpredictable.

Hormone therapy at the menopause can also improve, or worsen, migraine, although improvement is more usual and can be dramatic.

Oral contraception

The questions to consider are:
(a) Does oral contraception make migraine worse? (b) Does oral contraception induce migraine? (c) Is oral contraception dangerous in a migrainous person?

(a) Headaches of all kinds are common when using oral contraception, especially in women who had pre-existing headaches, and especially in the first three months of use, after which they tend to improve. Changing the particular oral preparation may cause the headaches to remit and some migraineurs do better on a continuous oral progestogen. A proportion of women suffering headaches on oral contraception are migraine subjects whose migraine has become more severe, especially in the 'pill-free' days. Women adversely affected in this way will bring their complaint to the doctor but do not necessarily give a correct picture of the prevalence of this adverse effect in migraine subjects. A year-long study in 362 women who had migraine before starting oral contraception found, indeed, that 11.6 per cent became headache-free and 24 per cent were improved as compared with only 18 per cent who worsened. The combined oral contraceptive preparations were those mainly associated with improvement as compared with the now obsolete sequential preparations. In a general practice survey of more than a thousand women on oral contraceptives, most for more than five years, only 1.9 per cent had migrainous headaches while 13.4 per cent had other types of headaches. This study confirmed the tendency for all headaches to cluster, or be more severe, in the pill-free days and for headaches to be more of a problem in those who had had headaches before taking oral contraceptives. Factors connected with worsening of migraine on oral contraception are increasing age and parity, and long menstrual cycles.

(b) It is, however, inescapable that oral contraception initiates migraine for the first time in a proportion of women. If this occurs and oral contraception is stopped the migraine usually disappears. Sometimes it may persist; this is unfortunate but where there is no pre-existing migraine it is impossible to predict this outcome.

(c) Even if migraine is a possible risk factor for cerebral infarction, though the evidence is inconclusive (Collaborative Group Study, 1973), it does not add further to the risk associated with oral contraception use. Nevertheless, it is sensible to discontinue oral contraception if migraine occurs for the first time, or neurological symptoms accompanying the attack become more severe. If focal neurological symptoms appear for the *first time*, this constitutes an imperative for stopping oral contraception. With the exception of these provisos, a migraine tendency need not be regarded as a bar to oral contraception.

TREATMENT

Headache sufferers swell the numbers of frequent or long-term attenders at the surgery and doubtless cause weariness of the spirit to the doctor. Many of these complainers are women, but this may be because the female hormones 'prime' the cerebral vasculature to abnormal sensitivity rather than because of psychological factors. It is as irrational to resent women with headaches as it would be to resent men with urinary symptoms or children with abdominal pain. It is the treatment difficulty which engenders despair or uninterest.

Migraine can usually be diagnosed by the description of the attacks and other special characteristics of time relations (weekends, menstruation) or obvious precipitating factors. Initially some time must be spent in explaining the illness, allaying anxiety, and holding out hope of improvement. The fact that the doctor seems familiar with the disorder, is not dismissive, and is willing to try and help can make the first interview the foundation of successful treatment. The 'helpless victim' attitude needs tackling since it is inimical to lasting improvement. Some responsibility for the patient's own treatment should be hinted at early in treatment. This includes any avoidable trigger factors such as missing meals. It is sensible to note down the alleged attack frequency since memories are short and at a later date denial of improvement may have to be rebutted gently. Diary cards may be very useful. Drug treatment can be very helpful, either prophylactically if attacks are frequent or symptomatically at the time of attack, or both.

Prophylaxis

Prophylaxis is usually called for if the attack frequency is twice a month or more but this needs to be discussed with the individual patient. There

Table 15.1 *Prophylactic drugs for migraine*

	Daily dose	Action	Length of use	Reported marked improvement in clinical trials	Side effects
Propranolol (Inderal, etc.)	30–100 mg	β-blocker Other actions stabilizes membranes	Indefinitely	50–65%	Rare at this dose. Cold extremities. faintness, slow pulse, low BP
Pizotifen (Sanomigran)	1.5 mg occasionally up to 3 mg	5–HT competitive inhibitor	Indefinitely	50–65%	Weight gain Drowsiness
Clonidine (Dixarit)	0.025–0.15 mg	Central-α-blocker	Indefinitely	?	Depression (rare) Brief hypertensive rebound on stopping (rare)
Methysergide (Deseril)	1–6 mg divided Usually 2–3 mg	5–HT peripheral antagonist	Not more than 6 months then 1 months break Dependence marked	70% or more	Malaise Rare-retroperitoneal, pleural, pulmonary fibrosis.
Promethazine (Phenergan, etc.)	10 mg mane 25 mg nocte Children 10 mg nocte	Antihistamine	Indefinitely	–	Drowsiness Skin photosensitivity is rare
Amitriptyline (Tryptizol, etc.)	25 mg nocte Children 5–10 mg nocte	Anxiolytic	6–18 months	–	Drowsiness

are a number of reasonably effective prophylactics, almost all with a high safety factor. The ones that I consider useful are listed in Table 15.1. Short courses of drugs for two or three weeks only are quite useless since most of the prophylactics take that time to become effective, the disorder is usually of long standing and fluctuates unpredictably, and the placebo effect in migraine is very high. The patient should be urged to persevere through the first two weeks, during which there may be mild side effects which later disappear, and not to report back for four to six weeks.

A brief expansion of the information in Table 15.1 may be of use. *Propranolol* is used in low dosage. The quantities used in hypertension and cardiovascular disease are quite out of place and are often accompanied by side effects. In low dosage it can be used safely for long periods if necessary and has a greater than 50 per cent success rate. *Pizotifen* is a 5-HT competitive antagonist and blocks platelet 5-HT receptors. Its central action has not been delineated but it causes appetite stimulation in most patients. The weight gain can usually be controlled by strict restriction of sucrose in the diet. Other forms of carbohydrate do not seem important in this respect. The dose is standard for the great majority of patients. It carries a more than 50 per cent success rate. *Clonidine* is a central α-receptor blocker but also seems to reduce vascular responsiveness in general. Again, the antihypertensive doses are inappropriate. As there is considerable individual variation in response it is always worth proceeding to the maximum dose (Table 15.1). The only side effect of consequence, and it is rare, is depression. If this occurs the drug is withdrawn and not reintroduced. It should always be tailed off on discontinuance since abrupt withdrawal may result in a brief but alarming hypertensive period. *Methysergide* is a 5-HT antagonist working at peripheral vessel level and having constrictor action in its own right. It is highly effective but the rare yet serious side effects of retroperitoneal, pulmonary, and/or pleural fibrosis limit its use to severe cases not responding to other drugs. Even then, treatment should be given for not more than six months on end with an obligatory break of one month before restarting it. Dependence may occur and the rebound headaches in the break periods are so intense that the patient may continue taking the drug clandestinely. The fibrotic process, in the early stages, resolves when the drug is stopped. *Promethazine* is useful in some adults and many children. It is the only safe prophylactic in pregnancy. Why an antihistamine is useful is not clear but some other antihistamines are helpful symptomatically in a mild attack. *Amitriptyline*, at night only, in low dosage is very useful in children. Some claim that it is of use in adults too. *Aspirin* use prophylactically is not generally accepted. Some migraineurs when they get older lose their headaches but suffer the aura symptoms. I find that a single tablet of aspirin daily will often abolish these annoying episodes. Possibly it acts to reduce the platelet aggregating tendency.

A preventative approach to migraine can give very satisfactory control in many subjects.

Symptomatic

Analgesics

If migraine attacks occur less than twice a month a symptomatic approach is the most suitable. A symptomatic approach may still be most appropriate if the attacks occurs more frequently as some women will not want to take daily medication. Discussion with the patient will clarify their attitude. Removal to a place of quiet and comfort and a simple analgesic may be all that is required if the attack is not long established, that is up to four to five hours. Paracetamol, or aspirin with codeine preparations are useful especially in effervescent form, if this does not cause vomiting. Paramax is paracetamol with metoclopramide and if the tablets seem ineffective then the powder form in sachets may be the answer, as the metoclopramide sometimes does not escape from the tablet rapidly enough. Much the best of these preparations is paracetamol, codeine, and caffeine (Solpadeine) which begins to exert its effect within 20 minutes. Why it is absorbed so much more quickly and completely than other similar products is not clear but long experience in its use at the Oxford Migraine Clinic bears it out. It should be given in half a glass of water only, flavoured if necessary, to try to avoid vomiting. *However, a severe migraine attack requires ergotamine.*

Another problem that confronts the family practitioner is the patient who has been suffering a severe attack for more than 24 hours and whose alarmed family has called for help. The patient is distraught, exhausted, often vomiting persistently and requires sleep above all. Little will be achieved by ergotamine at this late stage and treatment by injection of sedative or pain-killer is sensible. Every doctor has a favourite injection and it probably matters little what is used so long as the vomiting is stopped and the patient sleeps. Diazepam or chlorpromazine are good: papaveretum (Omnopon) is not to be despised, or dihydrocodeine tartrate (DF 118) but these two and other pain killers should be accompanied by metoclopramide or prochlorperazine maleate also by injection.

Ergotamine

Ergotamine is the most complete and successful treatment if it is given early enough, that is preferably within the first six to seven hours. Ergotamine is not an analgesic but a powerful vasoactive agent which in a migraine attack can constrict the external carotid artery. It has been shown in animals that though it constricts and reduces the bloodflow through the external carotid it nevertheless increases the perfusion of the carotid capillary bed. In subjects whose cerebral bloodflow was being measured during a migraine attack, injection of ergotamine reduced the external carotid flow and terminated the headache without causing any reduction in cerebral (internal carotid) flow. Fears about using ergotamine in patients with a marked vasospastic (aura) stage to their attack are probably groundless unless a β-blocker is being taken prophylactically.

Problems in the symptomatic use of ergotamine stem from the absorption difficulty in a migraine attack, which in the past was largely unrecognized and led to the recommended dosage being too high. Pharmaceutical manufacturers' guidelines still range from 4 mg to a horrifying 12 mg for an attack, whereas 1 mg is enough if it is fully and rapidly absorbed. The absorption difficulty may be explained by radiological evidence, although sparse, which shows the stomach during a migraine attack to have total absence of peristalsis, an 'hourglass' configuration, and a patent pylorus. When very large doses of ergotamine are given, only a little seeps through the pylorus but this is absorbed and terminates the headache. All the rest of the drug is then absorbed and causes vomiting, depression, and malaise, and lays the foundation for dependence. In recent years the use of metoclopramide with smaller doses of ergotamine has been a very great advance in treatment. Injection of this drug is impractical in the

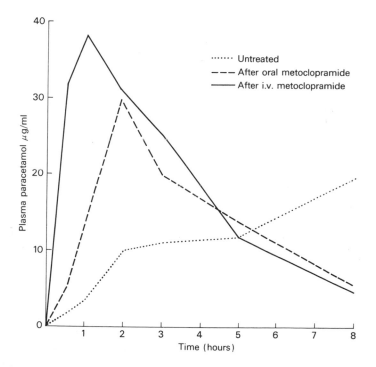

Fig. 15.2. Absorption of 1500 mg of paracetamol in a 71-year-old woman with delayed gastric emptying. . . . . . . before treatment. – – – – after 5 days on metoclopramide 10 mg t.d.s. _____ after i.v. injection of 10 mg metoclopramide superimposed on the daily treatment. (After Nimmo 1973.)

general management of attacks but oral metoclopramide is effective in most patients because, unlike most drugs, it is absorbed through the gastric mucosa. Metoclopramide promotes peristalsis and normal gastric motility, and is far more effective than centrally acting antinauseants. Figure 15.2 shows in a patient with gastric delay that the oral route for metoclopramide is satisfactory (Nimmo 1973). If 1 mg of ergotamine is given with 10–20 mg of metoclopramide it will alleviate a migraine attack in a reasonable time and without overdosage side effects. The two drugs should be given together; delaying the ergotamine by 15 minutes, as advocated by some clinicians, is illogical. The occasional patient has an idiosyncratic reaction to metoclopramide which precludes its use. An alternative preparation is effervescent ergotamine which, in its highly dispersed fluid form, seems to be able to escape through the open pylorus.

Vomiting can start so early in an attack, and be so severe, that oral administration fails. Table 15.2 lists other preparations, routes, and dosages. Ideally, not more than 2 mg should be used in a week, though this restriction can be eased if the headaches come in clusters over a short time with long attack-free intervals. It has been necessary to write in such detail about methods of use of ergotamine since the therapeutic boundaries are narrow and easily and commonly overstepped.

Ergotamine dependence and toxicity.   Excessive ingestion of ergotamine leads to a situation of dependence which is often not recognized because it is characterized by *headache*. The daily, or alternate day, headache is thought by the patient to be migraine, and a habit of taking daily ergotamine develops. Egotamine headaches can be distinguished from migraine by their very stereotyped time of appearance, severity, and generalized location. The unfortunate person feels unwell most of the time. Signs of toxicity, when severe, include hypertension, abdominal or leg cramps, painful lumps in the fingers or toes (vaso-occlusive lesions), and cyanosis of the nailbeds. Withdrawal of ergotamine is least painfully and most easily done by instituting effective prophylaxis for two weeks before beginning to withdraw the drug, as otherwise very severe rebound headaches may demoralize the patient. After a month's abstinence the person is allowed to use ergotamine for an attack in proper dosage. When the ergotamine has been withdrawn the patient begins to feel well and the migraine usually comes under control.

Prostaglandin inhibitors: menstrual migraine

The usual symptomatic treatments apply but in addition it is sometimes possible to prevent its occurrence, or reduce the headache to mild discomfort, by using a prostaglandin inhibitor from the day of the expected attack and continuing for three to six days, depending on the length of time that the person is usually at risk. Nine of 12 menstrual migraine

Table 15.2. *Ergotamine treatment of migraine attacks*

Route	Proprietary name	Ergotamine content	Instructions to patient	Maximum dose per week	Remarks
Oral	Cafergot	1 mg	Take together with 10–20 mg metoclopramide	2–3 mg	Use 1 mg (max: 2 mg) per attack Side effects with higher doses are: Vomiting Malaise Depression Burning sensation in throat
	Femergin	1 mg			
	Migril	2 mg			
	Effergot	2 mg	Effervescent dissolve in water		
Sublingual	Lingraine	2 mg	Place under tongue		
Suppository	Cafergot	2 mg	Cut across and use half		
Inhalation	Medihaler-ergotamine	0.36 mg per metered dose	2 doses at 5 minute interval Third dose later if necessary	Six metered doses	Effective in only a few patients
Injection (i.m)	Gynergen* (ergotamine tartrate)	0.5 mg ampoule	½–1 ampoule (never intravenous)	Two injections	Side effects short-lived, if any
	Dihydergot (dihydro-ergotamine)	1 mg ampoule	1–2 ampoules	Three injections	

* Imported only by Mawes and Proctor Pharmaceuticals, Gateshead.

patients had their migraine prevented or very much reduced in a double blind trial I made of mefenamic acid (Ponstan) against placebo. The dose used was 500 mg three times a day. Other workers have used flufenamic acid in a much larger number of patients and reported excellent results. It might be unwise to start the prostaglandin inhibitor more than two days before the expected menstruation as delay in the onset of bleeding has been reported.

Other treatments

I have not touched on other methods of treatment—biofeedback, acupuncture, relaxation methods, special diets—because my experience of, and faith in, them is limited. Biofeedback was disappointing in our hands (hand temperature training) though some felt they benefited from the learned relaxation they acquired during the procedure. Acupuncture is undoubtedly successful in some people though it seems usually to be rather temporary.

Good rapport with the patient is of the first importance in treatment, but no one doctor can achieve this with all patients. With explanation of the disorder, instruction about and provision of useful drugs, and the interest and encouragement of the doctor, most women learn to cope well with their individual migraine problem.

REFERENCES AND FURTHER READING

Collaborative group for the study of stroke in young women (1973). *N. Engl. J. Med.* **288**, 871.

Epstein, M. T., Hockaday, J. M., and Hockaday, T. D. R. (1975). Migraine and reproductive hormones throughout the menstrual cycle. *Lancet* **1**, 543–8.

Nimmo, J. (1973). The influence of metoclopramide on drug absorption. *Postgrad. med. J.* **49**, Suppl, 25–8.

Somerville, B. W. (1972). The influence of progesterone and oestradiol upon migraine. *Headache* **12**, 93–102.

Further reading for patients

Rose, F. Clifford and Gawel, M. (1979). *Migraine: the facts*. Oxford University Press.

Lambley, Peter (1980). *The headache book*. Star, London.

Sacks, Oliver (1981). *Migraine*. Pan, London.

Wilkinson, Marcia (1982). *Migraine and headaches*. Martin Dunitz

16 Health education

Hilary Graham

The archaic meaning of 'doctor' is 'teacher', and today, still, the giving of information, advice and support is seen to lie at the heart of general practice. This chapter discusses the role of doctor-as-teacher in the health education of women. Examining the role of the doctor involves a dual focus, on the general practitioners as the 'givers' (pp. 336–8) and the women as the 'receivers' (pp. 338–45). The first section tackles the question of what is health education? What is it trying to achieve? How does it work? The second section discusses this question in an epidemiological context, suggesting that women's health can only be understood in relation to their position within the family on the one hand, and their position within the class structure on the other. The third section illustrates the importance of these social and economic influences by examining two areas of current concern: smoking and infant feeding. The final section (Section 4) draws the arguments of the chapter together, and explores some future possibilities for health education. It notes the significant divergences between the model which underlies present health education programmes and the structures which underlie women's lives, and suggests ways in which doctors could become more effective and more supportive in their role as health teachers.

THE DOCTOR AND HEALTH EDUCATION

Given that 'health' is an ambiguous concept and that 'education' is similarly amorphous and ill-defined, it is not surprising to find that there is no clear consensus about the nature of 'health education'. A widely accepted (though vague) definition is that of Hochbaum: 'the task of health education is to equip people intellectually and emotionally to make sound decisions on matters affecting their health, safety and welfare' (Hochbaum 1971). Tuckett has specified the task more precisely, identifying three dimensions present to a greater or lesser extent in different campaigns (Tuckett 1979). First, there is health education as preventive medicine, which aims to reduce morbidity and mortality by modifying people's beliefs and patterns of behaviour (as, for example, in the campaign to combat lung cancer by reducing the incidence of smoking, a campaign in which general practitioners are centrally involved). Secondly, there is health education as better utilization of the services, which aims to help individuals to make more effective use of the National Health Service (by educating them as to when it is appropriate to visit the doctor or seek screening). Thirdly, and more broadly, there is health education as knowledge for living. This is the approach enshrined in health education programmes for schools (like the Health Education Council's *Living well* project), where teaching aims to promote a positive attitude to health and an ability to cope with the problems of everyday life.

Health professionals are clearly heavily involved in all three areas of health education. As one commentator puts it (Smith 1979):

The health educational activity of the N.H.S. is an inevitable consequence of the existence of the service which can not avoid exerting an influence on health knowledge, beliefs and behaviour. Within the service, professional health workers constitute the most important and potentially influential health education agents. Almost every act of doctors in the presence of patients . . . has an influence . . .

The role of the doctor has been spelt out by the Royal College of General Practitioners in a series of reports (Education Committee Study Group 1976; Working Party 1981 *a, b, c, d*). The 1976 report on the education of patients suggested that the trust and open access on which the doctor-patient relationship is built, makes the consultation an ideal setting for health education. The more recent 1981 reports of the RCGP's Working Party on Prevention pinpoint specific areas in which doctors can work actively to promote health: family planning, child health, psychiatric disorders, and arterial disease. The Health Education Council has similarly highlighted the role of the doctor, noting, in the context of advice on smoking:

the G.P. is in a unique position to help out in this way. Two out of three patients consult their G.P. at least once a year . . . The G.P.'s influence in health matters is unrivalled and face-to-face consultation is especially persuasive.

What kind of persuasive influence are general practitioners assumed to be exercising? As the most important and influential agents of health education, what are they teaching? At its simplest, the general practitioner is suggesting that health is something which is under people's control, and is therefore a personal responsibility. Although acknowledging the broader social and economic influences on health, the RCGP Working Party on Prevention (1981) argues that the doctor's role in prevention:

entails helping people to learn and to accept responsibility for their own well-being . . . It should not mean only care by the doctor or even the primary care team; it should increasingly imply the basic responsibility of every person to care for his or her own health and future.

The model is a 'do-it-yourself' one, where changes in lifestyle—in what individuals eat, drink, and smoke, in the exercise they take and in their routine visits to doctor and dentist—is seen to prevent and cure ill-health. This model neatly coincides with the cost-saving policy favoured by the present (1982) government. The opening paragraph of *Care in action*, the 1981 policy document for the new health authorities, for example, 're-minds us that we all have a personal responsibility for our own health' (DHSS 1981).

In stressing personal responsibility, current health education pro-grammes—like the health policies to which they are linked—make two cru-cial assumptions. They imply, firstly, that health is something which, like divine salvation, can be achieved by dint of individual effort and sacrifice. Health is presented as a choice: the public can either take it (and the hard work which goes with it) or leave it. Health education programmes suggest not only that health is individually determined, but, secondly, that individuals have the power and resources to determine it. Where bar-riers to health are recognized, they are seen to spring from ignorance and irresponsibility: it is lack of knowledge which prevents the public from in-stituting the changes in their lifestyle necessary to secure good health. According to the RCGP report on prevention (RCGP 1981*a*), 'barriers for patients appear to depend chiefly on their beliefs and knowledge', (Working Party Report No. 18) a point reiterated in *Care in action* (DHSS 1981):

There are plenty of risks to health which are within the individual's power to re-duce and avoid. Too many endanger their health through ignorance or social pressure.

If this is the kind of health education that general practitioners are giving, what does it mean for the receivers? It is their position and perspective which I discuss in the next two sections.

WOMEN AND HEALTH EDUCATION

The DHSS report on *Inequalities in health* (1980) demonstrated, yet again, the profound impact that social position has upon health. The risk of illness and premature death, among both young and old, is still strong-ly correlated with social class. Social position, however, is not simply a question of class: gender has also a pervasive influence on health. Although women live longer than men, they suffer more ill-health, visit their general practitioner more, and take more medication (Working Party on Health Inequality 1980). To understand women's health, we there-fore need to take account of two cross-cutting social structures: the struc-ture of class divisions and the structure of gender divisions. For it is where disadvantages of class coincide with disadvantages of sex that women (and their children) are most at risk.

Traditionally, while men are defined by their relation to the labour market—they are 'breadwinners' or 'unemployed', middle-class doctors or working-class milkmen—women are defined by their relation to their family—they are 'wives and mothers' or 'unmarried daughters'. About 85 per cent of British women *are* housewives, managing a home for husbands, children, and dependent relatives. However, in 1979, about 60 per cent of the women in the 20–35 year age group were also in paid employment—a picture changing rapidly with unemployment rising faster among women than men. Further the traditional role of the housewife—the bearing and raising of children—has also changed since the 1930s. Today women still have, on average, the same number of children, but they have them younger and they have them closer together. The typical mother spends only seven years carrying and caring for her two children until they enter school at five years old.

Despite these changes, inequalities remain, within both the labour market and the family. While men workers are found in every major sector of the economy, women are concentrated in a few 'women's' occupations. Three-quarters of all women workers are employed in the service industries, doing tasks very similar to those they perform in the home: cooking and catering, washing, cleaning, sewing, and nursing. They are concentrated in the low-paid and insecure jobs—and yet, it has been calculated, that without their earnings the incidence of family poverty would treble. Within the family, too, women are the 'poor relations'. Women spend, on average, upward of 50 hours a week on unpaid housework and caring for dependants. As the managers of the household budget, they are the ones who cut back when family resources are stretched—as, for example, when the family has to live on supplementary benefit. A recent study of families dependent on supplementary benefit found that around half of the families never or only occasionally ate cheese, cereals, fresh fruit, or meat; and that only half the mothers had three meals a day (a quarter had two meals, and a quarter only one). More starkly still, we now know that 25 per cent of all violent crime is wife-assault. Women living outside the nuclear family do not escape disadvantage: 90 per cent of single-parent families are headed by women, yet these families are three times more likely to be in poverty than ones headed by a man.

How are these structures of economic and social inequality reflected in the patterns of women's health? Focusing on specific areas of current medical concern is perhaps the clearest way of illuminating the links between social structure on the one hand and ill-health and health-damaging behaviour on the other.

First, women's disadvantaged position in society can help us to understand why women are particularly vulnerable to anxiety or depressive neurosis. Three times as many women as men are diagnosed by their GPs as suffering from depression (47 per 1000 compared with 13 per 1000). Class divisions reinforce those of sex. Brown and Harris in *The social origins of depression* (1978) found nearly four times as many cases of clinical depression among working-class women as among middle-class women

(230 per 1000 compared with 60 per 1000). Those most at risk were working-class women with young children at home. In this group, where financial hardship, housing problems, social isolation, and poor marital communication were most pronounced, 31 per cent (310 per 1000) experienced a depressive onset in the twelve months preceding the survey.

Secondly, the social and economic disadvantages that women face can help explain—in a paradoxical way—why women are increasingly taking up the health-damaging habits of men. Alcoholism and smoking, traditionally male forms of self-destruction, are increasing among women. The rate of alcoholism-admissions to mental hospitals among women, although half that among men, has doubled in eight years. In the most vulnerable age-group, the 35–44 year olds, the rate is now nearly 50 per 100 000 (the male rate for that age-group is 125 per 100 000). Alcohol is one of the ways women cope with the personal and emotional stresses and strains that their position in society creates for them. Significantly in view of Brown and Harris' findings on depression, although alcohol consumption is still highest among women in the upper social classes, Alcoholics Anonymous note the increase in referrals among women who give their occupation as 'homemaker'.

The patterns of smoking among women paint a similar picture. Sex differences in smoking have also narrowed—and with them, the rates of lung cancer. Thirty years ago, two-thirds as many women smoked as men (60 per cent of men compared with 40 per cent of women). Today, while the rates for men have fallen, the incidence of smoking among women has remained the same. Further, women are smoking younger and smoking more heavily than previously. Pronounced class differences have also emerged: smoking is more common among working class women (Table 16.1). Explanations of these patterns again draw attention to women's disadvantaged position within the labour market and the home. Smoking provides an individual strategy for handling problems and pressures which the woman can not prevent or control: problems with children and employers, with money and housing.

Thirdly, a recognition of gender and class divisions can help us understand why women engage in patterns of behaviour which places the

Table 16.1. *Cigarette smoking: by sex and social class 1978 (%)*

Social class	Women	Men
I and II	31	33
II non-manual	33	38
III manual	42	49
IV and V	41	55

Source: adapted from the General Household Survey (1978).
Total sample: women = 12 156
men = 10 480

health of their children at risk. It can illuminate the reasons why women, and particularly working-class women, fail to attend ante-natal and child health clinics, why they fail to breast-feed their babies, and why they introduce solid food and sugary snacks into their babies' diet. It can illuminate why these risk-taking activities are more common among working-class women—the class gradient in infant feeding, taken from the latest national survey, is revealed in Table 16.2. Non-attendance at clinic, bottle-feeding, and the early introduction of solid foods, although detrimental to the baby's health, allow the woman to find some kind of balance between the needs of her baby and the needs of the rest of her family. For a woman with many responsibilities and few resources, the costs of regular clinic attendance, breast-feeding, and the avoidance of solids and snacks are high; costs which can often be measured in the health of other members of the family (Graham 1980*a*).

Table 16.2. *Incidence of breast-feeding by social class: 1975 (%)*

Social class	Percentage breast-fed at birth
I and II	70
III non-manual	60
III manual	45
IV and V	39

Source: Martin (1978). Total sample = 1442

Doctors have a central role to play in relation to these three aspects of women's health, a role described in detail in the current series of RCGP reports on prevention (RCGP 1981 *a, b, c, d*). The section below considers two of the issues, looking at the risks women take with their own health (and focusing on why women smoke) and with the health of their children (focusing on infant feeding). In so doing, the section also sheds some light on the first issue: the way in which psychological disorders in women can be linked to their position within and beyond the home.

SPECIFIC EXAMPLES: EDUCATING WOMEN ON SMOKING AND INFANT FEEDING

This section examines two specific areas of health education for women, drawing together the issues raised in the previous sections about the nature of health education and the nature of women's lives.

I have suggested earlier that current programmes of prevention are concerned with initiating changes in individual behaviour rather than changes in our social environment. Unlike the public health movement of the nineteenth century which pressured governments to improve the sanitary and housing conditions of the working class, the health education movement of today directs its energies to 'helping individuals help themselves'. This individualism is highlighted in the current campaigns directed at women.

The first assumption of health education—that the barriers to health lie in the individual and not in their social environment—is implicit across the spectrum of current campaigns, from those which urge women to introduce low-cholesterol diets for the sake of their husband's health to those which aim to improve the uptake of maternity services. The Flora margarine publicity material assures women 'once you have decided to protect your family—your husband, your children and yourself—from the coronary epidemic, it is simply a matter of wise planning', while a popular BMA booklet tells its readers that, although all women should receive ante-natal care, 'through ignorance and irresponsibility those most in need do not receive it' (BMA).

The theme of ignorance and irresponsibility emerges, too, in the recent programmes to reduce smoking in pregnancy and encourage breast-feeding. The main posters used in the HEC's anti-smoking campaign confront the issues directly: tackling the question of irresponsibility in their captions and the problem of ignorance in their texts:

Is it fair to force your baby to smoke cigarettes?
This is what happens if you smoke when you're pregnant. Every time you inhale you fill your lungs with nicotine and carbon monoxide. Your blood carries these impurities through the umbilical cord into your baby's blood stream. Smoking can restrict your baby's normal growth inside the womb. It can make him underdeveloped and underweight at birth. Which, in turn, can make him vulnerable to illness in the first weeks of life. It can even kill him . . .

Do you want a cigarette more than you want a baby?
When a pregnant woman smokes she puts her unborn baby's life at risk. Every time she inhales, she poisons her baby's bloodstream with nicotine and carbon monoxide. Smoking can restrict your baby's growth inside the womb. It can make him underdeveloped and underweight at birth. It can even kill him . . .

The emphasis on irresponsibility is more muted in the campaigns to promote breast-feeding. As evidence has accumulated of the guilt engendered in mothers who decide against, or fail at, breast-feeding, campaigns have adopted a more sensitive and knowledge-oriented approach. Current literature no longer speaks of women's responsibilities to breast-feed, but tells mothers 'why breast feeding is best for your baby' (HEC/NCT).

These women's campaigns highlight, too, the second assumption of contemporary health education—that changes in lifestyle can follow directly and simply from changes in attitudes to health. In the publicity material, individuals appear on their own (jogging in the park or smoking while pregnant) or alone with their baby (breast-feeding)—enjoying a sense of freedom and privacy rarely experienced by women in the months before and after childbirth!

A number of recent studies challenge these assumptions, but here I will draw on two studies in which I was involved—one of women's experiences of pregnancy, the other of their experiences of early motherhood (Graham 1977; Graham and McKee 1980). These two surveys suggest first, that risk-taking behaviour can not be explained in terms of women's ignorance and irresponsibility, and secondly, that the majority of women have neither the resources nor the opportunity to adopt health-promoting lifestyles for themselves or their families.

The studies pointed to women's sense of responsibility for their children, a responsibility which surfaced at each stage of the survey: in women's worries that their baby would not be normal, in the acute sense of failure they felt when they were unable to comfort their baby when it cried and satisfy it when it was hungry, in their feelings of guilt when they became exasperated by the perpetual round of unsettled days and wakeful nights. However, these anxieties did not develop in a social vacuum, but were experienced alongside existing responsibilities which women had both in and beyond the home: responsibilities to other family members, to housework, and to paid employment. Although faced with multiple obligations, few women had access to the resources—of money, space, time, health, and energy—to cope with the conflicts and tensions which inevitably resulted. They had, therefore, to find strategies for resolving the conflicts alone. It was in this context that risk-taking behaviour often occurred, with smoking and bottle-feeding, for example, providing ways of balancing the competing demands of home and family.

Most respondents in the two surveys knew of the hazards of smoking—but, none the less, about 40 per cent continued to smoke (40 per cent in the 1974 survey and 37 per cent in the 1976 survey). Their explanations suggest that 'being responsible' involved not simply meeting the needs of the baby, but reconciling these needs with those of other members of the family. Reconciling needs demanded the constant presence and attention of the mother—and smoking offered a way of temporarily escaping without leaving the room. One expectant mother described the importance of cigarettes as follows:

after lunch, I'll clear away and wash up and put the telly on for Stevie (her son). I'll have a sit down on the sofa, with a cigarette and maybe a cup of tea. It's lovely, it's the one time in the day I really enjoy and I know Stevie won't disturb me.

Another summed up her feelings more precisely:

I couldn't stop, I just couldn't. It keeps me calm. It's me one relaxation is smoking.

In such circumstances, not surprisingly, attitudes to smoking were equivocal. Giving up smoking offered a way of promoting the health of their unborn baby, but only if the costs for the rest of the family were not too high:

I've cut down and I'm down to ten a day. If I cut down any more I take it out on my son which isn't fair on him. So it's one bairn or the other.

A recent study of women smokers paints a similar picture suggesting that smoking provides a means of containing—and surviving—the conflicts which spring from the roles which women perform (Jacobson 1981).

[women] use their smoking as a safety valve, an alternative to letting off steam. Not only do women smoke to keep their emotions in check, many dare not stop for fear of what may happen if they can't prevent their emotions from leaking out . . . One woman said 'Getting angry hurts others. When I smoke, I feel a release in my whole body from anger and tension. The cigarette won't hurt anybody but me'. 'Our husbands' said another' can explode when they come home, but we can't. We are supposed to absorb the frustrations of everyone else in the family and still maintain the image of the superwife and the supermother. I don't want to scream and yell at the family and hurt people, so I smoke.

Like smoking, the way women handle infant feeding reflects their experiences of the complex and competing responsibilities of the superwife and supermother (Graham 1980*b*). Like smoking, too, bottle-feeding and the early introduction of solid foods provide strategies by which these conflicts can be contained and diffused. Most of the respondents in the survey (60 per cent) wanted and attempted to breast-feed their babies. But by the end of the first month after birth, the proportion of the breast-feeders in the sample had fallen to 32 per cent, and by the end of the fifth month it was 20 per cent. For many mothers, breast-feeding proved to be a baby-oriented method of feeding which placed too high a premium on the baby's health, and in consequence, too high a cost on the mother and other members of the family. In such circumstances, mothers reported that, symbolically, their milk 'ran out' or they did not 'have enough'. As one respondent, having her second child, put it:

This time I was determined to succeed [at breast-feeding]. I thought 'this time I am really going to persevere'. But I got so tired, you can't rest when you have got two. I mean, I let the housework go, but I still had to do the ironing and the washing and cook a meal. I just could not, I did not have enough.

As this account indicates, few respondents had either the opportunity or the inclination to share the responsibilities of childcare and and housework with others. Instead, they had to find a way of coping with their responsibilities alone. Bottle-feeding—like smoking—provided such a strategy: it provided a way of meeting the needs of the baby without disrupting the fabric of family life. Life, for many respondents seemed easier 'on the bottle':

I fed her for about a month I think it was, but she messed me about that much and with Sarah (her older child) being so young, I just couldn't cope, because

Sarah used to pester. So I thought I'd be better on the bottle. The baby's no different but I feel better in myself, bottle feeding her. I've got a lot more patience . . .

CONCLUSION: ALTERNATIVES FOR HEALTH EDUCATION

This chapter has examined the model which underlies contemporary
health education, and the doctor's privileged position in facilitating
changes in individual attitudes and behaviour. It has suggested that two of
its central assumptions—concerning the barriers to health and the individual's ability to overcome them—are seriously out of line with the reality of most women's lives.

If the current model of prevention and health education assume a degree of individual freedom enjoyed by only a middle-class, male minority,
where does this leave the general practitioner attempting to provide sensible and meaningful advice to patients, most of whom are neither middle
class nor male? There are a number of avenues to be pursued. First, the
conventional health education model can be adapted to take account of
women's position in the family. This would involve adjusting the content
of health education literature—a greater realism is already in evidence in
the recent HEC material on infant feeding, where advice is increasingly
geared to the lifestyle (and income levels) of ordinary families. (For
example, the HEC's booklets *Starting your Baby on solid foods* and *Healthy
eating for your children*). It would involve, too, changes in the process as
well as the content of health education—with doctors participating in
neighbourhood health education and in community health projects.
Secondly, and still working within the individualistic model, there could
be a shift in emphasis from advice on prevention and cure to advice on
alleviation, at present a neglected area of professional intervention
(Smith 1979). Alleviation, however, is fundamental to women's work in
the home: relieving the stress of conditions which can neither be prevented nor cured. Alleviation may involve caring for elderly relatives or a
handicapped child, or it may involve reducing the toll which life on a low
income in a damp and overcrowded home takes upon husbands and children. Practical information and support could provide doctors with a vital
role in helping women cope with such problems, and the feelings of
anxiety and despondency which they often create. Thirdly, doctors could
move beyond the confines of the contemporary model of health education
(Draper, Griffiths, Dennis, and Popay 1980). They could seek to educate
the public not only in the need for self-help, but in the need for collective
action to achieve health-promoting changes in our social environment.
Doctors could themselves become involved in these broader strategies.
This wide involvement in health might arise out of participation in community health and education programmes or from pressure-group activity
within the professional medical bodies of the BMA or the RCGP. It

would mean, for example, campaigning around the production as well as the consumption of food and tobacco; campaigning around the national distribution of income and wealth as well as the personal patterns of spending. It would require programmes which examined the nature of work as well as the use of leisure time, the division of power between men and women as well as the nature of women's responsibilities in the home. Broadening the concept of health education in this way has inevitable political implications, implications which doctors have been urged not to ignore (Stacey 1980):

where health care professionals are clearly appraised of the social causes of disease, it seems proper that those in the N.H.S. who recognise the consequences of bad social conditions should act as a strong pressure group to try and get these remedied.

The role of doctor-as-teacher today, it appears, involves more than the education of patients. It demands, also, a commitment to continuing professional education; a commitment to the political responsibilities that go with a deeper understanding of the nature of health.

REFERENCES AND FURTHER READING

BMA (British Medical Association). *Our children's health*. British Medical Association, London.

Brown, G. and Harris T. (1978). *The social origins of depression*. Tavistock Publications, London.

DHSS (Department of Health and Social Security) (1981). *Care in action: A handbook of policies and priorities for the health and personal social services in England*. HMSO, London.

Draper, P., Griffiths, J., Dennis, J., and Popay, J. (1980). Three types of health education. *Br. med. J.* **281**, 493–5.

Education Committee Study Group of the Royal College of General Practitioners (1976). *The education of patients and public by general practitioners in the seventies*. London Royal College of General Practitioners, London.

Flora project for health disease prevention. *Coronary disease: how to protect your family*. The Flora Project, London.

Graham, H. (1977). Women's attitudes to conception and pregnancy. In *Equalities and inequalities in family life* (ed. R. Chester and J. Peel). Academic Press, London.

Graham, H. (1980*a*). Family influences in early years on the eating habits of children. In *Lifestyles and nutrition* (ed. M. Turner). Applied Science Publishers, London.

—— (1980*b*). Mothers' accounts of anger and aggression toward their baby. In *Psychological approaches to child abuse* (ed. N. Frude). Batsford Books, London.

—— and McKee, L. (1980). *The first months of motherhood*. Monograph Series No. 3. Health Education Council, London.

HEC (Health Education Council). *Starting your baby on solid foods, and healthy eating for your children*. Health Education Council, London.

——/Action on Smoking and Health. *Give up smoking—guide for general prac-*

titioners to help patients give up smoking. Health Education Council/Action on Smoking and Health, London.

——/NCT (National Childbirth Trust). *The best way to feed your baby*. Health Education Council/National Childbirth Trust, London.

Hochbaum, G. M. (1971). Measurement of effectiveness of health education attitudes. *Int. J. Hlth Educ.* **XIV**, 2.

Jacobson, B. (1981). *The ladykillers: Why smoking is a feminist issue*. Pluto Press, London.

Martin, J. (1978). *Infant feeding 1975: Attitudes and practice in England and Wales*. Office of Population, Census and Surveys, London.

Smith, E. (1979). Health education and the National Health Service. In *Health education: perspectives and choices* (ed. I. Sutherland). Allen and Unwin, London.

Stacey, M. (1980). Realities for change in child health care: existing patterns and future possibilities. *Br. med. J.* **280**, 1512–15.

Sutherland, I. (1979). *Health education: perspectives and choices*. Allen and Unwin, London.

Tuckett, D. (1979). Choices for health education: A sociological view. In *Health education: perspectives and choices*. (ed. I. Sutherland). Allen and Unwin, London.

Working Party of the Council of the Royal College of General Practitioners (1981*a*). *Health and prevention in primary care* Report from General Practice 18. Royal College of General Practitioners, London.

—— (1981*b*). *Prevention of arterial disease in general practice* Report from General Practice 19. Royal College of General Practitioners, London.

—— (1981*c*). *Prevention of psychiatric disorders in general practice* Report from General Practice 20. Royal College of General Practitioners, London.

—— (1981*d*). *Family planning—An exercise in preventive medicine* Report from General Practice 21. Royal College of General Practitioners, London.

Working Party on Health Inequality (1980). *Inequalities in health*. Department of Health and Social Security, London.

17 Eating problems

Elizabeth Mitchell

Nutrition is an integral part of a woman's life, not only in relation to her own needs, but also in relation to the needs of her family, friends, and acquaintainces. Women are traditionally the suppliers of food, and Orbach (1978) makes an important point when she states that being overweight in our society is related to being female. One can extend her arguments to encompass a wide variety of weight disorders, including anorexia nervosa, and bingeing, which are almost exclusively the domain of women. Neither is it necessary to adopt feminist principles to acknowledge the point. When her child is born, and even while she is still pregnant, a mother is bombarded with a wide variety of information on how to feed herself and her child. After the birth, she is given information about breast- or bottle-feeding, and the importance of feeding herself in relation to this, both from medical sources and non-medical sources, such as friends, her mother, and so on. One of the first tasks she must master is to differentiate cries of hunger from other cries, and her competence as a mother will at first be judged on the feeding of her child. Certainly there can be no doubt that adequate nutrition, especially in these first months, is an essential prerequisite for the baby's healthy physical and psychological development. I suspect, however, that these early interactions are also important in the development of women's attitudes towards their own and other's feeding, and their perception of their own competence. Attitudes within the medical profession towards certain foods are also important, as changes in eating patterns change in relation to the scientific literature, e.g. bowel cancer and dietary fibre, and cholesterol and heart disease. Surveys of food intake in the UK show that the intake of bran in the diet has recently increased, and another difference has been a huge increase in the consumption of chicken between the years of 1950 and 1973. Staples such as potatoes and bread still play a central although declining role in the British person's diet, and malnutrition is rare except perhaps in the elderly.

After birth, nutrition may become one of the first battlefields between a mother and her child, as she gradually learns to respond to the likes and dislikes of her baby, and progress is made from fluids to solids. The rejection of food is one of the baby's first means of self-assertion, even before speech has developed. Later on in life, in western culture certainly, food comes to be associated with a variety of functions, not all linked to the satisfaction of the primary drive of hunger. Family mealtimes may be a time for sharing and reciprocity, or the arena for rows and arguments. The part which food plays in any particular household is likely to be noted by the child; in the form of modelling or imitation, a well-established form of learning. As a child grows up, the differentiation of sexual roles may mean that a daughter is more actively engaged in the preparation and serving of food, and the old adage, 'The way to a man's heart is through his stomach', has yet to be replaced, even though it is no longer accepted. Parents, too, may still recall the impact of two world wars on food provisions, and the deprivation of rationing, which may not enable them to view food dispassionately.

Women's changing roles

It is still only relatively recently that an increasing number of married women are going out to work, either to supplement their family income or in response to the devaluation of the mothering role, or dissatisfaction at home. In the past women were often the seekers and gatherers of food, and even now when more women work outside the home they may still be responsible for the nutrition of their families. Thus women may push themselves to adopt more roles than they can realistically manage, at least not without recourse to drugs and other methods of coping.

Food within a family can be used in a number of ways, and one of the most common ones is as a reward for certain 'good' behaviours, or as a 'treat'. Most family celebrations are associated with the provision of food and drink from an early age, and it is difficult to think of social situations in which food or drink is absent. In other families, however, reinforcement might be more variable, for example a sweet, or a hug, or a story reading, or a trip to the park. Thus from an early age, rewards and food, and 'bad' behaviour and deprivation of food may be linked, such that the experience of emotions and food become interlinked.

Margaret Mead, the anthropologist, defines food habits as 'the culturally standardised set of behaviours in relation to food manifested by individuals who have been reared within a given culture'. Thus, to understand patterns of consumption, one needs to understand food ideology. For instance, in Britain the eating of horsemeat is viewed with distaste by most people, whereas in France it may be as absolutely acceptable as Sunday lunch!

Economic factors

Apart from cultural norms, economic and religious values also have an important bearing on patterns of food consumption. Britain's economy has shifted from one which was predominantly rural to one which is much more urban. Early in the nineteenth century, over 80 per cent of British residents inhabited rural areas, and Britain was virtually self-sufficient in terms of her food requirements. Meat consumption, however, was mostly restricted to the gentry and the better-off, and malnutrition was rife. With the onset of the Industrial Revolution, patterns of food consumption changed as wages increased. Food consumption since then has ebbed and flowed according to economic factors, and to the intervention of specific governments in for example, administering school meals and providing social services for the elderly and infirm or the needy.

Food through the ages: cultural perspective

Women are largely responsible for their families' diet. Women's attitudes are partly derived from parental attitudes to food, and the social class from which they come. Food habits tend to be passed on from one generation to the next, and families may pass on specific myths about the value of certain foods, and their relation to health. To a large extent, the woman is also held responsible for educating her family about food values, a factor which is recognized by the advertising industry, when they wish to introduce a new foodstuff such as 'soyameat', or other such foods. Many women, however, by virtue of the number of differing demands placed on them, and the variety of roles they perform, are often more dependent on 'fast' foods than their ancestors, and there is also a trend for them to have more labour-saving gadgetry, two factors which may not be conducive to maintaining average weights.

It may be useful at this stage to comment on pre-literate societies. In many of these the economy was a subsistence one, and much of the labour was related to food. Famine was common, and in view of this, gluttony at times of plentifulness was acceptable. Indeed, Kropf (1889) recorded a Trobriand Islander in the Pacific as saying 'We shall be glad, we will eat until we vomit.' Powdermaker (1973) discusses how food is the centre of a complex value system, and elaborate ideology, and 'How religious beliefs, rituals and etiquette, social organisation, prestige systems and group unity relates to food consumption in most parts of the world.' Distribution of food is also a measure of power, for example the selling of grain to the USSR by the USA.

It is only recently, too, that attitudes towards food consumption are changing and, although in some cultures obesity is still valued as a sign of wealth, for example in the Middle East, generally it is regarded negatively in our society. Of equal importance is the role of food in hospitality. Women again are largely responsible for entertaining with food and drink. The provision of food is associated in different cultures with a variety of functions, especially as a sign of caring and concern. Food is a part of religious ceremonies and religious rites may involve food taboos, for example in the Muslim and Hindu religion. Indian women may consume a different diet from that of the Western woman, and one based on different food ideology, myths, and beliefs. Fasting is a part of many religions and abstention from food is often viewed as pure and near to godliness.

It is therefore not surprising, against this backcloth, that the average woman has more than a passing aquaintainance with food, and that some women's relationship with food becomes problematical. The tasks of preparing it, buying it, and serving it, may be a daunting one when one considers the enormous range of functions it fulfills. Socially, too, a woman's competence will be judged partly on her food presentation and culinary skills, and her competence as a woman overall has traditionally been assessed in relation to food. It is a rare woman who dares to throw these rules aside.

The average size of the family has decreased recently as a result of economic and social changes, and the average size has decreased from six in 1880 to just over two today. The average family now spends more per capita on food than it could previously although this may now be spent much more on prepared foods, or 'fast foods'. As women are likely to have two jobs rather than one, they often have less time for leisure. Recent surveys of British women show that todays woman is more likely to be more peer-orientated and more likely to express herself through products, appearance, and possessions than the older woman (over 34 years). She trusts advertising more than her predecessors, and buys more convenience foods. She also shops less often. As most of these surveys are carried out by the food industry, perhaps they can very rightly claim that 'We know what makes women happy, unhappy and afraid.'

'Fads' and the role of the media

Educating women about their needs continues to be a theme which provides many journalists with jobs. Unlike men, who are not continuously subjected to magazines or advertisements telling them how to shave themselves or dress, women are told how to make-up, how to dress, and how to diet, stay fit, and be healthy. Clearly, at one level, women have accepted the view that they are somehow unable to look after themselves, since a good many buy these magazines. Success is equated with physical fitness and beauty, and the woman in the adverts bears little relation to the average woman.

Apart from magazines, information on nutrition is provided by a number of bodies, for example, the school, the general practitioner, and is not always associated with greater health, for example, as Greaves (1973) noted when he examined its association with increased food faddism. He gives as an example, the trend towards buying more vitamins and 'health foods'. Magazines in particular promote 'fad' diets, for example, 'the grapefruit diet', 'the drinking girls diet', 'the high energy diet', and so on. Certain foods may as a result, come to be linked to overweight or slimness. Grapefruit, for example, may be seen as a diet food. There are a huge numbers of diets available, all purporting to be a magical solution to weight loss. There is also a large number of books masquerading under 'medical' titles which are in fact not at all soundly based. Examples of books on diets include: *Calories don't count* [they do!], *The protein programming diet, The doctor's metabolic diet*, the *Snack diet*, and the *Scarsdale diet, Last chance refeeding diet*, and *Fasting is a way of life* [not for long!]. The latter three are in particular *dangerous to health*, and should not be recommended, even though they may be familiar names. Other fads may include the consumption of 'health' foods, or formula diets. The latter may be helpful for those who have a small amount of weight to lose, but are not advised by the American Medical Association for those who are moderately overweight, or who have a history of heart disease, diabetes, or kidney complaints. However, they do not encourage the development of alternative eating behaviour.

It is beyond the scope of this review to summarize all types of disorders of nutrition so I will concentrate on obesity, anorexia nervosa, and bulimia, all of which are increasingly common in women.

OBESITY

Obesity, like anorexia, is found more commonly in women than in men, although unlike anorexia, it is more usually a problem for women in social classes IV and V. It is generally accepted that obesity is a complex, multidetermined condition, emanating occasionally from some gross endocrine abnormality, but more usually from a discrepancy between energy input and output.

Classification

There are various types of obesity, which have an important bearing on the type of treatment prescribed. Table 17.1 below outlines classifications of obesity. Most types of obesity are polygenic in origin, although there are some rare conditions which are not, such as the Prader–Willi syndrome, where there is gross obesity, small extremities and voracious appetite.

While genetic studies of twins and foster children suggest a link between inheritance and environmental factors, the precise contribution of each is as yet unknown. It is interesting that the concordance rate for spouses is almost as high as that for families.

The debate regarding genetic–environmental effects continues, and a similar debate regarding fat cell number and size rages alongside of it. However most clinicians feel that one of the most helpful distinctions is

Table 17.1. *Classifications of obesity*

Anatomical
1. Descriptive
   (a) Generalized (quantitate anthropometrically)
   (b) Localized
2. Cellularity
   (a) Hypertrophic (increased size of fat cells)
   (b) Hyperplastic (increased number of fat cells)
Functional
1. Is patient diabetic?
2. Is patient hypertensive?
   (a) Impaired glucose tolerance
   (b) Gall bladder disease
   (c) Smoker
3. Is patient hyperlipidemic?
Aetiological
1. Endocrine
2. Hypothalamic
3. Genetic
4. Undetermined origin

between early and later onset obesity, the latter being much more amenable to treatment. Bray (1980) suggests that in cases of early-onset obesity, fat cell distribution is often more generalized, and he believes there to be a three to five times greater number of fat cells present in these women. While this is still controversial, chronic obesity is certainly more difficult to treat, if only because of its chronicity.

The degree of obesity is generally categorized in the following way:

mild obesity: 20 per cent overweight;
moderate obesity: 50 per cent overweight;
gross or massive obesity: 100 per cent overweight.

The most common method of estimating the percentage overweight and the easiest one is a comparison of height–weight ratios based on the tables of the Metropolitan Insurance Company. Table 17.2 outlines the prevalence of obesity in the UK and the USA, and most studies show that obesity rates are associated with age, in that older women are more likely to be obese. Women over 50 years in Western countries tend to be over-represented in the obese, and this may be partly attributable to a combination of diminishing energy expenditure while food intake remains constant.

Thus the prevalence of obesity is widespread, and represents a formidable challenge to the nation in terms of general health care, overall expenditure, and loss of working hours. Obese parents, too, are more likely to have obese children, and overweight children themselves are likely to become overweight adults. While mild obesity does not constitute a great health risk, moderate and especially massive obesity have a number of associations with ill-health, all of which place the obese at greater risk,

Table 17.2. *Prevalence of obesity in the UK and USA: studies*

Investigation	Age	Country	Obese females (%)
Metropolitan Life Insurance Co. (1960)	20–29	USA	12
	30–39		25
	40–49		40
	50–59		46
	60–69		45
Moore *et. al* (1962)		USA	42
National Health Survey (1964)		USA	29
Montegriffo (1968)	20–29	UK	21
	30–39		33
	40–49		53
	50–59		64
	60–69		60

and are costly and time-consuming for the health services, and in particular the general practitioner and his team. Table 17.3 below outlines a variety of disorders associated with obesity, which are either caused or exacerbated by it. In women, menstrual disorders such as amenorrhoea and dysmenorrhoea may occur and obesity in pregnancy presents special problems for the obstetrical team. Obesity here is linked to increased morbidity in the mother and her child, and obese women have more Caesarean sections. In pregnancy, obesity is defined as weight in excess of 20 per cent of the median weight for height.

Even in childhood, obesity may be associated with the development of physical problems. One study found that obesity was prevalent in 53 per cent of hypertensive children, while another reported a correlation of 0.58 between systolic blood pressure in adolescents and weight. Since obese women are also more prone to physical disorders, they may also be less attractive as employees. In childhood obesity attracts negative attitudes and the obese are the subject of ridicule and rejection. Eventually

Table 17.3. *Disorders caused or exacerbated by obesity*

Cardiovascular disease	Ventilation impairment
Diabetes mellitus	Organ compression
Hypertension	Water retention
Cerebrovascular disease	Venous stasis
Nephrotic syndrome	Menstrual disorders
Gallbladder disease and stones	Impaired fertility
Gout	Hirsutism
Osteoarthritis	Obstetrical complications
Skin problems	Surgical and anaesthetic risk

Increased risk of breast and endometrial cancer
The early development of obesity may be associated with:
Externally rotated feet, flat feet, knock knees
Back problems
Psychological problems

they may often come to accept these attitudes themselves, and may become self-denigrating and lacking in self-esteem. The obese, that is, women in the main, are stigmatized in our society, and the traditional stereotype of the obese as less intelligent, lazy, untidy, and generally less attractive is still upheld. Even professionals may view obesity as the result of poor self-control, and Canning and Meyer (1966) showed that obese women are even less likely than their normal weight counterparts to be admitted to college, despite the equivalence of their qualifications and ability. There is, however, little good evidence as yet in support of the notion that obese women consume larger quantities of food than women of normal weight. Clearly, however, they still consume more than their individual requirements, which still makes treatment for them a question of increasing their energy expenditure, or decreasing their calorie consumption, or both. The literature, too, on the role of emotional factors governing food intake is ambiguous.

Emotions and eating

Many women report an association between emotion and eating. Boredom, depression, anxiety, and tension may act to promote greater food intake. Experimentally, anxiety in particular is the subject of extensive investigation. Psychoanalysts have long hypothesized a relationship between these, seeing increased eating as a resolution of underlying conflicts. In a series of fascinating experiments, however, Pudel (1976) and others suggest that the influence of arousal on eating follows an inverted U-shaped curve, with moderate levels of arousal having the greatest effect on eating. Saliva, of course, may dry up at higher levels of autonomic arousal. Older women, too, appear to be less influenced by emotional arousal, or have developed different methods of dealing with it.

One of the major variables to receive attention lately in relation to arousal and food intake is the notion of restraint, which has been found to predict overeating in an experimental situation. Table 17.4 outlines the Stunkard (1981) questionnaire which is a useful aid in assessment. This questionnaire, when scored, yields a variety of scores. It has been found that scores on this test predict overeating better than weight alone. Thus, those highest in restraint are in fact bingeing–abstaining anorexics, and it is possible to find people of normal weight who are also high on restraint as well as obese women who are low in restraint. Alcohol and emotional states within this model are thought to reduce inhibition, and therefore restraint, weighting the see-saw in favour of overeating. Dieting, as one might expect then, paradoxically, increases the probability of binge-eating. Deprivation of any sort, of course, builds up a desire for the forbidden object.

Before going on to discuss treatment of obesity more specifically, I must say a word or two about social factors and food intake. As already

Table 17.4. *Eating inventory*

Directions: This table contains a number of statements. Each statement should be answered either *true* or *false*. Read each statement and decide how you feel about it in PART I.

If you agree with the statement, or if you feel that it is *true* about you, answer *true* by circling the T next to the statement.

If you disagree with a statement, or if you feel that it is *false* as applied to you, answer *false* by circling the F next to the statement.

PART I

		Factor number
1. When I smell a sizzling steak or see a juicy piece of meat, I find it very difficult to keep from eating, even if I have just finished a meal.	T F	3
2. I usually eat too much at social occasions like parties and picnics.	T F	2
3. I am usually so hungry that I eat more than three times a day.	T F	3
4. When I have eaten my quota of calories, I am usually good about not eating any more.	T F	1
5. Dieting is hard for me because I just get too hungry.	T F	3
6. I deliberately take small helpings as a means of controlling my weight.	T F	1
7. Sometimes things just taste so good that I keep on eating even when I am no longer hungry.	T F	2
8. Since I am often hungry, I sometimes wish that while I am eating an expert would tell me that I have had enough or that I can have something more to eat.	T F	3
9. When I feel anxious, I find myself eating.	T F	2
10. Life is too short to worry about dieting.	T F	1
11. Since my weight goes up and down, I have gone on reducing diets more than once.	T F	2
12. I often feel so hungry that I just have to eat something.	T F	3
13. When I am with someone who is overeating, I usually overeat too.	T F	2
14. I have a pretty good idea of the number of calories in common foods.	T F	1
15. Sometimes when I start eating I just can't seem to stop.	T F	2
16. Since I know how guilty I will feel afterward, I rarely go on eating binges.	T F	1
17. It is not difficult for me to leave something on my plate.	T F	2
18. At certain times of the day I get hungry because I have got used to eating then.	T F	3
19. Sometimes I get so nervous that I just have to eat something.	T F	2
20. While on a diet, if I eat a food that is not allowed I consciously eat less for a period of time to make up for it.	T F	1
21. Being with someone who is eating often makes me hungry enough to eat also.	T F	3
22. When I feel blue, I often overeat.	T F	2
23. I enjoy eating too much to spoil it by counting calories or watching my weight.	T F	1
24. When I see a real delicacy, I often get so hungry that I have to eat it right away.	T F	3
25. I often stop eating when I am not full as a conscious means of limiting the amount that I eat.	T F	1
26. I get so hungry that my stomach often seems like a bottomless pit.	T F	3
27. My weight has hardly changed at all in the last ten years.	T F	2
28. I am always hungry so it is hard for me to stop eating before I finish the food on my plate.	T F	3
29. When I feel lonely, I console myself by eating.	T F	3

Table 17.4 *Eating inventory* *(cont'd)*

30. I consciously hold back at meals in order not to gain weight.	T F	1
31. I sometimes get very hungry late in the evening or at night.	T F	3
32. I eat anything I want, any time I want.	T F	1
33. Without even thinking about it, I take a long time to eat.	T F	2
34. I count calories as a conscious means of controlling my weight.	T F	1
35. I do not eat some foods because they make me fat.	T F	1
36. I am always hungry enough to eat at any time.	T F	3
37. I pay a great deal of attention to changes in my figure.	T F	1
38. While on a diet, if I eat a food that is not allowed, I often then splurge and eat other high calorie foods.	T F	2

PART II

Directions: Please answer the following questions by circling the number above the response that is appropriate for you.

Factor number

39. How often are you dieting in a conscious effort to control your weight?   + 1

1	2	3	4
rarely	sometimes	usually	always

40. How many pounds over your desired weight were you at your maximum weight?   + 2

1	2	3	4	5	6
	less than	less than	less than	less than	less than
zero lb	5 lb	10 lb	15 lb	20 lb	35 lb

7	8	9	10
less than	less than	less than	greater than
50 lb	75 lb	150 lb	150 lb

41. Would a weight fluctuation of 5 lbs affect the way you live your life?   + 1

1	2	3	4
not at all	slightly	moderately	very much

42. How often do you feel hungry?   + 3

1	2	3	4
only at meal times	sometimes between meals	often between meals	almost always

43. What is your maximum weight loss within one month?   + 2

1	2	3	4	5	6	7
less than	less than	less than	less than	less than	less than	less than
2 lb	4 lb	6 lb	8 lb	10 lb	12 lb	15 lb

8	9	10
less than	less than	greater than
20 lb	30 lb	30 lb

44. Do feelings of guilt about overeating help you to control your food intake?   + 1

1	2	3	4
never	rarely	often	always

45. How difficult would it be for you to stop eating half-way through dinner and not eat for the next four hours?   + 3

1	2	3	4
easy	slightly difficult	moderately difficult	very difficult

Table 17.4 *Eating inventory* *(cont'd)*

46. How conscious are you of what you are eating?   + 1

1	2	3	4
not at all	slightly	moderately	extremely

47. How frequently do you skip a meal as a conscious means of limiting
your eating?   + 1

1	2	3	4
almost		at least	almost
never	seldom	once a week	everyday

48. What is your maximum weight gain within a week?   + 2

1	2	3	4	5	6	7
	less	less	less	less	less	less
	than	than	than	than	than	than
zero lb	1 lb	2 lb	3 lb	4 lb	5 lb	6 lb

8	9
less	greater
than	than
9 lb	9 lb

49. How frequently do you *avoid* 'stocking up' on tempting foods?   + 1

1	2	3	4
almost never	seldom	usually	almost always

50. In a typical week, how much does your weight fluctuate
(maximum-minimum)?   + 2

0	1	2	3	4	5	6
	less	less	less	less	less	greater
	than	than	than	than	than	than
zero lb	1 lb	2 lb	3 lb	4 lb	5 lb	5 lb

51. How likely are you to shop for low calorie foods?   + 1

1	2	3	4
unlikely	slightly likely	moderately likely	very likely

52. Do you eat sensibly in front of others and splurge alone?   + 2

1	2	3	4
never	rarely	often	always

53. How likely are you to consciously eat slowly in order to cut down
on how much you eat?   + 1

1	2	3	4
unlikely	slightly likely	moderately likely	very likely

54. How frequently do you skip dessert because you are no longer
hungry?   – 3

1	2	3	4
almost		at least	almost
never	seldom	once a week	every day

55. How likely are you to consciously eat less than you want?   + 1

1	2	3	4
unlikely	slightly likely	moderately likely	very likely

56. Do you go on eating binges even though you are not hungry?   + 2

1	2	3	4
never	rarely	sometimes	at least once a week

57. On a scale of 0 to 10, where 0 means no restraint in eating (eat
whatever you want, whenever you want it) and 10 means total
restraint (constantly limiting food intake and never 'giving in'),
what number would you give yourself?   + 1

0

Table 17.4 *Eating inventory* *(cont'd)*

eat whatever you want, whenever you want it
1
2
usually eat whatever you want, whenever you want it
3
4
often eat whatever you want, whenever you want it
5
6
often limit food intake, but often 'give in'
7
8
usually limit food intake, rarely 'give in'
9
10
constantly limiting food intake, never 'giving in'

58. To what extent does this statement describe your eating behaviour?
    'I start dieting in the morning, but because of any number of things
    that happen during the day, by evening I have given up and eat
    what I want, promising myself to start dieting again tomorrow.'   + 2

1	2	3	4
not like me	little like me	pretty good description of me	describes me perfectly

mentioned at the beginning of this chapter, food has a variety of complex functions. Socializing, and the provision of food and drink are closely linked, and the provision of food is an important statement of caring and love. It is only relatively recently that, for instance, fat babies are no longer seen as 'happy babies' and the product of their mother's love, but as a new generation of obese adults.

Orbach (1978), too, has written extensively on the role of women as care-givers and hence food-givers in our society. She particularly stresses the dual role of the woman as both mother and provider of food and as a sexual person too. This promotes a dual standard which Orbach views as a contributory factor in women's dilemma about feeding themselves and in viewing their own bodies. While her feminist views need not be accepted in their entirety, her proposed treatment of de-emphasizing food and shape and promoting self-acceptance, ties in with the experimental psychological literature on restraint.

Thus obesity has been and will continue to be the focus for prolonged and extensive investigation and treatment, leading as it can do to the development of physical and often psychological ill-effects. For women, in particular, there may be times when it is important to prevent the development of obesity or its exacerbation. These may be in pregnancy, in early childhood, and after hysterectomy or other operations which restrain activity levels. Many women will not in fact seek help at all from their general practitioners, but will instead consult a wide variety of profit-making organizations, many of which use principles of behaviour modification in their general approach to weight-reduction. These organizations include Weightwatchers, Silhouette, and Slimmer, and are a good option especially for those women who wish to lose a relatively small amount of weight, primarily for aesthetic reasons.

Adolescence

In adolescence the developing young woman lays down fat deposits, especially around the areas traditionally defined as sexual, i.e. the breasts, buttocks, thighs, and hips. This period with emerging adolescence may be associated with greater than normal weight gain for obese children, who in any case may have earlier onset of puberty than adolescents of normal weight. Many women who later go on to develop anorexia nervosa also experience earlier puberty, and many of these begin their spiral of uncontrolled dieting after their weight gain, and with it their emerging sexuality is commented on by others, and viewed with ambivalence by themselves. Puberty, for any young woman, is a crucial time for the development of self-esteem, derived most commonly from peer group identification, modelling, and testing of adult roles. Attitudes towards the body, or the development of body image is also important at this time, and negative attitudes in the family towards sexuality may all contribute towards stifling healthy development, and in the anorexic, to feelings of shame and disgust. These may culminate in loss of body weight and the shrinking of sexual areas in the anorexics, and to cycles of deprivation of food and bingeing in the obese teenager. Parents then can be encouraged to support their teenagers to lose weight sensibly if they are grossly overweight, and perhaps at the same time discuss the fact that body shape, despite society's emphasis, is only one aspect of the self. Adolescents, too, can be encouraged to take responsibility for themselves, learning to set realistic goals and to compare themselves less with outside norms to which they may never aspire. Assigning a point system for loss of weight and change of eating habits may be helpful. As with adults, it is important to ascertain the aims of weight loss, that is, to elicit appropriate expectations and to correct faulty assumptions about weight loss, which may reduce co-operation and compliance. Many obese women for instance will, when asked, produce a variety of reasons why they wish to lose weight, including greater sociability, improved marital relationships, greater confidence, etc. For some of these women weight loss will produce these changes while others may benefit from assertion training, or marital therapy, or anxiety management training. Where bingeing occurs, identifying the precipitants of these episodes may educate the woman about the chain of behaviours leading to overeating, and may help to induce greater feelings of self-control. Behavioural programmes which may help are detailed later on in this chapter.

Treatment

Many adult women can pinpoint times when their weight has increased dramatically, such as following a hysterectomy, or after their second child. A study of normal weight women found that they too may eat when bored or depressed, but more often eating for them is associated with pleasant rather than unpleasant affect. While some have suggested that the obese fail to discriminate between emotions and hunger, others have shown that the eating behaviour of people of normal weight is not solely a function of internal cues such as hunger, but is, as in the obese, a complex interaction of level of prior food deprivation, palatability, and accessibility of the food. Certainly, the obese are more finnicky than normals in their choice of foods. It seems likely too that restraint lowers blood-sugar levels and leads to binge-eating, mostly of carbohydrate, and to a constant preoccupation with food.

1. Dietetic advice

A vast array of professional and non-professionals are engaged in advising the mild to moderately obese how to lose weight. Nowadays, the general practitioner may not treat the patient, but may refer her to one of many outside agencies, such as Silhouette, Weightwatchers, or *Slimming magazine*. Alternatively the general practitioner may refer the patient to a dietician or health visitor where appropriate. Assessment may include a weight history to establish chronicity of weight gain, social factors which may have contributed, and lifestyle and value-system. A behavioural diary as outlined further on is an important part of assessment, and encourages self-monitoring of food intake, and a detailed examination of the antecedents and consequences of eating. The amount of physical activity should also be noted, and the amount of food required to lose and maintain weight losses. So often, the latter phase is overlooked in treatment, but is in fact one of the most important stages. Goals set should be realistic ones, and the number of factors governing weight loss explained. Fluid intake charts may be helpful.

As regards the content of any diet, it is useful to refer to the recommended daily dietary allowance chart of the Food and Nutrition Board to establish average requirements. Deprivation of any foods may be self-defeating in terms of the literature on restraint. In general, obese women can be encouraged to eat less, rather than to restrict foods of a specific category. Finally, cultural differences and expectations are relevant for consideration, for example West Indian families and other Indian families have different eating patterns which influence dieting behaviour.

Dwyer (1980), and others, provide excellent reviews on popular diets, and the advantages and disadvantages of these. These fall into four categories:

(a) diets which specify only certain foods, so that energy intake is reduced automatically;

(b) diets which claim to increase the efficiency of weight loss by energy expenditure;

(c) diets which include foods which are poorly absorbed;

(d) diets which encourage elimination of fluids.

There is no one diet which is more appropriate that any other but an example of a typical diet is given at the end of this chapter. 'Fad' diets were referred to earlier on in this chapter, and will not be discussed here.

2. *Psychological methods of weight control*

Psychotherapy. There is little evidence to show that psychotherapy is an effective or efficient method of weight control, either in the short term or the long term. In one study obese patients seen by analysts effectively reduced their weight, but this group does not represent the norm, in that they were in a high income bracket and did not present with concerns about their shape. This aside, however, there may indeed be some obese women who are so distressed by their weight, or have some severe personality problems such as to warrant referral for alternative treatments.

Behaviour therapy. The evidence in favour of the efficacy of behavioural treatments in the treatment of obese women is, however, considerable, at least in the short term. This should be as far as possible the treatment of choice for mildly and moderately obese women. There are many good books available, including self-help manuals, and these are detailed at the end of the chapter. The most commonly used is that of Stuart and Davis (1978), whose basic principles are outlined in Table 17.5. These stem from a number of assumptions, for example that eating is a behaviour which is reinforcing in the short term, and that the negative consequences of eating excessively are long term. Hence, short-term goals need to be established to harness motivation. A second assumption is that calorie intake is excessive. While there is no evidence for an 'obese eating style', the obese still consume more than their requirements. An individualized behavioural analysis can educate the woman about her needs, and about the specifics of her eating behaviour, since, like other habits, these may occur automatically.

Many of these principles are used in organizations such as Weight-watchers, and have their roots in learning theory. Dieticians, too, often make use of them as part of an overall treatment strategy. They have no side effects, and although comparisons with drugs suggest that drugs are

Table 17.5 *Stuart and Davis: Recommendations for treatment*

Behaviour:	Individual eating behaviour — Slow down rate of eating — Swallow foods already in the mouth before taking another bite — Chew foods before swallowing — Put down knife and fork between mouthfuls
Consequences:	Eating is controlled by its consequences Bring into focus ultimate aversive consequences of overeating (individualized list), e.g. health risks, embarrassments.
Antecedents:	Eating is elicited by certain situations. Reducing the cues leading to eating can prevent overeating, e.g. only eat in one place such as the kitchen, do nothing else whilst eating, shop when satiated rather than hungry; clear plates into the rubbish immediately after eating; always eat with a knife and fork.
Suppression of cues:	Use small plates, reprogramme social environment; have others monitor eating; control deprivation by regular meals.
Strengthening:	Assumes that responses which compete with inappropriate eating are elicited by antecedents. Provide reinforcement, enlist support, e.g. spouse or parent, offer reasonable choices of food.

as effective in the short term, behavioural treatment appears to be better at long-term follow-up. Realistically, average weight losses are in the region of 1 lb per week.

3. Drug therapy

Obese women are always asking for a pill to solve their weight problem, but such pills have little part to play. Drug therapy may be useful to control appetite, but the use of appetite suppressants is controversial, and although drug therapy may effect weight loss in the short term, recent studies show that behaviour therapy is better at maintaining weight loss. Drugs should *not* therefore be used as the treatment of choice only as a last resort when other methods fail. In this respect, like surgery and jaw-wiring, it is covered here largely for information. Table 17.6 outlines

Table 17.6 *Drugs for treatment of obesity*

	Example
Amphetamine	Benzedrine
Dextroamphetamine	Dexedrine
Amphetamine resin complex	Biphetamine
Benzphetamine complex	Didrex
Chlorphentermine	Pre-Sate
Clortermine	Voranil
Diethylpropion	Tenuate
Fenfluramine	Pondimin
Mazindol	Sanorex
Phendimetrazine	Plegine
Phenmetrazine	Preludin
Phentermine hydrochloride	Adipex
Phentermine resin	Ionamin

popular anorectic drugs, of which fenfluramine is a commonly used one. All drugs, of course, can produce side effects, and contraindications include coronary heart disease, severe hypertension, hyperthyroidism, glaucoma, agitated states, and a history of drug abuse or excessive dependence on other medications in the past. Fenfluramine may cause drowsiness and diarrhoea, while others may produce confusion, dizziness, tremor, palpitations, and hypertension. The use of diuretics, too, is not advisable unless necessary, as the weight loss is temporary, and quickly regained.

More commonly available, of course, are dietary supplements or alternatives which are freely available. These may include Methylcellulose in tablet form or in various 'slimming' foods. Suffice it to say, that these have no proven efficacy, and no foods are 'slimming'. The food industry's propaganda, however, continues to propagate the myth that this is so, and the diet revolution continues to pay them dividends.

There are, of course, some women who have what is termed an external locus of control, and do not in any way see themselves 'responsible' for their weight loss, and attribute their weight gain to 'glands' or 'hormones'. These women may seek drugs and respond to them as it fits in with their conceptual framework.

4. Jaw-wiring

Jaw-wiring has been shown to be effective in the short term, like most other treatments of obesity but not in the long term. Despite its drawbacks, such as impaired socializing, low aesthetic value, etc., it has been found to be useful with grossly obese women. Again it is open to abuse by the determined who may liquidize food.

5. Surgery

For the massively obese, surgery may be the only option available to them, to minimize the risks to their health. However, the dangers inherent in any surgery on the obese and especially innovative surgery, need to be weighed carefully before this option is pursued. Ileo-jejunal bypass surgery carries a not insubstantial mortality risk and is now being supplanted in Britain with gastric bypass surgery, which as yet has been shown to have fewer complications. Most surgeons acknowledge that surgery should be a last resort for obesity, and in their assessment of the obese they are always careful to note that all other avenues of treatment have been pursued. The function of gastric bypass surgery, is of course to reduce the amount of food entering the stomach at any one time as the top of the stomach is partitioned off. Determined ladies can by overeating burst their staples.

Summary of treatments

Behavioural treatment should be used where possible for mild and moderately obese women. Maintainance of weight lost in any treatment is still a problem. Involving the spouse does appear to be helpful in this respect. Exploring the reasons for weight loss may establish difficulties and lead to supplementary help as suggested. Some of these women may welcome sexual counselling but many obese women in fact enjoy an active sex life, and it may come as a surprise to others that a good sex life is not totally contingent on a particular weight. For some women, structured tasks aimed at helping them to accept their own bodies will elucidate negative attitudes and beliefs. Body perception is an important element in self-esteem, and attitudes towards these most commonly stem from the mother.

Finally, given that general practitioners may in fact re-refer a woman who seeks help for her obesity, their initial role is important. Establishing target weight is a crucial time, and should, where possible, be done with the help of the person to whom the woman is being referred, or not at all, since it can lead to faulty expectations, lowering of morale and attrition if it is fixed at too low a level. Intermittent requests for feedback from the referring agency may also stimulate and motivate the agent, for example the dietitian. It is a constant source of surprise to me that general practitioners function as well as they do, receiving minimal feedback from their 'well' patients. Other general practitioners may, however, wish to treat their patients themselves, or with a colleague, and group treatment is an efficient method of treatment. Indeed, following their treatment, some groups continue to meet intermittently on their own to reinforce weight loss or to provide a social function. Emphasis, too, should be placed on the development of areas of satisfaction other than food, and supporting the view that obese women can be attractive, sociable, feminine, and sexual, and that they have a choice about loss of weight, unless it is likely to radically impair their health. In this respect, the general practitioner is in a prime position to educate.

ANOREXIA

Anorexia is a Greek term used to describe a condition where there is a loss of appetite or desire. Such a loss of appetite may, of course, be present in any normal individual woman for a short time, as a result of physical ill-health, such as gastroenteritis, influenza, etc. When anorexia is prolonged, however, then it is usually referred to as either primary or secondary anorexia, according to its inferred aetiology.

Secondary anorexia is thought to be secondary to some other major problem, such as physical disease, for example carcinoma or where psychological factors other than anorexia nervosa are prominent, for example depression. Although it was previously thought that depression resulted mainly in a loss of appetite, some recent evidence suggests that whether or not weight is lost or gained in depression is to some extent a function of the level of restraint exercised prior to the onset of the depressive episode. Thus women who before they became depressed were commonly restraining themselves from eating are more likely to overeat while those who were not restraining themselves are more likely not to eat. This evidence is in agreement with the model of depression as a series of behaviours in which previously esteemed reinforcers are no longer reinforcing. Given the huge numbers of women with two pre-school children who are depressed, this suggests that manipulation of eating behaviour may be more common than supposed.

Before going on to discuss primary anorexia in detail, I would like to pause briefly to discuss the nature of appetite itself. While, from a physiological point of view, the workings of the hypothalamus are thought to be closely involved in the maintainence of appetite, appetite itself has often been confused with hunger. The latter involves sensations such as gastric contractions, feelings of emptiness, nausea, headache, low blood-sugar levels, etc., and is even in normal weight women a relatively poor predictor of food intake. Appetite on the other hand, or the desire to eat is determined by a complex number of factors in normals, the obese, and anorexics. It is influenced by the palatibility of the food, by its availability, by psychological factors such as the perception of the number of calories consumed, whether actual or presumed, and by external factors such as the time of day, social context, illumination of the food, and so on.

Primary

Primary anorexia is a condition which, in the main, like so many other disorders of nutrition, affects far more women than men. Indeed it is thought that men who suffer from anorexia nervosa are much more difficult to treat by virtue of the fact that ordinarily they are protected. Over the past ten years, anorexia has been the subject of increasing publicity, a move which cannot entirely be supported. Indeed, fashion magazines now often have, on alternate pages, articles expounding the virtues of slimness on the one hand, and the dangers of anorexia on the other, with minimal consideration for their incompatibility. It is easy to understand why editors of fashion magazines are anxious to know about the latest 'syndrome' in the field of weight disorders.

The symptoms of anorexia nervosa are well established, but often difficult to elicit from the sufferer, who so often does not appreciate the full extent of her problem, and indeed may not present, as is commonly the case, as a 'patient', but be brought along by parents or other members of her family.

It has been estimated that approximately 1 per cent of women suffer from anorexia nervosa. It is characterized by a number of features:

(1) marked loss of body weight often in excess of 25 per cent of average weight for height;

(2) avoidance of foods, or episodic bingeing and abstaining;

(3) amenorrhoea;

(4) no known medical illness which could account for the anorexia;

(5) no other psychological illness which could account for the loss of body weight;

(6) the presence of at least two symptoms such as: vomiting, hyperactivity, early morning wakening, bradycardia, episodic bingeing, and fine downy hair on the body and face

Metabolic changes can also include: hirsutism,
                                      abnormal insulin response
                                      tachycardia
                                      hypotension
                                      high serum cholesterol levels.

Anorexics often present with a physical complaint in the first instance, although they do not typically complain of poor sleep and early morning wakening. Rather they see the additional time spent up and awake as an opportunity for greater loss of weight.

There is also an increased incidence of epilepsy in anorexia, possibly as a result of the disturbance in electrolyte balance which may occur especially in the bingeing-abstaining mode.

As anorexia nervosa affects women in the main, so too is it more frequently found in social classes I and II. Perhaps the increasing numbers of anorexics in Britain is partly a reflection of the general emphasis on physical fitness and slimness, a move which in moderation is a good one. Anorexia is much less common in less affluent countries, and I doubt that an adolescent female in Biafra would be diagnosed as anorexic, for obvious reasons. Fashion, too, prescribes a certain shape, and it is not coincidence that one very successful fashion model at the height of her fame weighed only six and a half stone. Certain occupations prescribe certain body shapes. Thus, the idiosyncrasies of fashion must take their share of the blame for the increase in anorexia. Adolescence is a time of turbulence and change, especially around puberty, when shape changes dramatically. Many anorexics may delay this difficult period and even their bone development, such that after appropriate treatment and weight increase, they actually can be seen to grow.

The incidence of dieting is high at any rate in this population of young women, and it is as yet unknown why some dieters spiral downwards into anorexia. It is almost as if their success at dieting, somehow compensates for all the other perceived failures in their lives. Often these women are intelligent and successful, but immensely lacking in self-esteem. Certainly, no one would deny that not eating is a powerful means of self-expression.

Types of anorexia nervosa

It is probably most helpful to differentiate between two types of anorexia nervosa, although these need not necessarily be mutually exclusive.

Abstaining anorexics. These women commonly lose weight by, in the main restricting their intake of carbohydrate, and confining their eating to foods high in protein. Often these women are less chronically ill, and may be more sexually and socially naive. As a group, they are easier to treat.

Bingeing–abstaining anorexics. This may be a more chronic form of anorexia, or a different type altogether. These women typically restrict their food intake, but their restraint fails and they resort to bingeing quantities of food. It is always important to elicit the definition of a binge, since this may range from consuming an extra item, not on the list of foods to be eaten, or it may refer to the consumption of huge quantities of food such that the anorexic may resort to stealing, or get into debt. Shoplifting can occur, but it is not necessarily food which is shoplifted. Hoarding of food is characteristic, and despite the fact that anorexics may not themselves eat, they are intensely preoccupied with food and are happy to prepare it for others. This group of young women is often lacking in control in other areas of their lives, they may be sexually promiscuous, heavy drinkers, or both. Following an episode of bingeing they may attempt to reduce their weight by vomiting, purging with large quantities of purgatives, and/or abusing diuretics. This type of behaviour can, of course occur right across the weight disorders: at low body weight it is termed anorexia nervosa, at normal body weight 'dietary chaos syndrome', and at high body weight it would be one variant of obesity. It is unfortunate that with respect to the development of new 'syndromes' this may mean that a bizarre behaviour which could usefully be ignored at least for a time, gains the status of a psychiatric disorder, which carries more profound implications. Women in this area as in others, are very amenable to being classified as psychiatrically ill.

Physical presentation

Thus, since anorexics may not present with their eating behaviour, it becomes important to diagnose it adequately. Anorexics may present with complaints of diarrhoea, unexplained abdominal pain, vomiting, amenorrhoea, chilblains, hirsutism, or oedema. Crisp (1967) showed that women who are later diagnosed as having anorexia are more likely than their peers to have had their appendices removed. He has also suggested that thyrotoxicosis is occasionally diagnosed in anorexics who may seek help after a binge which results in sweating, tachycardia, and increased basal metabolic rate. Generally, anorexics will present when they are in an out-of-control phase and would welcome some external control, while still not admitting to the anorexia. Physical examination should lead to the exclusion of organic disease. From a physiological point of view, hormonal levels in anorexia may be substantially reduced. Seven stone, or thereabouts, is seen as a critical period for anorexics.

As discussed earlier in this chapter, appropriate feeding is an integral part of a mother's role, and anorexia is a powerful avoidance posture, and a position which few of us can afford to ignore, being associated as it is with a 5 per cent mortality rate. Death, if it occurs, is usually a result of inanition or suicide, most commonly when the anorexic woman sees her future as bleak, and anorexia as no longer a solution to her problems.

Psychological factors

Although psychoanalytic theorists view anorexia as linked to the satisfaction of oral dependency needs and impregnation fantasies, and where abstinence is seen as a defence against these, most people of a less fanciful disposition see anorexia as a complex phobic avoidance response, brought about by the traumas of adolescence. Precipitants may also include the break-up of an important relationship, exam anxiety, or marital disharmony. When anorexics have married at low body weights, their behaviour will be difficult to change if the spouse cannot adjust to the new body weight. This view of anorexia also upholds the idea that weight and sexuality are linked, and that anorexia prevents the development of maturity and is an avoidance of the female role. For some anorexics, this avoidance may reflect in negative attitudes about an aspect of the body, such as the stomach or the thighs. Or, the anorexic may view her emerging sexuality with diffidence and ambivalence, having as her models of femaleness perhaps a mother who has not herself come to terms with her shape. At any rate, the anorexic makes a basic mistake of logic in assuming that slimness is associated with all nature of successes, such as success in peer relationships. Body-image, too, is often distorted, and mirror-gazing is common, although weighing is not. Anorexics often perceive themselves as fat even at very low body weight.

Family dynamics

There is as yet little in the way of supporting the notion that parental attributes are linked to causality in anorexia. Patients may of course present in a number of ways, often relating to parents in bizarre ways. However, it is difficult to establish whether this is a product of the behaviour, or the reason for it. The family can be viewed as a system, the behaviour of one member reflecting on the others. It may be that anorexics somehow fulfil a necessary role as a scapegoat, which maintains homeostasis in the family. Like obesity, it is unlikely that any one factor is the major cause of anorexia. Rather, it is likely to be the result of a sequence of events and problems. In treatment, many of the physiological abnormalities return to normal, and an anorexic who has become ill very early on, may even grow during treatment, for example her shoe size or overall height may increase. It seems likely then that anorexia is the result of a number of events and beliefs some of which are overt and others which are not acknowledged. Within the latter are difficulties such as a fear of being independent, fear of success, of being let down in a relationship, or anxieties about facing up to adulthood. Sibling rivalry is a common theme, and some parents themselves may have frank psychological problems such as alcoholism or even anorexia.

Treatment

Treatment of primary anorexia is almost entirely psychological. Some clinicians do use antidepressants, but there is as yet little evidence in support of these. One aspect of this is that some antidepressants are associated with weight gain, a factor which will terrify the anorexic who is already terrified of a loss of control over her eating. The main deciding factor in treatment will be the severity of the weight loss. Anorexia nervosa is an extremely difficult condition to treat not least because they are unwilling to be treated and are manipulative. Patients who weigh less than six stone are often best treated in a specialist hospital, although in practice the general practitioner may end up treating severe cases because of long waiting lists, or because the patient has been discharged as 'untreatable' at some stage.

Treatment in general practice

Behavioural treatment. Behavioural treatments of anorexia nervosa have been almost exclusively used within in-patient settings, and have met with some success. However, as in the field of obesity, it is unhelpful to use only weight gain or loss as the main outcome measure, and in anorexia may even be harmful as an anorexic may resort to a number of measures in order to promote weight gain, which in themselves are not conducive to producing a good long-term outcome. Rather, social relationships, work adjustment, and return of menstruation are often better indices of the long-term outcome. Between 40 and 50 per cent of anorexics improve markedly or recover in treatment, while a further 20–35 per cent are improved. These results occur across a broad range of treatments, although there is some suggestion that the results of behavioural treatments are more consistent. As in obesity, however, individual variation is considerable. Particular care needs to be taken in methodology used, for example in separating bulimics from abstainers. Long-term follow-up is a necessity, not a luxury, if we are to understand the basic mechanisms involved. Depression after re-feeding and before discharge may be associated with a better outcome. Social skills treatment superimposed on other treatments, for example family and individual psychotherapy, does not improve outcome at one year follow-up but is associated with a more rapid reduction in levels of anxiety, depression, and fear of negative evaluation (Crisp and Pillay 1981). It is again unlikely that any one technique will be useful for all anorexics, and it would therefore seems useful to examine the role of optimum intervention periods, with specific subgroups.

Abstainers are likely to be easier to help in an out-patient setting. Bingeing anorexics are more difficult to treat, and may be referred to out-patient clinics for anorexia, or treated with caution. The aim is always the same, i.e. to restore body weight to normal levels, and to promote psychological readjustment. Although there are as yet no proven methods of efficacy, several guidelines may be helpful.

1. Establish an agreement or contract about target weight.
2. Outline areas of difficulty, apart from weight.
3. Encourage food intake via increasing portion size, rather than focusing on calories, e.g. an extra teaspoonful of butter, an extra slice of bread, etc. A recent hospital out-patient study suggested that dieticians using graded re-feeding as outlined, and acting in a generally supportive way rather than interpretive, could be as effective as a separate therapist who was engaged in traditional psychotherapy with anorectics and their families. These results are very interesting, and have direct applicability to the general practitioner's surgery.
4. There should be regular appointments, if possible once a week, for weighing and discussion. Charting of weight is essential, and often the anorexic will have her chart too. Too rapid an weight increase should be avoided and weight gain should be in the region of a maximum of 2 lb per week.
5. As treatment progresses, tasks can be set, e.g. shopping, etc. Many anorexics will find 7 st. a critical period, with its associations with return of menstruation. Consistency is a key word in treatment, and the general practitioner's task is one of imparting the view that control over weight increase can be established, and that the aim is not to promote obesity, but to help the anorexic level out at target weight.

'DIETARY CHAOS SYNDROME'

Some clinicians have noticed in the aftermath of anorexia, that there is an increasing number of women who have a normal weight, but control their food intake in a number of abnormal ways, for example by vomiting or purging. While there is no consensus about what constitutes normal eating behaviour, this is clearly not normal. However, in my opinion, the recent emphasis in the media on anorexia and bingeing must take some of the blame in drawing people's attention to these methods used to induce weight loss. This behaviour is extremely common in the USA, where the rate of obesity is high and 'fast foods' freely available. Preoccupation with weight here, as in other areas, is undoubtedly a reflection of dissatisfaction in some aspect of these women's lifestyles, but also, an excessive preoccupation with external norms, which bear little relationship to the real areas of importance in women's lives. General support and guidance are relevant here, depending on chronicity. With women who are chronically behaving in this way, identifying the precipitants may be helpful. Once more, it is not at all surprising that it is women in the main who, after reading articles in the press about this 'new disease' rapidly present themselves for treatment, which for them may be to recognize that the artificial standard imposed by the media is an unrealistic one.

Normal women may binge intermittently, but a characteristic of women who present with the more severe form is that they are usually at high average body weight, or have been overweight in the past and are unable to sustain what may be artificial levels of weight loss.

NUTRITION AND THE ELDERLY

It seems useful to comment on nutrition in the elderly, since women on average live longer. Although this area has been amply covered in other books, it is worth mentioning that malnutrition in the elderly is still fairly common, and may be associated with poor self-care, ignorance, general ill-health, lack of financial resources, social isolation, or mental disturbance. Secondary problems may include difficulty in chewing, reduced appetite, or malabsorption. Most commonly, this malnutrition is associated with a lack of protein, and often a deficiency in vitamins A and D. The DHSS has published a report on *Nutrition and old age*, and they conclude that the prevalence of malnutrition for the 70–80 age group of women is 5 per cent, whereas for the over-80s group it is 8 per cent. They discuss eleven risk factors, including living alone, having no regular cooked meals, being on supplementary benefit, belonging to social class IV and V, having a low IQ, and suffering from depression, emphysema, chronic bronchitis, poor dentition, difficulty in swallowing, partial gastrectomy, and being housebound. Since malnutrition correlates with poor health, and increasing dependency on the health and social services, this area is an important one, in which the health-care team can play a valuable role. In particular by recognizing deterioration at an early stage and providing support and perhaps health education or financial assistance via available subsidies or a meals-on-wheels service. This may prevent or at least delay hospitalization. The lack of facilities for the aged in our hospitals, the work on reality orientation in the elderly,* and the ever increasing numbers of aged women suggest that this task is worthwhile.

---

* Reality orientation is a form of treatment devised to assist the aged in the prevention of disorientation and further dementia as a result of admission to an institution. It is a system of teachings devised to present old people with information about the time of day, their environment, etc., and to help them to memorize this information.

APPENDIX

WEIGHT REDUCTION DIET (Merton, Sutton, and Wandsworth District Dietetic Dept.)

This diet is an example of a properly formulated diet, which although not universally appropriate, i.e. for those who have other problems, can be useful, supplemented by the behavioural principles outlined earlier.

Name .... Date ....

* If obesity has not already impaired your health, it will soon do so.
* You are overweight because you have been eating more food than you require.
* This tells you how to alter your eating habits so that you may safely lose weight.
* This diet, together with your co-operation, will certainly improve your health.
* Generally, on this diet, you should lose about 1½–2 lb per week.

1. Have three meals a day. Do not eat between meals, but you may have low calorie drinks.
2. At two or three meals, you should have moderate servings of protein-containing foods. These are meat, poultry, fish, eggs, cheese, and pulses, e.g. lentils. These may be cooked in any way you like, but do not fry or use breadcrumbs, batter, pastry, flour, or any thickening or serve with thick gravies or sauces.
3. Have vegetables or salad at least once a day.
4. Everyday you may have 3 small slices of bread–preferably wholemeal. Instead of one small slice of bread you may have:

½ large slice of bread or toast
2 small crispbreads or cream crackers
3 tablespoons breakfast cereal—preferably wholegrain.
4 tablespoons cooked porridge
1 small egg-sized potato
1 heaped tablespoon mashed potato
1 tablespoon cooked rice
1 tablespoon boiled pasta, e.g. spaghetti or noodles
1 small chapati

2 tablespoons baked beans
1 tablespoon yam, sweet potato, or plantain
1 carton plain yoghurt
1 extra serving fruit

5. Have up to three servings of fruit: fresh, unsweetened stewed fruit or small glass unsweetened fruit juice a day.
6. You may have half a pint of whole milk or 1 pint skimmed milk per day for use in tea, coffee and on cereal.
7. Only use a thin scraping of butter or margarine on bread.

Sample day's menu

Daily milk allowance: ½ pint whole milk or 1 pint skimmed
Breakfast
Fresh grapefruit or tomato juice if desired
1 egg or two rashers of bacon (grilled), or portion of fish, if desired
1 small slice bread or toast (with scraping butter) OR Alternative from list e.g. breakfast cereal
Tea or coffee with milk from allowance
Mid-morning
Tea, or coffee with milk from allowance, or oxo, bovril, marmite, low-calorie squash.
Lunch
Clear or unthickened soup if desired.
Moderate serving of lean meat, poultry, fish, egg, or cheese.
Large helping of vegetables or salad
1 small slice bread (with scraping of butter) OR alternative from list
Serving of fruit
Mid-afternoon
Drink as per mid-morning
Evening meal
Clear soup if desired
Moderate serving of lean meat, poultry, fish, egg, or cheese.
Large helping of vegetables or salad
1 small slice bread (with scraping of butter) OR alternative from list
Serving of fruit
Bed-time
Drink as per mid-morning.

CHOOSE YOUR MEAL FROM THESE FOODS

Meat
Moderate servings (3–4 oz. cooked) of lean meats, offal, or poultry

Fish
Good helping, (4–6 oz) white fish, or a smaller helping of oily fish, e.g. sardines, mackerel, herrings, kippers, cooked without extra fat
Eggs
Boiled, poached, scrambled, or omelette cooked without fat
Cheese
2 oz serving of any variety except cream cheese
4 oz cottage cheese may be taken instead
Vegetables and salad
All varieties
Fruit
Up to three pieces a day, e.g. apple, pear, orange, peach, or small banana
Allowed freely, grapefruit, lemon, melon, rhubarb, gooseberries, red- and blackcurrants cooked without sugar
Drinks
Water, tea, coffee, soda water, low-calorie and diabetic squash, tomato juice, slimline minerals and sugarless drinks, Oxo, Bovril, Marmite, un-thickened soups
Seasonings
Salt, pepper, vinegar, mustard, Worcester sauce, herbs, spices, chillies, curry powder, garlic, gherkins, pickled onions, gelatine
Sweeteners
Saccharine, Saxin, Sweetex, or Hermesetas liquid or tablets

DO NOT EAT THESE FOODS

Sugar
Sweets, chocolate, confectionary, glucose or honey, jams, marmalades, preserves, treacle, golden syrup, granulated sugar substitutes, and sorbital sweeteners
Cakes, pastries, biscuits, pies, puddings
Drinks
Fruit, squash, cordials, mineral waters and fizzy drinks, e.g. Lucozade, Coca-Cola, lemonade, Ribena, chocolate, cocoa, and malted milk drinks. All alcohol, particularly beer, ale, stout, cider, including diabetic beers and lager
Snack foods
Potato crisps, nuts, and other packet snack foods
Fruit
Grapes, tinned fruit in syrup, dried fruit
Convenience products
Condensed milks, ice-cream, fruit yoghurt, single and double cream

Fats and oils
Vegetable oil, dripping, cooking fats, salad cream, cream cheese
Proprietary foods
'Slimming Foods', Diabetic foods, except Diabetic squash

SAMPLE ANOREXIC DIET FOR USE IN THE SURGERY (Bowyer 1982 personal communication)

When initially seen, an anorexic may have a dietary pattern of abstinence from carbohydrate foods and commonly foods containing concentrated fat; she may eat nothing all day allowing herself to eat only at the end of the day; there may be days of fasting followed by binge-type eating in large quantities, but whatever the pattern of eating there is a very definite strictness in type and quantity of food and when it is eaten.

Initially it is important to advise regular meals (breakfast/mid-day/evening) and there is a need for them to include carbohydrate in the form of either bread, cereals, pasta, or potato at each meal usually starting with small quantities (e.g. 1 slice of bread or 1 tablespoon of potato) to give:

Breakfast	1 cup of cereal + milk OR/1 slice of bread with fat
Mid-day	meat or fish or cheese or eggs
Evening meal	vegetables—cooked or salad
	bread or rice or potato or pasta

It is imperative to work slowly but firmly in building up an anorexic's intake and hence weight gain, but also to reassure her that your advice is not going to lead to her becoming overweight. Weight gain also comes when an anorexic has confidence in the therapist.

Often diet sheets of 2000–4000 calories may be advocated but it is unrealistic to expect a person whose calorie intake may only be a fraction of this to be able to eat this quantity straight away within an out-patient programme, also weight gain can be expected on a much lower calorie intake. Diet sheets are unnecessary as all advice can be based on a regular meal pattern as mentioned which can then be increased in quantity and more foods introduced.

Aspects such as only eating dry bread or using watered-down milk can be highlighted by careful dietary-history taking, and targets such as using half a pint of whole milk instead of half a pint of milk and water can be worked towards by the following appointment time—from experience with working on one aspect like this at a time, advice is followed far better than asking an anorexic to make various changes all at once.

As there is a definite strictness surrounding an anorexic's intake they have clearly defined lists of 'allowed' and 'forbidden' foods—'allowed' foods generally consisting of very low-calorie, bulky foods and 'forbidden' foods consisting of high calorie-dense foods usually concentrated carbohydrates and foods containing concentrated fat. It is important to integrate these two lists so that the forbidden foods are slowly incorporated into the diet and viewed as part of a normal intake by advising the anorexic to eat e.g. a sweet food such as biscuits/cake/pudding after meals; however it is equally important not to emphasize these foods as those totally responsible for the weight gain, since this would only re-emphasize the concept of 'fattening' foods, but to stress instead that the overall increased food intake will produce a steady weight gain. It is important to establish if an anorexic does not like a particular group of foods, e.g. sugar-containing foods, and to ask her why. She may not like it because it is 'forbidden' to her, she may not like the taste, or there may be another reason; the first explanation will often be denied initially, but if the anorexic trusts the therapist she may eventually admit to it.

If an anorexic is asked to write down everything she eats she will generally do so with a good deal of honesty and by glancing at a breakfast of:

cereal and milk
boiled egg
toast, butter, and marmalade

which seems sufficient and may reflect the pattern for the rest of the day this actually could amount to:

1 dessertspoon of cereal + milk
1 boiled egg
½ slice of toast with scraping of butter and marmalade

So, without having to make drastic changes to the diet, breakfast could be in the same form but quantities defined and advised as

1 cup of cereal with 1 cup of milk
1 egg
1 slice of toast with 1 teaspoon each of butter and marmalade

which will increase the calories. The whole day's meals can be discussed thoroughly and increased in this manner.

When a regular meal pattern has been established and an anorexic is eating a protein/vegetable/starch at each meal together with calorie-dense foods such as cakes/biscuits/crisps/puddings/sweets or chocolates within the meal pattern and there is a steady weight gain, an anorexic will slowly become more confident in widening the choice of food she eats but the simple structure of regular meals built up slowly around our 'meat/vegetable/potato plus pudding' type of eating is a good basis for an anorexic to restart a less restrictive eating pattern in order to gain and hopefully then maintain a more normal weight.

REFERENCES AND FURTHER READING

Bray, G. A. (1980). In *Obesity* (ed. A. J. Stunkard). W. B. Saunders, London.
Canning, H. and Meyer, J. (1966). Obesity: its possible effect on college accept-

ance. *New Engl. J. Med* **275**, 1172–4.

Crisp, A. (1967). Anorexia nervosa. *Hosp. Med.* **5**, 713–8.

Crisp, A. and Pillay, H. (1981). The impact of social skills training within an established treatment programme for anorexia nervosa. *Br. J. Psychiat.* **139**, 533.

Dwyer, J. (1980). Sixteen popular diets: brief nutritional analyses. In *Obesity* (ed. A. J. Stunkard). W. B. Saunders, London.

Greaves, J. P. (1973). *British Foundation Nutrition Bulletin.* No. 9. Sept. In *Speaking to each other* (ed. Hoggan). Chatto & Windus, London.

Kropf (1889). In *The psychology of obesity, dynamics and treatment* (ed. N. Kiell) p. 75–83. Charles C. Thomas, London.

Montegriffo, V. M. E. (1968). Height and weight of a United Kingdom population with a review of anthropomorphic literature. *Ann. hum. Genet.* **31**, 389–99.

Moore, M. E. Stunkard, A. J., and Srole, L. (1962). Obesity, social class and mental illness. *J. Am. med. Assoc.* **181**, 962–6.

National Health Survey (1964). HMSO, London.

Orbach, S. (1978). *Fat is a feminist issue.* Paddington Press, New York.

Powdermaker, H. (1973). An anthropological approach to the problem of obesity. In *The psychology of obesity, dynamics and treatment* (ed. N. Kiell) pp. 75–83. Charles C. Thomas, London.

Pudel, V. E. (1976). In *Appetite and food intake* (ed. T. Silverstone).

—— (1977). *Int. J. Obesity* **1**, 369–86.

Stuart, R. B. and Davis, B. (1978). *Slim chance in a fat world, behavioural control of obesity.* Research Press, Champaign, Illinois.

Stunkard, A. J. (1981). 'Restrained eating' What it is and a new scale to measure it. In *The body weight regulatory system: normal and disturbed mechanisms* (ed. C. A. Cloffi, W. P. T. James, and T. B. V. Itallie). Raven Press, New York.

Diet books (not recommended)

Cott, L. (1977). *Fasting is a way of life.* Bantam Books, New York.

Kremor, W. L. (1975). *The doctors' metabolic diet.* Crown Publishers, New York.

Linn, R. (1977). *Last chance refeeding diet.* Bantam Books, New York.

Republican Drug Co. Protein programme reducing diet. In *Health brand protein powder pack.* Republican Drug Co., Buffalo, New York.

Snack (Wisconsin) diet (1970). McCalls.

Taller, H. (1961). *Calories don't count.* Simon and Schuster, New York.

Tarnower, M. D. and Sinclair Baker (1978). *Complete Scarsdale diet.* Bantam, New York.

Behavioural self-help texts for losing weight

Amit, Z., Sutherland, E. A., and Weiner, A. (1976). *Stay slim for good.* Charter Communications of Grosset and Dunlap, New York.

Fanburg, J. and Snyder, B. M. (1975). *How to be a winner at the weight loss game . . . and keep it off forever.* Ballentine Books, New York.

Ferguson, J. M. (1976). *Habits, not diets: the real way to weight control.* Bull Publishing Palo Alto, California.

Ikeda, J. (1978). *Change your habits to change your shape.* Bull Publishing, Palo Alto, California. (For teenagers only.)

Jeffrey, D. B. and Katz, R. C (1977). *Take it off and keep it off.* Prentice Hall, Englewood Cliffs, New Jersey.

Jordan, H. A., Levitz, L. S., and Gelman, S. (1976). *Eating is okay.* Rawson

Associates, New York. (Also a Signet paperback.)

LeBow, M. D. and Perry, R. P. (1977). *If only I were thin*. Prairie Publishing Co., Winnipeg.

Mahoney, M. J. and Mahoney, K. (1976). *Permanent weight control*. W. W. Norton, New York.

—— and Jeffrey, D. B. (1977). *A manual of self-control procedures for the overweight*. American Psychological Association (Catalog of Selected Documents in Psychology), Washington DC.

Nash, J. D. (1978). *Taking charge of your weight and wellbeing*. Bull Publishing, Palo Alto, California.

Stuart, R. B. and Davis, B. (1972). *Slim chance in a fat world*. Research Press, Champaign, Illinois. (Revised condensed edition 1978.)

—— (1978). *Act thin, stay thin*. W. W. Norton, New York.

Appetite disorders

Anorexia

Crisp. A. (1980). *Let me be*. Academic Press, London.

Palmer, R. (1980). *Anorexia nervosa*. Penguin, Harmondsworth.

Bulimia

Fairburn, C. (1981). A cognitive approach to the treatment of bulimia. *Psychol. Med.* **11**, 707–11.

Halmi, K. A., *et al.* (1981). Binge-eating and vomiting. A study of a college population. *Psychol. Med.* **11**, 697–706.

Wardle, J. (1980). Dietary restraint and binge eating. *Behav. Analysis Modification* **4**, 201–9.

Obesity

Israel, A. S. and Stolmaker, L. (1980). Behavioural treatment of obesity in children and adolescents. In *Progress in behaviour modification* Vol. 10, pp. 82–106. Academic Press, London.

Le Bow, M. D. (1981). *Weight control*. Wiley, Chichester.

Ley, P. (1980). The psychology of obesity. In *Contributions to medical psychology* Vol. 2. British Psychological Society and Macmillan, London.

Stunkard, A. J. (1980). *Obesity*. Saunders, London.

Mitchell, E. M. (1980). Psychological aspects and management of obesity. *Br. J. hosp. Med.* December, p. 23.

Index